THE
MATLAB® 5
H A N D B O O K

Eva Pärt-Enander and Anders Sjöberg

Uppsala University
Information Technology
Department of Scientific Computing
Sweden

Addison-Wesley

Harlow, England ● Reading, Massachusetts ● Menlo Park, California ● New York
Don Mills, Ontario ● Amsterdam ● Bonn ● Sydney ● Singapore
Tokyo ● Madrid ● San Juan ● Milan ● Mexico City ● Seoul ● Taipei

© Pearson Education Limited 1999
Addison Wesley Longman Limited
Edinburgh Gate
Harlow
Essex
CM20 2JE
UK

and Associated Companies throughout the World.

The rights of Eva Pärt-Enander and Anders Sjöberg to be identified as authors of this Work have been asserted by them in accordance with the Copyright, Designs and Patents Act 1988.

The programs in this book have been included for their instructional value. They have been tested with care but are not guaranteed for any particular purpose. The publisher does not offer any warranties or representations nor does it accept any liabilities with respect to the programs.

Many of the designations used by manufacturers and sellers to distinguish their products are claimed as trademarks. Pearson Education Limited has made every attempt to supply trademark information about manufacturers and their products mentioned in this book. A list of the trademark designations and their owners appears on page xv.

Typeset by 56
Printed and bound in Great Britain by Henry Ling Ltd, at the Dorset Press, Dorchester, Dorset

First printed 1999

ISBN 0-201-39845-1

British Library Cataloguing-in-Publication Data
A catalogue record for this book is available from the British Library.

1001559 186

Preface

What is MATLAB?

MATLAB is a product of The MathWorks, Inc. and is an advanced interactive software package specially designed for scientific and engineering computation. The MATLAB environment integrates graphics illustrations with precise numerical calculations, and is a powerful, easy-to-use, and comprehensive tool for performing all kinds of computations and scientific data visualization. MATLAB has proven to be a very flexible and usable tool for solving problems in applied mathematics, physics, chemistry, engineering, medicine, finance, and other application areas which deal with complicated numerical calculations. MATLAB is also an excellent pedagogical tool when teaching mathematics, numerical analysis, and engineering. The program is widely used at universities and colleges all around the world, and it is popular for industrial use. MATLAB is available on machines ranging from personal computers to supercomputers, as well as on most platforms, for example PC, Macintosh, and UNIX.

About MATLAB

The commands in MATLAB are expressed in a notation close to that used in mathematics and engineering. For instance, to solve a system of linear equations, written as $\mathbf{Ax} = \mathbf{b}$ in matrix/vector form, one first creates the coefficient matrix $\mathbf{A}$ and the right-hand side $\mathbf{b}$ and then simply types $x = A\backslash b$. In a similar way, one can use short notations for finding, for example, solutions of ordinary differential equations, eigenvalues of a matrix, and interpolating or curve fitting of some given data.

There is a very large set of commands and available functions, also known as MATLAB M-files, that make life easier. Hence, solving problems in MATLAB is generally much faster than traditional programming, and the code is clear and self-documented because of the natural notation. It is easy to modify these functions since most of the M-files are open. The algorithms used are robust and well-known numerical methods, programmed by leading experts in mathematical software. To obtain high performance, the MATLAB software is written in optimized C, with some important inner loops coded in assembly language.

MATLAB's two- and three-dimensional graphics engine is object oriented, making it a powerful environment for construction of high-quality images and graphs. MATLAB is both an environment and a matrix/vector-oriented programming language, allowing the user to build her or his own reusable tools. With MATLAB code, one can easily create special user-defined M-files, for example functions and programs, which solve certain problems. The graphics package contains functions for creating graphical user interfaces (GUIs), with buttons, menus and other accessories.

Furthermore, there exists a large set of optional 'toolboxes' of functions for specific application purposes, for example, signal processing, optimization, symbolic mathematics, financial analysis and image analysis. All of these are written on top of MATLAB, and the toolboxes can be combined to form high-performance tools for design and analysis.

There are two basic versions of the software: the professional version, distributed by The MathWorks, Inc., and the smaller Student Edition of MATLAB, distributed by Prentice Hall. The main restriction in the Student Edition is that the matrix size is limited to 16384 elements. However, this version of MATLAB contains three toolboxes, Signals and Systems Toolbox, the Control Systems Toolbox and the Symbolic Math Toolbox. The limitations and special functions are not discussed further since the full version of MATLAB is so widely available.

The MathWorks, Inc. has made an official Year 2000 statement that guarantees that the MATLAB date handling is fully millennium compliant.

The main features of MATLAB are:

- Advanced algorithms for high-performance numerical computations, especially in the field of matrix algebra.

- A large collection of predefined mathematical functions and the ability to define one's own functions.

- Two- and three-dimensional graphics for plotting and displaying data and for pedagogical, scientific, and aesthetic illustrations and visualizations.

- A complete help system based on HTML.

- Powerful matrix/vector-oriented high-level programming language for individual applications.

- Ability to cooperate with programs written in other languages and for importing and exporting formatted data.

- Toolboxes available for advanced problem solving in several application areas.

About The MATLAB 5 Handbook

This book provides practical guidance on the use of MATLAB and shows how to create user-defined programs in MATLAB code. It is based on MATLAB version 5.2, but can also be used with older versions and the Student version as well. The book is a concise reference book, but it also gives examples of how MATLAB commands can be used and it is therefore suitable as a handbook in courses about MATLAB.

The MATLAB 5 Handbook is a source of information that answers many of the frequently asked questions raised by both inexperienced and experienced MATLAB users. Basic knowledge of mathematics is required to understand most of the material; therefore an introduction to linear algebra is included in the book in Appendix B.

The specific characteristics of *The MATLAB 5 Handbook* are:

- It is discipline independent.

- It is a complete and reliable manual written in a succinct style.

- The MATLAB commands and functions are easy to locate and their descriptions simple to understand.

- Concepts and problem fields have been made easy to find to give the reader inspiration and enlightenment to solve actual problems.

- Conceptually close commands are grouped together in chapters, sections and tables, to assist problem solving.

- Each chapter, each section and each table starts with the most basic commands.

- It contains a number of straightforward examples and demonstrations of commands.

- The graphic commands of MATLAB are integrated into the text together with other commands, but they are also covered more completely in two separate chapters (13 and 14).

- One chapter is devoted to the usage of FORTRAN and C with MATLAB (Chapter 15).

- It contains definitions, basic concepts, and the theory of linear algebra in Appendix B.

- It contains a step-by-step introduction for beginners in Appendix A.

Audience

The MATLAB 5 Handbook is intended for all MATLAB users, from the beginner to those already familiar with the software. The book can be used by students of mathematics, engineering and natural sciences, but also applies to areas such as economics and statistics. It is also an invaluable reference guide for advanced MATLAB users, such as scientists and engineers.

How to use The MATLAB 5 Handbook

The material is logically organized and presented with examples throughout. It is comprehensive and self-contained. The chapters in *The MATLAB 5 Handbook* can be read virtually independently from each other. However, we recommend that a beginner starts with Chapter 1, which is a presentation of MATLAB, and follows on with Chapter 2, to learn the basics. It is recommended that a pure novice starts with Appendix A, which is a step-by-step introduction to MATLAB. There is also a list of references, a list of command and function tables and an index. Appendix B contains the basic definitions of concepts in linear algebra and Appendix C describes extension programs of MATLAB, that is, the currently available toolboxes and SIMULINK block-diagram modeling and simulation software. A quick reference to commands and functions can be found in Appendix D.

The history of MATLAB and The MATLAB 5 Handbook

MATLAB was originally written by Dr Cleve Moler, Chief Scientist at The MathWorks, Inc., to provide easy access to matrix software developed in the LINPACK and EISPACK projects. The very first version was written in the late 1970s for use in courses in matrix theory, linear algebra, and numerical analysis. MATLAB is therefore built upon a foundation of sophisticated matrix software, in which the basic data element is a matrix that does not require predimensioning. Over 400 000 persons in over 100 countries are using MATLAB today.

The Department of Scientific Computing at Uppsala University, Sweden, began using MATLAB in 1986 as a teaching tool in numerical analysis, especially in numerical linear algebra. The MATLAB software at that time was an academic version, written in FORTRAN code. Besides preparing exercises and assignments, the department also produced a handbook. This handbook has since then been updated and extended. The authors who have contributed material and/or editing over the years are Rickard Enander, Peter Hägglund, Pernilla Isaksson, Bo Melin, Peter Flink, Magnus Almgren, Patrik Forssén, Jacob Jonsson, Andreas Pihl, and Anna Sundström.

The present *MATLAB 5 Handbook*, written for MATLAB version 5.2, is a revised edition of The MATLAB Handbook, published by Addison Wesley Longman since 1996.

Acknowledgements

The authors are very grateful to the Department of Scientific Computing, Uppsala University, The MathWorks, Inc., and the Swedish distributor of MATLAB, Computer Solutions Europe AB in Stockholm. We would also like to thank the reviewers and of course Karen Mosman, Emma Mitchell and their colleagues at Addison Wesley Longman.

Eva Pärt-Enander   Anders Sjöberg

January 1999

Comments and further information

Further information about MATLAB can be found in the WWW home pages of The MathWorks, Inc. The MathWorks, Inc. also maintains an archive of M-files on the anonymous `ftp` server.

Comments on this book can be sent by e-mail or in an envelope marked 'MATLAB' to the following address:

Uppsala University
Information Technology
Department of Scientific Computing
Box 120
SE–751 04 Uppsala
Sweden
e-mail: `matlab@tdb.uu.se`
www: `http://www.tdb.uu.se/~matlab/`

Comments to The MathWorks, Inc. regarding MATLAB can be sent to:

The MathWorks, Inc.
24 Prime Park Way
Natick, MA 01760–1500
USA
phone: (508) 647 7000
fax: (508) 647 7001
e-mail: `info@mathworks.com`
www: `http://www.mathworks.com/`
ftp: `ftp.mathworks.com`

Contents

Trademark notice

The following product names are trademarks or registered trademarks of the organizations given in brackets after each: MATLAB (The MathWorks, Inc.); Borland C (Borland International Inc.); Cray (Cray Research, Inc.); FORTRAN and Pascal (Oracle Corporation UK Limited); IBM PC (International Business Machines Corporation); Lotus 123 (Lotus Development Corp.); Macintosh (Apple Computer, Inc.); Microsoft Internet Explorer, Microsoft Visual C, Windows and Microsoft Word (Microsoft Corporation); Netscape (Netscape Communications Corp); Solaris and Sun (Sun Microsystems, Inc.); SPARC (Sparc International Inc.); UNIX (licensed through X/Open Company Ltd); VAX (Digital Equipment Corporation).

What is MATLAB?

And none of this would have been any fun without MATLAB.

Nachtigal, M.N., Reddy, S.C. and Trefethen, L.N. (1990).
How Fast are Nonsymmetric Matrix Iterations?
In *Proc. Copper Mountain Conference on Iterative Methods*,
Copper Mountain CO, 1–5 April, 1990.

1.1 What can be done in MATLAB?

MATLAB is a program for computation and visualization. MATLAB is widely used and is available on all kinds of computers, ranging from personal computers to supercomputers.

MATLAB is controlled by commands, and it is programmable. There are hundreds of predefined commands and functions and these functions can be further enlarged by user-defined functions.

MATLAB has powerful commands. MATLAB can, for instance, solve linear systems with one single command, and perform a lot of advanced matrix manipulations.

MATLAB has powerful tools for graphics in two and three dimensions.

MATLAB can be used together with other programs. The graphics capabilities of MATLAB can, for instance, be used to visualize computations performed in a FORTRAN program.

There are about 25 different MATLAB toolboxes available for special application fields.

MATLAB is a very efficient tool for solving both small and large problems in a wide range of areas:

- Research and development in industry.

- Teaching mathematics, especially linear algebra. All basic concepts can be studied.

- Teaching and research in numerical analysis and scientific computing. Algorithms can be studied in detail and compared with each other.

- Teaching and research in engineering and scientific subjects, for example electronics, control theory and physics.

- Teaching and research in all other fields where computational problems occur, such as economics, chemistry and biology.

The building block in MATLAB is the matrix, and the name MATLAB is derived from MATrix LABoratory.

1.2 Some MATLAB examples

The examples in this section are just a brief presentation of what MATLAB can do. In some cases we have given the complete MATLAB commands and in other cases, for simplicity, only parts of the commands.

The MATLAB code is shown in this book in a specific font to distinguish it from the rest of the text. The MATLAB output is in *italics*. We thus have:

```
This style for commands that we give to MATLAB.
```
This style for what MATLAB gives as response.

The percentage sign % is used in MATLAB as a symbol for comments and this is used throughout the book. Other notations we have used are *italics* for scalars and predefined functions and **bold face** for matrices, vectors and user-defined functions. Matrices are named with a capital letter first, and vectors start with a lower-case letter. Cell matrices are thought of as matrices or vectors and are also in bold face, as are structs and objects. In the command tables we use *italics* for those function parameters which are optional; for instance for `command (par1, `*`par2`*`)` the parameter `par1` is always needed, but *`par2`* is optional.

■ **Example 1.1   Functions in 2D and 3D**

MATLAB can be used to calculate and graphically show functions in two and three dimensions. All elementary mathematical functions and a large number of advanced functions are included as MATLAB functions.

(a) We compute and plot $\sin(2x)$, $\sin x^2$ and $\sin^2 x$ in the interval $0 \le x \le 6$ by giving short MATLAB commands.

```
x  = linspace(0,6);     % Creates a vector x.
y1 = sin(2*x);          % The vector y1 contains the
                        % sin(2x) values at the
                        % x-coordinates defined by x.
y2 = sin(x.^2);         % The vector y2 contains the
                        % sin(x^2) ditto.
y3 = (sin(x)).^2;       % The vector y3 contains
                        % the (sin(x))^2 ditto.
```

The command `plot(x,y1)` plots the vector **y1** as a function of the vector **x**, the definition of the `plot` command can be found in Chapter 13. Thus we can easily draw the curves of $\sin(2x)$, $\sin x^2$ and $\sin^2 x$ in a graph and label them correctly (Figure 1.1).

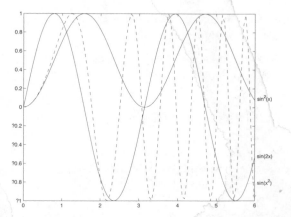

Figure 1.1 *Three curves in the same graph.*

(b) A function of two variables needs three dimensions to be properly visualized and MATLAB can give very good three-dimensional plots. In Figure 1.2 we show the function $f(x, y) = \cos(x) \cdot \sin(y)$ plotted in four different ways: with the surf command and shading interp upper left, with mesh upper right, with waterfall lower left and contour lower right. See Chapter 13 for more information on the graphics commands.

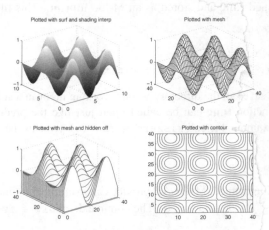

Figure 1.2 *A surface of a function of two variables plotted in four ways.*

(c) It is also possible to plot a parametric curve, for instance:

$$\begin{cases} x = \cos t - \sin 3t \\ y = \sin t \cos t - \cos 3t \end{cases}$$

The plot in the x–y plane is shown in Figure 1.3.

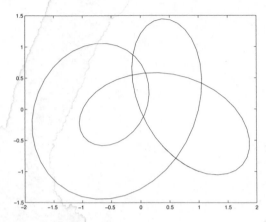

Figure 1.3 *A parametric curve.*

■

■ **Example 1.2   Analysis of functions**

The MATLAB commands `fzero` and `fmin` can be used to find zeros and minima of a function.

The function $xe^{x^2} - e^{x^2} - \sin x^3$ can be written as a user-defined function (see Section 2.9) called **func** and stored as an M-file **func.m**. This file consists of the following lines:

```
function y = func(x)
y = x.*exp(x.^2) - exp(x.^2) - sin(x.^3);
```

If this M-file is saved in the directory we are working in, or in a subdirectory called **matlab**, the function **func** can be called upon just like the predefined MATLAB functions, for example, the call `xiszero = func(0)` gives us the answer:

```
xiszero =
      -1
```

With this function defined, MATLAB provides an instrument to find the zeros of the equation $xe^{x^2} - e^{x^2} - \sin x^3 = 0$. The command: `xsolv = fzero('func',3)` gives us:

```
xsolv =
    1.2194
```

The second argument in the command, in this case with the value 3, is a first approximation to start the computations.

If we plot the function in the interval $-1 \le x \le 1.5$ we see that the answer is correct (Figure 1.4).

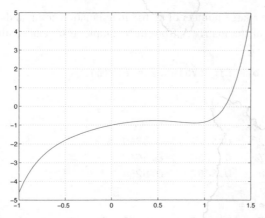

Figure 1.4 *The function* $xe^{x^2} - e^{x^2} - \sin x^3$ *plotted in the interval* $-1 \leq x \leq 1.5$.

The function seems to have a minimum between 0.5 and 1. To find out exactly where we can give the command `mpoint = fmin('func',0.5,1)`. The result is:

```
mpoint =
      0.8954
```

The commands for examining user-defined functions in MATLAB can be found in Chapters 10 and 11.

■

■ Example 1.3   Linear systems and eigenvalues

(a) MATLAB can solve linear systems with one single command line. Let the coefficient matrix **A** and the right-hand side **b** be defined as:

$$\mathbf{A} = \begin{pmatrix} 3 & 1 & -1 \\ 1 & 2 & 4 \\ -1 & 4 & 5 \end{pmatrix} \quad \mathbf{b} = \begin{pmatrix} 3.6 \\ 2.1 \\ -1.4 \end{pmatrix}$$

This corresponds to the linear system $\mathbf{Ax} = \mathbf{b}$ which looks like:

$$\begin{cases} 3x_1 + x_2 - x_3 = 3.6 \\ x_1 + 2x_2 + 4x_3 = 2.1 \\ -x_1 + 4x_2 + 5x_3 = -1.4 \end{cases}$$

and is solved by the command:

```
x = A\b
```

The result is:

```
x =
       1.4818
      -0.4606
       0.3848
```

(b) There is also a large number of matrix manipulation commands. For instance, the eigenvalues of the matrix **A** from the example in (a) can easily be found by the command:

```
[EigenVectors,EigenValues] = eig(A)
```

which gives:

```
EigenVectors =
   -0.9482   -0.3129   -0.0553
   -0.2887    0.7756    0.5613
    0.1328   -0.5482    0.8258


EigenValues =
    3.4445        0        0
        0   -1.2305        0
        0        0   7.7860
```

The columns of the matrix **EigenVectors** are the eigenvectors of **A** and the elements on the diagonal of **EigenValues** are the eigenvalues. Since the matrix **A** is symmetric all eigenvalues are real and the three eigenvectors are mutually orthogonal.

■

The basic concept in MATLAB is the matrix. Basic matrix instructions are presented in Chapter 3, and further commands are given in Chapters 4, 7, 8 and 9.

■ **Example 1.4   Curve fitting and interpolation**

(a) If we have a set of points in the x–y plane represented by two vectors **x** and **y**, then we can interpolate the points or fit a curve to them. Let

$$\mathbf{x} = (1 \quad 1.5 \quad 3 \quad 4 \quad 5 \quad 6 \quad 6.5 \quad 7 \quad 8)$$

$$\mathbf{y} = (1.2 \quad 1 \quad 1.7 \quad 2.5 \quad 2 \quad 2.3 \quad 2.5 \quad 3 \quad 3.1)$$

correspond to 9 points in the x–y plane. First, we show the linear function that fits the data in the least squares sense. This is obtained by three simple command lines in MATLAB:

```
p1 = polyfit(x,y,1);     % p1 = A vector containing the
                         % coefficients for a polynomial
                         % of degree one.
linc = polyval(p1,x);    % linc = A vector containing the
                         % values of the polynomial p1 in
                         % the points x.
plot(x,linc,x,y,'x')     % Plots the polynomial and the
                         % data marked by 'x'.
```

See Figure 1.5 (left) for the result.

We can fit polynomials of higher degrees to the set of points in the least squares sense. The command lines from above will have to be changed a little to obtain a polynomial of degree 7 instead:

```
p7 = polyfit(x,y,7);      % p7 = A vector containing the
                          % coefficients for a polynomial
                          % of degree 7.
xx = 1:0.25:8;            % xx = All points in which we
                          % want the polynomial computed.
polc = polyval(p7,xx)     % polc = A vector containing the
                          % values of the polynomial p7 in
                          % the points xx.
plot(xx,polc,x,y,'x')     % Plots the polynomial and the
                          % data marked by 'x'.
```

The result of this is shown in Figure 1.5 (right).

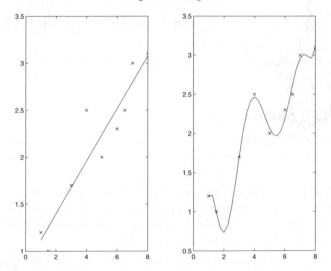

Figure 1.5 *Polynomials of first and seventh degree fitted to the set of data consisting of 9 points in the x–y plane.*

(b) MATLAB provides interpolation functions for both two and three dimensions. Given a set of points, (x_i, y_i), and some intermediate points, $\tilde{x}_i$, MATLAB can return the values in those intermediate points by interpolating the data. This can be done in different ways. As an example we will use the set of points from (a) to give the interpolated values in the following points:

$$\tilde{\mathbf{x}} = (\,1 \quad 1.1 \quad 1.2 \quad 1.3 \quad \ldots \quad 7.9 \quad 8\,).$$

In Figure 1.6 we show piecewise linear and cubic spline interpolation respectively. The 'x' marks represent the original set of data, and the dotted lines are the interpolated functions in the intermediate points.

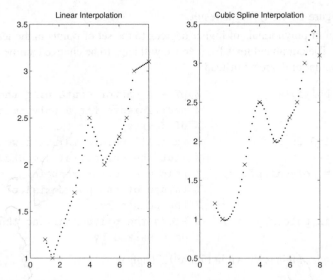

Figure 1.6 *Interpolation by piecewise linear functions (left) and cubic splines (right).*

More about interpolation and curve fitting can be found in Chapter 10.

■

■ **Example 1.5   Statistics**

MATLAB contains statistical commands. For example, we can easily find mean values and median values out of experimental data and also plot histograms or bar graphs.

Figure 1.7 displays the age of everyone in Littletown. The upper plot is a histogram where the number of persons of every age is shown. For instance, we can see that the two oldest persons are 92 years old. The histogram also shows that there is no one in Littletown of age 11 or 12 and seven children of age 7.

We can also see that there are as many people aged over 32 as there are under 32, since this is the median age. Furthermore, the average age is 35. This is also marked in the lower plot.

Furthermore, the lower plot shows the age of all inhabitants in Littletown. For example, if we knew the eleventh person to be listed we would also know that this person is just a baby, since the eleventh bar touches the *x* axis. This kind of plot is called a stairstep graph, that is, a bar graph with no internal lines. The statistics commands are presented in Chapter 6.

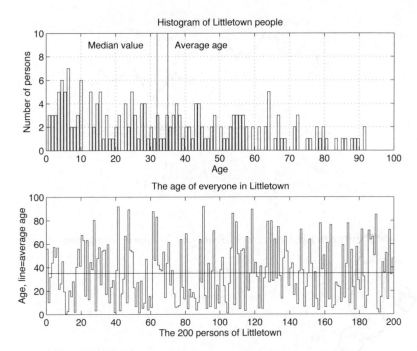

Figure 1.7 *A histogram and a graph of data from Littletown.*

◼

◼ Example 1.6   Fourier transform and signal analysis

MATLAB can compute a discrete Fourier transform using the Fast Fourier Transform, FFT. This can be used in signal analysis and in solving differential equations.

To demonstrate the Fourier transform in MATLAB we perturb the function $5\sin(x) + 2\sin(5x)$ using random numbers with expectation value 0 and variance 1:

```
x = linspace(0,2*pi,64);
signal = 5*sin(x) + 2*sin(5*x) + randn(x);
```

The perturbed and the original signal are shown in Figure 1.8 (upper).

Then we transform the signal and delete all high frequencies in the transformed signal, that is, the central part of the coefficient vector is set to zero.

```
transf = fft(signal);
filttransf(1:9) = transf(1:9);
filttransf(56:64) = transf(56:64);
```

The real part of the Fourier transform is shown in Figure 1.8 (lower) and the Fourier transform with the high frequencies deleted in Figure 1.9 (upper).

The vector with only the low frequencies is transformed by the inverse Fourier transform:

```
filtsig = ifft(filttransf);
```

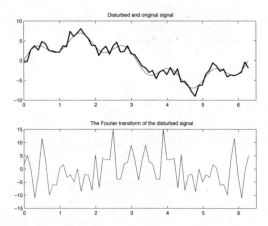

Figure 1.8 *A perturbed signal and its Fourier transform.*

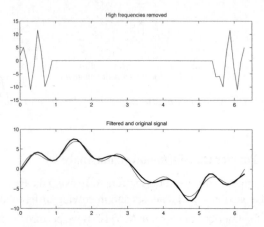

Figure 1.9 *The filtered Fourier transform.*

This filtered signal, along with the original signal, is shown in Figure 1.9 (lower). The filtered signal is smooth, as expected. It is not equal to the original signal since the perturbation also affected the low-frequency part of the signal.

In Section 10.5 the Fourier transforms that come as a part of MATLAB are presented. For more information about the Signal Processing Toolbox see Appendix C.

■

■ **Example 1.7   Ordinary differential equations**

MATLAB can solve ordinary differential equations numerically. As an example we show a cat chasing a mechanical toy mouse running on a circle. The position of the cat and the mouse is given by $(x(t), y(t))$ and $(X(t), Y(t))$ respectively. The velocity vector of the cat is parallel to the difference vector between the cat and the mouse.

The cat starts at (50, 40). This gives us the following system of differential equations:

$$\begin{cases} \dfrac{dx}{dt} = \dfrac{w}{\alpha}(X(t) - x(t)) \\[2mm] \dfrac{dy}{dt} = \dfrac{w}{\alpha}(Y(t) + y(t)) \\[2mm] x(0) = 40 \\[1mm] y(0) = 50 \end{cases}$$

where w is the velocity of the mouse and α is the distance between the cat and the mouse at the time t and is given by:

$$\alpha(t) = \sqrt{(X(t) - x(t))^2 + (Y(t) - y(t))^2}$$

The solution of the system is presented in Figure 1.10, where we can see that the cat does not succeed in catching the mouse since the mouse is too fast.

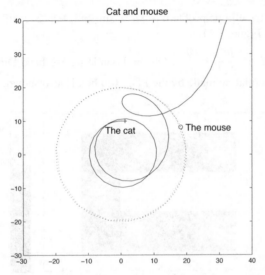

Figure 1.10 *A cat chasing a mechanical toy mouse. The small circle is the endpoint of the mouse and the cross is the endpoint of the cat.*

In Section 11.2 we show how to use MATLAB for ordinary differential equation problems in general.

■

■ Example 1.8   Partial differential equations

There are toolboxes in MATLAB for different applications. Here we give as an example the PDE Toolbox, which can solve elliptic, parabolic and hyperbolic equations in two-dimensional geometry by using the Finite Element Method. The region is divided into a large number of triangular subregions. For each triangle the solution is approximated by a simple function and the error will be smaller the more triangles we use.

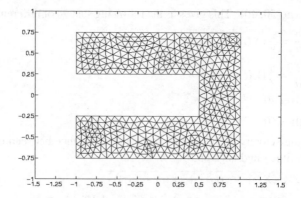

Figure 1.11 *Triangulation for FEM by the PDE Toolbox.*

We have solved the elliptic problem $-\Delta u = \sin(2\pi y + \pi/2)\cos(2\pi x + \pi/2)$ in the region shown in Figure 1.11.

The Laplacian Δ is $\dfrac{\partial^2}{\partial x^2} + \dfrac{\partial^2}{\partial y^2}$. On the boundaries we have Dirichlet conditions $u = 0$. The triangulation made by the PDE Toolbox is also shown.

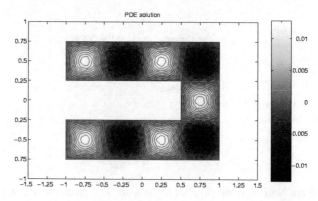

Figure 1.12 *A solution plot with contour lines computed by PDE Toolbox.*

The solution of the problem can be visualized as a 2D plot with contour lines as in Figure 1.12.

◼

◼ **Example 1.9   Programming in MATLAB**

MATLAB is programmable. Sequences of commands can be written in a text editor and then the user-defined function or program from the MATLAB command window can be called. The name of the file must have the extension **.m** and the file is called an **M-file**. These M-files can be used in the same way as all the standard MATLAB functions.

(a) The factorial, $n! = 1 \cdot 2 \cdot 3 \cdots \cdots n$, can be computed in different ways. Here we show a user-defined function which is recursive:

```
function p = factorial(nn)

% Computes the factorial of nn.

if  nn == 0
  p = 1;
else
  p = nn*factorial(nn-1);
end
```

The M-file is named **factorial.m** and a call to the function is made by:

```
fourfactorial = factorial(4)
```

The result is:

```
fourfactorial =
    24
```

(b) It is possible to use object oriented programming in MATLAB. We have a class **world** which simulates life and death in a small world. It is necessary to have some neighbors for an individual to be born in this world, but too many neighbors will make survival harder. The constructor of the class **world** is in the file **world.m** in the directory @**world**:

```
function w = world(Size, Density, nrCreate, nrSurvive)
% WORLD creates a world of Life.
%This is the constructor method.
% The Size gives the side of the world, which is square.
% Density    should be in the interval 0..1 and defines
%            the approximate ratio between filled and
%            empty squares.
% nrCreate   is the number of nearest neighbors that an empty
%            cell needs to grow life.
% nrSurvive  is the number of nearest neighbors that a filled
%            cell needs to survive and grow.

colormap('gray')
w.Size = Size;
w.nrCreate = nrCreate;
w.nrSurvive = nrSurvive;
w.Map = round( (-0.5+Density)+rand(Size,Size) );
w.NextY = zeros(Size,Size);
w = class(w,'world');
```

The methods that belong to the class are also defined in the directory @**world** but are not shown here. Now one may create the object **w** by the following command:

```
w = world(20,0.6,[2 4 5],[3 6 7]);
```

We now repeat

```
w = year(w)
```

ten times which is the same as ten years passing in our population, and we get
Figure 1.13.

Figure 1.13 *The population in the world* **w** *after 10 years.*

For more about programming in MATLAB, see Chapter 12.

■

■ **Example 1.10   Graphical user interface**

MATLAB offers an opportunity to design easy-to-use programs. Programs can be
manipulated by push buttons, pop-up menus, editable text, and so on, in a control
figure. This is described in Section 14.3. In Figure 1.14 we show an example of such
a graphical user interface designed by a Swedish scientist. The program is used for
solving a model equation on non-equidistant grids.

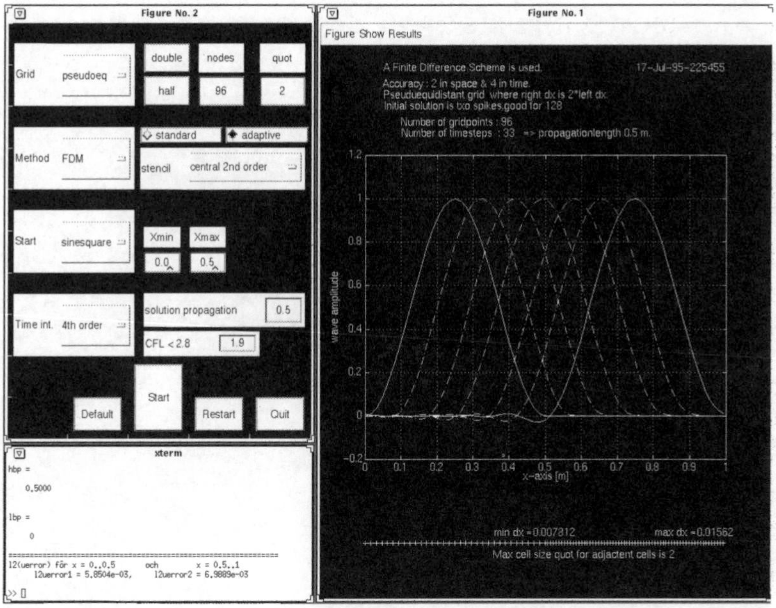

Figure 1.14 *A MATLAB program with graphical user interface applications.*

■

1.3 Help in MATLAB

This book is meant to show the commands available in MATLAB and explain how to use MATLAB. Most of the time this will be enough for the reader, but for those who want to learn more, there is help available in MATLAB. By typing the `help` command at the prompt, MATLAB gives an explanation of the command.

A powerful help database in HTML format is also included with MATLAB 5. This makes searching for a command much easier and helps follow up references. When the command `helpdesk` is given, a browser is started, e.g. Netscape Navigator or Microsoft Internet Explorer, which loads an index page.

If this is still not enough, MATLAB's complete manuals may be ordered from The Math-Works, Inc.; see the Preface.

Getting Started

First we describe how to start and, just as important, how to quit MATLAB. Then we describe how assignments and computations are made. We also demonstrate how to save results, get help and how to define your own functions. Some of the contents of this chapter may be skipped by experienced MATLAB users. However, we recommend a quick browse of the chapter. We also recommend the step-by-step introduction in Appendix A.

2.1 Starting and quitting MATLAB

How MATLAB is started varies between different computer systems. In Windows and Macintosh systems, the program is usually started by clicking on an icon. In UNIX systems the program is started by typing:

```
matlab
```

at the command line prompt. If none of the suggestions above works, ask the system manager. When starting MATLAB the files **matlabrc.m** and **startup.m** are executed if they exist. In these files one may give commands to adjust MATLAB to one's needs, e.g. constants, settings for the graphics etc. On a multi-user system the **matlabrc.m**-file is reserved for the system manager, but you may create the file **startup.m** for your own use, see Example 2.20 (c).

To quit MATLAB type `quit` or `exit`.

Commands 1	EXIT AND INTERRUPTION
`exit, quit`	ends the MATLAB session. The program finishes and values of variables are lost if not explicitly saved; see Section 2.8.
`Ctrl-c`	interrupts a MATLAB task, for instance when MATLAB is computing or printing, but the session is not ended.

Apart from this there are menu options specified for some systems. As an example, the option `quit` can be found under the `file menu` in Windows and Macintosh systems.

The following keyboard short-cuts are very useful when editing or executing MATLAB. When alternatives are given, it is usually because different keys are valid on different platforms. Try these keys on your system, and note which key combinations apply.

Commands 2	SPECIAL FUNCTION KEYS
↑ or `Ctrl-p`	recalls previous commands.
↓ or `Ctrl-n`	recalls commands typed later than the current command.
→ or `Ctrl-f`	moves one character right.
← or `Ctrl-b`	moves one character left.
`Delete, Backspace`	deletes character.
`Ctrl-l` or `Ctrl-←`	moves one word left.
`Ctrl-r` or `Ctrl-→`	moves one word right.
`Ctrl-a` or `Home`	moves to first character of line.
`Ctrl-e`	moves to end of line.
`Ctrl-k`	deletes to end of line.
`cedit`	toggles between different shortcuts. Type `help cedit` for more information.

2.2 Introduction to matrices and multidimensional matrices in MATLAB

The basic format for data in MATLAB is the **matrix**. A two-dimensional matrix is a rectangular table with the elements ordered in **rows** and **columns**. If it has m rows and n columns the matrix is said to have the **size** $m \times n$, or is of type $m \times n$. **Multidimensional matrices** have more than two dimensions and are said to have the size $m \times n \times \ldots \times p$.

■ **Example 2.1**

A 2×3 matrix can look like:

$$\mathbf{A} = \begin{pmatrix} 1 & 2 & 3 \\ 4 & 5 & 6 \end{pmatrix} = \begin{pmatrix} a_{11} & a_{12} & a_{13} \\ a_{21} & a_{22} & a_{23} \end{pmatrix}$$

The first row is $(1 \quad 2 \quad 3)$ and the second column is $\begin{pmatrix} 2 \\ 5 \end{pmatrix}$.

■

The **elements**, that is the numbers a_{ij}, of the matrix are usually real, but can also be complex numbers. An element a_{ij} is referred to by the row index i and the column index j. In Example 2.1, we have $a_{21} = 4$. In this chapter we only deal with **numerical matrices**, that is matrices containing only numbers. Matrices with text containing characters (see Commands 4, p. 24) and cell matrices, which may contain different kinds of data, are dealt with in Section 5.5, p. 109.

When the matrix consists of only one row it is a special case; then it is a **row vector**. If the matrix has only one column, we have a **column vector**. Vectors are special cases of matrices. The number of elements in a vector is the **length** of the vector.

If the matrix is of size 1×1 it is a **scalar**, that is, a number.

A variable is defined in MATLAB by assigning it a value. This is done as follows:

variable = *expression*

After *expression* press the 'carriage return' key. The *expression* can consist of numbers, variables, operators, functions, and so on.

An alternative way of defining a variable is to enter the term *expression*. MATLAB then assigns the value of the expression to the predefined variable **ans**, an abbreviation of 'answer'.

Assignment of a two-dimensional matrix can be done in several ways. The easiest is to give the elements row by row surrounded by brackets, [] (see also help paren). Brackets are not needed when a scalar is defined.

Elements in the same row are separated by one or more blanks ' ' or a comma, ','. Rows are seperated by semicolon, ';' or 'carriage return'. Each command given without a finishing semicolon displays the result on to the screen. With a semicolon at the end, the computation is performed, but the result is not displayed. A list of punctuation marks used in MATLAB is received with help punct.

The value of a variable is obtained by printing its name and pressing 'carriage return'. MATLAB answers by displaying both the variable name and the value. If the variable does not exist, an error message is displayed. An alternative way to display the contents of a variable is given in Section 5.1.3.

A specific element of a matrix or a vector is referred to by specifying its indices, for example a two-dimensional matrix:

variable(rowIndex,columnIndex)

If the variable is a vector, only one index is allowed. How to deal with multidimensional matrices is discussed in Example 2.3.

■ **Example 2.2**

(a) Assignment of a scalar. If x = 7 is written the following is printed on the screen:

    x =
       7

(b) If only 7 is written the result becomes:

```
ans =
      7
```

(c) The definition of a matrix, in this case of size 2×3, can be made by giving the elements row by row:

```
A = [1 2 3
4 5 6]
```

which gives the following on the screen:

```
A =
     1    2    3
     4    5    6
```

(d) It is also possible to give all the elements on the same line with semicolons to separate the rows:

```
A = [1 2 3;4 5 6];
```

A semicolon after the command suppresses the print-out of the result.

(e) Definition of a row vector and a column vector:

```
rowvec = [1.2 3.2 4];
colvec = [2.7;3.4;-9.2];
```

(f) Displaying the value of a variable. By writing `colvec` MATLAB displays:

```
colvec =
     2.7000
     3.4000
    -9.2000
```

(g) Assignment of a matrix element by element:

```
B(1,1) =   1;
B(1,2) =   7;
B(2,1) = -5;
B(2,2) =   0
```

gives us the result:

```
B =
     1    7
    -5    0
```

∎

Three-dimensional matrices and other data structures use the dimension order rows, columns and depth consequently in, for example, function arguments. There are two index principles for multidimensional matrices; the most natural, **matrix indexing**, gives the element a position in each dimension, e.g. the row and column index in the example above. This is shown in Figure 2.1 in which a $3 \times 3 \times 2$ matrix is visualized with indices for the different elements.

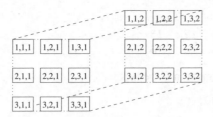

Figure 2.1 *Indices for the elements in a* $3 \times 3 \times 2$ *matrix.*

The other index principle is the **linear index method**. Some commands interpret the whole matrix as one long column of elements; one example of this is `reshape` (see Commands 37). Then it is reasonable to give the elements a linear index number describing which position a specific matrix index gets if all the elements were to be put in a row. This is illustrated in Figure 2.2.

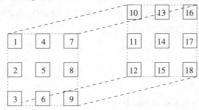

Figure 2.2 *Linear index in a* $3 \times 3 \times 2$ *matrix.*

There are several ways to create a multidimensional matrix.

■ **Example 2.3**

(a) With two two-dimensional matrices **A** and **B**:

   A=

1	2	3
4	5	6

  B=

11	12	13
14	15	16

we may easily construct a three-dimensional matrix **C**:

```
C(:,:,1) = A;
C(:,:,2) = B;
```

which gives:

`C(:,:,1)=`

1	2	3
4	5	6

$$C(:,:,2)=$$

11	12	13
14	15	16

(b) To change an element in **C** we type:

```
C(1,1,1) = 100;
```

and get:

$$C(:,:,1)=$$

100	2	3
4	5	6

■

MATLAB allows several variables to be defined on the same command line. It is also possible to continue a large assignment on the next line by typing three dots ' ... ...' before pressing 'carriage return'.

■ Example 2.4

(a) Several commands on the same line:

```
x = 7; y = 4.6735567; z = x^y;
```

(b) A long command divided into several lines:

```
mat1 = [1.2 1.1 -1.1 1.4 1.1 -1.1 -1.2 ...
-1.1 -1.3 1.7];
```

■

MATLAB remembers the sizes of the different matrix variables. To obtain the size of a certain variable the commands `size` and `length` are used.

Let **A** now be an $m \times n \times \ldots \times p$ matrix and **x** an $m \times 1$ matrix (a column vector) or a $1 \times n$ matrix (a row vector). MATLAB has the following commands:

Commands 3	SIZE OF VARIABLES
`size(A)`	gives a row vector containing the size of **A**. The first element in the returned vector is the number of rows, and the following is the number of columns, depth etc.
`[m,n,...,p] = size(A)`	gives the size of **A**, as the number of rows m and the number of columns n, that is two scalars. If too few arguments are given, the last dimensions are multiplied into the last argument.
`size(A,dim)`	gives the size of **A** in the dimension *dim*.

Commands 3	(CONTINUED)
size(x)	gives a row vector with the size or length of the vector **x**. If **x** is a column vector, the first element will be m and the second 1. If **x** is a row vector the first element is 1 and the second n.
length(x)	gives the length of a vector, that is n if **x** is a row vector and m if **x** is a column vector.
length(A)	gives the largest number of $m, n, \ldots$ and p.
ndims	returns the number of dimensions in the multidimensional matrix **A**. This function is equivalent to length(size(A)).
sub2ind(size,m, ,n,...)	gives the linear number of the index $(m, n, \ldots)$ in a matrix with size **size**.
[m,n, ...] = ind2sub (size,ind)	gives the index $(m, n, \ldots)$ for the element with linear index **ind**; to the imagined matrix to be interpreted as multidimensional the parameter **size** must be a vector.

Note: Sometimes the word 'dimension' is used instead of size and length. It is also common for length to be associated with a vector norm, and for the size of a matrix to be associated with a matrix norm. However, in this handbook size and length are used with the same meaning as size and length. When the concept length is used in the other sense, this is specified.

■ **Example 2.5**

(a) The command thesize1 = size(A), where **A** is the same as in Example 2.2 (c) above, returns:

```
thesize1 =
        2     3
```

The command thesize2 = size(C), where **C** is the three-dimensional matrix in Example 2.3, gives:

```
thesize2 =
        2     3     3
```

(b) To check if the information in Figure 2.2 is correct we use:

```
sub2ind([3 3 2],1,2,2)

ans =
    13
```

■

2.3 Variables in MATLAB

Identifiers, e.g. names of variables, can be 19 characters long in MATLAB. Letters A–Z, a–z, numbers, and the underscore sign '_' can be a part of it, but the first character has to be a letter. The name of a predefined function can also be used as a variable name, but this is not recommended since the function cannot be reached until the variable is deleted by the command `clear`.

MATLAB makes distinctions between upper-case and lower-case letters: for example the matrices a and A are not the same. MATLAB commands are normally written with lower-case letters. As an example, the command abs(A) gives the absolute value of **A**, but ABS(A) results in the following error message being displayed on screen:

```
??? Undefined variable or function ABS; Caps Lock may be on
```

The user does **not** need to specify the data type of a variable and it is not necessary to declare the variables before they are used. MATLAB has a number of different data types. It is valuable to be able to decide size and form of the variable, especially for the compound data types, matrices, cell matrices, structs and objects.

For each data type there is a function with the same name which converts the variable to that type. The different basic data types used are listed in the following table.

Commands 4   DATA TYPES AND CONVERTING FUNCTIONS

double	is a floating point number with double precision. Each number stored as `double` uses 64 bits.
char	is used to store characters. Each character stored uses 16 bits.
sparse	is used to store sparse matrices. The memory used by a sparse is 4+(number of non-zero elements*16).
uint8	is an eight bits integer without a sign. The mathematical functions are not defined for this data type which is used, e.g. for storing images.

The compound data types are described in Chapters 5 and 12.

There are a number of functions to help us find out if a variable is of a special type. There is also a special kind of logical vector in MATLAB, which is created with the command `repmat` (see Section 4.1).

Commands 5	LOGICAL FUNCTIONS
`iscell(x)`	returns 1 if **x** is a cell matrix, 0 otherwise. See also Section 5.5.
`isfield(x)`	returns 1 if **x** is a field in a struct, 0 otherwise. See also Section 12.5.
`isfinite(x)`	returns a vector of the same size as x containing 1 in the positions where **x** contains finite elements and 0 in the other positions.
`islogical(x)`	returns 1 if **x** is a logical vector, 0 otherwise.
`isnumeric(x)`	returns 1 if **x** is a numeric vector, 0 otherwise.
`isstr(x)`	returns 1 if **x** is a string, 0 otherwise. See also Section 5.1.
`isstruct(x)`	returns 1 if **x** is a struct, 0 otherwise. See also Section 12.5.
`isobject(x)`	returns 1 if **x** is an object, 0 otherwise. See also Section 12.6.
`locical(x)`	returns a logical vector that can be used, e.g. for logical indexing or logical tests.

■ **Example 2.6**

If a function is to be applied on every second element in a matrix it may be done like this:

```
data = rand(1,10)

data =
        0.6700    0.2009    0.2731    0.6262    0.5369    0.0595
        0.0890    0.2713    0.4091    0.4740
```

We create **x** by using `repmat`:

```
x = repmat([1 0],1,5)

x =
      1    0    1    0    1    0    1    0    1    0

filter = logical(x)

filter =
      1    0    1    0    1    0    1    0    1    0
```

To use the filter the following command is given:

```
halfdata = data(filter)
```

```
halfdata =
        0.6700 0.2731 0.5369 0.0890 0.4091
```

To use the filter together with the function round one types:

```
result = round(data(filter))
```

```
result =
        1    0    1    0    0
```

The command `repmat` generates block matrices and is further described in Section 4.1.

∎

There are a number of predefined variables in MATLAB as follows:

Commands 6	PREDEFINED VARIABLES IN MATLAB
ans	is assigned the value of the latest computed expression which is not given a name.
eps	returns the machine accuracy, defined as the distance between 1 and the closest representable floating point number. The number *eps* is used as tolerance in some commands. The user can assign a new value to *eps*, but note that the value of *eps* is not restored by the command `clear`.
realmax	returns the largest floating point number the computer can handle.
realmin	returns the smallest non-zero floating point number the computer can handle.
pi	returns π, that is 3.141 592 653 589 793, with an accuracy of about 16 decimals if *eps* is small enough.
inf	is defined as $1/0$. When division by zero occurs MATLAB returns *inf* and continues to compute without interrupting the execution.
NaN	is defined as 'Not a Number'. This non-number is either of the type $0/0$ or `inf/inf`.
i, j	are defined as $\sqrt{-1}$, the imaginary unit. We can assign i and j other values, and they will no longer be predefined constants. They are restored by the `clear` command; see below.

Commands 6   (CONTINUED)

`nargin`	gives the number of input arguments in a function call; see Section 12.3.
`nargout`	gives the number of output arguments in a function call; see Section 12.3.

To find which variables are defined the following commands may be used:

Commands 7   LIST OF VARIABLES

`who`	gives a list of the defined variables.
`who global`	does the same as `who` but only the global variables are listed; see Section 12.3.
`who a*`	gives a list of all variables beginning with an *a*.
`whos`	gives a more detailed list than the command `who`, for example the sizes of the matrices are shown.
`whos global`	does the same as `whos`, but only the global variables are listed; see Section 12.3.
`exist(namestr)`	returns different values depending on how the variable in the string **namestr** is defined. For more information about strings see Chapter 5. For now it is only important to note that the name of the variable should be given between quotation marks ' '. The function returns the value:
	1, if **namestr** is the name of a variable;
	2, if **namestr** is the name of an M-file (see Section 2.9);
	3, if **namestr** is the name of a MEX-file (see Chapter 15);
	4, if **namestr** is a compiled SIMULINK function;
	5, if **namestr** is the name of a predefined MATLAB function.
`inmem`	returns a cell vector with strings which contain the functions, M-files, currently in the memory. If two output parameters are given, the second contains a list of MEX-files currently in the memory.
`workspace`	gives a graphical interface to the information given by `whos`. The command `clear` is integrated in the environment. Works in UNIX despite the information given by `help workspace`.

Every variable that is defined will remain throughout the whole session if it is not deleted or renamed by the user. To delete variables, which is advisable, for example, when dealing with very large matrices, the command `clear` is used.

Commands 8	DELETING VARIABLES AND PACKING
clear	deletes all variables and restores all predefined variables except *eps*. See also Commands 111 (p. 250) on clear when running files.
clear name	deletes only the variable *name*.
clear name1 name2 ...	deletes the variables *name1*, *name2*, ...
clear a*	deletes all variables beginning with an *a*.
clear value	gives different results depending on *value*. Type help clear for details.
pack	rearranges and compacts the allocated memory, a so-called 'garbage collection'. When MATLAB's memory is full you can obtain more space with the command pack without clearing any variables. What happens is as follows: • all variables are saved on disk in a temporary file **pack.tmp**; • the contents of the primary memory are deleted; • all variables are loaded in primary memory from **pack.tmp**; • the file **pack.tmp** is deleted;
pack filename	rearranges and compacts the allocated memory by using the file **filename** as a temporary file.

Type help clear, help memory and help pack to get more information on how to save memory in MATLAB.

Remark: Commands in MATLAB are actually considered to be functions, taking strings as arguments. This means that the two statements:

```
command argument
```

```
command('argument')
```

are equal. For instance, clear name gives the same result as clear('name') and who global is equivalent to who('global'). Other examples can be found in several parts of the book, for example axis square and axis('square') in Section 13.3. The possibility of using the function/string formulation makes the MATLAB programming language very flexible, since command arguments may be created using string manipulation commands; see Chapter 5.

2.4 Arithmetic expressions and mathematical functions

Common conventions are used to write numbers in MATLAB. The decimal point is used and scientific notation makes it possible to write very large and very small numbers. Examples are 3.14 and $1.23E-6$, where the latter stands for 1.23×10^{-6}.

MATLAB has an extended set of **arithmetic operators**, and these are:

1. ^   power
2. *   multiplication
    /   right division (ordinary division)
    \   left division
3. +   addition
    −   subtraction

The operators are given in order of precedence, where 1 is of highest precedence. In expressions with operators of the same precedence they are executed from left to right. Parentheses, ( ), can be used to change the order of precedence.

In Section 3.3 we will see that it is useful to have two different kinds of division. For scalars the right division 2/5 giving 0.4 is the same as the left division 5\2. It is the expression or number that the slash 'leans on' that is the denominator.

■ **Example 2.7**

If we write a/b + c MATLAB reads it as $\dfrac{a}{b} + c$ but the expression a/(b+c) is read $\dfrac{a}{b+c}$.

If we use left division a\(b+c). MATLAB interprets it as $\dfrac{b+c}{a}$.

■

MATLAB contains predefined mathematical functions which can be used in arithmetic expressions. If the argument is complex, so, in most cases, is the answer.

MATLAB can also compute expressions containing predefined variables: for example an expression can be used as an argument of a function.

The predefined mathematical functions are listed in Commands 9. Even if these functions are described for scalar arguments, we shall see in Section 3.6 that they can handle vectors and matrices as well. Note that all trigonometric functions require that the arguments are given in radians.

Commands 9	MATHEMATICAL FUNCTIONS
abs(x)	gives the absolute value of x, that is $|x|$.
sign(x)	gives the sign of x, 1 if positive, -1 if negative and 0 if zero.
sqrt(x)	gives the square root of x, that is $\sqrt{x}$.
pow2(x,f)	gives $x \times 2^f$. This is a very efficient operation since it is performed as an addition of f to the exponent in the floating point format of x.
exp(x)	gives the exponential function of x, that is e^x.
log(x)	gives the natural logarithm of x, that is $\ln x$.
log10(x)	gives the base 10 logarithm of x, that is $\log_{10} x$.
log2(x)	gives the base 2 logarithm of x, that is $\log_2 x$.
sin(x)	gives $\sin x$, x in radians.
cos(x)	gives $\cos x$, x in radians.
tan(x)	gives $\tan x$, x in radians.
cot(x)	gives $\cot x$, that is $1/(\tan x)$, x in radians.
asin(x)	gives $\arcsin x$, that is $\sin^{-1} x$.
acos(x)	gives $\arccos x$, that is $\cos^{-1} x$.
atan(x)	gives $\arctan x$, that is $\tan^{-1} x$.
atan2(x,y)	gives $\arctan(x/y)$ and the result is in the interval $[-\pi, \pi]$.
acot(x)	gives $\operatorname{arccot} x = \arctan(1/x)$.
sec(x)	gives $1/(\cos x)$.
csc(x)	gives $1/(\sin x)$.
asec(x)	gives $\sec^{-1} x = \arccos(1/x)$.
acsc(x)	gives $\csc^{-1} x = \arcsin(1/x)$.
sinh(x)	gives $\sinh x$.
cosh(x)	gives $\cosh x$.
tanh(x)	gives $\tanh x$.
coth(x)	gives $\coth x$, that is $1/(\tanh x)$.
asinh(x)	gives $\sinh^{-1} x = \ln(x + \sqrt{1 + x^2})$.
acosh(x)	gives $\cosh^{-1} x = \ln(x + \sqrt{1 - x^2})$.
atanh(x)	gives $\tanh^{-1} x = 0.5 \ln((1 + x)/(1 - x))$.
acoth(x)	gives $\coth^{-1} x = 0.5 \ln((x + 1)/(x - 1))$.

sech(x)	gives $1/(\cosh x)$.
csch(x)	gives $1/(\sinh x)$.
asech(x)	gives $\operatorname{sech}^{-1} x = \ln((1 + \sqrt{1 - x^2})/x)$.
acsch(x)	gives $\operatorname{csch}^{-1} x = \ln((1 + \sqrt{1 + x^2})/x)$.

■ **Example 2.8**

(a) If we type sinepi = sin(pi) we get:

> *sinepi =*
> *1.2246e-16*

The result is not exactly 0 since pi is an approximation of π and we have round-off errors in the computation.

(b) logarithm = log10(100)

> *logarithm =*
> *2*

(c) e = exp(1)

> *e =*
> *2.7183*

■

There are several commands for rounding of numbers. In Commands 10, x is a floating point number or a matrix with floating point elements.

Commands 10 ROUNDING COMMANDS AND RELATED COMMANDS

round(x)	gives the integer closest to x. If **x** is a vector this holds for all components.
fix(x)	gives the integer closest to x in the direction towards 0; that means rounding upwards for negative x and downwards for positive.
floor(x)	gives the closest integer less than or equal to x.
ceil(x)	gives the closest integer greater than or equal to x.
rem(x,y)	gives the remainder of the integer division x/y.
gcd(x,y)	gives the greatest common divisor of the integers x and y.
[g,c,d] = gcd(x,y)	gives g, c, d such that $g = xc + yd$.
lcm(x,y)	gives the least common multiple of positive integers x and y, and can be used to determine the least common denominator.

Commands 10 (CONTINUED)

[t,n] = rat(x)	gives an approximation of x by the rational number t/n, where t and n are integers. The relative error is less than 10^{-6}. See also rats (Section 5.1.2) which gives the corresponding string.
[t,n] = rat(x,tol)	gives the same as above but with relative error less than *tol*.
rat(x)	gives a continued fraction representation of x.
rat(x,tol)	gives a continued fraction representation of x with relative error *tol*.

■ **Example 2.9**

(a) Rounding can be done in several ways. The commands:

```
x = -1.49;
rdx = round(x), fixx = fix(x), flx = floor(x), clx = ceil(x)

return

rdx =
     -1

fixx =
     -1

flx =
     -2

clx =
     -1
```

(b) We approximate $\sqrt{2}$ by a rational number t/n:

```
[t,n] = rat(sqrt(2))

t =
        1393

n =
      985
```

To compare with the true value we type `differ = sqrt(2) - t/n` which gives:

```
differ =
   3.6440e-07
```

As we can see, the difference is not large and will be even smaller if we specify a smaller value for the parameter *tol* in the function `rat`.

■

Complex valued expressions are allowed in most situations in MATLAB. The built-in variables *i* and *j* return the **imaginary unit**, that is the value of $\sqrt{-1}$, and can be used to generate complex numbers. It is possible to use the names *i* and *j* as names of variables and a new complex unit can be generated by:

```
ii = sqrt(-1);
```

One has to be careful with blanks when writing complex elements in a matrix since blanks will separate the elements; see Example 2.10(c) below.

■ **Example 2.10**

(a) `z = 3 + 4i`

```
z =
   3.0000 + 4.0000i
```

(b) A more complicated expression can look like:

```
w = r*exp(i*theta); comp = z*w;
```

where r and `theta` are already defined variables.

(c) Vectors can be complex as well:

```
complexvector = [1-i 2-2i 3 -3i]
```

returns:

```
complexvector =
  1.0000 - 1.0000i   2.0000 - 2.0000i   3.0000   0 - 3.0000i
```

Note that the blank between 3 and –3i forces MATLAB to read them as two separate complex numbers. We may see this if we type:

```
length(complexvector)
```

which gives us the result:

```
ans =
   4
```

■

There are some commands dealing with complex numbers and functions.

Commands 11	FUNCTIONS ON COMPLEX NUMBERS

`real(z)`	gives the real part of z.
`imag(z)`	gives the imaginary part of z.
`abs(z)`	gives the absolute value of z, that is $|z|$.
`conj(z)`	gives the complex conjugate of z, that is $\bar{z}$.
`angle(z)`	gives the phase angle of z, that is θ in $z = x + i\,y = re^{i\theta}$.
`unwrap(v)`	gives a vector of the same length as **v**, where the differences in phase angle between two consecutive elements have been changed so that the difference is at most π.
`unwrap(v,k)`	gives a vector just as above, but uses jump tolerance k instead of π.
`cplxpair(v)`	gives a vector where the elements of **v** have been sorted by increasing real parts and the complex numbers have been ordered in pairs with their complex conjugate. In one pair the negative imaginary part stands first. Real elements are sorted at the end in the vector. If a complex element of **v** has not got its complex conjugate in **v**, an error message is displayed.

■ **Example 2.11**

Let the complex number z be:

```
z = 1 + 2i;
```

(a) The real and imaginary parts of z are given by:

```
realpart = real(z), imagpart = imag(z)

realpart =
    1

imagpart =
    2
```

(b) The complex conjugate is given by `conjugate = conj(z)`

```
conjugate =
    1.0000 - 2.0000i
```

and the absolute value of z by `absz = abs(z)`

```
absz =
    2.2361
```

(c) The argument of a complex number, that is the phase angle in the complex plane, is given by `arg = angle(z)`

```
arg =
    1.1071
```

∎

There are also functions for transformations between coordinate systems. These functions can operate on vectors and matrices as well, and then the result will be of the same size as the input argument.

Commands 12   COORDINATE TRANSFORMATION

`[theta,r] = cart2pol(x,y)`	transforms from Cartesian coordinates to polar coordinates; the polar coordinates *theta* and r are given from the Cartesian x and y.
`[x,y] = pol2cart(theta,r)`	transforms from polar coordinates to Cartesian coordinates; the Cartesian coordinates x and y are given from the polar *theta* and r.
`[alpha,theta,r] = cart2sph(x,y,z)`	transforms from Cartesian coordinates to spherical coordinates; the angles *alpha*, *theta* and the length r are given from the Cartesian coordinates x, y and z.
`[x,y,z] = sph2cart(alpha, theta,r)`	transforms from spherical coordinates to Cartesian coordinates x, y and z.

There are also more advanced mathematical functions predefined in MATLAB.

Commands 13   SPECIAL MATHEMATICAL FUNCTIONS

`legendre(n,x)`	returns a vector of length $n + 1$ representing the values of associated Legendre functions of degree n and order 0 to n computed in x. If $x = \mathbf{x}$ is a vector the command returns a matrix, the columns of which are the associated Legendre functions computed for each element of $\mathbf{x}$. The elements of $\mathbf{x}$ must be in the interval $[-1, 1]$.

Commands 13   (CONTINUED)

`bessel(n,x)`	gives Bessel functions of the first kind. Both n and x can be vectors but n must increase in steps of one and be in the interval $[0, 1000]$. This command calls different routines depending on whether **x** is complex or not, but these routines can be called directly. Write `help bessel` for more information.
`bessely(n,x)`	gives Bessel functions of the second kind with the same arguments as `bessel`.
`gamma(x)`	gives the gamma function, that is for positive x:

$$\Gamma(x) = \int_0^\infty t^{x-1} e^{-t} \, dt$$

To obtain the definition for negative x, type `help gamma`.

`gammainc(x,a)`	gives the incomplete gamma function

$$\frac{1}{\Gamma(a)} \int_0^x t^{a-1} e^{-t} \, dt$$

`gammaln(x)`	gives the natural logarithm of the gamma function. Avoids overflow and underflow that may occur with `log(gamma(x))`.
`beta(x,y)`	gives the beta function, that is

$$\frac{\Gamma(x)\Gamma(y)}{\Gamma(x+y)}$$

The argument x must be in the interval $[0, 1]$. If the function is called by three arguments the command `betainc` below is used.

`betainc(x,a,b)`	gives the incomplete beta function, defined analogously to the incomplete gamma function.
`betaln(x,y)`	gives the natural logarithm of the beta function.
`expint(x)`	gives $\displaystyle\int_x^\infty \frac{e^{-t}}{t} \, dt$
`erf(x)`	gives the error function, that is the integral

$$\frac{2}{\sqrt{\pi}} \int_0^x e^{-t^2} \, dt$$

`erfinv(y)`	gives the inverse error function.
`erfc(x)`	gives the complementary error function $1 - \text{erf}(x)$.
`erfcx(x)`	gives the scaled complementary error function. Type `help erfcx` for more information.
`[k,e] = ellipke(m)`	gives complete elliptic integrals of the first and the second kind for $0 < m < 1$.
`[j1,j2,j3] = ellipj(x,m)`	gives the Jacobi elliptic functions.

In addition, you can define your own functions; see Section 2.9. Some of the special mathematical functions are also treated in Section 10.4.

2.5 Counting flops and time-keeping

MATLAB counts the number of arithmetic operations during a session, or parts of a session. This can be useful when comparing different algorithms to each other. To obtain an approximate number of floating point operations (flops) the command `flops` is used. Timing methods that show which parts of a MATLAB program take the most time are discussed in Section 12.7.

Commands 14	FLOPS COUNTER
`flops`	returns the approximate number of floating point operations completed since the counter last had the value 0, which is the default when starting MATLAB. Addition and subtraction count as one operation if the numbers are real, and two operations if the numbers are complex. Multiplication and division count as one operation if the numbers are real and six if they are complex. Calls to elementary functions count as one operation if the arguments are real, several if they are complex; the number depends on the function.
`flops(0)`	resets the counter to zero.

■ **Example 2.12**

Counting the number of operations. The following commands:

```
flops (0); x = 10 + 20 + 30*40/50;
numflops = flops
```

give, as expected, the result:

```
numflops =
    4
```

■

MATLAB can tell you date and time and give information about the computer. Together with the command `flops` these commands can be used to analyze the efficiency of an algorithm.

Commands 15	TIME AND DATE, PART 1
`tic`	starts a timer which can be read with the command `toc`.
`toc`	reads the timer, that is displays how much time has passed since it was started. If the timer is not running, `toc` returns no value.
`clock`	returns a row vector with six elements representing date and time in decimal form. The first five elements are integers. The seconds are given with an accuracy of several decimal points. The command `fix(clock)` rounds the seconds to the nearest integer.
`etime(t1,t2)`	computes the difference in seconds between **t1** and **t2**, where **t1** and **t2** are six element row vectors representing date and time.
`cputime`	returns the CPU-time in seconds that MATLAB has used since starting.

■ **Example 2.13**

Timing can be done in the following way:

Save current time by writing

```
t1 = clock
```

Write MATLAB commands and finish with

```
timedifference = etime(t1,clock);
```

to get the time difference, that is the time spent performing the commands in between.
■

MATLAB has built-in functions to handle dates. The sequences some functions use are composed of an integer part describing the date and a decimal part describing the time.

Commands 16	TIME AND DATE, PART 2
`date`	returns current date in a string of the form day–month–year.
`calendar(yyyy,mm)`	returns a 6 × 7 matrix over the weekdays in the month *mm* in the year *yyyy*.

| Commands 16 | (CONTINUED) |

`datenum(yyyy,mm,dd)` gives a sequence number for the day *dd* in the month *mm* in the year *yyyy*. The date 0000–01–01 has the daynumber 1.

`datestr(d,form)` returns the date with sequence number *d* at the format *form*, see Table 2.1.

`datetick(axis,form)` is used to write the data on the axis of a graph.

`datevec(d)` returns a vector [*yyyy mm dd ho mi se*] if *d* is either a sequence number or a date on a format returned by e.g. `datestr`.

`eomday(yyyy,mm)` returns the number on the last day in the month *mm* in the year *yyyy*.

`now` returns the sequence number of today and current time.

`[daynr dayname] =` `weekday(day)` returns *dayname* which tells whether the day *day* is a Sunday, Monday etc. and *daynr* equal to the sequence number of the day *day* in the week. Here *day* is a date on a stringformat or a sequence number.

The different date formats that may be used in `datestr` are listed in Table 2.1. We are using 02.14 Saturday the 26th of April 1986 as an example.

| Table 2.1 | DATE FORMAT |

0	gives the format *dd–mmm–yyyy HH:MM:SS*	`26--Apr--1986 02:14:00`
1	gives the format *dd–mmm–yyyy*	`26--Apr--1986`
2	gives the format *mm/dd/yy*	`04/26/86`
3	gives the format *mmm*	`Apr`
4	gives the format *m*	`A`
5	gives the format *m#*	`4`
6	gives the format *mm/dd*	`04/26`
7	gives the format *dd*	`26`
8	gives the format *ddd*	`Sat`
9	gives the format *d*	`S`
10	gives the format *yyyy*	`1986`
11	gives the format *yy*	`86`
12	gives the format *mmmyy*	`Apr86`
13	gives the format *HH:MM:SS*	`02:14:00`
14	gives the format *HH:MM:SS PM*	`2:14:00 AM`
15	gives the format *HH:MM*	`02:14`
16	gives the format *HH:MM PM*	`2:14 AM`
17	gives the format *QQ–YY*, where *QQ* is the number of the quarter	`Q2--86`
18	gives the format *QQ*	`Q2`

■ **Example 2.14**

To get the weekday for a particular date we use:

```
[dnr dname] = weekday('26--April--1986')

dnr =
            7

dname =
          Sat
```

In MATLAB, the week starts on Sunday, which makes Saturday weekday number 7.

■

2.6 Output formats

The result is usually displayed on the screen in integer format without decimals or in short floating point format with four decimals.

If all elements in a matrix are integers they are displayed in integer format, but if one or more of the elements is a non-integer all elements are displayed in floating point format. An exception is the number 0, which is always written in integer format.

The output format has nothing to do with the accuracy in the computation. MATLAB always performs the computations with full accuracy. For most computers MATLAB uses about 16 decimal places in computations.

The command `format` is used to change the output format. In the Windows and Macintosh versions, the output format can also be controlled through pull-down menus in the command window.

Commands 17	NUMERICAL OUTPUT FORMAT
`format defformat`	changes the output format to the format defined by *defformat*, which can be one of the following: `short`, `long`, `short e`, `long e`, `hex`, `+`, `bank`, `rat`. There are also `compact` and `loose`, which give a more compact, or loose, output format but do not affect the numerical output format. All examples in the book use `format compact`.
`more on`	stops displaying when the window is full and waits for a key stroke before further output is displayed. At the bottom of the window MATLAB prints —*more*— to indicate that there is more to be displayed.

Commands 17	(CONTINUED)
`more off`	gives output without considering whether the window is big enough or not.
`more(n)`	displays output in *n* lines if the output is longer than *n* lines.

■ **Example 2.15**

Suppose that p = 1 + 1/3; and that we first define format and then display *p* on the screen, then:

`format short`	gives	*1.3333*	4 decimals
`format long`	gives	*1.33333333333333*	14 decimals
`format short e`	gives	*1.3333e+00*	4 decimals
`format long e`	gives	*1.333333333333333e+00*	15 decimals
`format hex`	gives	*3ff5555555555555*	hexadecimal
`format +`	gives	*+*	positive: +,
			negative: − or zero: 0
`format bank`	gives	*1.33*	dollars and cents
`format rat`	gives	*4/3*	as a rational number

■

It is also possible to reduce the number of blanks that MATLAB uses in the output, and to direct the output when the line is too long for the window. In this book, `format compact` is used in the examples to reduce the number of blanks.

2.7 Help commands and demonstrations

Help can always be obtained by using any of the following commands.

Commands 18	HELP COMMANDS
`help`	gives a list of about 20 topics on which general information can be given. These topics are in directories and information about each topic is given by `help dir`, where `dir` is the directory.
`help command`	gives help for the specified `command`.
`help dir`	gives the contents of directory `dir`.
`hthelp`	opens a MATLAB GUI to a hyperlinked database. This command is replaced with `helpdesk` and may be removed in future versions.

Commands 18   (CONTINUED)

`htpp`	is a preprocessor to link helpfiles in `hthelp`.
`loadhtml`	is used by `hthelp` and `http` to load, interpret and show HTML files.
`helpdesk`	starts a web browser with the index page in MATLAB Help Desk.
`doc command`	gets the help page for the command *command* in MATLAB Help Desk.
`web URL`	directs the browser to *URL* and opens a browser if needed. See `help web` for more information.
`lookfor text`	searches the first line of all M-files for the string **text**.
`demo`	gives a demonstration of MATLAB's different commands, functions and application areas. The command `demo` runs MATLAB Expo. This displays a menu of different demonstration examples to select. A couple of simple games can also be found.
`expo`	runs MATLAB Expo; see also `demo`.
`info`	gives information about MATLAB, for example what kind of computers can run MATLAB, how to get more information about the current development and new releases of MATLAB, and so on.
`whatsnew`	gives information about the new commands in the new version.
`subscribe`	gives the opportunity to become a subscribing user of MATLAB.
`why`	explains why something went wrong.

MATLAB Help Desk is an HTML-based help system where a lot of the information available through `help` is supplied together with hyperlinks to references, pictures and formulas. It also includes a better search facility than provided by `lookfor`. It is important to note that MATLAB Help Desk uses JavaScript and this must therefore be enabled. If the `helpdesk` command is given and the browser does not look like Figure 2.3 and shows only the MATLAB logo it is probable that JavaScript has not been enabled. The choice of browser is determined in UNIX by an M-file named **docopt.m**; in Windows MATLAB uses the program associated with .htm files.

■ **Example 2.16**

(a) The command `help size` gives:

```
SIZE   Size of matrix.
    D = SIZE(X), for M-by-N matrix X, returns the two-element
```

row vector D = [M, N] containing the number of rows and
columns in the matrix. For N-D arrays, SIZE(X) returns
a 1-by-N vector of dimension lengths. Trailing singleton
dimensions are ignored.

[M,N] = SIZE(X) returns the number of rows and columns in
separate output variables. [M1,M2,M3,...,MN] = SIZE(X)
returns the length of the first N dimensions of X.

M = SIZE(X,DIM) returns the length of the dimension
specified by the scalar DIM. For example, SIZE(X,1)
returns the number of rows.

See also LENGTH, NDIMS.

```
Overloaded methods
    help zpk/size.m
    help tf/size.m
    help ss/size.m
```

Note that MATLAB writes the commands in capital letters in the help text although MATLAB does not accept commands given in capital letters.

(b) To start MATLAB Help Desk give the command `helpdesk` and MATLAB starts a browser (or uses one that is already running) as shown in Figure 2.3.

(c) To find information about the sine function we type:

lookfor sine which gives:

```
ACOS    Inverse cosine.
ACOSH   Inverse hyperbolic cosine.
ASIN    Inverse sine.
ASINH   Inverse hyperbolic sine.
COS     Cosine.
COSH    Hyperbolic cosine.
SIN     Sine.
SINH    Hyperbolic sine.
TFFUNC  time and frequency domain versions of
        a cosine modulated Gaussian pulse.
DST     Discrete sine transform.
IDST    Inverse discrete sine transform.
```

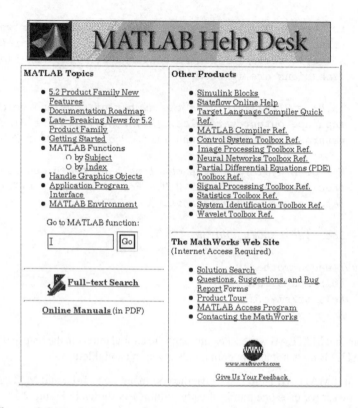

Figure 2.3 *The index page shown when* MATLAB Help Desk *is started.*

An excellent way to learn MATLAB commands is to run a couple of demonstration programs with the command demo, then examine interesting commands with the command help and finally start using the commands.

There are commands that give information about the computer on which you are running MATLAB.

Commands 19	COMPUTER INFORMATION

[str,n] = computer	gives a description of the computer on which MATLAB is running. The string **str** depends on the computer or operating system, for example VAX, Sun, PC, Macintosh and so on, and n is the total number of allowed elements in a matrix in the current installation of MATLAB.
isieee	returns 1 for computers with IEEE arithmetic, for example IBM PC, Macintosh, and 0 for computers without, for example VAX, Cray.
version	returns a string with current MATLAB version number.

Commands 19	(CONTINUED)
`ver`	displays current MATLAB and toolbox version numbers.
`hostid`	returns MATLAB server host identification number.
`getenv(str)`	returns text associated with **str**. Here, **str** is the name of a symbol or an environment variable.
`terminal`	configures MATLAB terminal settings.

■ **Example 2.17**

On a Sun workstation running Solaris 2 the command

`[comp,numb] = computer`

returns

```
comp =
     SOL2
numb =
     268435455
```

■

2.8 Saving and loading

MATLAB can keep a diary of what is displayed on the screen. This is done by the command `diary`. An exception is graphical output. To print or save graphs, see Section 13.7.

Commands 20	DIARY OF A SESSION
`diary filename`	stores the following session in file **filename**.
`diary off`	stops the recording.
`diary on`	starts the recording. Continues on current diary file.
`diary`	stores the following session in file **diary**, but is also a switch between `diary on` and `diary off`.

The resulting ASCII file can later be edited and included in documents. However, the values and results saved with the command `diary` cannot usually be read by MATLAB on a later occasion.

To save the variables and their contents so that they can be used in a later session, the commands `save` and `load` should be used. The name of the file, **filename** in the table, determines how MATLAB interprets the file. All files that end with **.mat** are interpreted as binary, and all files ending with something else, including **filename.**, are interpreted as ASCII files.

Commands 21	SAVING AND LOADING VARIABLES

`save`	saves all variables on the file **matlab.mat**.
`save filename`	saves all variables on the file **filename.mat**. If one writes **filename.**, with a dot at the end, or if another suffix is added, MATLAB does not add the suffix **.mat**.
`save filename v1 v2 ...`	saves the variables $v1$, $v2$, and ... etc. on file **filename.mat**.
`save filename v -ascii`	saves the values of variables v in readable ASCII-format on the file **filename.mat**. Write 8 decimals.
`save filename v -ascii -double`	saves the values of variables v in readable ASCII-format in double precision with 16 decimals on the file **filename**.
`load`	loads all variables from the file **matlab.mat**.
`load filename`	loads all variables from the file **filename.mat** to MATLAB. If **filename** does not have a suffix the file is created with `save`. If the file has a suffix but is still binary the option −mat should be used.
	If **filename** contains '.' and a suffix, for example **temp.dat**. the data are loaded from the corresponding ASCII-file to MATLAB as a matrix named **filename** without '.' and suffix. The file is either created by `save file var -ascii` or directly by using an editor or as an output file from another program.

■ **Example 2.18**

Suppose that the ASCII file **A.dat** is created by an editor or by a program, containing the following data:

```
1   4   5
4   2   9
```

In MATLAB we get the Matrix A by typing:

```
load A.dat, A
A =
     1          4          5
     4          2          9
```

■

For an example of saving data on a file when the filename is stored as a string, see Example 5.8 (b). See also Chapter 15, in which more sophisticated file handling, and how files are used in FORTRAN and C programs, are discussed.

2.9 Command files and function files

Instead of writing statements of MATLAB commands at the MATLAB prompter you can write them in a text file, created with an editor. These commands are executed by MATLAB when the user writes the file name and its arguments, if any. MATLAB reads the commands from the file instead of the terminal. When the last command in the file is executed, MATLAB can read commands from the terminal again. MATLAB will first look for the file in the current working directory; if it does not exist there all directories in the pathway are searched. The pathway is kept in `matlabpath`; see Commands 22. If one wants to execute a file which is not in a place where it is automatically looked for one may use the command `run`; see Chapter 12.

An M-file is a file of the kind:

filename.m

that is, it must have the suffix **.m**.

An M-file contains a number of consecutive MATLAB commands and it may refer to other M-files. It may even be recursive, that is to say, refer to itself.

There are a number of predefined M-files on MATLAB's 'utility-disk', for example **cond.m**, **demo.m**, **length.m** and **hilb.m**. To see the names of the files one uses the command `what`. Then the M-files defined by the user and stored in the MATLAB directory are listed.

An alternative to `what` is the command `dir`. This command is one of the file commands in MATLAB.

| Commands 22 | SYSTEM COMMANDS |

`what` *dirname*	lists all MATLAB files in the current directory. If **dirname** is given the files in the directory **dirname** are listed.
`dir`	lists all files in a directory or subdirectory. The command can be used with different path names and wild cards.
`ls`	also lists the files but in a different output format.
`pwd`	lists current working directory.
`delete filename`	deletes the file **filename**.
`cd`	changes current directory.

Commands 22   (CONTINUED)

`type filename`	displays the contents of the file **filename**. If no suffix is specified MATLAB reads **filename.m**.
`edit file`	opens an editor. If **file** is given this file is opened in the editor.
`copyfile(file1, file2)`	copies **file1** to **file2**. See `help copyfile` for error handling.
`which filename`	displays the search path of the function specified by **filename**.
`path`	displays MATLAB's directory search path. If the command is given with arguments the search path is changed. Type `help path` for more information.
`matlabpath`	works as `path` but without error handling when a new search path is given.
`genpath(directory)`	returns a new search path consisting of the old together with all directories under `MATLABROOT/toolbox`. If **directory** is given all directories under **directory** are added instead.
`pathsep`	lists the separation marks which separate directories in `matlabpath`.
`partialpath`	lists local search paths.
`editpath`	gives a graphic user interface where one may add and edit directories from MATLAB's search path.
`addpath(dir1, dir2,...,flag)`	adds the directories **dir1**, **dir2**, ... at the beginning of MATLAB's search path. If the string **flag** is given and is `begin` the directories are added at the beginning; if it is `end` at the end.
`rmpath dir`	removes the directory **dir** from MATLAB's search path.
`pathtool`	is a graphic tool to modify the search path. It works in UNIX although `help pathtool` suggests it will not.
`path2rc`	stores the current search path in the file **pathdef.m** from which the search path is read when starting MATLAB.
`dbtype filename`	displays the contents of the file **filename** with line number. If no suffix is given in **filename** MATLAB uses the suffix **.m**.
`dbtype filename r1:rn`	displays line $r1$ to line rn in **filename**, with line numbers.
`lasterr`	repeats the last error message.
`lastwarn`	repeats the last warning message.
`!`	interprets the line as operating system commands. This does not exist in the Macintosh version.
`isstudent`	returns 1 if The Student Edition of MATLAB (distributed by Prentice Hall) is used. Otherwise 0 is returned.
`isdir dirname`	returns 1 if **dirname** is a directory, otherwise 0.

Commands 22	(CONTINUED)
isppc	returns 1 if MATLAB is used on a Macintosh Power PC, otherwise 0.
isunix	returns 1 if MATLAB is used on a UNIX system, otherwise 0.
isvms	returns 1 if MATLAB is used on VMS, otherwise 0.
vms	runs a VMS DCL command from MATLAB. Is the same as ! but with the possibility to store data from the command in variables. Type `help vms` for more information. The command is only available on VMS systems.
dos	runs a DOS command from MATLAB. Is the same as !, see above, but with the possibility of storing data from the command in variables. Type `help dos` for more information. The command is only available on a PC.
applescript	loads an AppleScript file and runs it. See `helpdesk` for more information. The command is only available on a Macintosh.
unix	executes a UNIX operating system command from MATLAB, similar to !. Type `help unix` for more information.
tempdir	returns a string with the name of the temporary directory of the system (if there is one).
tempname	returns a string beginning with 'tp', MATLAB will check that the string is not a filename in the temporary directory of the system. Because of this the string is suitable to use as a name for a temporary file.
matlabroot	returns a string with the search path to the directory where MATLAB is installed.

It may be a good idea to create a directory named `matlab` to save one's M-files in. MATLAB looks automatically in this directory and finds the files.

■ **Example 2.19**

(a) To look at the contents of the file **sec.m**. included in MATLAB, we type:

```
type sec

function y = sec(z)
%   SEC    Secant.
%   SEC(X) is the secant of the elements of X.

%   Copyright (c) 1984-98 by The MathWorks, Inc.
%   $Revision: 5.3 $  $Date: 1997/11/21 23:28:33 $

y = 1./cos(z);
```

The comments in M-files, that is lines starting with %, are used as documentation in MATLAB. Preferably these comments should be informative, and not as in this example confuse **X** and **z**. The elementwise operator ./ is defined in Section 3.5.

(b) If help sec is written, the starting comment lines of the file **sec.m** are displayed:

```
SEC Secant.
    SEC(X) is the secant of the elements of X.
```

■

This is an example of a **function file**, a user-defined function, that is a special kind of M-file. Apart from the second kind of M-file, which we will call a **command file**, a function can have one or several arguments or parameters. These are given with separating commas ','. In the example sec, there is one parameter, namely **z**. The parameters must be surrounded by parentheses '( )'. Command files are also called script files. Type help script for more information about this.

Functions in MATLAB have a strong resemblance to functions in C or subroutines in FORTRAN. The function files must have certain properties:

- The first line in a function file must contain the word function; command files have no such demand. Therefore M-files without this first line are command files.

- The first line must specify the function name, the input arguments (parameters) and the output arguments (parameters). The input parameters are variables copied from MATLAB's workspace to the workspace of the function. The first line looks like:

```
function output = name(input)
```

- A function may have zero, one or several input parameters and return values.

- The equivalent to subroutine in FORTRAN, procedure in Pascal or void function in C/C++ is the following in MATLAB:

```
function = name(inputArguments)
```

A function M-file is called by writing

```
filename(inputArguments)
```

in MATLAB. It is recommended that name is the same as filename. The arguments, used when calling, do not need to have the same names as the formal argument in the function file.

The comments coming after the first line are displayed when help name is written. A similar convention is used for command files.

Function files and command files are executed just like ordinary MATLAB commands. The statements in the file are executed when the name of the file is written, together with the arguments if there are any.

All M-files are common ASCII files and can be created in a text editor. It might be good to write and test M-files from MATLAB using the command ! whenever an operating system command has to be called, for example when editing the text; see Commands 22.

■ **Example 2.20**

(a) Suppose that a certain matrix is often used. It can be created and then stored according to Section 2.8, and then loaded whenever needed. An alternative way is to create the matrix in an M-file. The following MATLAB command is stored in the file **Thematrix.m**, and creates a matrix that can be used frequently:

```
A = [-9 -3 -16;13 7 16;3 3 10];
```

By typing: Thematrix, the matrix **A** is assigned according to the line above. We show this by typing the command:

```
whos
```

```
    Name        Size          Bytes   Class

    A           3x3              72   double array

Grand total is 9 elements using 72 bytes
```

(b) Suppose that the following function is stored in the file **average.m:**

```
function y = average(A)
% The function computes the average of
% all elements of A, the result is a scalar.

[m,n] = size(A);
y = sum(sum(A))/m/n;
```

If the matrix from Example (a) is defined, the following command:

```
average_value = average(A)
```

gives as a result

```
average_value =
              2.6667
```

Another way of writing the function **average** is:

```
function y = average(A)
% The function computes the average of all elements
% of A, the result is a scalar.

y = mean(A(:));
```

The commands sum and mean are defined in Chapter 6, and the colon notation A(:) is presented in Section 4.3.

(c) **startup.m** is a special user-defined command file. It will run automatically each time you start MATLAB if it is situated in your MATLAB working directory. In it you can list your own predefined constants and settings or, as in this example, make MATLAB greet you as you start a wonderful, new MATLAB session!

```
% My first startup.m
disp ('Welcome to MATLAB!')
```

With this command file defined we will see this the next time we start MATLAB:

```
              < M A T L A B (R) >
        (c) Copyright 1984-98 The MathWorks, Inc.
                 All Rights Reserved
               Version 5.2.0.3084
                    Jan 17 1998


  To get started, type one of these: helpwin, helpdesk, or demo.
  For product information, type tour or visit www.mathworks.com.

Welcome to MATLAB!
>>
```

More about M-files can be found in Section 12.3.

Matrix Operations

Most of the operations in MATLAB can be applied directly on matrices. Apart from the arithmetic operations +, -, *, ^, /, \\, discussed in Section 2.4, there is the ' operator for transposition and conjugation, relational operators and logical operators.

Users of the Student Edition of MATLAB should be aware that the total number of elements in the matrices is limited to 16384.

Moreover there are arithmetical and logical functions on matrices. Some of these work on two-dimensional matrices only.

3.1 Addition and subtraction

The sum of two matrices, $\mathbf{A} + \mathbf{B}$, and the difference between two matrices, $\mathbf{A} - \mathbf{B}$, are defined if $\mathbf{A}$ and $\mathbf{B}$ are of equal size. The matrix $\mathbf{A} \pm \mathbf{B}$ has the elements $a_{ij\ldots p} \pm b_{ij\ldots p}$. In MATLAB, addition and subtraction can also be performed between an $m \times n$ matrix $\mathbf{A}$ and a scalar, that is a 1×1 matrix s. The matrix $\mathbf{A} + s$ has the same size as $\mathbf{A}$, and the elements are $a_{ij} + s$.

■ **Example 3.1**

Suppose that $\mathbf{A}$ and $\mathbf{B}$ are defined as:

$$\mathbf{A} = \begin{pmatrix} 1 & 2 \\ 3 & 4 \end{pmatrix} \quad \mathbf{B} = \begin{pmatrix} 5 & 6 \\ 7 & 8 \end{pmatrix}$$

The MATLAB commands

```
Add = A + B, Sub = A - B, Add100 = A + 100
```

give the results:

```
Add =
      6      8
     10     12


Sub =
     -4     -4
     -4     -4
```

```
Add100 =
    101    102
    103    104
```

■

3.2 Multiplication

Matrix multiplication, that is $C = AB$, is defined for two-dimensional matrices if the number of columns in A is equal to the number of rows in B. If this is not the case, MATLAB returns an error message. The only exception is when one of the matrices is 1×1, i.e. a scalar, which MATLAB accepts. The operator for multiplication is $*$ in MATLAB, so that the command is C = A*B.

The element c_{ij} is the **dot product** of the ith row in A and the jth column in B. See Commands 23 and Appendix B for definition of dot product. The matrix C has the same number of rows as A, and the same number of columns as B.

For square matrices the product BA is defined as well, but the result is in most cases different from AB.

■ **Example 3.2**

(a) Suppose that A and B are the same as in Example 3.1. The commands

    A, B, MultAB = A*B, MultBA = B*A

give the following result, displayed on the screen:

```
A =
     1     2
     3     4

B =
     5     6
     7     8

MultAB =
    19    22
    43    50

MultBA =
    23    34
    31    46
```

(b) Let **x** and **y** be:

$$\mathbf{x} = (1 \quad 2 \quad 3) \qquad \mathbf{y} = \begin{pmatrix} 1 \\ 10 \\ 100 \end{pmatrix}$$

The commands s = x*y, M = y*x result in:

```
s =
   321


M =
     1      2      3
    10     20     30
   100    200    300
```

■

MATLAB also includes other products. The command dot(x,y) gives the **dot product**, also called the **scalar product** or the **inner product**, of two vectors **x** and **y** with equal number of elements. If the dot product is zero the two vectors are **orthogonal**. The dot product of two matrices **A** and **B** is defined if **A** and **B** are of equal size, and is defined columnwise in MATLAB. The result is a row vector where the components are the dot products of the first columns, the second columns and so on. See also Appendix B.

Commands 23   THE DOT PRODUCT

dot(x,y)	gives the dot product of the vectors **x** and **y**.
dot(A,B)	gives a row vector of length n where the elements are the dot products of the corresponding columns in **A** and **B**. The matrices **A** and **B** must be of the same size $m \times n$. For multi-dimensional matrices, see helpdesk.
dot(A,B,dim)	gives the dot product of **A** and **B** in the *dim* dimension.

For two vectors **x** and **y** with three components each, the command cross(x,y) gives the **vector product**, or the **cross product**, that is:

$$\mathbf{x} \times \mathbf{y} = (x_2 y_3 - x_3 y_2 \quad x_3 y_1 - x_1 y_3 \quad x_1 y_2 - x_2 y_1)$$

The vector $\mathbf{x} \times \mathbf{y}$ is orthogonal to the vectors **x** and **y**.

The cross command can also be applied to $3 \times n$ matrices, then the result is a $3 \times n$ matrix where the ith column is the cross product of the ith columns in **A** and **B**.

Commands 24	THE CROSS PRODUCT
`cross(x,y)`	gives the cross product of the vectors **x** and **y**.
`cross(A,B)`	gives a $3 \times n$ matrix where the columns are the cross products of the corresponding columns in **A** and **B**. The matrices **A** and **B** must be of equal size $3 \times n$.
`cross(A,B,dim)`	gives the cross product between the vectors **A** and **B** in the *dim* dimension. **A** and **B** must have the same dimension, and both `size(A,dim)` and `size(B,dim)` has to be 3.

■ **Example 3.3**

Suppose:

$$\mathbf{x} = (1 \quad 0 \quad 0) \qquad \mathbf{y} = (0 \quad 1 \quad 0)$$

The command `crossprod = cross(x,y)` gives:

```
crossprod =
        0    0    1
```

which is orthogonal to both **x** and **y**, that is

`scalar1 = dot(x,crossprod), scalar2 = dot(y,crossprod)`

gives:

```
scalar1 =
        0
```

```
scalar2 =
        0
```

■

There is a function in MATLAB to perform a two-dimensional convolution of matrices. It is possible to use FIR filter (Finite Impulse Response) as an argument; this is described in `helpdesk`.

Commands 25	CONVOLUTION OF MATRICES
conv2(A,B)	returns the two-dimensional convolution of the matrices **A** and **B**.
conv2(hcol,hrow,A)	convolves the matrix **A** with the vector **hcol** columnwise and the vector **hrow** rowwise.
conv2(...,format)	gives a special form of the convolution. The parameter **format** must be one of the following strings:

	'same'	returns the part of the convolution that is closest to the center and the same size as **A**.
	'valid'	returns only the parts of the convolution that is calculated without zero-padded edges.

convn(A,B)	returns the multidimensional convolution of the matrices **A** and **B**.
convn(...,format)	gives a special form of the convolution, see above.

The Kronecker tensor product can be used to create large regular block matrices. It is given by the command kron(A,B). If **A** is an $m \times n$ matrix, and **B** is a $k \times r$ matrix the command returns an $m \cdot k \times r \cdot n$ matrix.

Commands 26	TENSOR PRODUCT
kron(A,B)	gives the Kronecker tensor product of **A** and **B**.

■ **Example 3.4**

Suppose:

$$A = \begin{pmatrix} 2 & 0 \\ -1 & 1 \end{pmatrix} \quad B = \begin{pmatrix} 1 & 2 & 3 \\ 1 & 0 & 1 \end{pmatrix}$$

Then the command K = kron(A,B) results in:

```
K =
     2     4     6     0     0     0
     2     0     2     0     0     0
    -1    -2    -3     1     2     3
    -1     0    -1     1     0     1
```

■

3.3 Division

There are two symbols for matrix division in MATLAB, **left division** \ and **right division** /. If **A** is a non-singular square matrix, then A\B and B/A correspond to left and right multiplication of **B** by the inverse of **A**, that is equivalent to the commands inv(A)*B and B*inv(A), respectively. However, MATLAB executes these differently, which is shown in Example 3.5. The inverse of **A**, inv(A) or $\mathbf{A}^{-1}$, is defined in Section 7.1.

If **A** is a square matrix then X = A\B is the solution $\mathbf{A}^{-1}\mathbf{B}$ of the matrix equation $\mathbf{AX} = \mathbf{B}$, where **X** is of the same size as **B**. In the special case where $\mathbf{B} = \mathbf{b}$ is a column vector, then x = A\b is the solution of the linear system $\mathbf{Ax} = \mathbf{b}$; see Section 7.2.

If **A** is a rectangular $m \times n$ matrix with $m > n$, X = A\B gives the least squares solution of the matrix equations $\mathbf{AX} = \mathbf{B}$; see also Section 7.7.

The solution of the matrix equation $\mathbf{XA} = \mathbf{B}$ is $\mathbf{X} = \mathbf{B}/\mathbf{A}$ which is the same as $(\mathbf{A}'\backslash\mathbf{B}')'$, that is right division can be defined by left division. Here, the apostrophe, ', denotes transposition and is explained in Section 3.4.

■ **Example 3.5**

(a) Let **A** and **B** be defined as in Example 3.1. The commands
A, B, Right = B/A, Left = A\B give:

```
A =
       1       2
       3       4

B =
       5       6
       7       8

Right =
      -1       2
      -2       3

Left =
      -3      -4
       4       5
```

If instead we type Right = B*inv(A) and Left = inv(A)*B, we get:

```
Right =
    -1.0000    2.0000
    -2.0000    3.0000
```

```
Left =
    -3.0000    -4.0000
     4.0000     5.0000
```

This is the same as the matrices computed by / and \ respectively, but the floating point format reveals that the computational procedures are different.

(b) Let us now take the following **A** and **b**:

$$A = \begin{pmatrix} 1 & 3 & 5 \\ 1 & 2 & 4 \\ 0 & 5 & 1 \end{pmatrix} \qquad b = \begin{pmatrix} 22 \\ 17 \\ 13 \end{pmatrix}$$

The solution of the system $Ax = b$ is typed in MATLAB as x = A\b, which gives us:

```
x =
    1.0000
    2.0000
    3.0000
```

(c) We use the same **A** and **b**. Let us investigate the number of operations to solve the system $Ax = b$.

The commands flops (0); x = inv(A)*b; flops give the result:

```
ans =
    109
```

and flops(0); x = A\b; flops give:

```
ans =
    72
```

therefore fewer operations are required in MATLAB to solve a system with left division than with inversion and multiplication. For a definition of the command flops see Section 2.5.

∎

3.4 Transposition and conjugation

An important operator is the one for transposition and conjugate transposition, which is written in MATLAB with an apostrophe '. In textbooks this combined operation is often denoted by * or ^{H}.

If **A** is real then row 1 becomes column 1, row 2 becomes column 2, and so on when it is transposed. An $m \times n$ matrix becomes an $n \times m$ matrix. If the matrix is square, the matrix is reflected in the main diagonal.

If the matrix **A** with elements a_{ij} is complex, then the elements are conjugated as well. The matrix A' contains $\overline{a_{ji}}$ on entry (i, j).

If only the transposition is desired, a point is typed before the apostrophe `.'`, writing `A.'` means transposing and gives the same result as `conj(A')`. If **A** is real then `A'` is the same as `A.'`.

■ **Example 3.6**

Suppose **A** and **b** are the same as in Example 3.5 (b).
`Transp = A'`, `Transpb = b'` then give:

```
Transp =
     1     1     0
     3     2     5
     5     4     1

Transpb =
    22    17    13
```

■

3.5 Elementwise arithmetic operations

Arithmetic operations can also be performed element-by-element. Matrices of equal size, that may be multidimensional, are required. If the operation is preceded by a point the operation is performed elementwise.

For addition and subtraction there is no difference between elementwise operation and matrix operation. The elementwise operators are:

```
+        -        .*       ./       .\       .^
```

Note that `.'` is not on the list. The point has a different meaning in that case. The operator gives only the transpose, as opposed to `'` which gives the conjugate transpose; see Section 3.4.

■ **Example 3.7**

Suppose that the following matrices are defined:

$$\mathbf{A} = \begin{pmatrix} 1 & 2 \\ -1 & 5 \end{pmatrix} \quad \mathbf{B} = \begin{pmatrix} 7 & 2 \\ 1 & 0 \end{pmatrix} \quad \mathbf{C} = \begin{pmatrix} 1+2i & 5-2i \\ 3+i & 1+3i \end{pmatrix}$$

(a) A.*B gives:

```
ans =
     7     4
    -1     0
```

(b) B./A gives:

```
ans =
     7     1
    -1     0
```

(c) B.^2 gives:

```
ans =
    49     4
     1     0
```

(d) A.^B gives:

```
ans =
     1     4
    -1     1
```

(e) The base can be scalar and the exponent a matrix: 2.^[1 2 3 4] gives:

```
ans =
     2     4     8    16
```

(f) C.' gives:

```
ans =
   1.0000 + 2.0000i   3.0000 + 1.0000i
   5.0000 - 2.0000i   1.0000 + 3.0000i
```

■

See also Example 13.1 which also uses elementwise operations.

3.6 Elementwise functions

The mathematical standard functions which are predefined in MATLAB (see Section 2.4), operate elementwise on matrices. If f is such a function and **A** is a matrix with the elements a_{ij} then $f(\mathbf{A})_{ij} = f(a_{ij})$. If the elements are complex then the resulting matrix can also be complex depending on the function. The size of the matrix is not changed.

■ **Example 3.8**

Let **A**, **B** and **C** be:

$$A = \begin{pmatrix} 0 & -3 \\ 5 & 1 \\ 4 & -6 \end{pmatrix} \quad B = \begin{pmatrix} \pi & 0 \\ \pi/2 & \pi/4 \end{pmatrix} \quad C = \begin{pmatrix} 1+i & -\pi i \\ 0 & 2-i \end{pmatrix}$$

(a) `abs(A)` gives:

```
ans =
     0     3
     5     1
     4     6
```

(b) `cos(B)` gives:

```
ans =
    -1.0000     1.0000
     0.0000     0.7071
```

(c) `sin(abs(C))` gives:

```
ans =
     0.9878     0.0000
          0     0.7867
```

■

Elementwise operators and functions are very useful in MATLAB and it is possible to define one's own elementwise functions and store them in M-files; see Section 2.9.

■ **Example 3.9**

The function $sincos(x) = \sin(x)\cos(x)$ is not a standard MATLAB function. However, you can define your own function *sincos*, and store it in the file **sincos.m**:

```
function y = sincos(x)
y = sin(x).*cos(x);
```

A call to *sincos* would look like:

```
y1 = sincos(pi), y2 = sincos([0 pi/4 pi/2])
```

```
y1 =
  -1.2246e-16
```

```
y2 =
        0    0.5000    0.0000
```

We see that $y1$, which should have been 0, is a very small number, in fact *eps* is larger. If we call *sincos* with a vector as an argument then the result is a vector since both sin and cos return vectors. This is very useful when plotting graphs of functions.

∎

Applications of M-files can be found in Chapters 12 and 13.

3.7 Powers and functions of matrices

For two-dimensional square matrices, the pth power of **A** can be executed with A^p. If p is a positive integer then the power is defined by a number of matrix multiplications. For $p = 0$ we get the identity matrix of the same size as **A**. When $p < 0$ then A^p is the same as inv(A)^(-p), and is defined if $\mathbf{A}^{-1}$ exists.

MATLAB expressions like exp(A) and sqrt(A) are regarded as elementwise operations (see Section 3.6); that is, they work on the elements one-by-one in **A**.

MATLAB can also treat functions of square matrices, for instance $\mathbf{A}^{1/2}$ (square root of **A**), or $e^{\mathbf{A}}$. For instance we have:

$$e^{\mathbf{A}} = I + \mathbf{A} + \frac{\mathbf{A}^2}{2!} + \frac{\mathbf{A}^3}{3!} + \cdots$$

Commands 27   MATRIX FUNCTIONS

expm(A)	computes $e^{\mathbf{A}}$ using the Padé approximation and is a built-in function.
expm1(A)	computes $e^{\mathbf{A}}$ using an M-file and the same algorithm as the built-in function.
expm2(A)	computes $e^{\mathbf{A}}$ using Taylor series.
expm3(A)	computes $e^{\mathbf{A}}$ using eigenvalues and eigenvectors.
logm(A)	computes the natural logarithm of **A**.
sqrtm(A)	computes $\mathbf{A}^{1/2}$. The square root is unique when **A** is symmetric and positive definite.

Commands 27	(CONTINUED)
funm(A,fcn)	computes the matrix function of **A** specified in the string **fcn**, see Section 5.1.4. The string **fcn** could be any of the elementary functions sin, cos, and so on; see Section 2.4. For example, expm(A) = funm(A,'exp').
[F, E] = funm(A,fcn)	computes the matrix function as above but returns the matrix **F**, the result, and the matrix **E**, an approximation of the residual.
polyvalm(p,A)	evaluates a polynomial of the matrix **A**. The vector **p** contains the coefficients of the polynomial; see Section 10.1.

It is important to make a distinction between expm and exp, logm and log, and so on.

■ **Example 3.10**

Suppose that:

$$\mathbf{A} = \begin{pmatrix} 1 & 0 \\ 0 & 2 \end{pmatrix}$$

Let us compare exp and expm:

```
Elementwise = exp(A), Operatorwise = expm(A)
```

give:

```
Elementwise =
    2.7183    1.0000
    1.0000    7.3891

Operatorwise =
    2.7183         0
         0    7.3891
```

3.8 Relational operators

MATLAB has six **relational operators** or **boolean operators** for comparisons between matrices. It is also possible to compare a matrix with a scalar: then each of the elements of the matrix is compared with the scalar.

The relational operators are:

> <   smaller than
> <=   smaller than or equal to
> >   greater than
> >=   greater than or equal to
> ==   equal to
> ~=   not equal to

The relational operators compare the corresponding elements and generate a matrix of the same size containing only ones and zeros. The elements are:

> 1   if the comparison is **true**
> 0   if the comparison is **false**

In an expression, arithmetic operators have the highest precedence, relational operators the second highest and logical operators the lowest. Parentheses are used to alter the precedence.

■ Example 3.11

(a) Compare the value of the predefined variable `pi` with the rational number that is an approximation of pi obtained by the command `rat`.

```
[t,n] = rat(pi), piapprox = t/n;
format long, piapprox, pi, piapprox == pi
```

gives:

```
t =
   355

n =
   113

piapprox =
   3.14159292035398

ans =
   3.14159265358979

ans =
   0
```

(b) Suppose:

$$A = \begin{pmatrix} 1 & 2 & 4 \\ 1 & 1 & 1 \\ 2 & 3 & 1 \end{pmatrix} \quad B = \begin{pmatrix} 2 & 2 & 2 \\ 2 & 2 & 2 \\ 2 & 2 & 2 \end{pmatrix}$$

Are there any elements in **A** that are greater than the corresponding elements in **B**?

```
Greater = A > B
```

gives:

```
Greater =
       0       0       1
       0       0       0
       0       1       0
```

that is the entries $(1, 3)$ and $(3, 2)$ are greater in **A** than in **B**.

(c) Let **A** be as in Example (b). Are there elements in **A** greater than 1?

```
GreaterThanOne = A > 1
```

gives:

```
GreaterThanOne =
       0       1       1
       0       0       0
       1       1       0
```

3.9 Logical operators

There are four **logical operators** in MATLAB:

&	**and**
|	**or**
~	**not**
xor	**exclusive or**

The logical operators have the lowest precedence of the operators. In an expression, both relational and arithmetic operations are performed prior to logical operations.

The difference between **xor** and **or** is that **or** is true if at least one of the expressions is true but **xor** is true if one of the expressions is true but not both.

The operators & and | compare two matrices of equal size. It is also possible to compare a scalar with a matrix, as in the previous section. The logical operators work elementwise. Components that are zero represent the logical value **false** and any other value of the component represents the logical value **true**. The result is a matrix containing ones and zeros.

Commands 28	LOGICAL OPERATORS
A & B	returns a matrix with the same size as **A** and **B**, which has ones at entries where both **A** and **B** have elements that are non-zero, and zeros at entries where either **A** or **B** is zero.
A | B	returns a matrix with the same size as **A** and **B**, which has ones at entries where at least one of **A** and **B** is non-zero, and zeros at entries where both matrices are zero.
~A	returns a matrix with the same size as **A**, which has ones where **A** is zero, and zeros where **A** is non-zero.
xor(A,B)	returns a matrix with the same size as **A** and **B**, which has zeros where **A** and **B** are either both non-zero or both zero, and ones on entries where either **A** or **B** is non-zero, but not both.

3.10 Logical functions

There are several **logical functions** in MATLAB. In the definitions of these functions below we assume that **A** is an $m \times n$ matrix and **x** a vector.

In some computations it is important to locate entries with certain properties in a given matrix. For example, in Gaussian elimination with partial pivoting we have to find the largest entry in the column we are working in. The MATLAB command find can be used for such cases.

Commands 29	FIND NON-ZERO ELEMENTS
find(x)	returns a vector containing the entries for non-zero components in **x**. If all the components are zero then an empty matrix is returned, that is [ ].
find(A)	returns a vector containing the entries for non-zero elements in a long vector built of the columns in **A**. The following command is preferable.
[u,v] = find(A)	returns the vectors **u** and **v**, containing the entries for non-zero elements in **A**, that is the entries (u_k, v_k) in **A** are non-zero.
[u,v,b] = find(A)	returns the vectors **u** and **v** containing the entries of the non-zero elements of **A**, and a vector containing the corresponding non-zero elements. The entries (u_k, v_k) in **A** are non-zero and can be found in b_k.

■ **Example 3.12**

Suppose **x** and **A** are:

$$\mathbf{x} = (3 \quad -4 \quad 0 \quad 6.1 \quad 0) \quad \mathbf{A} = \begin{pmatrix} 1 & 0 \\ 0 & 4 \end{pmatrix} \quad \mathbf{y} = \begin{pmatrix} 1 \\ 0 \\ 0 \\ 4 \end{pmatrix}$$

(a) `ind = find(x)`, `indcol = find(A)` give:

```
ind =
    1    2    4
```

```
indcol =
    1
    4
```

that is components 1, 2 and 4 are non-zero in the vector **x**. To obtain `indcol` we could as well have typed:

`find(y)`

(b) The command `find` can be used in combination with the relational operators, which makes the command very useful. For example, `index = find(x > 0.5)` returns:

```
index =
    1    4
```

If we type `greaterThan = x(index)` we get:

```
greaterThan =
    3.0000    6.1000
```

that is we use the vector **index** to find all elements greater than 0.5 in **x**.

If we just want to know how many elements in **x** are greater than 0.5 we can type:
`length (find(x > 0.5))` which for the example above would give:

```
ans = .
    2
```

(c) To obtain the index of all non-zero elements of **A** we type:
`[index1, index2] = find(A)` which gives us:

```
index1 =
    1
    2
```

```
index2 =
    1
    2
```

that is the components (1, 1) and (2, 2) are non-zero.

■

MATLAB has two functions, `any` and `all`, that test logical conditions for matrices and vectors. The result is boolean, which is either 1 or 0, **true** or **false**. They are especially useful in if-statements; see Section 12.1.

Commands 30	LOGICAL FUNCTIONS, PART 1
`any(x)`	returns 1 if any of the components in **x** is non-zero, otherwise it returns 0.
`any(A)`	operates columnwise on **A** and returns a row vector with ones and zeros, depending on whether the corresponding column contains as non-zero elements or not.
`all(x)`	returns 1 if all components are non-zero, otherwise a 0 is returned.
`all(A)`	operates columnwise on **A** and returns a row vector with ones and zeros, depending on whether the corresponding column has all elements as non-zero or not.

If one of the functions operates twice on a matrix, for example `any(any(A))` and `all(all(A))` a scalar is returned that is either 1 or 0.

■ **Example 3.13**

(a) All the components in a real vector **x** are smaller than or equal to 5 if `all(x < = 5)` returns the value 1. If the value 0 is returned at least one component is greater than 5. All elements of a matrix **A** is smaller or equal to 5 if `all(all(A < = 5))` returns the value 1.

(b) For a real square matrix **A**, **A** is symmetric if `all(all(A == A'))` returns the value 1.

(c) A square matrix **A** is upper triangular if `any(any(tril(A,-1)))` returns the value 0. Otherwise there is at least one non-zero element below the diagonal in **A**. An equivalent command is `all(all(A == triu(A)))` that returns 1 if **A** is upper triangular.

■

We have also the following logical functions:

Commands 31	LOGICAL FUNCTIONS, PART 2
`isnan(A)`	returns a matrix with size equal to **A**, having 1 on entries where **A** has 'NaN' and zeros elsewhere.
`isinf(A)`	returns a matrix with size equal to **A**, having 1 on entries where **A** has 'inf' and zeros elsewhere.

Commands 31	(CONTINUED)
isempty(A)	returns 1 if **A** is an empty matrix, otherwise zero.
isequal(A,B)	returns 1 if **A** and **B** are equal, that is are the same size and have the same contents, 0 otherwise.
isreal(A)	returns 1 if **A** is a real matrix with no imaginary part, otherwise zero.
isfinite(A)	returns a matrix with the same size as **A** with 1 on entries where the elements in **A** are finite and zeros elsewhere.

There are also logical functions that operate on strings and other data types, see Chapter 5.

Creating New Matrices

The basics of matrix definition and assignment are discussed in Section 2.2. It is also possible to create new matrices, for example by functions that return a new matrix or by using existing matrices.

4.1 Building new matrices

The **matrix of ones**, whose components are all ones, is created with the ones command. The **zero matrix** has all components equal to zero. It is created with zeros. The **identity matrix** has ones in the diagonal and zeros in all other entries. It is created with eye. In square matrix operations, the identity matrix of order n corresponds to the number 1 in scalar operations.

Commands 32 THE MATRIX OF ONES, THE ZERO MATRIX AND THE
IDENTITY MATRIX

`ones(n)`	gives an $n \times n$ matrix of ones.
`ones(m,n,...,p)`	gives an $m \times n \times \ldots \times p$ matrix of ones.
`ones(size(A))`	gives a matrix of ones of the same size as **A**.
`zeros(n)`	gives an $n \times n$ matrix of zeros.
`zeros(m,n,...,p)`	gives an $m \times n \times \ldots \times p$ matrix of zeros.
`zeros(size(A))`	gives a matrix of zeros of the same size as **A**.
`eye(n)`	gives an $n \times n$ identity matrix. Note that the eye command only may be used to create two-dimensional matrices.
`eye(m,n)`	gives an $m \times n$ identity matrix. Note that the eye command only may be used to create two-dimensional matrices.
`eye(size(A))`	gives an identity matrix of the same size as **A**.

■ **Example 4.1**

The commands:

```
OneMatrix  = ones(3,4,2)
ZeroMatrix = zeros(size(OneMatrix))
Identity   = eye(2)
Identity23 = eye(2,3)
Identity32 = eye(3,2)
```

give the following result on the screen:

```
OneMatrix(:,:,1) =
    1       1       1       1
    1       1       1       1
    1       1       1       1

OneMatrix(:,:,2) =
    1       1       1       1
    1       1       1       1
    1       1       1       1

ZeroMatrix(:,:,1) =
    0       0       0       0
    0       0       0       0
    0       0       0       0

ZeroMatrix(:,:,2) =
    0       0       0       0
    0       0       0       0
    0       0       0       0

Identity =
    1       0
    0       1

Identity23 =
    1       0       0
    0       1       0

Identity32 =
    1       0
    0       1
    0       0
```

A **random matrix** is a matrix in which all the components are random numbers. The rand command produces random numbers **uniformly distributed** between 0 and 1. There is also the command randn in MATLAB, which returns **normally distributed** random numbers, with the expected value 0 and variance 1.

Commands 33	RANDOM NUMBERS AND MATRICES

rand	gives uniformly distributed random numbers between 0 and 1; each call gives a new number.
rand + i*rand	gives a complex scalar random number.
rand(n)	gives an $n \times n$ matrix with the components uniformly distributed between 0 and 1.
rand(m,n,...,p)	gives an $m \times n \times \ldots \times p$ matrix with the components uniformly distributed between 0 and 1.
randn	gives normally distributed random numbers with expectation value 0 and variance 1.
randn(n)	gives an $n \times n$ matrix with normally distributed random numbers with expected values 0 and variance 1.
randn(m,n,...,p)	gives an $m \times n \times \ldots \times p$ matrix with normally distributed random numbers with expected values 0 and variance 1.

MATLAB 5 uses a new random number generator with several seeds. It can generate all floating point numbers in the closed interval $[2^{-53}, 1 - 2^{-53}]$. Theoretically it can generate more than $2^{1492} \simeq 10^{449}$ values before repeating itself. MATLAB 4 uses a random number generator with only one seed.

Commands 34	RANDOM NUMBER SEED

rand('state')	returns a vector with 35 elements containing the current state of the random state generator.
rand('state',s)	sets the state of the random seed generator to s.
rand('state',0)	sets the random seed generator to its original state.
rand('state',j)	sets, for an integer j, the random seed generator to its jth state.
rand('state', sum(100*clock))	sets the random seed generator to a new state each time, using the command clock; see Commands 15.
rand('seed',*arg*)	uses the random seed generator of MATLAB 4, see helpdesk for more information.
randn('state')	returns a vector with two elements containing the state of the normal random seed generator.
randn('state',arg)	sets the normal random seed generator according to **arg**, see rand.

■ **Example 4.2**

(a) The random seed generator may, for example, give the result below. We have only printed the first five elements (of 35) of the `state` vector.

```
astate = rand('state'); astate(1:5), Random = rand(2,3)
ans =
    0.6923
    0.1646
    0.5676
    0.3609
    0.8557
Random =
    0.4565    0.8214    0.6154
    0.0185    0.4447    0.7919
```

(b) To avoid starting with the same seed and always getting the same sequence of random numbers, the built-in function `clock` in MATLAB can be used:

```
rand('state',sum(100*clock)); R = rand('state'); R(1:5)
ans =
    0.8010
    0.4701
    0.5052
    0.0707
    0.4643
```

The `clock` command is defined in Section 2.5.

■

In MATLAB there are also commands that create new matrices using parts of existing matrices. Suppose A is an $m \times n$ matrix, and x is a vector with n components. Then the command `diag` produces new matrices as described in Commands 35.

Commands 35 NEW MATRICES FROM OLD MATRICES, PART 1

`diag(A)`	gives a column vector containing the elements on the main diagonal of A. This diagonal always starts in the upper left-hand corner. For square matrices it ends in the lower right-hand corner.
`diag(x)`	gives a square diagonal matrix of order n in which the main diagonal is the vector x and all other elements are zero.
`diag(A,k)`	gives a column vector containing the elements on the kth diagonal in A. If $k = 0$ the main diagonal is referred to, if $k < 0$ it is a diagonal below the main diagonal and if $k > 0$ a diagonal above the main diagonal.
`diag(x,k)`	gives an $(n + \text{abs}(k)) \times (n + \text{abs}(k))$ matrix with the elements of the vector x on the kth diagonal. All other elements are 0. Concerning the parameter k, see the previous command.

■ **Example 4.3**

Suppose:

$$A = \begin{pmatrix} 1 & 2 & 3 & 4 \\ 5 & 6 & 7 & 8 \\ 9 & 10 & 11 & 12 \\ 13 & 14 & 15 & 16 \end{pmatrix} \qquad x = (-5 \quad -10 \quad -15)$$

(a) The command `diag_element = diag(A)` gives:

```
diag_element =
     1
     6
    11
    16
```

(b) `Diag_matrix = diag(diag(A))` returns:

```
Diag_matrix =
     1     0     0     0
     0     6     0     0
     0     0    11     0
     0     0     0    16
```

(c) The command `Dmatrixx = diag(x)` or `Dmatrixx = diag(x')` gives:

```
Dmatrixx =
    -5     0     0
     0   -10     0
     0     0   -15
```

(d) If we type `superDiagElement = diag(A,2)` the output is:

```
superDiagElement =
     3
     8
```

(e) `NewMatrix = diag(diag(A,2))` returns:

```
NewMatrix =
     3     0
     0     8
```

Note that the size of this matrix is determined by the vector `diag(A,2)`.

(f) `SuperDiagonalMatrix = diag(diag(A,2),2)` returns the following matrix:

```
SuperDiagonalMatrix =
     0    0    3    0
     0    0    0    8
     0    0    0    0
     0    0    0    0
```

The second superdiagonal of **A** has length 2. Thus the created matrix is of type 4×4.

■

Triangular matrices are created in MATLAB with `triu` and `tril`.

Commands 36	NEW MATRICES FROM OLD MATRICES, PART 2

`triu(A)`	gives an upper triangular matrix of the same size as **A**. The elements on and above the main diagonal are the same as in **A**.
`triu(A,k)`	generates a matrix of the same size as **A**, where the elements on and above the kth diagonal are the same as in **A**. Negative numbers of k refer to diagonals below the main diagonal. All other elements are zero. The command `triu(A,0)` is equivalent to `triu(A)`.
`tril(A)`	gives a lower triangular matrix of the same size as **A**. The elements on and below the main diagonal are the same as in **A**.
`tril(A,k)`	generates a matrix of the same size as **A**, where the elements on and below the kth diagonal are the same as in **A**. Negative numbers of k refer to diagonals below the main diagonal. All other elements are zero. The command `tril(A,0)` is equivalent to `tril(A)`.

The following relation is true for every square matrix **A**:

```
A = triu(A) + tril(A) - diag(diag(A))
```

The strictly upper triangular part of **A** is defined as `triu(A,1)` and the strictly lower triangular part of **A** is defined as `tril(A,-1)`. Hence, the following relation is true for every square matrix **A**:

```
A = triu(A,1) + tril(A,-1) + diag(diag(A))
```

Decomposition of matrices in this manner is of importance when systems of linear equations are solved by iterative methods, for example Gauss–Seidel, Jacobi or Successive Over Relaxation (SOR).

■ **Example 4.4**

Suppose:

$$\mathbf{B} = \begin{pmatrix} 9 & 8 & 7 & 6 \\ 1 & 3 & 0 & 7 \\ -4 & 7 & 1 & 9 \end{pmatrix}$$

(a) then `UpperTriangular = triu(B)` returns:

```
UpperTriangular =
     9      8      7      6
     0      3      0      7
     0      0      1      9
```

(b) and `LowerTriangular = tril(B,-1)` results in:

```
LowerTriangular =
     0      0      0      0
     1      0      0      0
    -4      7      0      0
```

■

There are some commands for reshaping matrices.

| Commands 37 | ROTATING AND RESHAPING MATRICES |

`fliplr(A)`	gives the elements in the rows of the two-dimensional matrix **A** in reversed order, that is $b_{ij} = a_{i,n-j+1}$. Here 'lr' is short for left–right.
`flipud(A)`	gives the elements of the columns of the two-dimensional matrix **A** in reversed order, that is $b_{ij} = a_{m-i+1,j}$. Here 'ud' is short for up–down.
`flipdim(A,dim)`	returns a multidimensional matrix where the elements of **A** have reversed order in the dimension *dim*. The command `flipdim(A,1)` is the same as `flipud(A)` and `flipdim(A,2)` is the same as `fliplr(A)`.
`rot90(A)`	gives a 90 degree rotation of **A** counter-clockwise. The element in the upper right-hand corner is placed in the upper left-hand corner. See also Section 13.5.
`rot90(A,k)`	gives a $k \times n$ degree rotation of **A** counter-clockwise. See also Section 13.5.
`reshape(A,m,n, ...,p)`	returns a $m \times n \times \ldots \times p$ multidimensional matrix containing the elements of **A** taken in linear index order; see Figure 2.2 on how a linear index works. An error message is returned if **A** does not contain $m \cdot n \cdot \ldots \cdots p$ elements.

| Commands 37 | (CONTINUED) |

`repmat(A, [m n ... p])`	creates a multidimensional matrix with $m \times n \times \ldots \times p$ blocks with the same elements as **A**.
`repmat(x, [m n ... p])`	creates a $m \times n \times \ldots \times p$ multidimensional matrix with the scalar x in all positions. This is faster than `x*ones([m n ...])` for large matrices.
`shiftdim(A,n)`	shifts the orders of the dimensions n steps. A positive n shifts left, a negative n shifts right.
`squeeze(A)`	returns **A** without empty dimensions.
`cat(dim,A,B)`	gives a multidimensional matrix with **A** and **B** concatenated in the dimension *dim*.
`permute(A,order)`	alters the orders of the dimensions in **A** according to the vector **order**.
`ipermute(A,order)`	returns the inverse of the command `permute`. If one gives the command `ipermute(permute(A,order),order)` one gets **A**.

■ **Example 4.5**

(a) Suppose we have the multidimensional matrix **OneMatrix** in the Example 4.1. It may be reshaped into a two-dimensional matrix with, for example the command `B = reshape(OneMatrix,3,8)` giving the following result:

```
B =
    1    1    1    1    1    1    1    1
    1    1    1    1    1    1    1    1
    1    1    1    1    1    1    1    1
```

(b) To add a layer of zeros to **B** we first create a matrix with zeros with the command `C = zeros(3,8)`. We then get a concatenated matrix by typing:

```
D = cat (3, B, C)

D(:,:,1) =
    1    1    1    1    1    1    1    1
    1    1    1    1    1    1    1    1
    1    1    1    1    1    1    1    1

D(:,:,2) =
    0    0    0    0    0    0    0    0
    0    0    0    0    0    0    0    0
    0    0    0    0    0    0    0    0
```

(c) To quickly reshape **D** so it corresponds to the answer from `cat(3,C,B)` we use:

```
flipdim(D,3)

ans(:,:,1) =
     0     0     0     0     0     0     0     0
     0     0     0     0     0     0     0     0
     0     0     0     0     0     0     0     0

ans(:,:,2) =
     1     1     1     1     1     1     1     1
     1     1     1     1     1     1     1     1
     1     1     1     1     1     1     1     1
```

(d) The result from reshaping matrices with `permute` and `shiftdim` is shown here:

```
size(shiftdim(D,2))

ans =
     2     3     8

size(permute(D,[2 1 3]))

ans =
     8     3     2
```

■

In MATLAB a matrix or a vector can be extended by new elements, rows or columns. MATLAB changes the size of the matrix automatically. In this way it is easy to create new matrices using parts of old matrices, which is very useful in many applications.

To build a matrix from old ones is like defining a new matrix. Elements are separated by a blank or a comma and rows are separated by a semicolon or a 'carriage return'; see Section 2.2. In Section 4.3 the opposite procedure, to define submatrices from larger matrices, is covered.

■ **Example 4.6**

Suppose these matrices are already defined:

$$\mathbf{A} = \begin{pmatrix} 1 & 2 \\ 3 & 4 \end{pmatrix} \quad \mathbf{B} = \begin{pmatrix} 5 & 6 \\ 7 & 8 \end{pmatrix} \quad \mathbf{x} = (9 \quad 10) \quad \mathbf{y} = \begin{pmatrix} 11 \\ 12 \end{pmatrix} \quad \mathbf{z} = (13 \quad 14)$$

(a) There are several ways of extending the row vector **x** to 1×4. Suppose that we want the new vector to be:

$$\mathbf{xnew} = (9 \quad 10 \quad 0 \quad 15)$$

The following three methods give us the desired result:

    (i) `xnew = x; xnew(3) = 0; xnew(4) = 15;`

    (ii) `xnew = [x 0 15];`

    (iii) `temp = [0 15]; xnew = [x temp];`

(b) To extend **A** with a new row, for example the vector **z**, we have these two alternatives:

    (i) `Anew1 = [A; z];`

    (ii) `Anew1 = [A; [13 14]];`

In both cases the following is shown on the screen:

```
Anew1 =
     1     2
     3     4
    13    14
```

We may add more than one row at a time like this:

```
Anew2 = [A; x; z; [0 0]]
Anew2 =
     1     2
     3     4
     9    10
    13    14
     0     0
```

To extend **A** with a column, for example **y**, we have:

```
Anew3 = [A y] or Anew3 = [A [11; 12]]
```

Both cases give:

```
Anew3 =
     1     2    11
     3     4    12
```

To extend with a matrix is similar. By typing

```
ABvert = [A;B] and ABhoriz = [A B]
```

we obtain:

```
ABvert =
     1     2
     3     4
     5     6
     7     8

ABhoriz =
     1     2     5     6
     3     4     7     8
```

For **ABvert** the number of columns has to be equal in the two matrices **A** and **B** and for **ABhoriz** the number of rows must be equal.

■

To generate regular block matrices `repmat` is used in the following way:

■ **Example 4.7**

(a) The command `repmat([1 0;0 1],3,3)` returns:

```
ans =
    1    0    1    0    1    0
    0    1    0    1    0    1
    1    0    1    0    1    0
    0    1    0    1    0    1
    1    0    1    0    1    0
    0    1    0    1    0    1
```

(b) In Example 3.2 we used `repmat([1 0],1,5)` which returns:

```
ans =
    1    0    1    0    1    0    1    0    1    0
```

(c) If one wants to create a matrix with only one value one may use `repmat(42,[2 2])`, which gives the following result:

```
ans =
    42    42
    42    42
```

■

4.2 Empty matrices

One way to define empty matrices in MATLAB is `A = []`. It is also possible to create multidimensional matrices in which some dimensions are empty, for example a $0 \times 1 \times 0$ matrix. See also the command `isempty` in Commands 31.

■ **Example 4.8**

To create a matrix with the size 1-2-0-0-2 one may type `zeros(1,2,0,0,2)`. This results in:

```
ans =
    Empty array: 1-by-2-by-0-by-0-by-2
```

Empty row vectors and column vectors are defined with zeros:

```
rowvect = zeros(1,0)

rowvect =
   Empty matrix: 1-by-0

colvect = zeros(0,1)

colvect =
   Empty matrix: 0-by-1
```

The size of these vectors are now:

```
size(rowvect), size(colvect)

ans =
      1      0
ans =
      0      1
```

An empty matrix may be created with:

```
A = []

A =
     []
```

The command whos now gives us:

```
   Name         Size        Bytes        Class

   A            0x0           0          double array
   colvect      0x1           0          double array
   rowvect      1x0           0          double array

Grand total is 0 elements using 0 bytes
```

■

Some functions return constant answers working on empty matrices, which is often useful when programming. Let **E** be an empty matrix in Commands 38. To clear a matrix of empty dimensions the command squeeze is used.

Commands 38	FUNCTIONS ON EMPTY MATRICES
`squeeze(A)`	returns **A** without empty dimensions.
`sum(E)`	returns 0.
`prod(E)`	returns 1.
`max(E)`	returns **E**.
`min(E)`	returns **E**.

4.3 Generating vectors and submatrices

In MATLAB a colon, ':', is used to represent a series of values. Colon notation can be used to define a submatrix for instance. The use of colons to define vectors is first shown.

Commands 39	SEQUENCES OF NUMBERS, PART 1
`i:k`	gives a sequence of numbers from i to k in steps of one, that is $i, i+1, i+2, \dots, k$. If $i > k$ MATLAB returns an empty matrix, that is `[]`. The numbers i and k do not have to be integers. The last number in the sequence is less than or equal to k.
`i:j:k`	gives a series of values from i to k in steps of j, that is $i, i+j, i+2j, \dots, k$. For $j = 0$ an empty matrix is returned. The numbers i, j and k do not have to be integers. The last number in the sequence is less than or equal to k.

■ **Example 4.9**

(a) If we type `vect = 2:7` or `vect = 2:7.7` MATLAB returns in both cases:

```
vect =
     2     3     4     5     6     7
```

(b) Negative step: `vect2 = 6:-1:1` generates:

```
vect2 =
     6     5     4     3     2     1
```

(c) Real numbers: `realVect = 1.2:-0.8:-3.2` results in:

```
realVect =
    1.2000    0.4000   -0.4000   -1.2000   -2.0000   -2.8000
```

Note that the last number is −2.8.

(d) The command `realVect2 = 0:pi/4:pi` gives:

```
realVect2 =
        0     0.7854     1.5708     2.3562     3.1416
```

(e) Colon notation can be used to define matrices:

```
Mat1 = [2:4 0.1:1:2.1; 1:6]
```

returns:

```
Mat1 =
    2.0000    3.0000    4.0000    0.1000    1.1000    2.1000
    1.0000    2.0000    3.0000    4.0000    5.0000    6.0000
```

(f) Colon notation can be used to generate function tables, for example sine:

```
a = 0.0; b = 2*pi; n = 11; x = (a:(b-a)/(n-1):b)';
y = sin(x); Ftable = [x y]
```

gives:

```
Ftable =
        0          0
   0.6283     0.5878
   1.2566     0.9511
   1.8850     0.9511
   2.5133     0.5878
   3.1416     0.0000
   3.7699    -0.5878
   4.3982    -0.9511
   5.0265    -0.9511
   5.6549    -0.5878
   6.2832    -0.0000
```

■

There are also some predefined functions which can be used to generate sequences. It is possible to create linear sequences and logarithmic sequences which can be useful when plotting functions.

Commands 40   SEQUENCES OF NUMBERS, PART 2

`linspace(a,b)`	returns a vector with 100 equally spaced values in the interval $[a, b]$.

Commands 40	(CONTINUED)
`linspace(a,b,n)`	returns a vector with n elements in the interval $[a, b]$. The command works just like the colon notation but gives direct control of the number of elements in the vector.
`logspace(a,b)`	returns a vector with 50 elements whose values are logarithmically distributed in the interval $[10^a, 10^b]$. An exception is if b = `pi`, then the function returns a vector with logarithmically distributed values in the interval $[10^a, \pi]$.
`logspace(a,b,n)`	returns a vector with n elements logarithmically distributed in the interval $[10^a, 10^b]$, with the same exception as in the previous command.

The matrix **D** is called a submatrix of **C** if **D** can be obtained from **C** by removing rows and/or columns. The rows and the columns of **C** are also submatrices of **C**. A matrix may have many submatrices. This can be generalized to multidimensional matrices. Planes and dimensions may be removed or reduced. In Commands 41 the two-dimensional commands are presented.

To get the last element in a dimension one may give the value end. If **A** is a $4 \times 3 \times 2$ matrix, for example, `A(end,2,1)` gives the element a_{421} and `A(end,end,end)` gives a_{432}.

When a colon is used to define a submatrix of the matrix **A** we use the notation shown in Commands 41 below.

Commands 41	TO DEFINE A SUBMATRIX
`A(i,j,...,k)`	returns the element at entry $(i, j, \ldots, k)$ in the multidimensional matrix **A**, see also Section 2.3.
`A(:,j)`	returns the jth column of the two-dimensional matrix **A**.
`A(i,:)`	returns the ith row of the two-dimensional matrix **A**.
`A(:,j:k)`	returns the submatrix of the two-dimensional matrix **A** consisting of the columns $j, j + 1, \ldots, k$.
`A(i:k,:)`	returns the submatrix of the two-dimensional matrix **A** consisting of the rows $i, i + 1, \ldots, k$.
`A(i:k,j:l)`	returns the submatrix of the two-dimensional matrix **A** consisting of the elements in the rows i to k and in the columns j to l.
`A(:,:,...,:)`	returns the matrix **A** unchanged.
`A(:)`	returns the matrix **A** as one long column by concatenating the columns of **A** to each other.
`A(j:k)`	returns the elements from j to k of `A(:)` as a row vector.

Commands 41   (CONTINUED)

`A([j1 j2 ...])`	returns the elements $j1$, $j2$, and so on of `A(:)` as a row vector.
`A(:,[j1 j2 ...])`	returns the columns $j1$, $j2$, and so on of the matrix **A**.
`A([i1 i2 ...],:)`	returns the rows $i1$, $i2$, and so on of **A**.
`A([il i2 ...],` `[j1 j2 ...])`	returns the submatrix of the matrix **A** consisting of the elements in the rows $i1$, $i2$, and so on and the columns $j1$, $j2$, and so on.

See also `help colon`.

■ **Example 4.10**

Suppose that **Ftable** in Example 4.8(f) is defined.

(a) Then the statement `Submatrix = Ftable(2:4,:)` results in the output:

```
Submatrix =
    0.6283    0.5878
    1.2566    0.9511
    1.8850    0.9511
```

that is every column from row 2 to row 4.

(b) To get to the $3 \times 3 \times 3$ cube in the corner furthest away from origin in a $i \times j \times k$ cube we use:

```
A(end-2:end, end-2:end, end-2:end).
```

(c) The colon notation can be used together with relational operators, see Section 3.8. We can sort out the rows in **Ftable** where the element in column 2 has a value greater than 0 by the short command:

```
Selected = Ftable(Ftable(:,2) > 0,:)
```

which produces:

```
Selected =
    0.6283    0.5878
    1.2566    0.9511
    1.8850    0.9511
    2.5133    0.5878
    3.1416    0.0000
```

■

Composition of lists can be done with comma notation, see `help lists` for more information.

4.4 Special matrices in MATLAB

The zero matrix, the identity matrix and the matrix of ones are special matrices presented in Section 4.1. In the same section the commands for random matrices can be found.

In addition, MATLAB has commands for generating test matrices. The **Hilbert matrix**, that is a matrix **H** whose elements are $h_{ij} = 1/(i + j - 1)$ is used as a test matrix since it is ill-conditioned; see Section 7.6.

Commands 42	THE HILBERT MATRIX

`hilb(n)`	gives the Hilbert matrix of size $n \times n$.
`invhilb(n)`	gives the inverse of the Hilbert matrix of size $n \times n$. The elements are integers.

■ **Example 4.11**

If we type H = hilb(3), Hinv = invhilb(3) MATLAB responds with:

```
H =
    1.0000    0.5000    0.3333
    0.5000    0.3333    0.2500
    0.3333    0.2500    0.2000

Hinv =
      9     -36      30
    -36     192    -180
     30    -180     180
```

We see that the Hilbert matrix and its inverse are symmetric matrices; see Appendix B.

■

A **Toeplitz matrix** is defined by two vectors: a row vector and a column vector. A symmetric Toeplitz matrix is defined by a single vector.

Commands 43	THE TOEPLITZ MATRIX

`toeplitz(k,r)`	gives a non-symmetric Toeplitz matrix which has **k** as first column and **r** as first row. All other elements are defined by the element in the neighboring entry to the left and above.
`toeplitz(c)`	gives a symmetric Toeplitz matrix defined by the vector **c**.

■ **Example 4.12**

Let x = [1 2 3 4]; y = [9 8 7 6]; then

Toepmatrix1 = toeplitz(x,y), Toepmatrix2 = toeplitz(y,x)

gives:

```
Column wins diagonal conflict.
Toepmatrix1 =
     1    8    7    6
     2    1    8    7
     3    2    1    8
     4    3    2    1


Column wins diagonal conflict.
Toepmatrix2 =
     9    2    3    4
     8    9    2    3
     7    8    9    2
     6    7    8    9
```

■

A large library with special matrices is available through the gallery command. To find out which matrix families are available type help gallery and for information on a specific family type help private/family. The family specific commands are remnants from older versions and should be avoided.

The other special matrices in MATLAB are given in Commands 44 below.

Commands 44   OTHER SPECIAL MATRICES

compan(p)	returns the companion matrix to the polynomial **p**. That is a matrix whose characteristic polynomial is **p**. Here **p** is a vector containing the coefficients of the polynomial; see Section 10.1.
gallery(n)	returns $n \times n$ test matrices known from numerical analysis. For the moment only $n = 3$ and $n = 5$ exist: $n = 3$: ill-conditioned matrix; $n = 5$: interesting eigenvalue problem.
gallery family	returns a matrix from the family *family*; see Table 4.1.
hadamard(k)	returns a Hadamard matrix of order $n = 2^k$. The matrix is defined only when n is divisible by 4.
hankel(x)	returns a square Hankel matrix defined by the vector **x**. The matrix is symmetric, the elements defined by $h_{ij} = x_{i+j-a}$. The first column is the vector **x**, the elements below the anti-diagonal are zero.

Commands 44	(CONTINUED)
hankel(x,y)	returns an $m \times n$ Hankel matrix in which the first column is **x** and the last row is **y**.
magic(n)	gives a magic square of size $n \times n$.
pascal(n)	returns a Pascal matrix of size $n \times n$, that is a symmetric positive definite matrix whose elements come from Pascal's triangle. The elements of the inverse matrix are integers.
pascal(n,k)	gives for $k = 1$ a lower triangular Cholesky factor of the Pascal matrix above. Note that MATLAB normally uses upper triangular Cholesky factors. For $k = 2$ a permuted version of the same is given.
rosser	gives the Rosser matrix, a classic and troublesome symmetric eigenvalue problem. The Rosser matrix has size 8×8.
vander(x)	returns a Vandermonde matrix in which the last but one column is the vector **x**. An element, $v_{i,j}$ in the matrix is defined by: $v_{i,j} = x_i^{n-j}$, where n is the length of **x**.
wilkinson(n)	returns the Wilkinson eigenvalue test matrix of size $n \times n$.

■ **Example 4.13**

A magic square of size $n \times n$ is a matrix with the integers 1, 2, ... , n^2 as elements, and with equal row and column sums. To create a magic 3×3 square, we type magic(3), which gives the result:

```
ans =
     8     1     6
     3     5     7
     4     9     2
```

■

■ **Example 4.14**

To be able to get a Householder matrix we first run help private/house which gives us information on which specific arguments we have to give. The following creates the Householder matrix **H**.

```
x = [2; 5; 3];
[V, BETA] = gallery('house',x);
H = eye(3,3) - BETA*V*V'
```

$H =$

$$\begin{array}{rrr} -0.3244 & -0.8111 & -0.4867 \\ -0.8111 & 0.5033 & -0.2980 \\ -0.4867 & -0.2980 & 0.8212 \end{array}$$

In Table 4.1 we have listed the most common families available through the `gallery` command.

Table 4.1   MATRIX FAMILIES AVAILABLE THROUGH THE COMMAND `gallery`.

`circul`	gives cyclic permuted matrices. The first column may be given as an argument, the matrix then is built of columns with the same values permuted.
`dorr`	gives an ill-conditioned tridiagonal matrix.
`house`	gives a Householder matrix.
`invhess`	gives an inverse upper Hessenberg matrix.
`jordblock`	gives a Jordan matrix.
`poisson`	gives a sparse tridiagonal block matrix which comes up when solving Poisson's equation with finite differences.
`vander`	gives a Vandermonde matrix.
`wilk`	gives a Wilkinson matrix.

Strings and Other Datatypes

5

It is possible to operate on characters and strings in MATLAB. Strings can be displayed on the screen and can be used to construct commands which are evaluated or executed within other commands. Cell matrices, or cell arrays, are untyped matrices where the elements may be of any type. MATLAB also includes a number of functions suited for bitwise operations and also more general integer functions. It is also possible to treat vectors as sets.

5.1 Strings

A **string** is text stored in a row vector in which each entry represents a **character**. In reality, the elements contain the internal code of the characters, that is the ASCII code. When the value of a string variable is displayed on the screen the text is shown, not the ASCII numbers. Since strings are stored as vectors, we can refer to any element in a string by giving its index.

Matrices of characters are also allowed but must have the same number of characters in each row.

5.1.1 Assignment

A string in MATLAB is defined by apostrophes:

```
NameOfVariable = 'text'
```

where `'text'` could be letters, numbers and special characters.

■ **Example 5.1**

(a) A simple assignment, `name = 'John Smith'`, gives the following display on the screen:

```
name =
John Smith
```

(b) If just `'John Smith'` is typed, the variable *ans* is assigned the string:

```
ans =
John Smith
```

(c) Assignment of a character. If **name** from (a) exists then name(3) = 'a' gives:

```
name =
Joan Smith
```

(d) To reverse the order of the components for the string **name** from previous examples we type:

```
for i = length(name):-1:1
   eman(i) = name(length(name)+1-i);
end
eman
```

This will give us the string **eman** with the value:

```
eman =
htimS naoJ
```

See Section 12.2 for more about for-loops. The same result can also be obtained with eman = fliplr(name); see Section 4.1.

(e) The length of a string: namelen = size(name) gives:

```
namelen =
     1     10
```

(f) The apostrophe character is typed in a string by doubling it:

```
whoscat = 'Joan''s cat'
```

becomes:

```
whoscat =
Joan's cat
```

(g) Strings can be composed just like numerical matrices:

```
name1 = 'Joan'; name2 = 'John'; heart = 'is in love with';...
sentence = [name1,' ',heart,' ',name2]
```

gives:

```
sentence =
Joan is in love with John
```

See also the commands strcat and strvcat in Commands 47.

(h) It is also possible to use colon notation just like in numerical matrices:

```
name = 'Charles Johnson'; firstname = name(1:7) give:
firstname =
Charles
```

(i) text1 = 'John'; text2 = 'Joan'; couple = [text1;text2]

gives:

```
couple =
John
Joan
```

5.1.2 String commands

There are several commands for converting strings to other forms of representation.

<table>
<tr><td>Commands 45</td><td colspan="2">TO CONVERT A STRING</td></tr>
<tr><td><code>abs(str)</code></td><td>returns a vector with the ASCII codes for the characters in the string str.</td></tr>
<tr><td><code>char(x)</code></td><td>converts the integers in the vector x to characters according to a chosen set of characters. This is the inverse of the command <code>abs</code>. The old MATLAB command <code>setstr</code> is still working, but will be removed.</td></tr>
<tr><td><code>num2str(f)</code></td><td>converts the scalar f to a string representation in floating-point format, consisting of four digits and exponent if required. The command is often used together with <code>disp</code>, <code>xlabel</code> and other output commands; see Example 13.9 in Section 13.3.</td></tr>
<tr><td><code>num2str(f,k)</code></td><td>converts the scalar f to a string representation in floating-point format, consisting of k digits.</td></tr>
<tr><td><code>num2str(f,format)</code></td><td>converts the scalar f to a string. The format of the string is set according to format which works as in the function <code>sprintf</code>, see below.</td></tr>
<tr><td><code>int2str(n)</code></td><td>converts the integer n to a string representation of the integer.</td></tr>
<tr><td><code>rats(x,strlen)</code></td><td>converts the floating point number x to a string representation containing the rational approximation of x. The integer strlen is the number of positions the result is allowed to have, default is 13.</td></tr>
<tr><td><code>hex2num(hstr)</code></td><td>converts the hexadecimal number in the string hstr to the corresponding floating point number (IEEE double precision).</td></tr>
<tr><td><code>hex2dec(hstr)</code></td><td>converts the hexadecimal number in the string hstr to an integer.</td></tr>
<tr><td><code>dec2hex(n)</code></td><td>converts the integer n to the corresponding hexadecimal number. The result is a string.</td></tr>
<tr><td><code>base2dec(str,base)</code></td><td>converts the number in the string str from the base base to a decimal number.</td></tr>
<tr><td><code>dec2base(n,base)</code></td><td>converts the integer n to the base base.</td></tr>
<tr><td><code>bin2dec(str)</code></td><td>converts the binary number in the string str to a decimal number.</td></tr>
<tr><td><code>dec2bin(n)</code></td><td>converts the integer n to a binary number.</td></tr>
<tr><td><code>mat2str(A,n)</code></td><td>converts the matrix A to a string. If the argument n is given it represents the number of correct figures.</td></tr>
</table>

Commands 45	(CONTINUED)
str2num(str)	returns the numerical value of the string **str**. The content of the string can be numbers, decimal point, starting signs, an *e* followed by a power of ten and the imaginary part *i*.
str2rng(str)	converts a spreadsheet area **str** to a vector at the form [*R*1 *C*1 *R*2 *C*2] which gives start and end row and column for the area specified in the string **str**.
strjust(str)	returns a string with the same content as **str** but right adjusted.
sprintf(formatstr, A)	returns the elements of the matrix **A** in a string of the format defined in the format string **formatstr**, similar to format control in the programming language C. The command performs just like fprintf but the result is a string instead of a file; see Section 15.4.
[Str,E] = sprintf(...)	returns the string **str** as above, and a matrix **E**, containing an error message string if an error occurred. If the conversion is correct the empty matrix **E** is returned.
sscanf(str, formatstr,mn)	returns a matrix whose elements are read from the string **str** according to the string **formatstr**. The maximum number of elements read is *mn*, but this parameter is optional. The command performs like fscanf, but operates on a string instead of a file; see Section 15.4.
[A,nm,E,next] = sscanf(str, formatstr,mn)	returns a matrix **A** just like sscanf, but also returns the number of correctly converted elements *mn*, and the errors in the matrix **E**. The scalar *next* is index to the next element in the case when all the elements are not read.

■ Example 5.2

Let these variables be defined: str = 'ABC'; float = 1.25;

(a) The command x = abs(str) then returns:

```
x =
      65    66    67
```

that is ASCII codes for the characters A, B and C.

(b) If we type number = hex2dec(str), MATLAB gives:

```
number =
       2748
```

(c) The commands:

```
numstr = num2str(float)
disp(['Number as a string = ',numstr,'!']);
```

result in:

numstr =
1.25

Number as a string = 1.25!

To show that **numstr**, in fact, is a string, we type char = numstr(4) and MAT-LAB gives:

char =
5

The commands ischar(numstr) and whos also tells us that **numstr** is a string.

(d) The command numinfo = sprintf('The number = %5.2e',float) gives:

numinfo =
The number = 1.25e+00

(e) The command rational = rats(0.979796) will give us a string containing the rational approximation of the floating point number 0.979 796:

rational =
*   4995/5098*

The optional number 5 in the command littleRat = rats(0.979796,5) will restrict the string length to 5.

littleRat =
*   48/49*

In Section 2.4 the command rat is defined.

■

■ **Example 5.3**

Let **A** be defined as:

$$\mathbf{A} = \begin{pmatrix} 1 & 1 & 3 \\ 2 & 4 & 7 \end{pmatrix}$$

mat2str(A) now gives:

```
ans =
[1 1 3;2 4 7]
```

Let x = 4.12345, then mat2str(x) gives:

```
ans =
4.12345
```

```
num2str(x,2)
```

```
ans =
4.1
```

■

There are also logical functions that operate on strings and functions to extract substrings. In Commands 46 below, let **str** be a string.

| Commands 46 | FUNCTIONS OF STRINGS, PART 1 |

`blanks(n)`	returns a string with *n* blanks.
`deblank(str)`	returns the string **str** without trailing blanks.
`lower(str)`	changes all letters in **str** to lower-case letters.
`upper(str)`	changes all letters in **str** to upper-case letters.
`ischar(s)`	returns 1 if *s* is of the data type char, 0 otherwise. The old `isstr` command is still available but will be removed in future versions.
`isletter(str(i))`	returns a 1 if the *i*th character in **str** is a letter.
`isspace(str)`	returns a vector of the same size as **str**, whose elements are 1 if the corresponding character in **str** is a blank, tabular or line feed, otherwise 0.
`strcmp(str1,str2)`	compares **str1** and **str2**. If they are equal, 1 is returned otherwise 0.
`stricmp(str1,str2)`	works as `strcmp` but interprets lower- and upper-case letters as the same.
`str2mat(str1,str2, ...)`	creates a string matrix with **str1**, **str2**, and so on. If the strings **str**$_i$ are of different sizes, MATLAB completes the shorter ones with blanks in the end. The function handles at most 11 arguments but those can themselves also be string matrices.
`findstr(str1,str2)`	returns a vector containing the start positions for the substring **str2** in **str1**.
`strrep(str1,str2, str3)`	returns a modified string **str1** with all occurrences of **str2** replaced with **str3**.

Commands 46	(CONTINUED)
strtok(str1,str2)	returns the part of **str1** that remains when the trailing part after the first appearance of **str2** has been removed. If **str2** is not specified MATLAB uses blanks, that is selects the first sequence in **str1** that does not contain a blank.
[outstr,rstr] = strtok(str1,str2)	returns the string **outstr** as above but also the removed part in the string **rstr**.
lasterr	returns a string containing the last error message.
lastwarn	returns a string containing the last warning.

■ **Example 5.4**

(a) name = upper('matlab') gives:

```
name =
MATLAB
```

(b) fun = strrep('hahaha','a','i')

```
fun =
hihihi
```

(c) Let the string variables:

```
greet = 'Welcome', where = 'to Joan''s', party = ...
'birthday party!'
```

be defined. Then the command str2mat(greet,where,party) gives:

```
ans =
Welcome
to Joan's
birthday party!
```

(d) It is possible to extract information from a string with the contents separated by commas by using the command strtok. We define a string **text** as:

```
text = ...
'Monday,Tuesday,Wednesday,Thursday,Friday,Saturday,Sunday';

[day,rest] = strtok(text,',')

day =
Monday
rest =
,Tuesday,Wednesday,Thursday,Friday,Saturday,Sunday
```

By calling `strtok` with the string **rest** we can find next day and so on: `[day2,rest]` `= strtok(rest,',')` gives:

```
day2 =
Tuesday
rest =
,Wednesday,Thursday,Friday,Saturday,Sunday
```

Note that the command reads until the second comma, since the first, in the first position of the string, does not separate any part of the string.

∎

Two commands for concatenating strings are available: `strcat` for concatenating strings and `strvcat` for concatenating strings to a column vector. To analyze the content of a string one may use `strmatch` and `strcmp`.

Commands 47	FUNCTION OF STRINGS, PART 2
`strcat(str1,str2,...)`	concatenates the strings **str1** and **str2**. Is different from `cat` in the handling of cell matrices.
`strvcat(str1,str2,...)`	concatenates **str1** and **str2** to a column vector. The strings **str1** and **str2** must have the same number of characters. The number of rows must not be the same, and the number of rows in the result is the sum of number of rows in the arguments.
`strmatch(key, strs)`	searches the rows in **strs** for **key** and returns a vector with the row numbers of the strings beginning with **key**.
`strncmp(str1,str2,n)`	compares the *n* first characters in **str1** and **str2**. If they are the same 1 is returned, otherwise 0 is returned.
`strncmpi(str1,str2,n)`	works like `strncmp` but interprets lower- and upper-case letters as the same.

■ **Example 5.5**

(a) Suppose **A** is defined as in Example 5.3. Then:

```
text1 = 'ResultMatrix = ';
text2 = mat2str(A);
restext = strcat(text1,text2)
```

becomes

```
restext =
ResultMatrix =[1 1 3; 2 4 7]
```

Note that there is no blank between the equal sign and the left bracket. This is because `strcat` removes all preceding blanks. If one wants to keep the blanks one should use the command `cat`.

(b) Consider the following statements.

```
head = ['First name' '  ' 'Last name'];
boss = ['John' '              ' 'Smith'];
workers = ['Arthur' '          ' 'Moore ';
           'Joseph' '          ' 'Jonson';
           'Daniel' '          ' 'Smart '];
```

The string in the middle of each row contains two tab signs to make the table straight.

```
Table = strvcat(head,boss,workers)

Table =
First name     Last name
John           Smith
Arthur         Moore
Joseph         Jonson
Daniel         Smart
```

For **Table** it is now true that:

```
whos Table

  Name        Size      Bytes      Class

  Table       5x20        200      char array

Grand total is 100 elements using 200 bytes
```

Note that the size depends on the longest line and that therefore it is better to store this type of list separately.

∎

■ **Example 5.6**

Consider the following statements:

```
carVocabulary = strvcat('car','carpool','police car')

carVocabulary =
car
carpool
police car
```

```
strmatch('car',carVocabulary)

ans =
      1
      2
```

The result is the row numbers of the strings beginning with 'car'.

■

5.1.3 Display and input

To display the contents of a numerical matrix or a string vector one can simply type the variable name; see Section 2.3. The result is that both the variable name and the contents are shown.

Another way of displaying the value of a variable is to use the command disp. In this case only the contents of the variable are shown on the screen. This will be useful, especially in string applications.

Commands 48	DISPLAY

disp(A)	displays the contents of the matrix **A**. If **A** is a string, the text is displayed.

Input from the terminal is received with the input command. This also displays text and a prompter; see examples in Section A.6. The command disp in combination with num2str and int2str is demonstrated in Example 13.9.

Commands 49	INPUT

input(out, *in*)	displays the text in the string **out** on the screen and waits for an input from the terminal. If the variable **in** is 's' the result will be stored as a string. MATLAB will normally evaluate the expression as far as possible before storing. The string **out** can be several rows if the same controlling signs as for sprintf are used, e.g. '\n'.

■ **Example 5.7**

(a) Read a real number **x**:

```
x = input('Give a number x: ')
```

results in:

Give a number x: 2.0944

x =

    2.0944

(b) Read a matrix **A**. A semicolon after the command `input` suppresses the printing of the result.

```
A = input('Give the matrix A row by row: ');
```

gives:

Give the matrix A row by row: [1 2;3 5]

(c) It is also possible to use arithmetical expressions and functions:

```
A = input('Please give me a matrix: ');
```

gives:

Please give me a matrix: rand(4)*hilb(4)

(d) The input command may have more than one argument:

```
[m,n] = input('Give the size of A: ');
```

gives:

Give the size of A: size(A)

(e) Evaluation of logical expressions:

```
s = input('MATLAB input\nWrite an expression: ')
```

MATLAB input

Write an expression: log2(8) + 7 < 10

s =

    0

(f) To read a string:

```
name = input('What is your last name? ');
```

gives:

What is your last name? 'Smith'

Note that the string in this case must be enclosed by ' '. If the command looks like:

```
strname = input('What is your last name? ','s');
```

the name can be written directly:

What is your last name? Smith

■

It is also possible to read strings in other ways in MATLAB, for example with a menu; see Section 14.3.

5.1.4 Evaluation of strings

MATLAB commands can be written and stored as strings. These command strings can be evaluated by the `eval` command.

| Commands 50 | EVALUATION OF STRINGS |

eval(str)	executes the MATLAB commands contained in **str** and returns the results.
eval(str1,str2)	executes the MATLAB commands in **str1**. If all works without errors, this is the same as eval(str1). If the first string is an error in the evaluation of **str1**, the string **str2** will be evaluated, that is given an error message or something else.
[*x1,x2,*...] = evalin(aa,str)	works as eval but makes it possible to decide in which workspace **str** is to be evaluated in, i.e. where to read/write variables. The **aa** string can be either 'caller' (evaluates in the workspace where evalin was called) or 'base' (evaluates in MATLAB's commando area). Resulting data, if any, are stored in **x1**, **x2**, ...
evalin(aa,str,alt)	tries to evaluate the string **str** in the workspace **aa** (see above), and if that does not work the string **alt** is evaluated.
assignin(aa, name, val)	assigns the variable **name** the value **val**. If the variable does not exist it is created. The argument **aa** states the workspace; see evalin.
g = inline(str, *arg1,arg2,*...)	creates a so called inline function **g** from the string **str**, i.e. a function stored in the working memory, which can be called with g(val1,val2,...). The names of the parameters of the function can be given in the strings **arg2**, **arg2**, ... If they are not given, MATLAB will look for lower-case letters in **str** and suppose that these are the arguments.
g = inline(str,n)	creates an inline function **g** with $n + 1$ arguments called x, $P1$, $P2, \ldots, Pn$.
argnames(g)	returns a cell matrix with the names of the arguments of the inline function **g**.
vectorize(g)	puts a dot, '.', in front of *, / and ^ and thereby creates a vectorized version of the inline function **g**, so that operations are performed elementwise.
formula(g)	returns the inline function **g** as a string.
char(g)	is equivalent to formula(g).

The eval command makes MATLAB a flexible programming language. The command is useful, for example, for calls to functions which are not predefined in MATLAB; see Section 12.4.

■ **Example 5.8**

(a) Suppose that we want a simple program for matrix arithmetic which reads the matrices **A** and **B** and lets the user decide whether to perform addition or multiplication. This could look like this:

```
disp('Matrix analysis program. Give two matrices:');
A = input('A = ');
B = input('B = ');

choice = input('Choose one: 1 = A+B, 2 = A*B: ');

switch choice
  case 1, eval('disp(''Addition: ''); A+B');
  case 2, eval('disp(''Multiplication: ''); A*B');
end;
```

Note that the apostrophe ' should be repeated twice in order not to end the string. The disp and input commands are described in Section 5.1.3 and switch-case in Section 12.1.

Unfortunately some errors may develop because of wrong matrix dimensions, e.g., for the matrix multiplication **AB** it is required that the inner matrix dimensions should agree. By using a second string as a parameter to eval we can get an error message. We complete the old program and get:

```
disp('Matrix analysis program. Give two matrices:');
A = input('A = ');
B = input('B = ');

choice = input('Choose one: 1 = A+B, 2 = A*B :');

switch choice
  case 1, eval('disp(''Addition: ''); A+B','catchInfo');
  case 2, eval('disp(''Multiplication: ''); A*B', 'catchInfo');
end;
```

We now let eval call the user-defined function **catchInfo**, stored in the file **catchInfo.m**:

```
function catchInfo

errStr = lasterr;
dimStr = findstr(errStr,'dimensions must agree');

if ~isempty(dimStr)                % If wrong dimensions...

  if ~isempty( findstr(errStr,'Inner'))
```

```
      disp('Error!  A*B requires A:m*n, B:n*p.');
   else
      disp('Error! Addition requires A:m*n, B:m*n.');
   end
end
```

The string variable **lasterr** contains the latest error message from MATLAB. Suppose we give the matrices

```
A = [1 2 3; 4 5 6; 7 8 9], B = [1 2; 3 4].
```

Addition then gives:

```
Addition:
Error! Addition requires A:m*n, B:m*n.
```

and multiplication gives:

```
Multiplication:
Error!  A*B requires A:m*n, B:n*p.
```

(b) String variables can be combined with strings. If we have a variable name
file = 'myfile.mat' and wish to save the current session to this file, we type
eval(['save ',file]). This is the same as typing save myfile.mat. The
save command is defined in Section 2.8.

(c) MATLAB can also evaluate vector functions. Let **str1** be 'b.*sin(k.*x)'. If **b**,
k and **x** are vectors:

```
b = [1 2 3]; k = [2 2 2]; x = [1.2 1.5 1.2];
```

the command

```
values = eval(str1)
```

gives:

```
values =
    0.6755     0.2822     2.0264
```

(d) Let us create a string:

```
fcn = 'input(''Give a function'',''s'')';
```

The input command is presented in Section 5.1.3. Now an optional function can
be chosen from the terminal and evaluated. The command

```
fplot(eval(fcn),[0,4])
```

gives the following result, printed on screen:

```
Give a function
```

If we write sin then MATLAB opens a graphical window and displays the sine
function.

Suppose an M-file (see Section 2.9), named **sinx2.m** is defined according to:

```
function y = sinx2(x)
y = sin(x.^2);
```

See Section 12.3 for more information on M-files. If we write `sinx2` after the text *Give a function* we get a graph of the function $\sin x^2$; see Figure 5.1.

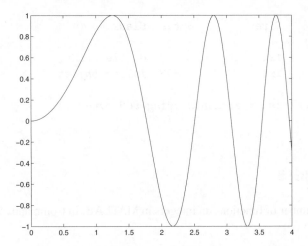

Figure 5.1 *The function* $\sin x^2$ *between 0 and 4.*

■

The strings which are evaluated can also contain MATLAB programming structures, such as `if`, `while`, `for` and others; see Chapter 12.

■ **Example 5.9**

To create an inline function **g** that calculates the expression $3\sin(x) + 5\cos(y)$ we type:

```
g = inline('3*sin(x)+5*cos(y)','x','y')

g =
     Inline function:
     g(x,y) = 3*sin(x)+5*cos(y)

argnames(g)

ans =
     'x'
     'y'

g(pi,2*pi)
```

```
ans =
    5
```

If we now type whos we get:

```
Name        Size            Bytes  Class

ans         1x1                 8  double array
g           1x1               898  inline object

Grand total is 75 elements using 906 bytes
```

■

5.2 Integers

There are a number of functions on integers in MATLAB. In Commands 51 *a* and *b* are integers.

Commands 51	FUNCTIONS ON INTEGERS
mod(a,b)	returns the remainder when dividing *a* and *b*.
factor(a)	returns the prime factors of *a*.
primes(a)	returns a row vector with prime numbers less or equal to *a*.
isprime(a)	returns 1 if *a* is a prime number.
nextpow2(a)	returns the smallest integer such that two raised to that integer is greater than *a*.
perms(c)	returns all possible permutations of the vector **c**.
nchoosek(A,k)	returns a matrix where each row has *k* elements and each possible combination of *k* elements from the matrix **A** is represented.

The functions perms and nchoosek returns answers that grow very fast with the input and therefore may require very long computation times.

■ **Example 5.10**

Is 4567 a prime number? The command isprime(4567) gives:

```
ans =
    1
```

What factors are there in 4569? We type `factor(4569)` and get:

```
ans =
        3       1523
```

∎

5.3 Bitwise operations

MATLAB may perform bitwise operations on integer variables. MATLAB returns 1 if the answer is true and 0 if it is false.

Commands 52   BITWISE OPERATORS

`bitand(a,b)`	returns the value of the bitwise operation a **and** b.
`bitor(a,b)`	returns the value of the bitwise operation a **or** b.
`bitxor(a,b)`	returns the value of the bitwise operation a **xor** b.
`bitget(a,bit)`	returns the value of the bit in position *bit* in the integer a.
`bitset(a, bit, newbit)`	gives the bit in position *bit* in the integer a the value *newbit*.
`bitshift(a,n)`	performs an n steps shift operation on a. If n is positive a is shifted left, otherwise a is shifted right.
`bitcmp(a,n)`	returns an n bits integer with the bitwise complement to a.
`bitmax`	returns the largest integer possible in floating point form.

∎ **Example 5.11**

Let a = 7, b = 3, c = 4. In binary code this is: a = 111, b = 011 and c = 100. Type `bitand(a,b)`:

```
ans =
    3
```

```
bitor(b,c)
```

```
ans =
    7
```

```
bitset(a,2,0)
```

```
ans =
    5
```

∎

5.4 Sets

MATLAB 5 has a number of functions that interpret vectors and cell matrices as sets and operates on these. In Commands 53 the variables **a** and **b** are vectors. Note that all of these commands can operate on matrices by adding the string `'rows'` as a last argument. In that case each row is interpreted as a single set and the function works on one set at a time. The returned set has the numbers sorted and each number only occurs once.

Commands 53	SETS
`intersect(a,b)`	returns the intersection of the sets **a** and **b**.
`ismember(a,s)`	returns a vector with the same size as **a** with ones in the positions where **a** has elements included in **s** and zeros otherwise.
`setdiff(a,b)`	returns the values that exist in **a** but not in **b**.
`setxor(a,b)`	returns the values that exist in **a** but not in **b** and the values that exist in **b** but not in **a**.
`union(a,b)`	returns the union of the sets **a** and **b**.
`unique(a)`	returns the same values as in **a** but removes all duplicate values so that in the returned set each value only occurs once.

■ **Example 5.12**

Let a = [12 24 42 24 12]; b = [96 42 64];
Then `union(a,b)` gives us:

```
ans =
    12    24    42    64    96
```

`unique(a)`

```
ans =
    12    24    42
```

`intersect(a,b)`

```
ans =
    42
```

■

5.5 Cell matrices

Cell matrices, or **cell arrays**, are matrices which can hold different kinds of data in different positions (cells) which make them different from 'ordinary' so called **numerical matrices**, which only consist of numbers, and **text matrices** with only strings. A cell matrix may therefore contain, for example, a string, two numbers and another cell matrix. Cell matrices may be multidimensional just like the numerical matrices. A one-dimensional cell matrix is called, analogous with the numerical case, a cell vector.

We can create a cell matrix in three different ways. The first way is to use braces, '{' and '}', just as numerical matrices are created with brackets, '[' and ']'. The second way is to assign the values cell by cell, so called cell-wise assignments. The third way is to create an empty matrix of the desired size. As with matrices all rows must have the same number of cells.

■ **Example 5.13**

A direct assignment with different data types may look like this:

```
A = {'John' 'Smith' 38 11.21; 'Paul' 'Anderson' 41 23.12}
```

or like this:

```
A = {'John','Smith',38,11.21; 'Paul','Anderson',41,23.12}

A =
    'John'      'Smith'         [38]      [11.2100]
    'Paul'      'Anderson'      [41]      [23.1200]
```

If one cell should contain a cell matrix the assignment may look like this:

```
B = { {2 2; 1 3} 22.3; 42 21 }

B =
    {2x2 cell}      [22.3000]
    [        42]    [      21]
```

By assigning a certain cell a value one may create a full cell matrix.

```
C{2,1} = 12.2

C =
              []
    [12.2000]
```

To create an empty cell matrix with size 2×4 we use:

```
D = cell(2,4)

D =
      []      []      []      []
      []      []      []      []
```

■

There are some functions that only work on cell matrices. Some other functions, e.g. `cat` and `strcat`, have been extended to work on cell matrices.

Commands 54	CELL MATRICES

`cell(m,n)`	creates an empty $m \times n$ cell matrix.
`cell2struct(cell, posts,dim)`	creates a struct with the help of the elements in the cell matrix **cell** and the fields **posts**. The elements are taken according to *dim* where 1 means that the first column in **cell** should be struct number one. To take the elements columnwise *dim* should be 2.
`celldisp(cell)`	goes through all elements in **cell** and prints them one by one. The `celldisp` command shows also the elements in a cell matrix in **cell**.
`cellplot(cell)`	shows a graphics plot of **cell**.
`cellstr(s)`	creates a cell vector where each row in **s** is a cell. The `char` command is the inverse of this function.
`iscellstr(cell)`	returns 1 if **cell** consists only of strings. If **cell** consists of both cell matrices and strings, 0 is returned.
`num2cell(A,dim)`	returns a cell matrix with the same size as the matrix **A**. If the argument *dim* is given, the whole dimension *dim* is put as a vector in its own cell which has the result that the returned matrix is not the same size as **A**.
`[out1,out2,...] = deal(in1,in2,...)`	copies input to output, i.e., the same as out1 = in1; out2 = in2;. See `helpdesk` for examples with cell matrices and structs.

■ **Example 5.14**

We can get a graphics plot of the content in the cell matrix **B** from Example 5.13:

```
cellplot(B)
```

The result is shown in Figure 5.2.

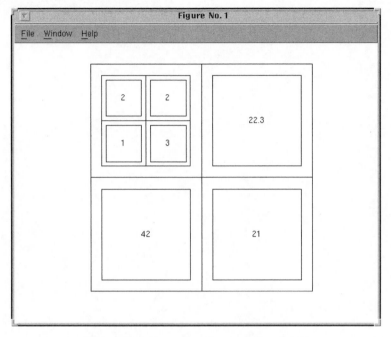

Figure 5.2 *The result from* cellplot *(B)*.

To view all of the content we may use celldisp(B):

```
celldisp(B)

B{1,1}{1,1} =
      2
B{1,1}{2,1} =
      1
B{1,1}{1,2} =
      2
B{1,1}{2,2} =
      3
B{2,1} =
     42
B{1,2} =
   22.3000
B{2,2} =
     21
```

Figure 5.9 ...

Data Analysis and Statistics

*In this chapter, MATLAB commands for data manipulation and statistical analysis are presented. Throughout the chapter **A** and **B** are, if nothing else is stated, multidimensional $m \times n \times \ldots \times p$ matrices and **x** is a vector.*

6.1 Maximum and minimum

Maximum is obtained as shown in Commands 55 below.

Commands 55	MAXIMA AND MINIMA
`max(x)`	returns the largest element of **x**. If **x** is complex the value of `max(abs(x))` is returned.
`max(A)`	returns a $1 \times n \times \ldots \times p$ matrix containing the maxima of the first dimension of **A**. In the two-dimensional case a row vector is returned, where the first element is the largest element in the first column of **A**, etc. If **A** is complex, `max(abs(A))` is returned.
`[y,ind] = max(A)`	returns a $1 \times n \times \ldots \times p$ matrix **y** containing the maxima of the first dimension of **A** and stores the row index of the largest number in each column in the row vector **ind**.
`max(A,B)`	gives a matrix of the same size as **A** and **B** with the elements at each position beeing the largest of the elements in **A** and **B** at the same position.
`C = max(A,[],dim)`	gives the maxima of **A** in the dimension specified by *dim*, e.g., `max(A,[],1)` gives the maxima of the rows of **A**.
`min(x)`	returns the smallest element in the vector **x**. The `min` command can be used just like `max` with respect to matrices. If **x** is complex the value of `min(abs(x))` is returned.

■ **Example 6.1**

We create a three-dimensional matrix **A**:

```
A(:,:,1) = [1 2 3;2 3 1;3 2 1];
A(:,:,2) = [2 4 6;4 6 2;6 4 2];
```

which gives us:

```
A(:,:,1) =
     1     2     3
     2     3     1
     3     2     1
A(:,:,2) =
     2     4     6
     4     6     2
     6     4     2
```

The maximum values are given by:

```
max(A)
```

```
ans(:,:,1) =
     3     3     3
ans(:,:,2) =
     6     6     6
```

The whos command now gives us:

```
  Name        Size              Bytes  Class

   A          3x3x2               144  double array
   ans        1x3x2                48  double array

Grand total is 24 elements using 192 bytes
```

■

6.2 Sums, products and differences

Different kinds of sums are obtained by the commands sum and cumsum.

Commands 56   SUMS

sum(x)	returns the sum of the components in the vector **x**.
sum(A)	returns a $1 \times n \times \ldots \times p$ matrix containing the sums of the columns of **A**.

Commands 56	(CONTINUED)
`cumsum(x)`	returns a vector containing the cumulative sum of the components in **x**, that is the second element is the sum of the first two components in **x**, and so on.
`cumsum(A)`	returns a matrix of the same size as **A** whose columns are the cumulative sums of the columns of **A**.
`cumsum(A,dim)`	gives the cumulative sum of the elements in the *dim* dimension of **A**. `cumsum(A)` is the same as `cumsum(A,1)`.

■ **Example 6.2**

An example of ordinary and cumulative sums with **A** as in Example 6.1:

```
TheSum = sum(A), TheCsum = cumsum(A)
```

```
TheSum(:,:,1) =
      6     7     5
TheSum(:,:,2) =
     12    14    10

TheCsum(:,:,1) =
      1     2     3
      3     5     4
      6     7     5
TheCsum(:,:,2) =
      2     4     6
      6    10     8
     12    14    10
```

■

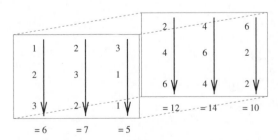

Figure 6.1 *Plot of how* `sum(A)` *works in three dimensions.*

Figure 6.1 illustrates how MATLAB calculates sum(A). The columns are summed and the answer is the three-dimensional matrix **TheSum** above, which is a $1 \times 3 \times 2$ matrix.

Products are computed in a similar way.

Commands 57	PRODUCTS
prod(x)	returns the product of the elements in **x**.
prod(A)	returns a multidimensional matrix whose elements are the column products.
prod(A,dim)	gives the product of the elements in the dimension *dim*.
cumprod(x)	returns a vector with the cumulative products of the element in **x**, that is the second element is the product of the first two components in **x**, and so on.
cumprod(A)	returns a matrix in which the columns are the cumulative products of the columns of **A**.
cumprod(A,dim)	gives the cumulative product in the dimension *dim*.

■ **Example 6.3**

Let us use the matrix **A**, defined in Example 6.1. The commands:

```
TheProd = prod(A), TheCprod = cumprod(A)
```

return:

```
TheProd(:,:,1) =
      6      12       3
TheProd(:,:,2) =
     48      96      24

  TheCprod(:,:,1) =
      1       2       3
      2       6       3
      6      12       3
  TheCprod(:,:,2) =
      2       4       6
      8      24      12
     48      96      24
```

■

Differences are computed with diff and there are also some other commands related to diff.

Commands 58	DIFFERENCES AND GRADIENT
diff(x)	gives for the vector **x** of length n a vector of length $n-1$ containing differences between adjacent components in **x**. If $\mathbf{x} = (x_1 \quad x_2 \quad \ldots \quad x_n)$, then we have diff(**x**) $= (x_2 - x_1 \quad x_3 - x_2 \quad \ldots \quad x_n - x_{n-1})$.
diff(A)	computes the difference of adjacent elements in the first dimension of **A**. For two-dimensional matrices we have diff(A) = A(2:m,:) - A(1:m-1,:).
diff(x,k)	gives the kth difference, that is diff(x,2) is equivalent to diff(diff(x)).
diff(A,k,dim)	gives the kth difference in the dimension *dim*.
[DAdx,DAdy, DAdz,...] = gradient(A)	returns the partial derivatives of the matrix **A** in the matrices **DAdx**, **DAdy**, **DAdz**, etc., which contains $\partial A/\partial x$, $\partial A/\partial y$, $\partial A/\partial z$, etc., on the corresponding entries. Type help gradient in MATLAB to get more information. See also Example 13.16.
[DAdx,DAdy, DAdz,...]= gradient(A,h1, h2,h3,...)	returns the partial derivatives $\partial A/\partial x$, $\partial A/\partial y$, $\partial A/\partial z$, etc. If the arguments $h1, h2, h3, \ldots$ are given these are used as step lengths for each variable.
del2(A)	returns the discrete Laplacian, that is a matrix whose elements have the value of the differences between the elements in **A** and the average of its four neighbors.

The gradient-command has been used in Figure P.5 in the color plate section to visualize the gradient of a function $z = f(x, y)$ with four extrema.

■ **Example 6.4**

Differences are easily computed and can be used as approximations of derivatives:

```
x = [1 4 9 16 25];
d1 = diff(x), d2 = diff(d1), d3 = diff(d2)
```

give the result:

```
d1 =
      3    5    7    9

d2 =
      2    2    2

d3 =
      0    0
```

Note that if the computed differences are to be used as approximations of derivatives they must be divided by the distance between the points.

■

6.3 Statistics commands

In the previous section commands operating columnwise on matrices, for example max, min, sum, and prod, were presented. Here we give a description of commands for statistical analysis of data.

The following commands give mean values, medians and standard deviation.

Commands 59	MEAN VALUE, MEDIAN VALUE AND STANDARD DEVIATION
mean(x)	gives the arithmetic mean value of the vector **x**.
mean(A, *dim*)	gives a $1 \times n \times \ldots \times p$ matrix containing the mean values of each of the first dimension of **A**. If *dim* is given the mean values in the dimension *dim* are computed.
median(x)	gives the median value of the elements in the vector **x**.
median(A, *dim*)	gives a $1 \times n \times \ldots \times p$ matrix containing the median values of each of the columns of **A**. If *dim* is given the median values in the dimension *dim* are computed.
std(x)	gives the standard deviations of the elements in the vector **x**.
std(A, *dim*)	gives a $1 \times n \times \ldots \times p$ matrix containing the standard deviations of each column of **A**. If *dim* is given the standard deviations in the dimension *dim* are computed.

■ **Example 6.5**

Let **A** be defined as:

$$\mathbf{A} = \begin{pmatrix} 1 & 1 \\ 2 & 2 \\ 3 & 3 \\ 4 & 100 \end{pmatrix}$$

Then the commands

```
average = mean(A), med = median(A), dev = std(A)
```

```
return
```

```
average =
     2.5000    26.5000

med =
     2.5000     2.5000

dev =
     1.2910    49.0068
```

■

In MATLAB the commands cov and corrcoef are used to obtain the covariance and the correlation coefficients. Note that these commands only work on two-dimensional matrices.

Commands 60   COVARIANCE AND CORRELATION

cov(x)	returns the variance for the components of the vector **x**.
cov(A)	returns the covariance matrix. The elements of the diagonal are the variances for the columns of **A**.
cov(x,y)	is equivalent to cov([x y]), where **x** and **y** are column vectors.
corrcoef(A)	returns the correlation matrix.
corrcoef(x,y)	is equivalent to corrcoef([x y]), where **x** and **y** are column vectors.

■ **Example 6.6**

Let us define the following vectors:

$$\mathbf{x} = \begin{pmatrix} 1 \\ 1 \\ 1 \end{pmatrix} \qquad \mathbf{y} = \begin{pmatrix} 1 \\ 2 \\ 2 \end{pmatrix} \qquad \mathbf{z} = \begin{pmatrix} 0 \\ -1 \\ 1 \end{pmatrix}$$

(a) We get the variances by:

```
varx = cov(x), vary = cov(y), varz = cov(z)

varx =
      0

vary =
      0.3333

varz =
      1
```

(b) The covariances:

```
Cvxy = cov(x,y), Cvxz = cov(x,z), Cvyz = cov(y,z)

Cvxy =
        0         0
        0    0.3333


Cvxz =
        0     0
        0     1


Cvyz =
    0.3333        0
        0    1.0000
```

(c) The correlation matrices are obtained by:

```
Corrxy = corrcoef(x,y), Corrxz = corrcoef(x,z), ...
Corryz = corrcoef(y,z)

Warning: Divide by zero.
> In /opt/matlab52/toolbox/matlab/datafun/corrcoef.m at line 31
Corrxy =
    NaN    NaN
    NaN     1


Warning: Divide by zero.
> In /opt/matlab52/toolbox/matlab/datafun/corrcoef.m at line 31
Corrxz =
    NaN    NaN
    NaN     1


Corryz =
      1     0
      0     1
```

■

6.4 Sorting

With MATLAB it is possible to sort data by using the command sort.

Commands 61	SORTING
sort(x)	returns a vector in which the elements of the vector **x** are sorted in ascending order. If the components are complex the absolute values are used, that is sort(abs(x)).
[y,ind] = sort(x)	returns, in addition to the sorted components of **x** in the vector **y**, a vector **ind** of indices such that y = x(ind).
sort(A,*dim*)	returns a matrix where each column of **A** is sorted in ascending order. Note that the rows are changed. If *dim* is given the sorting is performed in the dimension *dim*.
[B,Ind] = sort(A)	returns the sorted columns of **A** in the matrix **B** and the matrix **Ind**. Each column in the matrix **Ind** corresponds to the column **ind** in the vector case above.
sortrows(X,col)	sorts the matrix **A** in a rowwise ascending order. If the elements in the row are complex they are sorted primarily according to abs(x) and secondly to angle(x). If *col* is given the rows are sorted according to the column number specified by it.

■ **Example 6.7**

Suppose **A** is defined by:

$$A = \begin{pmatrix} 0 & 4 & 4 \\ 2 & 0 & 2 \\ 4 & 2 & 0 \end{pmatrix}$$

(a) [Ascend,Ind] = sort(A) gives as result:

```
Ascend =
     0    0    0
     2    2    2
     4    4    4

Ind =
     1    2    3
     2    3    2
     3    1    1
```

(b) If we want to sort in descending order instead, the following command can be used: Descend = flipud(sort(A)), giving:

```
Descend =
      4    4    4
      2    2    2
      0    0    0
```

The command flipud is defined in Section 4.1.

■

6.5 Histograms and bar graphs

A set of data can be visualized with histograms and bar graphs using the commands hist, bar, and stairs.

Commands 62	HISTOGRAMS AND BAR GRAPHS
hist(x)	plots a histogram with 10 intervals for the data stored in **x**.
hist(x,n)	plots a histogram with *n* intervals for the data stored in **x**.
hist(x,y)	plots a histogram for the data in **x** with the intervals defined by the vector **y**, a vector with elements in ascending order.
bar(x)	plots a bar graph of the values in **x**.
bar(z,x)	plots a bar graph of the values in **x** in the positions defined in vector **z**. The values in **z** have to be uniformly distributed in ascending order.
bar(x,...,str)	plots a bar graph as above but with the colors and shapes defined by the string **str**. Regarding values of **str**, see Section 13.1.
bar(A)	plots a bar graph of the values in the two-dimensional matrix **A** grouped by row.
stairs(x)	plots a stair-step graph, that is a bar graph without internal lines.
stairs(z,x)	plots a bar graph of the data stored in **x** in positions defined by **z**.
barh(x,A,*format*)	plots the $m \times n$ matrix **A** as *m* groups of *n* bars. The string **format** may be color type, see Section 13.1, or the string 'stacked' which stacks the values on top of each other.
barh(A)	works as barh but uses x=1:m.
stem(y)	plots the discrete data stored in **y** as lines emerging from the *x* axis terminating at the *y* value as a circle.

Commands 62	(CONTINUED)

`stem(z,y)`	plots the discrete data stored in **y** as lines emerging from the x axis in the positions specified by the vector **x** and terminated with a circle at the y value.
`pareto(y,`*x*`)`	plots the bars for the elements in the vector **y** in descending order. The vector **x** may be given and should then contain the index for the x axes. If x is not given the element index from the vector y is used. The `pareto` command also draws a line with the cumulative element sum.
`pie(x,`*extract*`)`	plots a pie graph of the vector **x**. Is `sum(x) <= 1` an incomplete graph is produced. The vector **extract** is of the same size as **x** and for each non-zero element in **extract** the equivalent element for **x** will be extracted.

The commands `hist`, `bar` and `stairs` can also be used to store data in vectors for further use. Some of these commands, e.g. `bar` and `pie`, also have a three-dimensional version; see Section 13.5.

Commands 63	DIAGRAMS

`[m,y] = hist(x)`	creates a histogram with 10 uniform intervals between max and min for **x**. The result is a vector **y** with 10 equidistant values between $\min(x)$ and $\max(x)$ and the vector **m** which contains the number of values in each interval. The histogram can be shown by `bar(y,m,'.')`.
`[m,y] = hist(x,n)`	creates a histogram with n uniform intervals.
`[m,y] = hist(x,y)`	creates a histogram with the intervals defined by the vector **y**.
`[xb,yb] = bar(y)`	creates a bar graph of the values in **y**. The bar graph can be displayed by `plot(xb,yb)`.
`[xb,yb] = bar(x,y)`	creates a bar graph of the values in **y** in positions defined by **x**.
`[xb,yb] = stairs(y)`	creates a stair-step graph of the values in **y**.
`[xb,yb] = stairs(x,y)`	creates a stair-step graph of the values in **y** in positions defined by **x**.

■ **Example 6.8**

Let **x** be defined as:

```
x = [1 1 3 4 5 1 9 8];
```

(a) Then `hist(x); title('Histogram of x using hist(x)');`
give us the graph of Figure 6.2.

The command `title` gives the text above the figure; see Section 13.3.

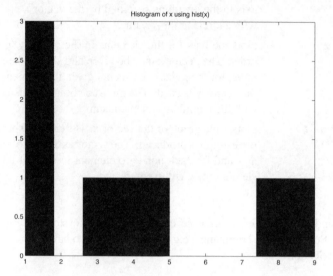

Figure 6.2 *Histogram with the standard interval length.*

(b) If we want three intervals we type:

`hist(x,3); title('Histogram of x using hist(x,3)')`
which result in the graph of Figure 6.3.

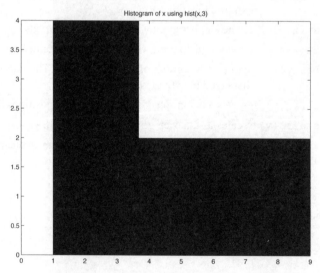

Figure 6.3 *Histogram with three intervals.*

(c) To draw bar graphs is just as easy:

bar(x); title('bar(x)');

give the graph in Figure 6.4.

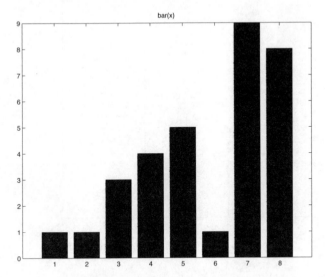

Figure 6.4 *Bar graph of x.*

(d) If we type [m,y] = hist(x); MATLAB creates the vectors **m** and **y**. If we continue with bar(y,m,'w') the histogram is plotted again; see Figure 6.5. To make it more interesting we make the histogram white instead of black. Other colors can be found together with the command plot in Section 13.1.

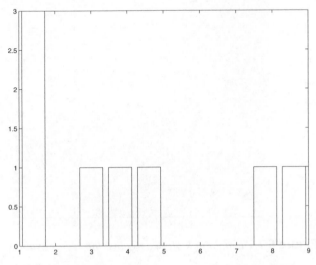

Figure 6.5 *Histogram plotted with the bar command.*

(e) If we still use the vector **x** but use the command `stem(x)` to display the data the result will be as in Figure 6.6.

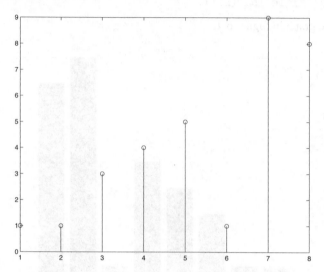

Figure 6.6 *The data in* **x** *plotted with* `stem`.

If we have an additional vector defined by:

`xvalues = [1.1 1.3 2 2.4 2.5 1.8 3 3.2];`

representing the points of the x axis, where the data are found, then the command `stem(xvalues,x,'-.')` results in the graph in Figure 6.7.

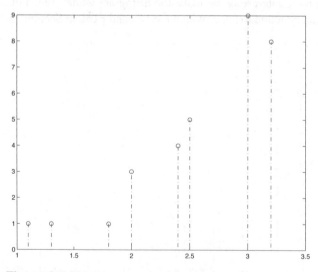

Figure 6.7 *The data in* **x** *plotted against the vector* ***xvalues***.

Note that the elements of the vector **x** do not have to be in ascending order. The command stem can have a third argument specifying line type and color in the plot just like the command bar.

■

6.6 Triangulation of regions

The following commands for triangulation of regions are available in MATLAB.

Commands 64   TRIANGULATION

TRI = delaunay(x,y, 'sorted')	returns the triangles which connect the vectors **x** and **y**. If the argument *'sorted'* is given the function assumes no duplicate values and that data is sorted for ascending **y** and for equal values of **y** for ascending **x** values.
voronoi(x,y,TRI)	plots the so called Voronoi diagram for the data sets **x** and **y**. If **TRI** is given it should be a Delaunay triangulation for **x** and **y**.

There are two functions using delaunay triangulations to give information on sets in relation to the triangulated set.

Commands 65   SEARCH FUNCTIONS WHEN TRIANGULATING

dsearch(x,y,TRI, px,py)	returns index for the point defined by the vectors **x** and **y** closest to (px, py). The matrix **TRI** is the triangulation of **x** and **y**.
tsearch(x,y,TRI, px,py)	returns index for the triangle defined by the sets in the vectors **x** and **y** and the triangulation **TRI** closest to the point (px, py). The matrix **TRI** is the triangulation of **x** and **y**.

6.7 Polygon analysis

Two functions to study the properties of polygons have been implemented.

Commands 66   POLYGONS

polyarea(x,y)	returns the area of the polygon defined by the set in the columns of **A** and **B**. If *dim* is given the polygon defined in the dimension *dim* is used.

Commands 66	(CONTINUED)
`polyarea(A,B,dim)`	returns the area of the polygon defined by the set in the first dimension of **A**. If *dim* is given the polygon defined by the dimension *dim* is returned.
`IN = inpolygon(x,y,` `px,py)`	returns **IN** which is of the same size as **x** and **y**. If (**x**, **y**) is inside the polygon defined by the vectors **px** and **py** the equivalent element in **IN** is given the value 1. If a point is on the polygon it gets the value 0.5 and outside it gets the value 0.
`rectint(x,y)`	returns the area of the region defined by the vectors **x** and **y**.
`rectint(A,B)`	returns an $n \times m$ matrix with all combinations of possible areas from `rectint(A(i,:),B(j,:))` if **A** is an $n \times 4$ matrix and **B** is an $m \times 4$ matrix.
`convhull(x,y,TRI)`	returns index to the points defined by **x** and **y** and which are on the convex hull of the set. If **TRI** is given it is used, otherwise a triangulation is computed.

■ **Example 6.9**

A square dart board may be defined according to the matrix **DartBoard**:

```
DartBoard(1,:,1) = [ 2 3 3 2 2 ];
DartBoard(2,:,1) = [ 2 2 3 3 2 ];
DartBoard(1,:,2) = [ 1 4 4 1 1 ];
DartBoard(2,:,2) = [ 1 1 4 4 1 ];
```

See Figure 6.8.

We now have:

```
DartBoard(:,:,1) =
     2      3      3      2      2
     2      2      3      3      2

DartBoard(:,:,2) =
     1      4      4      1      1
     1      1      4      4      1
```

The following function file can be useful to know how skilful a dart player you are.

```
function answer = dartresult(x,y, DartBoard)
% Returns a value corresponding to the score.

answer =
      2*sum(inpolygon(x,y,DartBoard(1,:,1),DartBoard(2,:,1)))+...
      3*sum(inpolygon(x,y,DartBoard(1,:,2),DartBoard(2,:,2)));
```

We now let MATLAB throw some darts.

```
RandomDarts(1,:) = 5.*rand(1,5);
RandomDarts(2,:) = 5.*rand(1,5)

RandomDarts =
    4.7506    1.1557    3.0342    2.4299    4.4565
    3.8105    2.2823    0.0925    4.1070    2.2235
```

We can get a nice picture and the result with the following sequence, where the darts are plotted as stars and an empty stripe surrounds the dart board. The result is put in the heading of the picture.

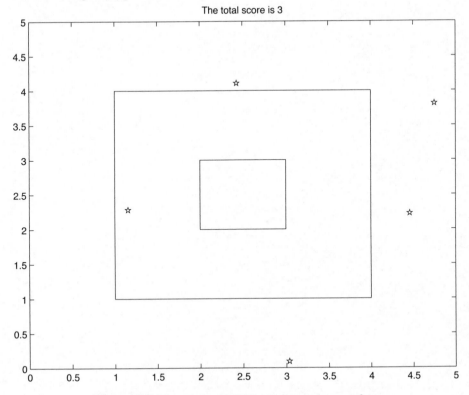

Figure 6.8 *The result of MATLAB throwing some darts.*

```
plot(DartBoard(1,:,1),DartBoard(2,:,1),'r',...
    DartBoard(1,:,2),DartBoard(2,:,2),'b')
hold on
plot(RandomDarts(1,:),RandomDarts(2,:),'pentagram')
axis([0 5 0 5])
title(cat(2,'The total score is ',num2str(...
dartresult(RandomDarts(1,:),RandomDarts(2,:),DartBoard))))
```

The result is Figure 6.8.

■

Systems of Linear Equations

Systems of linear equations are probably the most common computational problems. They arise as subproblems in almost all applications. Usually MATLAB solves systems of linear equations by division from the left with the operator \. Overdetermined systems can also be solved in the same manner as well as underdetermined.

Important concepts in the theory of linear systems are determinant, inverse, and rank. First, MATLAB commands for these are defined, while solving of systems begins in Section 7.2. Some factorizations are presented, followed by definitions of the norm and the condition number. The last section deals with overdetermined and underdetermined systems.

Note that all commands in this chapter only operate on two-dimensional matrices.

7.1 Determinant, inverse, and rank

The following commands are used to compute the determinant, the inverse, and the rank of a matrix **A**.

Commands 67	SOME FUNCTIONS ON MATRICES
`det(A)`	gives the determinant of the square matrix **A**.
`rank(A)`	gives the rank of **A**, that is the number of linearly independent rows and columns of **A**.
`inv(A)`	gives the inverse of the square matrix **A**. An error message is given if **A** is singular or almost singular.
`pinv(A)`	gives the pseudo-inverse of **A**. The pseudo-inverse is of size $n \times m$ if **A** is an $m \times n$ matrix. For non-singular matrices **A** we have `pinv(A) = inv(A)`.
`trace(A)`	gives the trace of **A**, that is the sum of the diagonal elements.

■ **Example 7.1**

Suppose we have the following matrices:

$$\mathbf{A1} = \begin{pmatrix} 1 & 3 \\ 2 & 4 \end{pmatrix} \quad \mathbf{A2} = \begin{pmatrix} 1 & 3 \\ 2 & 6 \end{pmatrix} \quad \mathbf{A3} = \begin{pmatrix} 1 & 3 & 2 \\ 2 & 7 & 6 \end{pmatrix}$$

Let us try the commands `det`, `inv`, `rank`, and a few other commands on these matrices.

(a) `det1 = det(A1), det2 = det(A2), det3 = det(A3)`

give:

```
det1 =
    -2

det2 =
    0
```

```
??? Error using ==> det
Matrix must be square.
```

The determinant is only defined for square matrices.

(b) The inverse is only defined for square matrices:

`Inv1 = inv(A1), Inv2 = inv(A2), Inv3 = inv(A3)`

give:

```
Inv1 =
   -2.0000    1.5000
    1.0000   -0.5000
```

```
Warning: Matrix is singular to working precision.
Inv2 =
    Inf    Inf
    Inf    Inf
```

```
??? Error using ==> inv
Matrix must be square.
```

However, the pseudo-inverse is defined for all matrices:

`Pinv1 = pinv(A1), Pinv2 = pinv(A2), Pinv3 = pinv(A3)`

give:

```
Pinv1 =
   -2.0000    1.5000
    1.0000   -0.5000
```

```
Pinv2 =
    0.0200    0.0400
    0.0600    0.1200
```

```
Pinv3 =
    0.9048   -0.3333
    1.0476   -0.3333
   -1.5238    0.6667
```

Note that the inverse of **A1** is the same as the pseudo-inverse of **A1**.

(c) The determinant of the inverse of **A**, $\det(\mathbf{A}^{-1})$, is the same as $\dfrac{1}{\det(\mathbf{A})}$, if the inverse exists:

```
detinv1 = det(inv(A1))
```

detinv1 =
  -0.5000

(d) The rank of a matrix is the same as the rank of its transpose:

```
rank1 = rank(A1), rank2 = rank(A2), rank3 = rank(A3)
```

give:

rank1 =
  2

rank2 =
  1

rank3 =
  2

and

```
rankT1 = rank(A1'), rankT2 = rank(A2'), rankT3 = rank(A3')
```

give:

rankT1 =
  2

rankT2 =
  1

rankT3 =
  2

(e) The determinant of a real matrix is the same as the determinant of its transpose:

```
detT1 = det(A1'), detT2 = det(A2'), detT3 = det(A3')
```

detT1 =
  -2

detT2 =
  0
??? Error using ==> det
Matrix must be square.

Two linear subspaces associated with linear systems are the **range** and the **null space**. If A is an $m \times n$ matrix with rank r, the range of A is the linear space spanned by the columns of A. The dimension of this space is r, that is the rank of A. The columns of A are linearly independent if $r = n$. The MATLAB command `orth` gives an orthonormal basis in the range of A.

The null space of A is the linear subspace of all vectors x for which $Ax = 0$. In MATLAB, an orthonormal basis in the null space is obtained with the command `null`.

If we have a set of vectors $v_1, v_2, \dots, v_n$ it is possible to check if they are linearly dependent by defining the matrix $B = (v_1 \quad v_2 \quad \dots \quad v_n)$. For instance, if the rank of B is $n - 1$, one of the vectors v_i can be written as a linear combination of the others.

The angle between two vectors, or in general between two subspaces, can be determined by the command `subspace`.

Commands 68	RANGE, NULL SPACE, AND ANGLE BETWEEN SUBSPACES
`orth(A)`	gives a matrix whose columns form an orthonormal basis in the range of A. The number of columns is equal to the rank of A.
`null(A)`	gives a matrix whose columns form an orthonormal basis in the null space of A. The number of columns is equal to the dimension of the null space.
`subspace(x,y)`	gives the angle between the column vectors x and y. The lengths of the vectors have to be the same.
`subspace(A,B)`	gives the angle between the subspaces spanned by the columns of A and B. The lengths of the columns have to be the same.

■ **Example 7.2**

We try the commands `orth`, `null` and `subspace` on the same matrices as in Example 7.1:

(a) First we try `orth`:

```
Range1 = orth(A1), Range2 = orth(A2), Range3 = orth(A3)
```

give:

```
Range1 =
     0.5760     0.8174
     0.8174    -0.5760
```

```
Range2 =
    0.4472
    0.8944

Range3 =
    0.3667   -0.9303
    0.9303    0.3667
```

(b) Secondly we try rank:

```
rank1 = rank(orth(A1)), ...
rank2 = rank(orth(A2)), rank3 = rank(orth(A3))
```

give:

```
rank1 =
    2

rank2 =
    1

rank3 =
    2
```

The rank of the range of a matrix is, of course, the same as the rank of the matrix itself.

(c) Then we try null:

```
nullSpace1 = null(A1), ...
nullSpace2 = null(A2), nullSpace3 = null(A3)
```

give:

```
nullSpace1 =
    Empty matrix: 2-by-0

nullSpace2 =
   -0.9487
    0.3162

nullSpace3 =
   -0.8729
    0.4364
   -0.2182
```

Here `Empty Matrix` indicates that the null space is empty. The zero vector is the only vector that results in the zero vector when **A1** operates on it.

(d) Some more examples with null:

```
nullSpaceT1 = null(A1'), ...
nullSpaceT2 = null(A2'), nullSpaceT3 = null(A3')
```

give:

```
nullSpaceT1 =
   Empty matrix: 2-by-0

nullSpaceT2 =
   -0.8944
    0.4472

nullSpaceT3 =
   Empty matrix: 2-by-0
```

(e) Examples with orth:

```
RangeT1 = orth(A1'), ...
RangeT2 = orth(A2'), RangeT3 = orth(A3')
```

give:

```
RangeT1 =
     0.4046      0.9145
     0.9145     -0.4046

RangeT2 =
     0.3162
     0.9487

RangeT3 =
     0.2197     -0.4357
     0.7508     -0.4958
     0.6229      0.7513
```

(f) Finally with subspace

```
angle = subspace(null(A2),orth(A2'))
```

gives:

```
angle =
     1.5708
```

The angle is $\pi/2$. This implies that the two spaces are orthogonal. Note that the command subspace requires columns of equal length.

■

7.2 Solving linear systems and LU factorization

Linear systems are solved in MATLAB with the operator \, which is a very powerful and intelligent operator. It is often valuable to study the computing process in more detail. There are several commands in MATLAB which make this possible.

Let **A** be an $n \times n$ matrix, and let **b** and **x** be column vectors with n elements. As an alternative, **B** and **X** can be matrices with n rows and p columns. In MATLAB, the system $\mathbf{Ax} = \mathbf{b}$ is solved with the command:

```
x = A\b
```

The more general system $\mathbf{AX} = \mathbf{B}$, that is with multiple right-hand sides, $\mathbf{B} = (\ \mathbf{b}_1 \quad \mathbf{b}_2 \quad \dots \quad \mathbf{b}_p \ )$, is solved in the same manner by:

```
X = A\B
```

If **A** is singular, or almost singular, an error message is given.

■ Example 7.3

Let us solve the following system in MATLAB:

$$\begin{cases} 2x_1 + 3x_2 = 7 \\ 4x_1 + \ x_2 = 9 \end{cases}$$

We form the coefficient matrix **A**, and the right-hand side **b**:

$$\mathbf{A} = \begin{pmatrix} 2 & 3 \\ 4 & 1 \end{pmatrix} \qquad \mathbf{b} = \begin{pmatrix} 7 \\ 9 \end{pmatrix}$$

The unknown vector $\mathbf{x} = (\ x_1 \quad x_2\ )'$ is sought, and can be obtained by: `x = A\b`

```
x =
    2
    1
```

■

MATLAB uses different methods to solve linear systems, depending on the coefficient matrix **A**. If possible, MATLAB exploits the structure of the matrix. For instance if **A** is symmetric and positive definite, MATLAB uses Cholesky factorization.

If MATLAB does not find an alternative method, the computations are carried out with Gaussian elimination and partial pivoting. This process is mainly an **LU factorization** or **LU decomposition** of **A**. Basically, it holds that **A** = **LU**, where **U** is an upper triangular matrix and **L** is a lower triangular matrix with a unit diagonal.

However, to guarantee stability in the computations, partial pivoting is used. This means that **L** is usually a permuted lower triangular matrix, that is, some rows are interchanged. Thus, **L** might appear to lack structure. These permutations define a **permutation matrix**, **P**.

A permutation matrix **P** of size $n \times n$ has n unit entries placed in an order where each row and column have all zeros except for exactly one unit entry. The inverse of a permutation matrix is the same as its transpose.

The LU factorization can now be expressed by the non-permuted lower triangular matrix $\mathbf{L}_l$ as:

$$\mathbf{PA} = \mathbf{L}_l\mathbf{U}$$

that is, our permuted matrix **L** is given by $\mathbf{L} = \mathbf{P}'\mathbf{L}_l$.

In MATLAB the command `lu` makes it possible to obtain **U** and either the permuted or the non-permuted lower triangular matrices **L**. In the latter case the permutation matrix **P** is also given.

Commands 69	LU DECOMPOSITION
`[L,U] = lu(A)`	gives an upper triangular matrix **U**, and a permuted lower triangular matrix **L**, that is **L** is the product of a lower triangular matrix with a unit diagonal and a permutation matrix, the inverse of **P**, see next command.
`[L,U,P] = lu(A)`	gives an upper triangular matrix **U**, a lower triangular matrix **L** with a unit diagonal, and a permutation matrix **P**, so that $\mathbf{LU} = \mathbf{PA}$.

■ **Example 7.4**

If **A** is defined by `A = [1 2 3;4 5 6;7 8 0];` and we type `[L,U] = lu(A)` the result is:

$L =$

0.1429	1.0000	0
0.5714	0.5000	1.0000
1.0000	0	0

$U =$

7.0000	8.0000	0
0	0.8571	3.0000
0	0	4.5000

Here the inverse of the permutation matrix is:

$$\mathbf{P}^{-1} = \mathbf{P}' = \begin{pmatrix} 0 & 1 & 0 \\ 0 & 0 & 1 \\ 1 & 0 & 0 \end{pmatrix}$$

Let us perform this Gaussian elimination in detail, and follow what really took place:

$$\mathbf{A} = \begin{pmatrix} 1 & 2 & 3 \\ 4 & 5 & 6 \\ 7 & 8 & 0 \end{pmatrix} \quad \mathbf{A1} = \begin{pmatrix} 7 & 8 & 0 \\ 4 & 5 & 6 \\ 1 & 2 & 3 \end{pmatrix} \quad \mathbf{A2} = \begin{pmatrix} 7 & 8 & 0 \\ 0 & 0.4286 & 6 \\ 0 & 0.8571 & 3 \end{pmatrix}$$

$$\mathbf{A3} = \begin{pmatrix} 7 & 8 & 0 \\ 0 & 0.8571 & 3 \\ 0 & 0.4286 & 6 \end{pmatrix} \quad \mathbf{A4} = \begin{pmatrix} 7 & 8 & 0 \\ 0 & 0.8571 & 3 \\ 0 & 0 & 4.5 \end{pmatrix}$$

We start with the matrix **A**. The first pivot element is in position (1, 1). By inter-changing the first and the third row, we get the largest possible pivot element, that is 7. This is the first permutation, and we get the matrix **A1**. The first elimination step gives us the matrix **A2**.

The second pivot element is in position (2, 2). We interchange rows two and three, to get the matrix **A3**, and the elimination gives us **A4**, which is the same as our matrix **U**.

We performed two permutations. First interchange of rows one and three, that is:

$$\mathbf{P1} = \begin{pmatrix} 0 & 0 & 1 \\ 0 & 1 & 0 \\ 1 & 0 & 0 \end{pmatrix}$$

and second interchange of rows two and three, that is:

$$\mathbf{P2} = \begin{pmatrix} 1 & 0 & 0 \\ 0 & 0 & 1 \\ 0 & 1 & 0 \end{pmatrix}$$

The product of **P1** and **P2** forms **P**:

$$\mathbf{P1} * \mathbf{P2} = \mathbf{P} = \begin{pmatrix} 0 & 0 & 1 \\ 1 & 0 & 0 \\ 0 & 1 & 0 \end{pmatrix}$$

and its inverse is:

$$\mathbf{P}^{-1} = \begin{pmatrix} 0 & 1 & 0 \\ 0 & 0 & 1 \\ 1 & 0 & 0 \end{pmatrix}$$

If we type `[L,U,P]` = `lu(A)` the result is as expected:

```
L =
      1.0000           0           0
      0.1429      1.0000           0
      0.5714      0.5000      1.0000


U =
      7.0000      8.0000           0
           0      0.8571      3.0000
           0           0      4.5000


P =
      0      0      1
      1      0      0
      0      1      0
```

■

There are a number of methods to solve the problem $\mathbf{Ax} = \mathbf{b}$ where $\mathbf{A}$ is a $n \times n$ matrix and $\mathbf{b}$ is a column vector with length n. A more thorough description of the algorithms is out of the scope of this book. See MATLAB Help Desk if you need more information.

Commands 70	METHODS FOR SOLVING SYSTEMS OF EQUATIONS
x = bicg(A,b,*tol*, *maxit*,M)	solves the system with the so called biconjugate gradient method. If *tol* is given it specifies the tolerance of the method, this is compared to `norm(b-A*x)/norm(b)` to see if the solution is acceptable. If *maxit* is given this is used as the maximum number of iterations. To use a preconditioner, specify it in the matrix **M**.
bicg(A,b, ... ,M1, M2,*x0*)	operates as above but uses the matrices **M1** and **M2** as preconditioners. The matrices **M1** and **M2** and the preconditioner **M** are related as $\mathbf{M} = \mathbf{M1} \cdot \mathbf{M2}$. If **x0** is given it is used as an initial vector to start the iterations with.

Commands 70 (CONTINUED)

`[x,flag,relres,`
`iter,resvect] =`
`bicg( ... )`
	returns the solution of the problem in **x**. Information on the convergence of bigc is stored in *flag*. The relative residual norm of the result is stored in *iter*. The value *resvect* is the norm of each iteration. All variables in the result vector may be omitted.

`bicgstab( ... )`	solves the system with the so called stabilized biconjugate gradient method, and is called in the same way as `bicg` and returns the results in the same form.
`cgs( ... )`	solves the system with the so called squared conjugate gradient method, and is called in the same way as `bicg` and returns the results in the same form.
`gmres(A,b,restart,` `... )`	solves the system with the so called generalized minimum residual method. It is called in the same way as `bicg` and returns the results in the same form except that the argument *restart* may be given. The solver will restart itself at iteration *restart* using that iterate as its new initial guess.
`pcg( ... )`	solves the system with the so called preconditioned conjugate gradients method, and is called in the same way as `bicg` and returns the results in the same form.
`qmr( ... )`	solves the system with the so called quasi-minimal residual method. It is called in the same way as `bicg` and returns the results in the same form.

7.3 Row echelon matrices

An alternative method to the LU factorization is to reduce the coefficient matrix **A** to the row echelon form. This is more general since it can be applied to rectangular matrices. A lot of useful information about the linear system is given by the echelon matrix.

To every $m \times n$ matrix **A** there is a permutation matrix **P**, a lower triangular matrix **L** with unit diagonal, and an $m \times n$ echelon matrix **R** such that $PA = LR$.

A matrix is said to be in **reduced row echelon form** if the following is true:

1. Zero rows, if there are any, are placed at the bottom of the matrix.

2. The first non-zero element of each row is a 1. This element is referred to as the leading element of the row.

3. The leading element of every row is placed to the right of the leading element of the previous row.

4. In a column with a leading 1 all following elements are zeros.

We can use the command `rref` in MATLAB to analyze the system $\mathbf{Ax} = \mathbf{b}$.

Commands 71	REDUCED ROW ECHELON FORM
`rref(A)`	gives the reduced row echelon form of $\mathbf{A}$, computed by Gauss–Jordan elimination and row pivoting.
`rref(A,tol)`	gives the same as the previous, but uses the tolerance *tol*. The tolerance is used to determine when an element is considered negligible.
`rrefmovie(A)`	computes the reduced row echelon form, and shows step by step how the computations are progressing.

Normally the tolerance used is `tol = max(size(A))*eps*norm(A,inf)`. The command `norm` is defined in Section 7.6.

■ **Example 7.5**

Let

$$A = \begin{pmatrix} 1 & 3 & 3 & 2 \\ 2 & 6 & 9 & 5 \\ -1 & -3 & 3 & 0 \end{pmatrix} \quad B = \begin{pmatrix} 2 & 1 & 1 \\ 4 & 1 & 0 \\ -2 & 2 & 1 \end{pmatrix}$$

(a) We know that some of the rows of the matrix $\mathbf{A}$ are linearly dependent if the matrix given by `rref(A)` contains one or more zero rows. The same test can be carried out on the columns of $\mathbf{A}$ by the command `rref(A')`. The commands `Aref = rref(A)`, `Bref = rref(B)` give:

```
Aref =
    1.0000    3.0000         0    1.0000
         0         0    1.0000    0.3333
         0         0         0         0
```

```
Bref =
    1    0    0
    0    1    0
    0    0    1
```

(b) One way to determine the rank of a matrix $\mathbf{A}$ is to count the number of non-zero rows in the reduced row echelon form of $\mathbf{A}$. In the current example, we see that $\mathbf{A}$ has rank two, and $\mathbf{B}$ has rank three. We verify this with the commands `rankA = rank(A)`, `rankB = rank(B)` which give:

```
rankA =

          2

rankB =

          3
```

■

The command `rref` may be used to investigate a system of linear equations. Let $\mathbf{Ax} = \mathbf{b}$ be a system of linear equations, and form the matrix $\mathbf{B} = (\mathbf{A} \quad \mathbf{b})$. The command C = `rref(B)` gives a matrix $\mathbf{C}$ in reduced row echelon form. Then the following hold:

- If $\mathbf{C}$ contains one or more rows with all zeros, the system contains redundant information. This means that one or more of the equations can be removed.

- If $\mathbf{C}$ contains a row where all elements but the last are zero, that is $(0, 0, \ldots, 0, 1)$, the system contains a contradiction, and no solution exists.

- If the system has a unique solution, it is found in the last column of $\mathbf{C}$.

7.4 Cholesky factorization

If a matrix $\mathbf{A}$ is symmetric and **positive definite**, that is $\mathbf{A} = \mathbf{A}'$ and $\mathbf{x}'\mathbf{Ax} > 0$ for every $\mathbf{x} \neq \mathbf{0}$, then there exists an upper triangular matrix $\mathbf{G}$ with positive diagonal elements such that $\mathbf{G}'\mathbf{G} = \mathbf{A}$.

This special case of LU factorization is called **Cholesky factorization**, and requires only about half as many arithmetic operations as the normal LU factorization. Note that the Cholesky factorization in some textbooks is defined in terms of lower triangular matrices.

Cholesky factorization is used automatically by MATLAB when symmetric positive definite systems are solved with left division, \.

The command `chol` can be used to compute the Cholesky factorization of a positive definite matrix $\mathbf{A}$.

Commands 72	CHOLESKY FACTORIZATION
`chol(A)`	gives an upper triangular matrix which is the Cholesky factor of $\mathbf{A}$. An error message is given if $\mathbf{A}$ is not positive definite.
`[G,err] = chol(A)`	gives the Cholesky factor $\mathbf{G}$ of the matrix $\mathbf{A}$. No error message is given if $\mathbf{A}$ is not positive definite, instead *err* is set non-zero.
`R1 = cholupdate(R,x)`	returns the upper triangular Cholesky factor $\mathbf{R1}$ for $\mathbf{A} + \mathbf{xx}'$ if $\mathbf{R} = $ `chol(A)` and $\mathbf{x}$ is a column vector of the same length as the columns of $\mathbf{A}$.

| Commands 72 | (CONTINUED) |

| R1 =
cholupdate(R,x,
'-') | returns the upper triangular Cholesky factor **R1** for **A** − **xx**′ if
R = chol(**A**) and **x** is a column vector of the same length as
the columns of **A**. |

■ Example 7.6

(a) b = [-1 -1 -1]; A = 4*eye(4) + diag(b,-1) + diag(b,1),...
    G = chol(A)

give:

```
A =
        4     -1      0      0
       -1      4     -1      0
        0     -1      4     -1
        0      0     -1      4
```

```
G =
    2.0000   -0.5000         0         0
         0    1.9365   -0.5164         0
         0         0    1.9322   -0.5175
         0         0         0    1.9319
```

We check this result by typing Test = G'*G and get:

```
Test =
    4.0000   -1.0000         0         0
   -1.0000    4.0000   -1.0000         0
         0   -1.0000    4.0000   -1.0000
         0         0   -1.0000    4.0000
```

Thus we get the matrix **A** back again.

(b) To study the difference in the number of arithmetic operations between the LU factorization and the Cholesky factorization we type:

```
flops(0), lu(A); flops, flops(0), chol(A); flops
```

and get:

```
ans =
        34
ans =
        30
```

However, the difference is more obvious for larger systems.

■

7.5 QR factorization

A third alternative, in addition to the LU and Cholesky factorizations, is to use **QR factorization** or **QR decomposition**, when linear systems are solved.

Let **A** be an $n \times n$ matrix. Then **A** can be factorized as:

$$\mathbf{A} = \mathbf{QR}$$

where **Q** is a unitary matrix and **R** is an upper triangular matrix of the same size as **A**. The system $\mathbf{Ax} = \mathbf{b}$ can be written as $\mathbf{QRx} = \mathbf{b}$ or equivalently:

$$\mathbf{Rx} = \mathbf{Q'b}.$$

This is an upper triangular system, and thus easy to solve.

The main advantage of QR factorization in comparison with Gaussian elimination, is a higher numerical stability. However, it is also more expensive in terms of arithmetic operations.

The QR factorization can be obtained in MATLAB with the command qr. Note that it is also possible to decompose $m \times n$ matrices. Thus we treat this general case and assume that **A** is an $m \times n$ matrix.

Commands 73	QR FACTORIZATION

`[Q,R] = qr(A)`	gives an $m \times m$ matrix **Q** whose columns form an orthonormal basis, and an upper triangular $m \times n$ matrix **R**, so that $\mathbf{A} = \mathbf{QR}$.
`[Q,R,P] = qr(A)`	gives a matrix **Q**, with orthonormal columns, an upper triangular matrix **R** with diagonal elements decreasing in magnitude, and a permutation matrix **P** so that $\mathbf{AP} = \mathbf{QR}$.
`[Q,R] = qr(A,0)`	gives a QR factorization economized in arithmetic operations and storage. If the number of rows is less than the number of columns in the $m \times n$ matrix **A**, then only the first n columns of **Q** are calculated, and thus **Q** is of the same size as **A**. Can also be obtained with a permutation matrix; see above or type `help qr`.
`[Q1,R1] = qrdelete(Q,R,j)`	gives a new QR factorization of the matrix made out of **A** with the jth column in the matrix **A** removed. The matrices **Q** and **R** are the QR factors of **A**.
`[Q1,R1] = qrinsert(Q,R,b,j)`	gives a new QR factorization of the matrix made out of **A** with an extra column **b** inserted before the jth column in the matrix **A** where **Q** and **R** are the QR factors of **A**. If $j = n+1$ the new column is the last one.

■ **Example 7.7**

(a) Let us solve $\mathbf{A}\mathbf{x} = \mathbf{b}$, where $\mathbf{A}$ and $\mathbf{b}$ are given by:

$$\mathbf{A} = \begin{pmatrix} 1 & 2 & 2 \\ 3 & 2 & 2 \\ 1 & 1 & 2 \end{pmatrix} \qquad \mathbf{b} = \begin{pmatrix} 7 \\ 9 \\ 5 \end{pmatrix}$$

```
[Q,R] = qr(A), x = R\Q'*b
```

give:

```
Q =
    -0.3015     0.9239    -0.2357
    -0.9045    -0.3553    -0.2357
    -0.3015     0.1421     0.9428


R =
    -3.3166    -2.7136    -3.0151
          0     1.2792     1.4213
          0          0     0.9428


x =
     1
     2
     1
```

This is the same as we get by the command A\b.

(b) Let us compare the number of arithmetic operations required to solve a linear system using the QR factorization and using the left division. To emphasize the difference we apply the methods to a larger system:

```
A = rand(10,10); b = rand(10,1); flops(0); ...
x = A\b; lureq = flops
```

give:

```
lureq =
        1506
```

and

```
flops(0), [Q,R] = qr(A); x = R\Q'*b; qrreq = flops
```

give:

```
qrreq =
        5285
```

■

QR factorization can be used to solve overdetermined systems, that is systems with more equations than unknowns (see Section 7.7) and when computing eigenvalues and eigenvectors (see Section 8.2).

One of several ways to compute the QR factorization of a matrix is to apply a series of **Givens rotations**. Givens rotations applied to vectors of length two can be obtained with the command `planerot`. To apply a Givens rotation to a matrix, the colon notation must be used.

<table>
<tr><td>Commands 74</td><td>GIVENS AND JACOBI ROTATIONS</td></tr>
</table>

`planerot(x)`	gives a Givens rotation in a 2×2 matrix that clears the second element of the two-element vector **x**. The command is used by the MATLAB functions `qrinsert` and `qrdelete`.
`[G,y] = planerot(x)`	gives the Givens rotation as above in **G**, and the result in $\mathbf{y} = \mathbf{Gx}$.
`rjr(A)`	applies a Jacobi rotation to **A**. The angle and plane where the rotation is applied is random. Eigenvalues, singular values and symmetry are preserved.

■ **Example 7.8**

A Givens rotation can be described as a plane rotation. Let the 2×2 matrix **A** have the vectors **x** and **y** as columns.

$$\mathbf{A} = \begin{pmatrix} 1 & 1 \\ -1 & 2 \end{pmatrix} \qquad \mathbf{x} = \begin{pmatrix} 1 \\ -1 \end{pmatrix} \qquad \mathbf{y} = \begin{pmatrix} 1 \\ 2 \end{pmatrix}$$

If we type `G = planerot(x)`, that is **G** rotates the vector **x** (the first column of **A**) to the x axis, and let **G** operate on **A** by `Anew = G*A` we obtain as result:

```
G =
    0.7071   -0.7071
    0.7071    0.7071

Anew =
    1.4142   -0.7071
         0    2.1213
```

We see that the vector norms of the columns in **A** and **Anew** are the same by giving the commands:

```
xnorm = norm(x), ynorm = norm(y), ...
xnewnorm = norm(Anew(:,1)), ynewnorm = norm(Anew(:,2))


xnorm =
    1.4142

ynorm =
    2.2361

xnewnorm =
    1.4142

ynewnorm =
    2.2361
```

that is the norm (also called length) of each column is unchanged. The command norm is defined in Section 7.6. In Figure 7.1 we see that the rotation is the same for both of the columns in **A**.

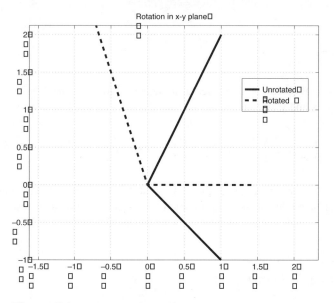

Figure 7.1 *Givens rotation of two vectors in the x−y plane.*

To apply Givens rotation on a matrix and in order to reduce the elements in the matrix we have to do some programming. For this, see the example on planerot in Section 12.2.

7.6 Norms and condition numbers

A **vector norm** is a scalar, that is a measure of the magnitude or length of a vector, and should not be confused with length as the number of elements in a vector. Various norms can be obtained in MATLAB with the command `norm`.

Commands 75	VECTOR NORMS

`norm(x)`	gives $\|\mathbf{x}\|_2 = \sqrt{\sum_k \|x_k\|^2}$, that is the Euclidean norm.
`norm(x,inf)`	gives $\|\mathbf{x}\|_\infty$, that is the maximum norm, the same as `max(abs(x))`.
`norm(x,1)`	gives $\|\mathbf{x}\|_1$, that is $\sum_k \|x_k\|$.
`norm(x,p)`	gives $\|\mathbf{x}\|_p$, that is $\sqrt[p]{\sum_k \|x_k\|^p}$. Thus `norm(x,2) = norm(x)`.
`norm(x,-inf)`	gives the smallest element by absolute value, that is `min(abs(x))`. Note that this is not a vector norm.

■ **Example 7.9**

Let

```
x = [3 4 5];

norm1   = norm(x,1),    norm2  = norm(x,2), ...
norminf = norm(x,inf), nonorm = norm(x,-inf)
```

This gives:

```
norm1 =
    12

norm2 =
    7.0711

norminf =
    5

nonorm =
    3
```

■

A **matrix norm** is a measure of the size of a matrix, not to be mixed up with size in the sense of the number of rows and columns. Matrix norms are often used in estimating errors due to perturbations in data or in numerical computations.

The *p*-norms of a square matrix are defined by the vector norms:

$$\|\mathbf{A}\|_p = \sup_{\mathbf{x} \neq \mathbf{0}} \frac{\|\mathbf{Ax}\|_p}{\|\mathbf{x}\|_p}$$

These definitions are not actually used in the computations. Instead the expressions in Commands 76 are used. These are equivalent to the definitions above if the matrices are square but they can also be used to compute norms of non-square matrices.

Since the computation of the Euclidean norm is an expensive operation, there is also a command to compute an estimate of the Euclidean norm, `normest`.

Commands 76   MATRIX NORMS

`norm(A)`	gives $\|\mathbf{A}\|_2$, that is the Euclidean norm, which is the same as the largest singular value of **A**; see Section 8.3.
`norm(A,1)`	gives $\|\mathbf{A}\|_1$, that is the largest column sum of **A**. Column sum means the sum of the absolute values of each element in the column.
`norm(A,2)`	gives $\|\mathbf{A}\|_2$, the same as `norm(A)`.
`norm(A,inf)`	gives $\|\mathbf{A}\|_\infty$, that is the largest row sum of **A**. Row sum means the sum of the absolute values of each element in the row.
`norm(A,'fro')`	gives $\|\mathbf{A}\|_F = \sqrt{\sum_i \sum_j |a_{ij}|^2}$, the Frobenius norm. This cannot be obtained by the definition of the matrix *p*-norm above.
`normest(A)`	estimates the Euclidean norm of **A**. The relative error is less than 10^{-6}.
`normest(A,tol)`	estimates the Euclidean norm of **A**. The relative error is less than *tol*.

■ **Example 7.10**

(a) Let

```
A = [1 1;2 3];

norm1   = norm(A,1),    norm2 = norm(A,2), ...
norminf = norm(A,inf), normf = norm(A,'fro')
```

give:

```
norm1 =
     4
```

```
norm2 =
     3.8643
```

```
norminf =
     5
```

```
normf =
     3.8730
```

(b) Let us compare the number of arithmetic operations required to compute the Euclidean norm and an estimate of the Euclidean norm of a large matrix.

```
A = rand(100);
flops(0), norm2 = norm(A), expensive = flops
```

give:

```
norm2 =
    49.8483
```

```
expensive =
       2948409
```

and

```
flops(0), normapprox = normest(A), cheaper = flops
```

give:

```
normapprox =
    50.6701
```

```
cheaper =
       133211
```

∎

Let $\mathbf{Ax} = \mathbf{b}$ be a linear system of equations. The **condition number** of a system is a real number greater than or equal to 1, measuring the sensitivity of the solution $\mathbf{x}$ with respect to perturbations in the data, that is in $\mathbf{A}$ and/or $\mathbf{b}$. A badly conditioned system has a large condition number. The definition is:

$$\text{cond}(\mathbf{A}) = \|\mathbf{A}\| \|\mathbf{A}^{-1}\|$$

The command cond(A) gives the condition number in the Euclidean norm, which can be expressed as the quotient of the largest and the smallest singular value of $\mathbf{A}$; see Section 8.3.

Commands 77	CONDITION NUMBERS
cond(A)	gives the condition number of **A** in the Euclidean norm.
cond(A,p)	gives the condition number in the norm specified by p, which may have the values 1, 2, *inf* and *'fro'*; see norm in Commands 76.
condest(A)	gives a lower bound estimate in the one-norm (1-norm) of the condition number of the matrix **A**.
[c,v] = condest(A)	gives a lower bound estimate of the condition number c in the 1-norm of **A**, and also computes a vector **v**, where $\|\mathbf{Av}\| = \frac{\|\mathbf{A}\|\cdot\|\mathbf{v}\|}{c}$.
[c,v] = condest(A,tr)	gives c and **v** as above, but also displays information about the steps in the calculations. If $tr = 1$ information on every step is displayed, and if $tr = -1$ the quotient c/rcond(A) is displayed.
rcond(A)	gives another estimate of the sensitivity of a system defined by the matrix **A**. A badly conditioned matrix **A** gives a number close to 0, while a well conditioned matrix gives a number close to 1.

■ **Example 7.11**

Let us try the Hilbert matrix (see Section 4.4):

bad = cond(hilb(5))

gives:

bad =
    4.7661e+05

This implies that in the worst case a perturbation in the right-hand side or in the coefficient matrix can be multiplied by the number *bad*, and five decimal places might be lost.

■

7.7 Overdetermined and underdetermined systems

A linear $m \times n$ system of equations $\mathbf{Ax} = \mathbf{b}$ is said to be **overdetermined** if $m > n$, that is if it has more equations than unknowns. These equations are usually inconsistent, and thus the system does not have an exact solution. This is, for instance, a frequent problem when fitting curves to experimental data.

The key is to try to find the vector **x** that minimizes the total error in the m equations. There are several ways to do this, but the most frequently used is to minimize the sum of the squares of the errors:

$$e = \sum_{i=1}^{m} \left(b_i - \sum_{j=1}^{n} a_{ij} x_j \right)^2 = \|\mathbf{b} - \mathbf{Ax}\|_2^2$$

This is the **method of least squares**, and a **least squares solution** can be obtained with either the operator \ or in special cases with the commands nnls and lscov. It is also possible to exploit the sparse matrices discussed in Chapter 9, and here we mention the command spaugment which gives a sparse matrix used in the computations.

Commands 78	SOLUTIONS BY LEAST SQUARES
A\b	gives the solution in the sense of least squares. See also Section 3.3. If **b** = **B** is a matrix, then the system corresponding to each column in **B** is solved.
spaugment(A,c)	gives the square symmetric sparse matrix T = [c*I A; A' 0]. The overdetermined system **Ax** = **b** can now be solved by T\z where **z** is the vector **b** with trailing zeros. The parameter c can be left out, MATLAB then uses a value according to the setting in spparms. Type help spparms.
nnls(A,b)	gives a solution of the least squares problem under the additional constraint that all the components of the solution must be non-negative. Type help nnls to get more information.
lscov(A,b,V)	returns the least squares solution when the covariance **V** is known. This means that $(\mathbf{b} - \mathbf{Ax})'\mathbf{V}^{-1}(\mathbf{b} - \mathbf{Ax})$ is minimized. Type help lscov for more information.

MATLAB usually performs a QR factorization when division from the left is used to solve overdetermined systems. If the system does not have full rank, and lacks a unique least squares solution, undetermined values are set to zero. A warning message is then issued.

■ **Example 7.12**

Let:

$$A1 = \begin{pmatrix} 1 & 1 \\ 1 & 2 \\ 1 & 3 \end{pmatrix} \qquad A2 = \begin{pmatrix} 1 & 3 \\ 1 & 3 \\ 1 & 3 \end{pmatrix} \qquad b = \begin{pmatrix} 2 \\ 0 \\ -1 \end{pmatrix}$$

```
fullrank = A1\b, notfullrank = A2\b
```

give:

```
fullrank =
    3.3333
   -1.5000
```

```
Warning: Rank deficient, rank = 1   tol = 3.4613e-15.
```

```
notfullrank =
         0
    0.1111
```

■

If $n < m$, then the system $\mathbf{Ax} = \mathbf{b}$ is **underdetermined**. Such systems usually have infinitely many solutions, and MATLAB selects one. No warning message is given.

■ **Example 7.13**

(a) Let:

$$A = \begin{pmatrix} 1 & 1 & 1 \\ 1 & 2 & 3 \end{pmatrix} \qquad b = \begin{pmatrix} 2 \\ 3 \end{pmatrix}$$

```
x = A\b
```

gives:

```
x =
    1.5000
         0
    0.5000
```

Unfortunately MATLAB cannot give the general solution. The solubility may be studied with the `rref` command; see Section 7.3. By typing:

```
UnderSol = rref([A~b])
```

we get

```
UnderSol =
     1     0    -1     1
     0     1     2     1
```

With this we may find the general solution which, for example, is

$$\mathbf{x} = \begin{pmatrix} 1+t \\ 1-2t \\ t \end{pmatrix} \qquad \text{for all } t$$

If we now have $t = 0.5$ we get the MATLAB solution.

(b) Let:

$$\mathbf{a} = \begin{pmatrix} 1 \\ 2 \\ 3 \end{pmatrix} \qquad \mathbf{b} = \begin{pmatrix} 2 \\ -2 \\ 2 \end{pmatrix}$$

We can now study the result of various matrix divisions, **b** divided by **a**.
Division from the left gives:

```
left = a\b
```

```
left =
    0.2857
```

or 2/7, which is the solution of the overdetermined system $\mathbf{ax} = \mathbf{b}$.
Division from the right gives:

```
Right = b/a
```

```
Right =
         0           0      0.6667
         0           0     -0.6667
         0           0      0.6667
```

which is the same as `(a'\b')'`, that is one solution of the underdetermined system
$\mathbf{a'x'} = \mathbf{b'}$.

Elementwise division from the left:

```
elementWiseLeft = a.\b
```

```
elementWiseLeft =
     2.0000
    -1.0000
     0.6667
```

which is the same as the elementwise division from the right:

```
elementWiseRight = b./a
```

```
elementWiseRight =
     2.0000
    -1.0000
     0.6667
```

Eigenvalues and Eigenvectors

In MATLAB there are efficient commands for the computation of eigenvalues and eigenvectors. Different subresults and factorizations can also be obtained. This can be useful for instance when teaching linear algebra. Note that the commands in this chapter only operate on two-dimensional matrices.

8.1 Computation of eigenvalues and eigenvectors

Let **A** be an $n \times n$ matrix. The eigenvalue problem of **A** is to find the solution of the system:

$$\mathbf{A}\mathbf{x} = \lambda\mathbf{x}$$

in which λ is a scalar and **x** is a non-zero column vector of length n. The scalar λ is an **eigenvalue** of **A**, and **x** is the corresponding **eigenvector**. Also for real **A**, the eigenvalues and eigenvectors may be complex. An $n \times n$ matrix has n eigenvalues denoted by $\lambda_1, \lambda_2, \ldots, \lambda_n$.

In MATLAB there is a command, `eig`, for determining the eigenvalues and the eigenvectors of **A**. The eigenvectors are normalized, that is the Euclidean norm of each eigenvector is 1; see Section 7.6.

The command `eig` automatically performs a balancing of **A**. This means that MATLAB determines a **similarity transformation Q** such that $\tilde{\mathbf{A}} = \mathbf{Q}^{-1}\mathbf{A}\mathbf{Q}$. The eigenvalue problem of $\tilde{\mathbf{A}}$ usually has a better condition than **A**. In cases when **A** has components of the same size as the machine error, the balancing could be bad for the computational process. The `eig` command with the parameter `nobalance` computes the eigenvalues and eigenvectors without this transformation.

Commands 79   EIGENVALUES AND EIGENVECTORS

`eig(A)`	returns a vector containing the eigenvalues of **A**.
`[X,D] = eig(A)`	returns a diagonal matrix **D** with the eigenvalues of **A** in its diagonal and a matrix **X**, whose columns are the corresponding eigenvectors of **A** such that $\mathbf{AX} = \mathbf{XD}$. A similarity transformation is performed in order to obtain a matrix with better conditioned eigenvalues.

Commands 79   (CONTINUED)

`[X, D] =` `eig(A,'nobalance')`	determines the eigenvalues and eigenvectors as above, but **A** is not balanced, that is no balancing similarity transformation is performed.
`balance(A)`	gives a balanced matrix.
`[T,B] = balance(A)`	gives a diagonal similarity transform **T** and a matrix **B** such that $\mathbf{B} = \mathbf{T}^{-1}\mathbf{A}\mathbf{T}$. Thus **B** is the balanced matrix of the previous command.
`eigs(A)`	returns a vector with a few of the eigenvalues of the matrix **A**. The command works like `eig` but does not return all eigenvalues. If no arguments are given the eigenvalues with the largest magnitude are calculated. Six eigenvalues are calculated if the rank of **A** is not less than 6 when all eigenvalues are calculated.
`eigs(f,n)`	returns a few of the eigenvalues of **A**. The string **f** contains a name of an M-file using a linear operator on the columns of a matrix, named in the M-file, and *n* gives the order of the problem. This method is much faster than first applying the operator and then finding the eigenvalues.
`eigs(A,B,k,sigma)`	returns a few of the eigenvalues of **A**. The matrix **B** has the same size as **A**; if not given $\mathbf{B} = \text{eye(size(A))}$ is used and *k* is the number of eigenvalues to be calculated. If *k* is not given the smaller of the numbers 6 and `rank(A)` is used. The variable *sigma* is a real or complex shift parameter or one of the following text strings that states which type of eigenvalue is wanted: `'lm'` largest magnitude (default) `'sm'` smallest magnitude `'lr'` largest real part `'sr'` smallest real part `'be'` both ends
`condeig(A)`	returns a vector with the condition numbers of the eigenvalues of the matrix **A**.
`[V,D,s] =` `condeig(A)`	returns `[V,D] = eig(A)` and `s = condeig(A)`.

If **A** is real, MATLAB uses the QR factorization in the computations, otherwise the QZ factorization is used.

The **left eigenvectors** are non-zero row vectors **y** that satisfy:

$$\mathbf{y}\mathbf{A} = \lambda\mathbf{y}.$$

The left eigenvectors can also be computed by eig if we use $\mathbf{A}'$, since:

$$\mathbf{A}'\mathbf{y}' = \bar{\lambda}\mathbf{y}'$$

where the apostrophe, ', represents transposition and complex conjugation of the matrix (see Section 3.4), and the overbar denotes complex conjugation. The set of eigenvalues of a matrix is called the **spectrum** of the matrix. The **spectral radius**, $\rho(\mathbf{A})$, is defined as max(abs(eig(A))). The product of the eigenvalues of $\mathbf{A}$ is equal to det(A), and the sum of the eigenvalues is equal to trace(A), that is the sum of the elements on the main diagonal of $\mathbf{A}$.

If $\mathbf{X}$ is a matrix whose columns are the eigenvectors of $\mathbf{A}$ and the rank of $\mathbf{X}$ is n, then the eigenvectors are linearly independent. If this is not the case, the matrix is called **defective**. If $\mathbf{X}'\mathbf{X} = \mathbf{I}$, then the eigenvectors are orthonormal. This is, for instance, true for symmetric matrices.

■ **Example 8.1**

Let $\mathbf{A}$ be defined as:

$$\mathbf{A} = \begin{pmatrix} -9 & -3 & -16 \\ 13 & 7 & 16 \\ 3 & 3 & 10 \end{pmatrix}.$$

(a) The command [Evect,Evalue] = eig(A) gives:

```
Evect =
    -0.7071    -0.5774    -0.5774
     0.7071     0.5774    -0.5774
     0.0000     0.5774     0.5774


Evalue =
    -6.0000          0          0
          0    10.0000          0
          0          0     4.0000
```

The eigenvalues are non-zero and the matrix has full rank, which can be confirmed by therank = rank(Evect),

```
therank =
     3
```

We also have M = Evect'*Evect

```
M =
     1.0000     0.8165    -0.0000
     0.8165     1.0000     0.3333
    -0.0000     0.3333     1.0000
```

that is the eigenvectors are not mutually orthogonal.

(b) determinant = prod(diag(Evalue)), ...
determinant2 = det(A)

give:

determinant =
  -240.0000

determinant2 =
  -240

We see that the determinant is equal to the product of the eigenvalues.

(c) theTrace = trace(A), theTrace2 = sum(diag(Evalue))

give:

theTrace =
    8

theTrace2 =
    8.0000

We can see that the trace is equal to the sum of the eigenvalues.

■

If **A** is real, but has complex eigenvalues, these eigenvalues appear as complex conjugate pairs. If [X,D] = eig(A), it is possible to transform **D** to a real block diagonal matrix with the cdf2rdf command. Instead of a complex conjugate pair of eigenvalues we obtain a real 2 × 2 block on the diagonal.

Commands 80	COMPLEX DIAGONAL TO REAL BLOCK DIAGONAL FORM

[Y,E] = cdf2rdf(X,D)	converts a complex diagonal matrix **D** to a real block diagonal matrix **E**. The columns of **Y** are not eigenvectors of **A**.

■ **Example 8.2**

Suppose that **A** is defined as:

$$A = \begin{pmatrix} 0 & 1 & 0 \\ -1 & 0 & 0 \\ 0 & 0 & 3 \end{pmatrix}$$

then [X,D] = eig(A) returns:

X =

0.7071	0.7071	0
0 + 0.7071i	0 - 0.7071i	0
0	0	1.0000

D =

0 + 1.0000i	0	0
0	0 - 1.0000i	0
0	0	3.0000

Both **X** and **D** are complex. The command: `[Y,E] = cdf2rdf(X,D)` gives the results:

Y =

0.7071	0	0
0	0.7071	0
0	0	1.0000

E =

0	1	0
-1	0	0
0	0	3

which happens to be the matrix **A** again.

∎

Note: The eigenvalues are the zeros of the characteristic polynomial, $\det(\lambda\mathbf{I}-\mathbf{A})$, where **I** denotes the identity matrix. The `poly` command gives the characteristic polynomial; see Section 11.1. The eigenvalues can then be computed with the `roots` command, but the `eig` command is a far more accurate and efficient method.

The **generalized eigenvalue problem** is to find non-trivial solutions to the system

$$\mathbf{Ax} = \lambda\mathbf{Bx}$$

where **B** also is an $n \times n$ matrix. The λ-values and the vectors **x**, which solve the system, are called generalized eigenvalues and generalized eigenvectors, respectively.

If **B** is singular the **QZ algorithm** is used.

Both the standard and the generalized eigenvalue problems can be characterized as special cases of matrix polynomial eigenproblems. These can be solved with the command `polyeig`.

Commands 81	GENERALIZED EIGENVALUES AND EIGENVECTORS

eig(A,B)	returns a vector containing the generalized eigenvalues if **A** and **B** are square matrices.
[X,D] = eig(A,B)	returns a diagonal matrix **D** with the generalized eigenvalues in the diagonal and a matrix **X** whose columns are the corresponding eigenvectors such that $\mathbf{AX} = \mathbf{BXD}$.
[X,v] = polyeig(A0,A1,..., Ak)	gives eigenvalues and eigenvectors to the eigenproblem of degree k: $(\mathbf{A}_0 + \lambda\mathbf{A}_1 + \lambda^2\mathbf{A}_2 + \cdots + \lambda^k\mathbf{A}_k)\mathbf{x} = \mathbf{0}$. The vector **v**, of length nk, contains the eigenvalues, and the $n \times nk$ matrix **X** has the eigenvectors as its columns. If $\mathbf{A}_0 = \mathbf{A}$, and $\mathbf{A}_1 = -\mathbf{I}$, then it is the standard eigenvalue problem.

To check the condition or sensitivity of the eigenvalues compute the condition number, $\text{cond}(\mathbf{X}) = \|\mathbf{X}\|\|\mathbf{X}^{-1}\|$, where **X** is a matrix whose columns are eigenvectors of **A**. A high value of the condition number signals bad condition, that is high sensitivity to perturbations.

To check the condition or sensitivity of the eigenvectors look at the separation of the eigenvalues. Multiple eigenvalues or eigenvalues which are close to each other indicate ill-conditioned problems.

■ **Example 8.3**

Suppose:

$$\mathbf{A} = \begin{pmatrix} 3.75 & -0.5 & -0.375 & 0.495 & -1.37 \\ 0.25 & 2.5 & 0.375 & -0.495 & -0.63 \\ 1.25 & -0.5 & 2.875 & 0.495 & -2.12 \\ 0.25 & -0.5 & -0.625 & 2.505 & 0.37 \\ 0.25 & -0.5 & -0.625 & 0.495 & 2.38 \end{pmatrix}$$

The command [XX,DD] = eig(A) gives:

```
XX =
  -0.0000   0.0000 - 0.4472i   0.0000 + 0.4472i   -0.4472    0.4472
   0.5000  -0.0000 + 0.4472i  -0.0000 - 0.4472i   -0.4472   -0.4472
   0.5000   0.0000 - 0.4472i   0.0000 + 0.4472i   -0.4472    0.4472
  -0.5000   0.0000 - 0.4472i   0.0000 + 0.4472i   -0.4472   -0.4472
  -0.5000   0.0000 - 0.4472i   0.0000 + 0.4472i   -0.4472    0.4472
```

Observe that two eigenvectors are non-real, namely column 2 and column 3.

```
DD =
    4.0000         0                0              0       0
         0    3.0000 + 0.0000i       0              0       0
         0         0          3.0000 - 0.0000i      0       0
         0         0                0          2.0000       0
         0         0                0              0    2.0100
```

We see that the eigenvalues are 2, 2.01, 3, 3, and 4, that is the eigenvector problem is supposed to be ill-conditioned. To get the condition number we type `badMatrix = cond(XX)` which gives:

```
badMatrix =
    5.0156e+07
```

Compare this number with the condition of the eigenvalues of the matrix in Example 8.2 which is `niceMatrix = cond(X)`:

```
niceMatrix =
              1.0000
```

There is a difference!

∎

8.2 Upper Hessenberg form, QR, and QZ factorizations

If only the eigenvalues and eigenvectors themselves are of interest, the methods from the previous section are recommended. However, sometimes it can be of interest to look more closely at the computational process. We define commands for that purpose in this and the next section.

A matrix **H** is an **upper Hessenberg matrix** if all elements below the first lower bi-diagonal are zero. A symmetric matrix in upper Hessenberg form is therefore tridiagonal. MATLAB can transform a matrix to this form by a similarity transformation.

Commands 82	UPPER HESSENBERG FORM
`hess(A)`	returns a similarity transformation of **A** into upper Hessenberg form.
`[P,H] = hess(A)`	returns the unitary transformation matrix **P** and an upper Hessenberg matrix **H**. These satisfy $\mathbf{A} = \mathbf{PHP}'$ and $\mathbf{PP}' = \mathbf{I}$.

The **QR algorithm** is a general and efficient numerical method that MATLAB uses to compute all eigenvalues of a matrix, that is when the command `eig` is given. In this method, it is advisable to transform the matrix to a similar upper Hessenberg form; see Example 8.4.

The QR algorithm is based on the QR factorization. Each $m \times n$ matrix $\mathbf{A}$ can be written as the product:

$$\mathbf{A} = \mathbf{QR},$$

where $\mathbf{Q}$ is a unitary $m \times m$ matrix, and $\mathbf{R}$ is an upper triangular $m \times n$ matrix. If $\mathbf{A}$ is a square matrix then so is $\mathbf{R}$. MATLAB returns the matrices $\mathbf{Q}$ and $\mathbf{R}$ when the `qr` command is used; see also Example 7.7.

Commands 83	QR FACTORIZATION
`[Q,R] = qr(A)`	gives a unitary $m \times m$ matrix $\mathbf{Q}$, and an upper triangular $m \times m$ matrix $\mathbf{R}$ such that $\mathbf{A} = \mathbf{QR}$.
`[Q,R,P] = qr(A)`	produces a unitary $m \times m$ matrix $\mathbf{Q}$, whose columns are orthonormal, an upper triangular $m \times n$ matrix $\mathbf{R}$ with descending diagonal elements and a permutation matrix $\mathbf{P}$ such that $\mathbf{AP} = \mathbf{QR}$.
`[Q,R] = qrinsert(Q,R,j,b)`	gives a new QR factorization as if an extra column b had been placed after the column j in the matrix $\mathbf{A}$ and where $\mathbf{Q}$ and $\mathbf{R}$ are given by the QR factorization of $\mathbf{A}$. If $j = n + 1$ the new column is put last.
`[Q,R] = qrdelete(Q,R,j)`	gives a new QR factorization as if the column j in the matrix $\mathbf{A}$ were removed and where $\mathbf{Q}$ and $\mathbf{R}$ are given by the QR factorization of $\mathbf{A}$.
`[Q1,R1] = qrupdate(Q,R,x,y)`	returns the QR factorization of $\mathbf{A} + \mathbf{xy'}$, i.e. the factorization of $\mathbf{A}$ modified with a matrix with the rank one.

If $\mathbf{A}$ is an upper Hessenberg matrix, then $\mathbf{Q}$ is also of the same form. This is used in the QR algorithm for which we now give a short and incomplete description.

QR Algorithm:

0. Let $\mathbf{A}_0 = \mathbf{A}$, $k = 0$.

1. Find the factorization of $\mathbf{A}_k : \mathbf{A}_k = \mathbf{Q}_k \mathbf{R}_k$.

2. Compute the next matrix in the iteration sequence by: $\mathbf{A}_{k+1} = \mathbf{R}_k \mathbf{Q}_k$.
   Let $k = k + 1$.

3. Go to 1.

This method, called the unshifted QR method, converges under certain circumstances towards an upper triangular matrix. Since all matrices $\mathbf{A}_k$ are similar to $\mathbf{A}_0 = \mathbf{A}$, that is have the same eigenvalues as the original matrix, the diagonal entries of the resulting upper triangular matrix are the eigenvalues of $\mathbf{A}$.

If the matrix is transformed first to upper Hessenberg form with zeros in almost half of the entries, and since this property remains throughout the algorithm, the number of arithmetic operations is reduced considerably. The QR method, as the one built-in in MATLAB, also uses shifts in order to accelerate the convergence.

■ **Example 8.4**

Let us compute the eigenvalues of the matrix

$$\mathbf{A} = \begin{pmatrix} -9 & -3 & -16 \\ 13 & 7 & 16 \\ 3 & 3 & 10 \end{pmatrix}$$

which is used in Example 8.1 as well, by executing some steps of the unshifted QR algorithm.

The correct eigenvalues are $\lambda_1 = 10$, $\lambda_2 = 4$ and $\lambda_3 = -6$.

```
A0 = hess(A); [Q0,R0] = qr(A0); A1 = R0*Q0
```

return:

```
A1 =
    1.7992   26.8770  -12.6126
    2.3625    4.5085   -0.1434
         0    4.9518    1.6923
```

We carry out a second step, `[Q1,R1] = qr(A1); A2 = R1*Q1` and obtain:

```
A2 =
   17.6077   11.3432    5.0128
  -15.3516  -13.6557   -5.8721
         0    1.0748    4.0480
```

At the beginning of the process it is not possible to see what the matrix will converge to but after 10 steps with the algorithm we can see that the components of the lower bidiagonal are small.

```
[Q9,R9] = qr(A9); A10 = R9*Q9
```

gives:

```
A10 =
     10.1297    22.6238    15.3505
     -0.0924    -6.1616    -5.8036
           0     0.0562     4.0319
```

Note that the upper Hessenberg form is preserved throughout the process.

■

An iterative process like the previous one can be written concisely in MATLAB using the built-in programming language. Examples are shown in Section 12.2.

The **QZ algorithm** is used to compute the **complex eigenpairs** of complex matrices and the generalized eigenvalues. In MATLAB the qz command can be called according to Commands 84 below.

Commands 84	QZ ALGORITHM

| `[C,D,Q,Z,V] = qz(A,B)` | gives upper triangular matrices **C** and **D**, whose diagonal elements are the generalized eigenvalues, and **V** containing the generalized eigenvectors. The matrices **Q** and **Z** are the transformations such that $\mathbf{QAZ} = \mathbf{C}$ and $\mathbf{QBZ} = \mathbf{D}$. |

The QZ method is based on the QZ factorization.

8.3 Schur decomposition and singular value decomposition

If **A** is a square matrix, then there is a unitary matrix **U** such that:

$$\mathbf{U}^{-1}\mathbf{AU} = \mathbf{U}'\mathbf{AU} = \mathbf{T}$$

where **T** is upper triangular. This is a similarity transform, so the matrices **A** and **T** have the same eigenvalues and since **T** is a triangular matrix the eigenvalues are located on the diagonal.

If **A** is real and symmetric then **T** has diagonal form, and the columns of **U** are the eigenvectors of **A**.

If **A** is real, but has complex eigenvalues, then **T** is a complex matrix. To avoid complex arithmetic, every pair of complex conjugated eigenvalues can be represented by real 2×2 matrice; see Example 8.2 for instance. In that case the matrix **T** is block triangular and real. In MATLAB it is possible to perform a **Schur decomposition** of a matrix **A** with the schur command, which exists in real and complex versions.

If **A** is real schur(A) returns the real Schur form, but if **A** is complex the complex form is returned. The difference is that the real Schur form represents the complex conjugate pairs of eigenvalues as real 2×2 blocks in the diagonal, but the complex form returns complex diagonal elements. The function rsf2csf converts from real to complex form.

Commands 85	SCHUR DECOMPOSITION
schur(A)	returns the Schur decomposition of **A**, that is the matrix **T** as above.
[U,T] = schur(A)	returns the Schur decomposition of **A** and the unitary matrix **U** such that $\mathbf{A} = \mathbf{UTU'}$.
[V,S] = rsf2csf(U,T)	converts matrices **U** and **T** in the real Schur form to the matrices **V** and **S** in the complex Schur form.

■ **Example 8.5**

Define **A1**, **A2** and **A3** by:

$$\mathbf{A1} = \begin{pmatrix} 2 & 1 \\ 1 & 2 \end{pmatrix} \quad \mathbf{A2} = \begin{pmatrix} 2 & 1 \\ 0 & 2 \end{pmatrix} \quad \mathbf{A3} = \begin{pmatrix} 0 & 1 \\ -1 & 0 \end{pmatrix}$$

The commands:

```
Sch1 = schur(A1), Sch2 = schur(A2)}, ...
[U,Sch3] = schur(A3)
```

give:

```
Sch1 =
       1      0
       0      3

Sch2 =
       2      1
       0      2
```

```
U =
      1      0
      0      1


Sch3 =
      0      1
     -1      0
```

We can see that the matrix **Sch3** is not upper triangular due to the complex eigenvalues. To see this we type: [V,S] = rsf2csf(U,Sch3) and get:

```
V =
          0 + 0.7071i     0.7071
     -0.7071                   0 - 0.7071i


S =
          0 + 1.0000i          0
          0                    0 - 1.0000i
```

that is, the eigenvalues are i and $-i$.

∎

MATLAB can also compute the **singular value decomposition**, **SVD**, and the singular values of matrices. These are non-negative numbers. In special cases they are the same as the eigenvalues. Similar to the eigs command there is also a command svds which returns a few singular values.

Let **A** be an $m \times n$ matrix in the following command table.

| Commands 86 | SVD DECOMPOSITION |

svd(A)	returns a vector containing the singular values of **A**.
[U,S,V] = svd(A)	returns a diagonal matrix **S** and two unitary matrices **U** and **V**, of size $m \times m$ and $n \times n$, respectively. The matrix **S** is of the same size as **A**, that is $m \times n$, containing the singular values of A on the diagonal. The singular values are non-negative and in descending order. The matrices are such that $\mathbf{A} = \mathbf{USV}'$ and $\mathbf{U}'\mathbf{AV} = \mathbf{S}$.
[U,S,V] = svd(A,0)	returns a more 'economic' alternative to the previous command. Only the first n columns of **U** are computed. Here the **S** matrix is $n \times n$.
svds(A,k,0)	computes the k largest singular values and the corresponding vector of the matrix **A**. If k is not given the value 5 is used. If a zero is given as the last argument the values with the smallest magnitude are computed, otherwise the largest.

Commands 86	(CONTINUED)
gsvd(A)	gives the generalized singular decompositions; see help gsvd for more information.

The pseudo-inverse of **A** is computed by the pinv(A) command. MATLAB uses the SVD decomposition to compute the pseudo-inverse; see also Section 7.1.

If s_i are the singular values then $\|A\|_2 = \max s_i = s_1$, $\|A^{-1}\|_2 = (\min s_i)^{-1} = s_n^{-1}$ and $\text{cond}(A) = s_1/s_n$, where s_n is the smallest singular value. The last expressions are true for non-singular matrices and also for rectangular matrices of full rank with $m > n$.

■ **Example 8.6**

Let us define these matrices:

$$A = \begin{pmatrix} 1 & 1 \\ 1 & 2 \\ 1 & 3 \end{pmatrix} \quad B = \begin{pmatrix} 1 & -1 & 0 \\ 1 & 2 & 0 \\ 1 & 3 & 0 \end{pmatrix}$$

(a) We compute the singular value decomposition by:

```
[Ua,Sa,Va] = svd(A), [Ub,Sb,Vb] = svd(B)

Ua =
      0.3231   -0.8538    0.4082
      0.5475   -0.1832   -0.8165
      0.7719    0.4873    0.4082


Sa =
      4.0791         0
           0    0.6005
           0         0


Va =
      0.4027   -0.9153
      0.9153    0.4027


Ub =
     -0.1641    0.9668    0.1961
      0.5653    0.2551   -0.7845
      0.8084    0.0178    0.5883
```

```
Sb =
      3.9116           0           0
           0      1.3036           0
           0           0           0
```

```
Vb =
      0.3092      0.9510           0
      0.9510     -0.3092           0
           0           0      1.0000
```

We can see that both **A** and **B** have two non-zero singular values, that is they have rank 2.

(b) The inverses of these matrices cannot be computed, but the pseudo-inverses are obtained by PseudoA = pinv(A), PseudoB = pinv(B):

```
PseudoA =
      1.3333      0.3333     -0.6667
     -0.5000      0.0000      0.5000
```

```
PseudoB =
      0.6923      0.2308      0.0769
     -0.2692      0.0769      0.1923
           0           0           0
```

(c) The norms and the condition number are given by:

```
normA = norm(A), normB = norm(B), ...
condA = cond(A), condB = cond(B)
```

```
normA =
      4.0791
```

```
normB =
      3.9116
```

```
condA =
      6.7930
```

```
condB =
      Inf
```

We can see that the Euclidean norm is equal to the largest singular value and that the condition number is equal to s_1/s_n.

Sparse Matrices

There are several problems that give rise to matrices in which most of the elements are zero. These matrices are called sparse. One example is the numerical solution of ordinary or partial differential equations. To save memory and computing time MATLAB has special commands where the sparsity of the matrices is considered. It is only possible to have two-dimensional sparse matrices in MATLAB.

9.1 Why sparse matrices?

A **sparse matrix** has most of the entries equal to zero. This can be used with advantage in computations and in storing the matrix. If we ask MATLAB to treat a matrix as sparse, only the m non-zero entries are stored in an $m \times 3$ matrix. The first column contains the row indices, the second the column indices and the third the non-zero elements. The zero entries are not stored. If we suppose that a floating point number requires 8 bytes to be stored, and the indices 4 bytes each, the whole matrix requires $16 \times m$ bytes in memory.

■ **Example 9.1**

```
A = eye(1000);
```

is a 1000×1000 identity matrix that requires about 8 Mb memory. If we use the command

```
B = speye(1000);
```

it is represented by a 1000×3 matrix instead, each row containing a row index, a column index and the element itself. Now only about 16 kb memory is required to store the 1000×1000 identity matrix, that is only about 0.2% of the memory for the full matrix. The same can be done for more general matrices as well.

■

The computation with sparse matrices is faster since MATLAB only has to operate on the non-zero elements; this is the second great advantage with sparse matrices.

■ **Example 9.2**

Suppose that **A** and **B** are defined as in Example 9.1.

Then the operation 2*A requires one million flops, but the operation 2*B requires only 2000 flops.

■

We have to use special commands to get sparse matrices since MATLAB does not create sparse matrices automatically. These commands are presented in the following section. All arithmetic and logical operations from previous chapters can be applied to sparse matrices.

9.2 To create and convert sparse matrices

To create a sparse matrix in MATLAB the command `sparse` is used.

Commands 87	CREATING SPARSE MATRICES
`sparse(A)`	returns the matrix **A** in sparse form by removing all non-zero elements. If **A** is already sparse, **A** itself is returned.
`sparse(m,n)`	gives a zero matrix of size $m \times n$ in sparse representation.
`sparse(u,v,a)`	gives a sparse matrix defined by the vectors **u**, **v** and **a** of the same length, where **u** and **v** are integer vectors and **a** is a real or complex vector. The entry (u_i, v_i) has the value a_i. If an element in **a** is zero it is excluded. The matrix gets the size $\max(u) \times \max(v)$.
`sparse(u,v,a,m,n)`	gives a sparse $m \times n$ matrix in which the entry (u_i, v_i) has the value a_i. The vectors **u**, **v** and **a** must be of the same length.
`sparse(u,v,a,m,n,` `nzmax)`	returns a sparse $m \times n$ matrix in which the entry (u_i, v_i) has the value a_i. There is also memory allocated for *nzmax* non-zero elements, and the value of *nzmax* must be larger than or equal to the lengths of the vectors **u** and **v**.
`find(x)`	returns the indices of the non-zero components of the vector **x**. If **x** = **X** is a matrix, the columns of **X** are considered as one long vector.
`[u,v] = find(A)`	returns the indices of the non-zero elements of the matrix **A**.
`[u,v,s] = find(A)`	returns the indices of the non-zero elements of the matrix **A**, with the values of the elements in the vector **s** and the corresponding indices in **u** and **v**, that is the vectors **u**, **v** and **s** can be used as parameters to the command `sparse`.

| Commands 87 | (CONTINUED) |

spconvert(D)   converts a matrix with three columns to a sparse matrix. The first column of **D** contains the row indices, the second column the column indices and the last column the elements.

Furthermore, a sparse matrix can be converted to a full matrix by using the command full.

| Commands 88 | CONVERTING TO A FULL MATRIX |

full(S)   returns the full matrix defined by the sparse matrix **S**.

■ **Example 9.3**

(a) We create a 5 × 5 identity matrix:

```
A = eye(5);
```

The matrix **A** can be converted to a sparse matrix **B** by

```
B = sparse(A)
```

```
B =
     (1,1)        1
     (2,2)        1
     (3,3)        1
     (4,4)        1
     (5,5)        1
```

(b) Suppose that these commands are given in MATLAB:

```
ind1 = [1 2 3 3 4 2];
ind2 = [1 2 1 4 5 3];
number = [0 1 2 3 0 5];
```

In this case we have row vectors but column vectors can also be used. The command Smatrix = sparse(ind1,ind2,number) results in:

```
Smatrix =
     (3,1)        2
     (2,2)        1
     (2,3)        5
     (3,4)        3
```

The two zero elements are excluded. To convert the matrix to a full matrix we type:

```
Fullmatrix = full(Smatrix)
```

which gives:

```
Fullmatrix =
     0    0    0    0    0
     0    1    5    0    0
     2    0    0    3    0
     0    0    0    0    0
```

Note that the size of the sparse matrix, and consequently the size of the full matrix, is defined by the largest element in **ind1** and **ind2** respectively, even if the corresponding value is zero and excluded in the displayed sparse matrix.

If we type the command whos we will get:

Name	Size	Bytes	Class
A	5x5	200	double array
B	5x5	84	sparse array
Fullmatrix	4x5	160	double array
Smatrix	4x5	96	sparse array
ind1	1x6	48	double array
ind2	1x6	48	double array
number	1x6	48	double array

```
Grand total is 74 elements using 684 bytes
```

We can see that the sizes of the two matrices are the same but the sparse matrix requires fewer bytes of memory.

(c) The find command is useful when dealing with sparse matrices. The command returns the same result independent of the form of the matrix, sparse or full. The three vectors that are returned can be used directly to recreate the matrix in sparse form. Let **Smatrix** be defined as in Example (b). The commands:

```
[ind1,ind2,number] = find(Smatrix);
Smaller = sparse(ind1,ind2,number)
```

give as result:

```
Smaller =
    (3,1)        2
    (2,2)        1
    (2,3)        5
    (3,4)        3
```

This is not the same matrix as **Smatrix**, which the following command shows:

```
Fullsmall = full(Smaller)

Fullsmall =
     0    0    0    0
     0    1    5    0
     2    0    0    3
```

Compare with Example (b).

■

9.3 Sparse matrix operations

The operations and functions on full matrices in MATLAB can also be applied on sparse matrices. Whether the result is sparse or full depends on the operator or function and the operands according to the following:

- Functions which have a matrix as argument and return a scalar or a vector of given size always return a full matrix, for example the command `size`.

- Functions which have a scalar or vector as argument and return a matrix as result also always return a full matrix, for example the command `eye`. There exist special commands for obtaining a sparse matrix, for example the command `speye`.

- Other functions with one argument return in general a result of the same form as the argument, for example `diag`.

- Operations or functions that require two arguments return, if the two arguments are of the same form, the result in that form. In case the two arguments are of different form the result is full if the sparsity is not conserved by the command.

- The uniting of two matrices, [A B], results in a full matrix if at least one of **A** or **B** is full.

- Colon notation in the right-hand side of an expression is considered as an operation with one argument and follows the rules for such operations.

- Colon notation in the left-hand side of an expression does not change the form of the matrix.

■ **Example 9.4**

Suppose that we have:

```
A = eye(5); B = sparse(A); h = [1;2;0;4;5];
```

that is one full 5 × 5 identity matrix and the corresponding sparse matrix.

(a) C = 5*B gives as a result:

```
C =
    (1,1)        5
    (2,2)        5
    (3,3)        5
    (4,4)        5
    (5,5)        5
```

which is a sparse matrix.

(b) D = A + B gives:

```
D =
    2    0    0    0    0
    0    2    0    0    0
    0    0    2    0    0
    0    0    0    2    0
    0    0    0    0    2
```

which is a full matrix.

(c) x = B\h gives:

```
x =
    1
    2
    0
    4
    5
```

which is a full vector.

■

There are a number of commands that handle the non-zero elements.

Commands 89	NON-ZERO ELEMENTS OF A MATRIX
nnz(A)	gives the number of non-zero elements in the matrix **A**. The command works for both full and sparse matrices.
spy(A)	displays the structure of the sparse matrix **A**. The spy command can also be used on full matrices. In that case only non-zero elements are displayed.
spy(A,cstr,size)	displays the structure as above but in colors defined by **cstr** (see Table 13.1), and size according to *size*.
nonzeros(A)	gives the non-zero elements in **A** ordered columnwise.
spones(A)	returns a matrix with the non-zero elements of **A** replaced with ones.

Commands 89   (CONTINUED)

spalloc(m,n,nzmax)	returns an $m \times n$ sparse zero matrix with allocated memory for *nzmax* non-zero elements. This reduces the need for large and time-consuming rearrangement of memory and filling in of new elements to a matrix is done with considerably more speed.
nzmax(A)	gives the memory allocated for the non-zero elements of **A**. Does not have to be the same as nnz(A); see sparse or spalloc.
issparse(A)	returns 1 if **A** is stored in sparse form, otherwise 0.
spfun(fcn,A)	evaluates the function **fcn** for all non-zero elements of **A**. Works also if the function is not defined for sparse matrices.
sprank(A)	returns the structural rank of the sparse matrix **A**. For all matrices sprank(A) $\geq$ rank(A).

■ **Example 9.5**

We define a sparse bidiagonal matrix with the following command:

```
A = sparse(diag(ones(5,1),1)) + sparse(diag(ones(5,1),-1));
```

Now we create a larger matrix with the command:

```
Big = kron(A,A)
```

What does **Big** look like? The Kronecker product gives a larger matrix with the structure defined by the arguments. We know it is sparse, and in sparse form, since both arguments are sparse. This can also be verified with the commands whos and issparse.

To see the structure we type spy(Big), and we get Figure 9.1.

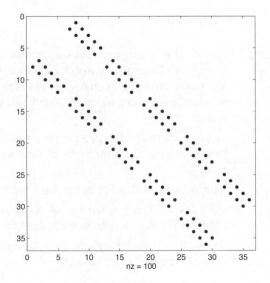

Figure 9.1 *The* spy *command displays the structure of a matrix.*

We can see that **Big** is block bidiagonal.

∎

9.4 Special cases of sparse matrices

There are four elementary sparse matrices in MATLAB, **identity matrix**, **random matrices**, **symmetric random matrices** and **diagonal matrices**.

Commands 90	SPARSE IDENTITY MATRICES
speye(n)	returns a sparse identity matrix of size $n \times n$.
speye(m,n)	returns a sparse identity matrix of size $m \times n$.

The command speye(A) gives the same result as sparse(eye(A)), but without the step involving storage of a full matrix.

Commands 91	SPARSE RANDOM MATRICES
sprand(A)	gives a sparse random matrix with the same structure as **A** and with uniformly distributed random numbers.

Commands 91 (CONTINUED)

`sprand(m,n,dens)`	gives a sparse uniformly distributed random matrix of size $m \times n$ of which a part *dens* is non-zero, that is there are $dens \times m \times n$ non-zero elements, $0 \leq dens \leq 1$. The parameter *dens* is the density of the non-zero elements.
`sprand(m,n,dens, rc)`	gives a sparse random $m \times n$ matrix with the approximate condition number $1/rc$. If $rc = $ **rc** is a vector of length $l \leq \min(m, n)$ the matrix gets rc_i as its l first singular values. All other singular values are zero.
`sprandn(A)`	gives a sparse matrix with same structure as **A** and with normally distributed numbers.
`sprandn(m, n, dens, rc)`	gives a sparse matrix with normally distributed numbers in the same way as `sprand`.
`sprandsym(S)`	gives a symmetric sparse matrix whose lower triangle and main diagonal have the same structure as **S**. The numbers are normally distributed.
`sprandsym(n,dens)`	gives a symmetric sparse matrix of size $n \times n$ and with density *dens*. The numbers are normally distributed.
`sprandsym(n,dens, rc)`	gives a symmetric sparse matrix of size $n \times n$ with the condition number $1/rc$. The numbers are symmetrically distributed around 0, but not normally distributed. If $rc = $ **rc** is a vector, the matrix has the eigenvalues rc_i, that is if **rc** is a positive vector then the matrix is positive definite.
`sprandsym(n,dens, rc,k)`	gives a positive definite matrix. If $k = 1$ the matrix is generated by random Jacobi rotation of a positive definite matrix. The condition number is exactly $1/rc$. If $k = 2$ the matrix is created by shifted sums of outer products. The condition number is approximately $1/rc$.
`sprandsym(S,dens, rc,3)`	gives a sparse matrix with the same structure as **S** and the approximate condition number $1/rc$. The parameter *dens* is ignored, but has to be there so that the function identifies the two last arguments correctly.

■ **Example 9.6**

(a) Suppose that the following matrix is defined:

$$A = \begin{pmatrix} 0 & 1 & 0 & 0 \\ 1 & 0 & 0 & 0 \\ 0 & 1 & 0 & 0 \\ 0 & 0 & 1 & 0 \end{pmatrix}$$

We can get a random sparse matrix by typing `Random = sprandn(A)`

```
Random =
    (2,1)       -0.4326
    (1,2)       -1.6656
    (3,2)        0.1253
    (4,3)        0.2877
```

with the random numbers at the same positions as the non-zero elements of **A**.

(b) If **A** is the same as in (a) and we type:

`B = sprandsym(A)`

we obtain:

```
B =
    (2,1)       -1.1465
    (1,2)       -1.1465
    (3,2)        1.1909
    (2,3)        1.1909
    (4,3)        1.1892
    (3,4)        1.1892
```

that is the lower triangle and the main diagonal of **A** are used to create a symmetric matrix, with random numbers at the non-zero entries.

∎

With the `spdiags` command, diagonals can be selected and diagonal and band matrices created. Suppose that **A** is an $m \times n$ matrix which has non-zero elements in p diagonals, and that **B** is a matrix of size $\min(m, n) \times p$, whose columns are diagonals of **A**. The vector **d** has length p, and integer components that define the non-zero diagonals of **A** according to:

$d_i < 0$ a lower diagonal, in relation to the main diagonal. As an example, $d_i = -1$ refers to the first lower diagonal.

$d_i = 0$ the main diagonal.

$d_i > 0$ an upper diagonal, in relation to the main diagonal.

| Commands 92 | DIAGONALS AND SPARSE MATRICES |

`[B,d] = spdiags(A)`	finds all non-zero diagonals of **A** and stores them as defined above, that is the diagonals are stored in the matrix **B** and the positions of these diagonals in the vector **d**.
`spdiags(A,d)`	gives a matrix with the diagonals defined by the vector **d** of the matrix **A**.
`spdiags(B,d,A)`	gives the matrix **A**, but with diagonals defined by **d** replaced with the columns of **B**.
`A = spdiags(B,d,m,n)`	gives a sparse $m \times n$ matrix defined by the diagonals stored in **B** in positions defined by **d**.

Example 11.4 shows how one may use the `spdiags` command when solving ordinary differential equations numerically.

9.5 Linear systems with sparse matrices

In many applications the sparse structure is kept, but the sparsity can be reduced as a result of fill-ins during the computations, for example in LU decomposition. This leads to an increase of floating-point operations and memory storage. To avoid this there are functions in MATLAB that rearrange the matrices. These are briefly described in Commands 93 below. Write `help` for each command to obtain more information, or see `helpdesk`.

Commands 93	PERMUTATIONS
`colmmd(A)`	returns a permutation vector which gives the column minimum degree ordering of **A**.
`symmmd(A)`	returns a symmetric minimum degree ordering.
`symrcm(A)`	gives the inverse Cuthill–McKee-transform of **A**. The non-zero elements of **A** are located around the main diagonal.
`colperm(A)`	returns a vector which gives a column permutation of **A**. The columns are ordered in increasing number of non-zero elements. This is sometimes a useful transformation prior to an LU factorization, when `lu(A(:,j))` is used. If **A** is a symmetric matrix both rows and columns are ordered, which is sometimes useful prior to a Cholesky factorization, `chol(A(j,j))`.
`randperm(n)`	gives a random permutation of the integers $1, 2, \ldots, n$. This can then be used to create a random permutation matrix.
`dmperm(A)`	performs a Dulmage–Mendelsohn-decomposition of the matrix **A**. Write `help dmperm` for more information.

■ **Example 9.7**

We want to create a permutation matrix of order 4. We type:

```
i = [1 2 3 4]; aa = ones(1,4); perm = randperm(4)
P = sparse(i,perm,aa)
```

Once `perm = randperm(4)` gave:

```
perm =
     4     1     3     2
```

which gave us the permutation matrix:

```
P =
   (2,1)        1
   (4,2)        1
   (3,3)        1
   (1,4)        1
```

If the matrix **A** is defined by:

$$\mathbf{A} = \begin{pmatrix} 7 & 4 & 3 & 4 \\ 5 & 2 & 4 & 2 \\ 5 & 6 & 3 & 1 \\ 8 & 1 & 1 & 2 \end{pmatrix}$$

then the commands:

```
RowChange = P*A, ColChange = A*P
```

result in:

```
RowChange =
      5      6      3      1
      5      2      4      2
      8      1      1      2
      7      4      3      4

ColChange =
      4      4      7      3
      2      2      5      4
      1      6      5      3
      2      1      8      1
```

■

There are two commands for incomplete factorizations. These are suitable to use as preconditioners for large systems of linear equations. Give the `helpdesk` command for more information.

Commands 94   INCOMPLETE FACTORIZATIONS

`cholinc(A,opt)`	gives an incomplete Cholesky factorization. The variable **opt**, if given, can have one of the following values:

`droptol`	The drop tolerance of the incomplete factorization, a zero gives the complete factorization.
`michol`	Removed elements are subtracted from the diagonal if `michol` is 1.
`rdiag`	Zeros on the upper triangular factor are replaced by `sqrt(droptol*norm(X(:,j)))` where j is the column of the element that is zero.

`[L,U,P]=` `luinc(X,opt)`	returns three matrices **L**, **U** and **P** that describe an incomplete LU factorization of the matrix **X**. The fields in the struct **opt** are:

`droptol`	The tolerance of the factorization.
`milu`	Modifies the factorization so that the element removed from a column are subtracted from the diagonal in the upper triangular factor.
`udiag`	Replaces zeros on the diagonal in the upper triangular factor with the *droptol* value.
`thresh`	The pivot threshold.

Sparse linear systems can be solved with the left division operator but there are also some special commands.

Commands 95   SPARSE MATRICES AND LINEAR SYSTEMS

`spparms(keystr,op)`	sets parameters used in algorithms for sparse matrices. Write `help spparms` for more information.
`spaugment(A,c)`	creates a sparse matrix according to `[c*1 A; A' 0]` that expresses a least squares problem as a quadratic linear system. See also Section 7.7.
`symbfact(A)`	performs a symbolic factorization analysis of Cholesky and LU factorizations of sparse matrices. Type `help symbfact` for more information.

Norms of sparse matrices are computed just like norms of ordinary full matrices with one important exception. The Euclidean norm of a sparse matrix cannot be computed directly. If the sparse matrix is small, the norm can be computed by `norm(full(A))`, but for large matrices this is not always possible. However, MATLAB can compute an approximation of the Euclidean norm. The condition numbers have similar restrictions.

Commands 96	APPROXIMATION OF EUCLIDEAN NORM AND CONDITION NUMBER FOR SPARSE MATRICES
normest(A)	gives an approximation of the Euclidean norm of **A**. Uses tolerance 10^{-6}.
normest(A,tol)	as the previous command, but uses tolerance *tol* instead of 10^{-6}.
[nrm,nit] = normest(A)	gives an approximation of the norm *nrm*, and also the number of iterations *nit* needed to obtain the norm.
condest(A)	gives a lower bound estimate in the one-norm (1-norm) of the condition number of the matrix **A**.
[c,v] = condest(A, *tr*)	gives a lower bound estimate of the condition number *c*, in the one-norm of **A**, and also computes a vector **v**, where $\|\mathbf{Av}\| = (\|\mathbf{A}\| \cdot \|\mathbf{v}\|)/c$. If *tr* is given, it displays information about the steps in the calculations. If *tr* = 1 information on every step is displayed, and if *tr* = −1 the quotient c/rcond(A) is displayed.

■ **Example 9.8**

Suppose

    Sprs = speye(4); Sprs(4,1) = 19; Sprs(3,2) = 4;

is given. Then normApprox = normest(Sprs) gives:

    normApprox =
       19.0525

and theNorm = norm(full(Sprs))

    theNorm =
       19.0525

To find the difference we type difference = theNorm - normApprox which gives:

    difference =
       8.5577e-09

Here, and in most of the applications, `normest` is a good approximation of the Euclidean norm. The number of arithmetic operations required is less than for `norm`; see also Section 7.6.

With the `etree` command an elimination tree of a square symmetric matrix can be found. The tree is represented by a vector **f** and can be plotted using the `etreeplot` command. The element f_i is the column index of the first non-zero entry in row i of the upper triangular Cholesky factor of the matrix. If there are no non-zero elements then $f_i = 0$. The elimination tree is constructed as follows:

Node i is a child of f_i or if $f_i = 0$ then node i is a root node of the tree.

Commands 97	ELIMINATION TREE OF MATRIX
`etree(A)`	returns the vector **f** of **A**. The command can also have optional arguments; type `help etree` for information.
`etreeplot(A)`	plots the elimination tree defined by the vector **f**.
`treeplot(p,c,d)`	plots a tree of the vector of pointers **p**. The arguments c and d define colors on the nodes and branches. The command is called by `etreeplot`.
`treelayout`	gives a layout of a tree. The command is called by `treeplot`.

■ **Example 9.9**

Let the symmetric sparse matrix **B** be defined.

$$
\mathbf{B} =
\begin{pmatrix}
5 & 1 & 0 & 0 & 1 & 0 & 0 & 1 \\
1 & 5 & 0 & 0 & 0 & 0 & 1 & 0 \\
0 & 0 & 5 & 0 & 1 & 1 & 1 & 0 \\
0 & 0 & 0 & 5 & 0 & 0 & 1 & 1 \\
1 & 0 & 1 & 0 & 5 & 0 & 0 & 0 \\
0 & 0 & 1 & 0 & 0 & 5 & 1 & 0 \\
0 & 1 & 1 & 1 & 0 & 1 & 5 & 0 \\
1 & 0 & 0 & 1 & 0 & 0 & 0 & 5
\end{pmatrix}
$$

The command `btree = etree(B)` gives:

```
btree =
      2     5     5     7     6     7     8     0
```

The number 2 at the beginning is not so hard to understand. It is the row number of the first non-zero element in the first column in the matrix and the first row of the Cholesky factor will have its first non-zero element in column 2 due to this. But for the number 5 in the second column we must consider what happens when we reduce the elements in the first column. Due to fill-in the element in row position 5 of column 2 will be non-zero after reduction in **B**. Thus element 2 in the `etree` vector is 5. The structure of the Cholesky factor can be seen by `spy(chol(B))`. The result is given in Figure 9.2.

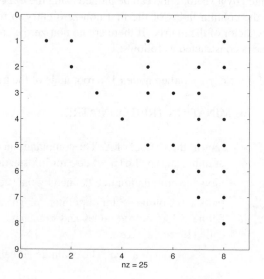

Figure 9.2 *Structure of the Cholesky factorization.*

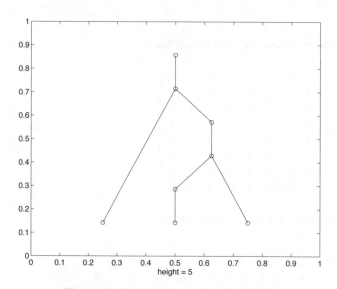

Figure 9.3 *Elimination tree of matrix* **B**.

The elimination tree of this vector is constructed as follows: there is only one row with zero elements in the upper triangular, node 8, so that is our only root. Node number 1 is a child of node number 2. Nodes 2 and 3 are children of node 5 that is a child of node 6. Nodes 4 and 6 are children of node 7 that is a child of node 8, the root.

If we give the command `etreeplot(B)` we get the structure of the tree, as illustrated by Figure 9.3.

The shape of the elimination tree depends on the ordering of the rows and the columns and it is used to analyze the elimination process.

■

With the `gplot` command it is possible to draw connections between coordinate pairs by using a matrix. To do this, n coordinates in an $n \times 2$ matrix are given. Each row of this matrix defines one point. Then an $n \times n$ matrix is created that indicates which points are connected. If point 4 is connected to point 8 the entry $(4, 8)$ gets the value 1. Since the matrix can be large, with few non-zero elements, it should be created as a sparse matrix.

This graph can illustrate **network problems**, for example transport problems. The graph also contains information of dependence between the unknowns in a linear system.

Commands 98	NETWORK GRAPHS
`gplot(A,K)`	draws a graph where point k_i is connected with point k_j if entry (i, j) in **A** is non-zero. Here **K** is an $n \times 2$ matrix with the coordinates of the points, and **A** is an $n \times n$ matrix indicating the connections.
`gplot(A,K,str)`	draws a graph as the previous command but in color and form defined by **str**. For values of that string, see Table 13.1.
`[X,A] = unmesh(E)`	returns the Laplace matrix **A** and the mesh vertex coordinate matrix **X** for the edge matrix **E**.

■ **Example 9.10**

Suppose that the following coordinate pairs **K** and connection matrix **A** are defined:

$$
\mathbf{K} = \begin{pmatrix} 0 & 1 \\ 1 & 0.2 \\ 1.3 & 0.9 \\ 2 & 0 \\ 2 & 1.9 \\ 3 & 2 \\ 4 & 1 \end{pmatrix}
\qquad
\mathbf{A} = \begin{pmatrix} 0 & 1 & 1 & 0 & 1 & 0 & 0 \\ 0 & 0 & 0 & 1 & 0 & 0 & 0 \\ 0 & 0 & 0 & 1 & 0 & 0 & 1 \\ 0 & 0 & 0 & 0 & 0 & 0 & 1 \\ 0 & 0 & 0 & 0 & 0 & 1 & 1 \\ 0 & 0 & 0 & 0 & 0 & 0 & 1 \\ 0 & 0 & 0 & 0 & 0 & 0 & 0 \end{pmatrix}
$$

The matrix **A** can be sparse. Then the command `gplot(A,K)` draws Figure 9.4, which illustrates what possible routes there are between point (0, 1) and point (4, 1) in a system.

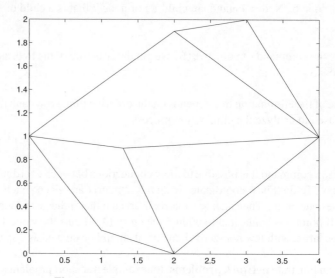

Figure 9.4 *An example of the use of* `gplot`.

Analysis of Functions, Interpolation, and Curve Fitting

MATLAB has commands for handling polynomials with or without evaluation. There are also powerful commands for analyzing functions, such as finding zeros and minima. MATLAB does also provide several commands and functions for interpolation and curve fitting of data sets. The classical Bessel functions are also represented.

10.1 Polynomials in MATLAB

A **polynomial**, $p(x)$, of degree n is in MATLAB stored as a row vector, **p**, of length $n + 1$. The components represent the coefficients of the polynomial and are given in descending order of the powers of x, that is:

$$\mathbf{p} = (\, a_n \quad a_{n-1} \quad \cdots \quad a_1 \quad a_0 \,)$$

is interpreted as:

$$p(x) = a_n x^n + a_{n-1} x^{n-1} + \cdots + a_1 x + a_0$$

Let **A** be a square matrix, and let the vectors **p** and **q**, of length $n+1$ and $m+1$, represent polynomials of degree n and m, respectively. In MATLAB the following commands are used to handle polynomials:

Commands 99   POLYNOMIALS

`polyval(p,x)`	evaluates the polynomial **p**. If x is a scalar the value of the polynomial in the point x is returned. If **x** is a vector or a matrix the polynomial is evaluated for all components of **x**.
`[y,err] = polyval(p,x,E)`	evaluates the polynomial **p** for the vector **x**, as above, and returns the result in **y**, but it also returns the error estimate vector **err**, according to the matrix **E** given from the `polyfit` command. See `help polyval` and `help polyfit` and Section 10.4.

Commands 99	**(CONTINUED)**

`polyvalm(p,A)`	operates on the entire matrix **A** directly, and does not work element-by-element as the previous command, that is it evaluates $p(\mathbf{A}) = p_1\mathbf{A}^n + p_2\mathbf{A}^{n-1} + \cdots + p_{n+1}\mathbf{I}$.
`poly(A)`	returns a vector representing the characteristic polynomial of the matrix **A**. See also Section 8.1.
`poly(x)`	returns a vector of length $n + 1$ representing a polynomial of degree n. The roots of that polynomial are given in the vector **x**, of length n.
`compan(p)`	returns the companion matrix **A** to the polynomial **p**, that is a matrix whose characteristic polynomial is **p**.
`roots(p)`	returns a vector of length n with the roots of the polynomial **p**, that is the solutions of the equation $p(x) = 0$. The expression `poly(roots(p))` = **p** is true. The result may be complex.
`conv(p,q)`	gives the product of the polynomials **p** and **q**, it can also be regarded as the convolution of **p** and **q**.
`[k,r] = deconv(p,q)`	divides the polynomial **p** by **q**. The quotient polynomial is represented by **k** and the remainder polynomial by **r**. The operation can also be regarded as the deconvolution of **p** and **q**.
`[u v k] =` `residue(p,q)`	returns a partial fraction expansion of $p(x)/q(x)$: $$\frac{p(x)}{q(x)} = \frac{u(1)}{x - v(1)} + \frac{u(2)}{x - v(2)} + \cdots + \frac{u(j)}{x - v(j)} + k(x).$$ The vectors **p** and **q** represent the coefficients of $p(x)$ and $q(x)$, respectively. The residues are returned in the vector **u**, the pole locations in the vector **v**, and the quotient polynomial in the vector **k**.
`[p q] =` `residue(u,v,x)`	returns two polynomials, **p** and **q**, from a partial fraction expansion **u**, **v** and **x**, as above.
`mpoles`	gives information on multiplicity of poles, see `help mpoles`.
`polyder(p)`	returns a vector of length n that represents the derivative of the polynomial whose coefficients are stored in the vector **p**.
`polyder(p,q)`	returns a vector representing the derivative of the polynomial defined by `conv(p,q)`.
`[u,v] =` `polyder(p,q)`	returns two vectors, which in the form **u/v** represent the derivative of the polynomial defined by `deconv(p,q)`.

■ **Example 10.1**

We apply some polynomial commands to the following polynomials:

$$p2(x) = 3x^2 + 2x - 4 \qquad p3(x) = 2x^3 - 2$$

In MATLAB these polynomials are represented by the following vectors:

```
p2 = [3 2 -4];
p3 = [2 0 0 -2];
```

Let us now suppose that they are defined.

(a) To evaluate the polynomials in $x = 1$ we type:

```
value2 = polyval(p2,1), ...
value3 = polyval(p3,1)
```

and get:

```
value2 =
    1
```

```
value3 =
    0
```

(b) Just as easily we can evaluate the polynomials for a vector or a matrix.

```
x = [1 2 3]';
values2 = polyval(p2,x), values3 = polyval(p3,x)
```

result in:

```
values2 =
    1
   12
   29
```

```
values3 =
    0
   14
   52
```

(c) If we multiply two polynomials, a new polynomial is obtained:

```
p5 = conv(p2,p3)
```

gives:

```
p5 =
    6    4   -8   -6   -4    8
```

(d) The roots of the polynomials are found with the roots command:

```
roots2 = roots(p2), roots3 = roots(p3)
```

gives:

```
roots2 =
   -1.5352
    0.8685

roots3 =
   -0.5000 + 0.8660i
   -0.5000 - 0.8660i
    1.0000
```

We show the two polynomials in Figure 10.1.

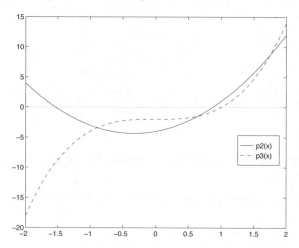

Figure 10.1 *The polynomials* $p2(x) = 3x^2 + 2x - 4$ *and* $p3(x) = 2x^3 - 2$.

(e) One Newton–Raphson iteration applied on the polynomial $p(x)$, represented by the vector **p**, can be written as:

```
q = polyder(p);
xnext = x - polyval(p,x)/polyval(q,x);
```

(f) The command `roots(poly(A))` returns the eigenvalues of the matrix **A**. Suppose the matrix **A** is defined by:

$$\mathbf{A} = \begin{pmatrix} -9 & -3 & -16 \\ 13 & 7 & 16 \\ 3 & 3 & 10 \end{pmatrix}$$

then the command:

```
usedRoots = roots(poly(A))
```

give:

```
usedRoots =
   10.0000
    4.0000
   -6.0000
```

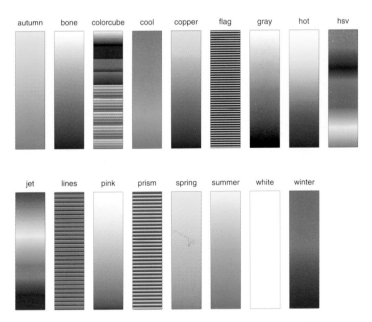

Figure P.1 *Seventeen different predefined MATLAB colormaps (defined in Section 13.6, Table 13.2). Commands used:* `colormap`, `pcolor`, *and* `subplot`. *Note that the command* `contrast` *also will create a custom-made colormap for a certain image.*

Figure P.2 *A cartoon-like geometrical object created with commands* `sphere`, `mesh`, `light`, `view`, `axis`, *and the use of graphics handles.*

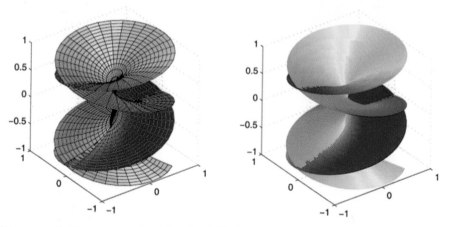

Figure P.3 *Riemann surface for the 3.75th root using the commands* cplxroot, *subplot,* shading faceted *(left), and* shading interp *(right).*

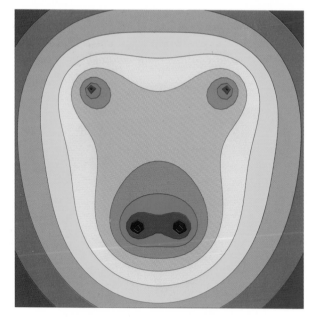

Figure P.4 *Contour plot of a function of two variables* $z = f(x, y)$ *using command* contourf. *The regions between the level curves of* z *are filled. Other commands used:* meshgrid, colormap, *and* axis.

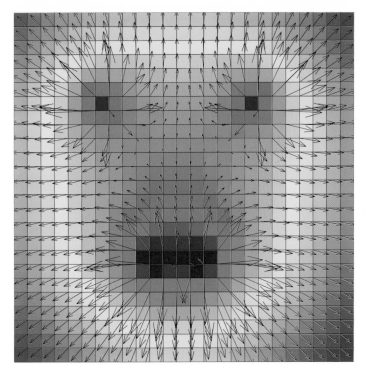

Figure P.5 *Plot of gradient vectors of a function of two variables $z = f(x, y)$ using commands* meshgrid, pcolor, hold, gradient, *and* quiver.

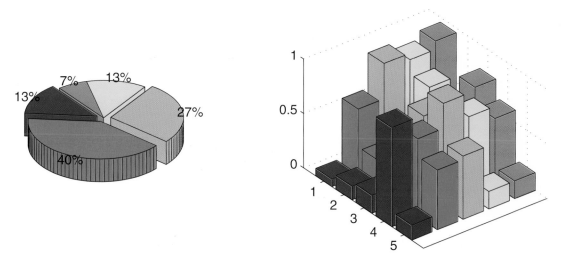

Figure P.6 *Command* subplot *used to show a 3D pie plot (left) and a 3D bar graph (right). Other commands used:* pie3, bar3, colormap, *and* caxis.

Figure P.7 *Display an image using MATLAB. Commands used:* `load earth`, `image`, `colormap`, *and* `axis`.

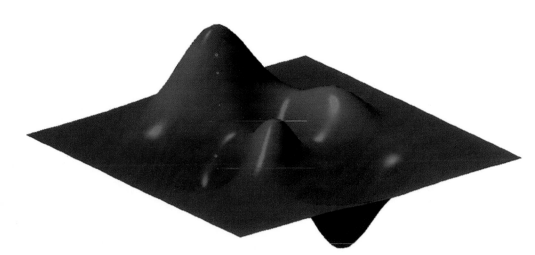

Figure P.8 *Surface plot of a function of two variables* $z = f(x, y)$ *using handle graphics and light objects. There is one red and one blue light source. Commands used:* `meshgrid`, `peaks`, `surf`, `colormap`, `material`, *and* `light`.

However, this way of obtaining eigenvalues is less efficient and less accurate than the MATLAB command eig(A):

```
usedEig = eig(A)
```

gives:

```
usedEig =
    -6.0000
    10.0000
     4.0000
```

which is the same result but in reversed order.

(g) For all matrices **A** the following is true: polyvalm(poly(A),A) = 0. This is the Cayley–Hamilton theorem. We try the theorem on a magic square of order 5.

```
Magical = magic(5);
AlmostZero = polyvalm(poly(Magical),Magical)
```

```
AlmostZero =
   1.0e-07 *
     0.2794    0.3551    0.1723    0.1770    0.2654
     0.2765    0.2887    0.2049    0.2142    0.2561
     0.1775    0.2468    0.2701    0.3073    0.2375
     0.1942    0.2744    0.2759    0.2608    0.2282
     0.2082    0.3120    0.2608    0.2515    0.2049
```

■

10.2 Zeros of functions

Mathematical functions can be represented by M-files in MATLAB; see Section 2.9. The function:

$$g(x) = \frac{5x - 6.4}{(x - 1.3)^2 + 0.002} + \frac{9x}{x^3 + 0.03} - \frac{x - 0.4}{(x - 0.92)^2 + 0.005}$$

is available to MATLAB if we type the following M-file stored as **g.m**:

```
function y = g(x)

y = (5.*x-6.4)./((x-1.3).^2+0.002) + ...
    (9.*x)./(x.^3+0.03) - ...
    (x-0.4)./((x-0.92).^2+0.005);
```

The MATLAB function **g** has been defined using the elementwise operators `.*`, `./`, `.^`, `+`, and `-`. Consequently, if the function is called by a vector the result is a vector. All MATLAB functions that are described in this chapter require that the mathematical functions are defined in this way.

The function can be plotted using the `plot` command:

```
x = linspace(0,2);          % Creates the x vector.

plot(x,g(x));               % Plots graph g(x).
grid;                       % Draws grid.
title('The g(x) function');  % Write title.
```

or by using the `fplot` command:

```
fplot('g',[0 2]);           % Plots the graph g(x).
grid;                       % Draws grid.
title('The g(x) function');  % Write title.
```

which results in Figure 10.2. Both the commands `plot` and `fplot` are defined in Section 13.1.

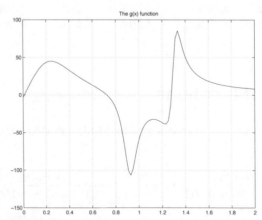

Figure 10.2 *A plot of* $g(x)$, *generated by* `fplot`.

To find the **zeros** of the function $f(x)$ is equivalent to solving the equation $f(x) = 0$. The zeros of a function of one variable can be found by the MATLAB command `fzero`. For polynomials the `roots` command should be used, see Section 10.1. The algorithm used by `fzero` is iterative, and requires an initial guess not too far from the desired zero.

Commands 100	ZEROS OF FUNCTIONS

`fzero(fcn,x0)`	returns one of the zeros of the function defined by the string **fcn**. The command requires an initial value $x0$. The relative error of the approximation is eps.
`fzero(fcn,x0,tol)`	returns one of the zeros of the function defined by the string **fcn**. The command requires an initial value $x0$. The relative error of the approximation is *tol*, defined by the user.
`fzero(fcn,x0,tol, pic)`	returns one of the zeros of the function defined by the string **fcn** as in the previous command, but also plots the iteration process if `pic` is non-zero.
`fzero(fcn,x0,tol, pic, p1,p2,...)`	can be used if the function **fcn** is a function of several variables, i.e., **fcn** = **fcn**$(x0, p1, p2, \dots)$. Send empty matrices for `tol` and `pic` if they are not given, e.g., `fzero(fcn,x0,[],[],p1)`.

The zerodemo command gives a demonstration.

■ **Example 10.2**

(a) We want to find the zeros of the function $g(x)$, defined at the beginning of this section:

```
x1 = fzero('g',0), x2 = fzero('g',0.5), x3 = fzero('g',2)
```

give:

```
x1 =
    0.0112
```

```
x2 =
    0.7248
```

```
x3 =
    1.2805
```

(b) To find the intersection of the functions $\sin x$ and $2x - 2$, that is to find the solution of the equation $\sin x = 2x - 2$, we define the function $sinm(x)$, and store it in the M-file **sinm.m** as follows:

```
function s = sinm(x)
```

```
s = sin(x) - 2.*x + 2;
```

Plotting the curve is a good way to find a starting value, therefore:

```
fplot('sinm',[-10 10]);
grid on;
title('The sin(x) - 2.*x + 2 function');
```

which results in Figure 10.3. We can see that 2 is an acceptable first guess, and type:

```
xzero = fzero('sinm',2)
```

and get:

```
xzero =
    1.4987
```

which is the solution of the equation $\sin x = 2x - 2$.

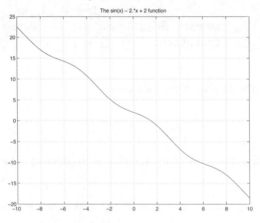

Figure 10.3 *The* $sinm(x)$ *function.*

10.3 Minimum and maximum of a function

Optimization is finding the optimal solution, that is finding the maximum or minimum of a function in an interval, with or without constraints. MATLAB uses numerical methods to find the minima of functions. The algorithms are iterative, that is some process is repeated a number of times. Now, suppose that we want to find a minimum x_{min} of the function f in an interval.

$$f(x_{min}) = \min_x f(x)$$

An iterative method needs an initial guess x_0. From this first value, x_0, one finds a new value, x_1, which, it is hoped, is closer to x_{min}. How the better approximation x_1 is found depends on which numerical method is used. The iterations continue until an approximation x_i with enough accuracy is found, that is $|x_{min} - x_i|$ is small enough.

If there are several local minima `fmin` will find one of them. There is also a special Optimization Toolbox for MATLAB; see Appendix C.

Here we mention two commands for optimization that are a part of the standard MATLAB system. The `fmin` command is used to determine a minimum of a function of one variable and the `fmins` command to determine the minimum of a function of several variables. The latter command requires a starting vector.

There is no command to determine the maximum of a function f. Instead, the minimum of the function $h = -f$ can be determined.

| Commands 101 | MINIMUM OF A FUNCTION |

`fmin(fcn,x1,x2)`	returns a minimum of the function in the string **fcn** in the interval $x1 < x < x2$. If there is no local minimum the smallest x value on the interval is returned. The approximation has a relative error less than 10^{-4}.
`fmin(fcn,x1,x2, options)`	returns a minimum of the function in the string **fcn** in the interval $x1 < x < x2$. If there is no local minimum the smallest x value on the interval is returned. The vector **options** contains control parameters, e.g., **options(1)** $= 1$ displays intermediate results, **options(2)** is the termination tolerance for x, default is 10^{-4}. Type `help foptions` for more information.
`fmins(fcn,x0)`	returns a minimum of the function **fcn**. A starting guess, i.e. the vector **x0**, has to be given by the user. The relative error is 10^{-4}.
`fmins(fcn,x0, options)`	gives the same as the previous but with some optimization option. Write `help fmins` and `help foptions` for details. As an example, it is possible to control the number of iterations and the tolerance of the computations of the function to be minimized.

■ **Example 10.3**

(a) We determine the minimum of the cosine function in the interval $[0, 2\pi]$.

```
cosmin = fmin('cos',0,2*pi)    % Gives minimum of cos.
cosmin =
    3.1416
```

which is the expected result.

(b) It is just as simple to determine the minimum of a more advanced function. The function $g(x)$ was defined earlier in Section 10.2. We search for a minimum of g in the interval $[0, 2]$.

```
gmin = fmin('g',0,2)
```

gmin =
     1.2277

Note that this is just one local minimum and not necessarily the one that minimizes the function in the interval. If we study Figure 10.2 we see that a smaller interval gives us the second minimum, which is smaller than the first:

```
gmin2 = fmin('g',0,1)
```

gmin2 =
     0.9260

(c) The `fmin` command can also be used to find maxima of functions, but first a new function returning $-g(x)$ must be written. That function is here stored in the M-file **minusg.m**.

```
function y = minusg(x)
```

```
y = -g(x);
```

To find the minimum of this function is equivalent to finding the maximum of the g function.

```
gmax = fmin('minusg',0,2)
```

gives:

gmax =
     0.2433

Here we have several maxima in the interval. It is the first maximum that MATLAB finds, not necessarily the global maximum of the function, that is returned.

(d) If we want to minimize a function of several variables we use `fmins`. Suppose that the function is:

$$f(x_1, x_2) = x_1^2 + x_2^2 - 0.5x_1x_2 - \sin x_1$$

We write the M-file **fx1x2.m**:

```
function f = fx1x2(x)
```

```
f = x(1).^2 + x(2).^2 - 0.5.*x(1).*x(2) - sin(x(1));
```

The function `fmins` requires a starting guess, so we try $(1, 0)$:

```
fx1x2min = fmins('fx1x2',[1,0])
```

gives:

```
fx1x2min =
     0.4744      0.1186
```

To plot the function we type the following program:

```
x = linspace(-1,1,50);   % Creates x vector. Assume y = x.

for i = 1:50                   % Computes fx1x2 in each node.
   for j = 1:50
      Z(i,j) = fx1x2([x(i) x(j)]);
   end
end

meshc(x,x,Z);            % Plots graph with contour lines
view(80,10);             % and gets a better view.
```

The command meshc gives the surface of the function plus contour lines in the xy plane below it. The commands meshc and view are defined in Section 13.5. The command linspace is presented in Section 4.2. The result will be Figure 10.4, where the minimum can be seen.

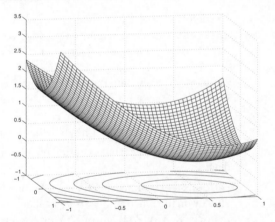

Figure 10.4 *The function* $x_1^2 + x_2^2 - 0.5x_1x_2 - \sin x_1$ *for the interval* $[-1, 1] \times [-1, 1]$.

■

10.4 Interpolation, curve fitting, and surface fitting

If a function is given in a finite number of points it is possible to find approximations for the intermediate points by interpolation. The easiest way is to use the two adjacent points and make a linear interpolation. The interp1 and interp2 commands have special algorithms for faster interpolation of equidistant data points. To use this, one has to put an asterisk, '*', in front of the name of the method, e.g., `interp1(x,Y,xx,'*cubic')`.

There are several functions in MATLAB which perform interpolation of data in different ways:

Commands 102	INTERPOLATION

`interp1(x,y,xx)`	returns a vector **f(xx)** of the same length as the vector **xx**, where the function **f** is defined by the vectors **y** and **x** such that **y** = **f(x)**. The values are computed with linear interpolation. For a correct result the vector **x** must be in descending or ascending order.
`interp1(x,Y,xx)`	returns a matrix **F(xx)** corresponding to the vector in the previous command. Each column of the matrix **Y** is a function of **x**, and the values of **xx** are interpolated for each such function. The resulting matrix has the same number of rows as the length of **xx**, and the same number of columns as the matrix **Y**.
`interp1(x,y,xx, metstr)`	performs a one-dimensional interpolation. The string **metstr** defines what method to use, and the possibilities are:

`'linear'`	linear interpolation.
`'nearest'`	nearest neighbor interpolation.
`'spline'`	cubic spline interpolation. Does also accept extrapolation.
`'cubic'`	cubic interpolation, requires equidistant values of **x**.

For all of the alternatives **x** has to be monotonous.

`interp1q(x,y,xx)`	works like `interp1` but is faster for non-uniformly spaced data.
`interp2(X,Y,Z,Xx, Yy)`	performs a two-dimensional interpolation of the matrices **Xx** and **Yy** on the function $Z = f(X, Y)$ that is represented by the matrices **X**, **Y** or **Z**. If any of **X**, **Y** or **Z** is a vector it is applied in the corresponding rows and columns.
`interp2(X,Y,Z,Xx, Yy,metstr)`	performs a two-dimensional interpolation where the string **metstr** defines what method to use according to:

`'linear'`	linear interpolation.
`'nearest'`	interpolation between adjacent points.
`'spline'`	cubic spline interpolation.
`'cubic'`	cubic interpolation.

Commands 102 (CONTINUED)

VV = interp3(X,Y,Z, V,XX,YY,ZZ,metstr)	performs an interpolation of the values in **V** representing the value of the function in **X**, **Y** and **Z**. **XX**, **YY** and **ZZ** are the points to be interpolated to. The string **metstr** defines what method to use according to:

'nearest' uses the value of the nearest point.
'linear' uses the eight nearest points and linear interpolation.
'spline' cubic spline interpolation.
'cubic' uses the 64 nearest points and cubic interpolation.

VV = interpn(X1,X2,X3, ... ,V,Y1,Y2,Y3, ... ,method)	works like interp3 but **V** and **VV** may be multidimensional. If **X1**, **X2**, **X3**, ... , are equidistant the calculation may be fastened by using *, e.g., '*cubic'.
interpft(y,n)	performs interpolation with the Fast Fourier Transform method and returns a vector of length n, computed from **y**. Requires that the values of **y** are equidistant, and that the result is computed in the same interval as **y**.
griddata(x,y,z, Xx,Yy,'method')	returns a matrix of the same size as **Xx** and **Yy** that represents a mesh, on which the function $z = f(x, y)$ is interpolated. The vectors **x**, **y** and **z** contain the x, y and z coordinates in the three-dimensional space. The string **method**, if given, defines how the surface is interpolated according to:

'linear' triangle-based linear interpolation.
'nearest' nearest neighbor interpolation.
'cubic' triangle-based cubic interpolation.
'v4' interpolation method used by MATLAB 4.

[X1,X2,X3,...] = ndgrid(x1, x2,x3,...)	transforms the domain given by the vectors **x1**, **x2**, **x3**, ... , for the matrices **X1**, **X2**, **X3**, ... , which may be used for evaluation of functions of several variables and multidimensional interpolation. The nth dimension in the matrix **Xn** is a copy of the elements is the vector **xn**.
[X1,X2,...] = ndgrid(x)	is the same as [X1,X2,...] = ndgrid(x,x,x,...).

■ **Example 10.4**

We make a table of $\sin x^2$ for 40 values between 0 and 2π.

```
x = linspace(0,2*pi,40); y = sin(x.^2);
```

(a) Now we can compute $\sin x^2$ for intermediate points using `interp1`, instead of `sin`. The command:

```
values = interp1(x,y,[0 pi/2 3])
```

gives:

```
values =
        0     0.6050     0.3559
```

We compare with the correct results:

```
correct = sin([0 pi/3 3].^2)
```

```
correct =
        0     0.8897     0.4121
```

The accuracy could be made better by using more values in the table.

(b) With spline interpolation we should obtain more accurate results. Suppose the vectors **x** and **y** are defined as above. Then:

```
better = interp1(x,y,[0 pi/2 3],'spline')
```

results in:

```
better =
        0     0.6241     0.4098
```

which is a better approximation.

■

The command `griddata` creates a function out of a set of arbitrary points in three dimensions.

■ Example 10.5

If we generate three vectors with 10 components with values distributed between 0 and 1:

```
x = rand(10,1); y = rand(10,1); z = rand(10,1);
```

we can interpolate a surface between these points with the command `griddata` if we first create a mesh to compute the surface in. We show some different ways to do this below:

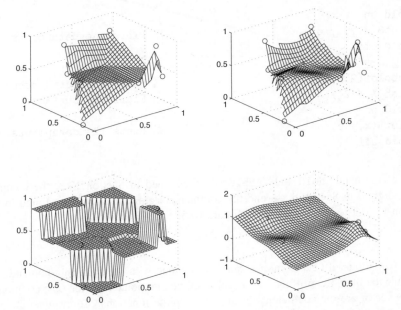

Figure 10.5 *Interpolation of 10 random points with* griddata, *plotted with* 'linear' *top left, with* 'cubic' *top right, with* 'nearest' *bottom left and* 'v4' *bottom right.*

```
stps = 0:0.03:1;                          % A vector with values in
                                          % [0,1].
[X,Y] = meshgrid(stps);                   % A mesh in [0,1] x [0,1].
Z1 = griddata(x,y,z,X,Y);                 % Interpolates, same as
                                          % 'linear'.
Z2 = griddata(x,y,z,X,Y,'cubic');         % Cubic interpolation.
Z3 = griddata(x,y,z,X,Y,'nearest');       % Nearest neighbor
                                          % interpolation.
Z4 = griddata(x,y,z,X,Y,'v4');            % MATLAB 4 griddata method.

subplot(2,2,1);                           % Plots in first subplot.
mesh(X,Y,Z1);                             % Plots the surface.
hold on                                   % Holds the picture.
plot3(x,y,z,'o')                          % Plots the datapoints.
hold off                                  % Releases the picture.

subplot(2,2,2);                           % Plots in second subplot.
mesh(X,Y,Z2);                             % Plots the surface.
hold on
plot3(x,y,z,'o')                          % Plots the datapoints.
hold off

subplot(2,2,3);                           % Plots in third subplot.
mesh(X,Y,Z3);                             % Plots the surface.
```

```
hold on
plot3(x,y,z,'o')                        % Plots the datapoints.
hold off

subplot(2,2,4);                         % Plots in fourth subplot.
mesh(X,Y,Z4);                           % Plots the surface.
hold on
plot3(x,y,z,'o')                        % Plots the datapoints.
hold off
```

The commands `hold` and `subplot` are described in Section 13.3, the command `meshgrid` in Section 13.4, and the commands `mesh` and `plot3` are found in Section 13.5. The result is shown in Figure 10.5.

■

Approximation with cubic splines can also be done with the `spline` command. It is possible to obtain the **pp-form** of the cubic spline interpolated vector. The components of the vector are the coefficients of the cubic spline functions. To evaluate the cubic spline functions the `ppval` command is used.

Commands 103	CUBIC SPLINE DATA INTERPOLATION
`spline(x,y,xx)`	is equivalent to `interp1(x,y,xx,'spline')`, but does only accept vectors as argument.
`spline(x,y)`	returns the pp-form of the cubic spline interpolating vector that approximates $y = f(x)$. The abbreviation pp stands for 'piecewise polynomial' and the components of the returned vector contain, among other things, the coefficients of the computed cubic spline. This can be used with the `ppval` function.
`YI = splncore(X,Y,XI)`	interpolates n dimensional data in **Y** as a function of the cell array **X** to the new set of definition **XI**. The function is used by `interp2`, `interp3` and `interpn`.
`ppval(pp,xx)`	evaluates cubic spline functions. If a cubic spline `pp = spline(x,y)` is defined then `ppval(pp,xx)` gives the same result as `spline(x,y,xx)`.
`p = mkpp(points, coeff,d)`	returns a piecewise polynomial by creating a pp-function from the given points, where **coeff(i,:)** contains coefficients for the ith polynomial. The number of polynomials is given by `l = length(points)-1` and the order of the ith polynomial is `n = length(coeff(:))/l`.
`[points,coeff,l, n,d] = unmkpp(p)`	returns information on piecewise polynomials; see above.

A polynomial can be fitted to data by **least squares approximation** (see also Section 7.7) with the polyfit command.

POLYNOMIAL CURVE FITTING

polyfit(x,y,n)	returns a vector with the coefficients of the polynomial of degree *n* which is the best least squares approximation to the set of data $\{(x_i,\ y_i)\}$.
[p,E] = polyfit(x,y,n)	returns a polynomial represented by the vector **p** as above, and a matrix **E**, that are used by the polyval function to estimate errors.

■ **Example 10.6**

The following commands return a picture showing the polynomials of third, fourth, and fifth degree approximating the data in some vectors **x** and **y**. The data set $(x_i,\ y_i)$ and the polynomials are plotted for each case above.

```
x = [-3 -1 0 2 5.5 7];
y = [3.3 4.5 2.0 1.5 2.5 -1.2];

p3 = polyfit(x,y,3);        % Fits the polynomial
p4 = polyfit(x,y,4);        % to the data
p5 = polyfit(x,y,5);        % given in x and y.

xcurve = -3.5:0.1:7.2;      % Creates x-values.
p3curve = polyval(p3,xcurve); % Computes the polynomial in
p4curve = polyval(p4,xcurve); % these x-values.
p5curve = polyval(p5,xcurve);

plot(xcurve,p3curve,'--',xcurve,p4curve,'-.', ...
     xcurve,p5curve,'-',x,y,'*');

lx = [-1 1.5]; ly = [0 0]; hold on;

plot(lx,ly,'--',lx,ly-1.3,'-.',lx,ly-2.6,'-');

text(2,   0,'degree 3');
text(2,-1.3,'degree 4');
text(2,-2.6,'degree 5');
hold off;
```

The result is shown in Figure 10.6.

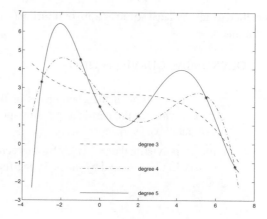

Figure 10.6 *Approximation by polynomials of different degrees.*

As expected, the accuracy is better for polynomials of higher degrees. The polynomial of the fifth degree passes all six points, that is it is the **interpolation polynomial** for this particular set of data. For more information on the graphics commands, see Chapter 13.

■

In MATLAB, the **Legendre functions** are computed for a scalar or a vector with the `legendre` command. The Legendre functions are systems of orthogonal polynomials that form complete orthogonal sets in chosen intervals. The **Legendre polynomials**, that is the Legendre functions of order zero, can be used for curve fitting on a given set of data. The **Bessel functions** are classical special functions that, among other things, can be used in mathematical physics.

Commands 105	THE LEGENDRE AND BESSEL FUNCTIONS

`legendre(n,x)`	returns a matrix with the values of the associated Legendre functions of degree n and order $m = 0, 1, \ldots, n$ computed in **x**. The components of **x** must be in the interval $[-1, 1]$. The first row corresponds to $m = 0$ and contains the Legendre polynomial of degree n evaluated in **x**.
`besselj(order,z)`	computes Bessel functions of the first kind. The variable *order* gives the order of the function and **z** are the elements which the function operates on.
`bessely(n,x)`	computes Bessel functions of the second kind. The variable *order* gives the order of the function and **z** are the elements which the function operates on.
`besselh(order,k,z)`	returns the value of the Hankel function (Bessel functions of the third kind) for elements in the vector **z**. The variable k defines which kind of Hankel function is to be used.

Commands 105   (CONTINUED)

`besseli(order,z)`	returns modified Bessel functions of the first kind. The variable *order* gives the order of the function and **z** are the elements which the function operates on.
`besselk(order,z)`	returns modified Bessel functions of the second kind. The variable *order* gives the order of the function and **z** are the elements which the function operates on.
`w = airy(k,z)`	returns the Airy function $\mathbf{w} = Ai(z)$ if $k = 0$ or if k is not given. If $k = 1$ the derivative $Ai'(z)$ is returned. If $k = 2$ the Airy function of the second kind, $Bi(z)$, is returned, and if $k = 3$ the derivative $Bi'(z)$ is returned.
`[w,err] = airy(...)`	returns an array of error flags in *err*.

10.5 Signal analysis

Here we give a short description of a few of the MATLAB commands for **signal analysis**. More information can be obtained by the `help` and `demo` commands. See also the 'Signal Processing Toolbox' and its manual. The commands for complex numbers (Section 2.4), and for convolution (Section 10.1), may also be of interest.

Commands 106   SIGNAL ANALYSIS

`fft(x)`	returns a vector containing the discrete Fourier transform of the vector **x**. If the length of the vector is a power of two the Fast Fourier Transform, FFT, is used. Note that the transform is not normalized.
`fft(x,n)`	returns a vector of length *n* with the discrete Fourier transform of the *n* first components of **x**. If **x** has $m < n$ components, the last $m + 1, \ldots, n$ elements are supposed to be zero.
`fft(A)`	returns a matrix with the discrete Fourier transform of the columns of the matrix **A**.
`fft(A,n,dim)`	returns a matrix with the discrete Fourier transform of the columns in the dimension *dim* of the multidimensional array **A**. This is the same as `fft(x,[],dim)`.
`ifft(x)`	returns the inverse discrete Fourier transform of **x**, normalized with the factor $1/n$, where *n* is the length of the vector. Can also transform matrices and vectors with a fixed vector length like the `fft` command.

Commands 106	(CONTINUED)

`fft2(A)`	returns a matrix which is the two-dimensional discrete Fourier transform of the matrix **A**. This matrix is not normalized. If $A = a$ is a vector this command is equal to the `fft(a)` command.
`fft2(A,m,n)`	returns an $m \times n$ matrix, which is the two-dimensional discrete Fourier transform of the corresponding components of the matrix **A**. This matrix is not normalized. If **A** is a smaller matrix the remaining entries are supposed to be zero. If possible MATLAB uses the Fast Fourier Transform, FFT.
`ifft2(A)`	returns a matrix which is the two-dimensional inverse discrete Fourier transform of the matrix **A**, normalized with a factor $1/nm$. The dimensions to be transformed can be changed as for `fft2`.
`fftn(A,Size)`	gives a n-dimensional array with the discrete Fourier transform of the n-dimensional array **A**. If **A** is a vector the answer is of the same form. If the array **Size** is given **X** is reshaped to the same size as **Size**.
`ifftn(A,Size)`	gives a n-dimensional array with the inverse discrete Fourier transform of the n-dimensional array **A**. If **A** is a vector, the answer is of the same form. If the array **Size** is given **X** is reshaped to the same size as **Size**.
`fftshift(A)`	returns an array where the first and the third quadrants and the second and the fourth quadrants of **A** are swapped. If **A** is a vector, a vector where the left and right sides are swapped is returned. If **A** is an n-dimensional array (and $n > 2$) an array of the same size where the half sides in each dimension are swapped is returned.
`ifftshift(A)`	performs the inverse of the `fftshift(A)` command.
`filter(b,a,x)`	returns the data from **x** filtered with the filter described by the vectors **a** and **b**. See `help filter` for more information.
`Y = filter2(h,X)`	filters the data in **X** with the two-dimensional FIR filter in the matrix **h**. The result **Y** is achieved with a two-dimensional correlation, and contains the central part of the correlation with the same size as **X**.

Commands 106	(CONTINUED)

Y = filter2(h,X,form)	returns the part of **Y** that is specified by the **form** parameter. *form* is a string with one of the following values:

'full'	returns the whole two-dimensional correlation. In this case **Y** is bigger than **X**.
'same'	is the same as Y = filter2(h,X).
'valid'	returns only the parts of the correlation which are calculated without zero padded edges. In this case **Y** is smaller than **X**.

■ Example 10.7

We create a 'hat function' and its Fourier transform. Our hat function is zero at 0 and 1, and one at 0.5.

The hat function is created with linspace:

```
x = linspace(0,1,100);
y = [linspace(0,1,50) linspace(1,0,50)];
```

We plot this function, illustrated by Figure 10.7, with the command:

```
subplot(1,3,1); plot(x,y);
title('A hat function');
```

and the Fourier transform, in the same figure, with:

```
subplot(1,3,2); plot(x,fft(y));
title('The Fourier transform');
```

This Fourier transform is complex valued but only the real part is displayed. Finally, we make sure that the retransformation gives us our hat function in return:

```
subplot(1,3,3); plot(x,ifft(fft(y)));
title('Retransformed hat function');
```

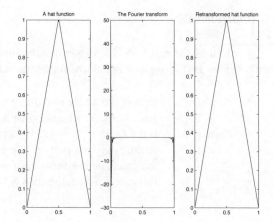

Figure 10.7 *The Fourier transform of a hat function.*

All plot commands are defined in Chapter 13.   ∎

Integrals and Differential Equations

Numerical solutions of definite integrals and ordinary differential equations can be computed and plotted with the help of efficient MATLAB commands.

11.1 Integration

In MATLAB we can solve definite integrals of the kind:

$$q = \int_a^b g(x)\, dx$$

numerically.

There are several methods for numerical integration also called numerical quadrature. If we want MATLAB to take care of the whole computation the quad command is used. We can also compute the values of the integrand **g** and then let MATLAB compute the integral using the trapezoidal rule and the command `trapz`. This can be useful when there are only discrete points of data and the integrand is not known as a mathematical expression.

Commands 107	COMPUTATION OF DEFINITE INTEGRALS
`trapz(x,y)`	computes the integral of **y** as a function of **x**. The vectors **x** and **y** have the same length and (x_i, y_i) represents a point on a curve. The spacing between the points does not have to be equidistant and the x values do not have to be sorted. However, negative intervals and subintervals are considered as negative integrals.
`trapz(y)`	computes the integral of **y** as above, but the x values are considered to be spaced with distance 1.
`trapz(x,A)`	computes the integral of each column in **A** as a function of **x**, and returns a row vector containing each result of the integrations. The columns of **A** must have the same length as the vector **x**.
`Z = trapz(x,A,dim)`	integrates over the dimension of **A** specified by *dim*. The length of **x**, if **x** is given, must be the same as `size(A,dim)`.

Commands 107   (CONTINUED)

`cumtrapz(A,dim)`	returns an array of the same size as **A** with the cumulative values of the integral of **A** calculated with trapezoidal integration. If *dim* is given the calculation is performed in the *dim* dimension.
`quad(fcn,a,b)`	returns an approximation of the integral of **g** on the interval $[a, b]$. The string **fcn** contains the name of a MATLAB function, that is a predefined function or an M-file, corresponding to **g**. The function must return a vector when a vector is passed to it. MATLAB performs a recursive adaptive integration with Simpson's rule; the tolerance is 10^{-3}.
`quad(fcn,a,b,tol)`	returns an approximation to the integral of **g** where the relative error is defined by the parameter *tol*. Otherwise it is the same as above.
`quad(fcn,a,b,tol, pic)`	returns an approximation to the integral of **g** where the relative error is defined by the parameter *tol*. If the parameter *pic* is non-zero a picture, displaying which points are evaluated, is shown.
`quad( ... ,trace)`	if *trace* is non-zero a graph illustrating the integral is plotted.
`quad8(...)`	can be used with the same combinations of parameters and returns the same result as quad, but uses a method with a higher order of accuracy. Therefore, when the derivative of the integrand is infinite in some part of the interval, for example for $q = \int_0^1 \sqrt{\sin x} \, dx$, this command will be better. Both quad and quad8 demand the integrand to be finite in the whole interval.
`dblquad(f,min1, max1,min2,max2, tol,trace,order)`	calculates the double integral of **f** which is a function of two variables. The first argument in the function is used in the inner integration. The inner integration is performed between *min1* and *max1* and the outer integration between *min2* and *max2*. The variable *tol* gives the relative error. It is possible to use *trace* as in quad. With the string **order** dblquad may be told to use quad, quad8 or some user-defined quadrature method with the same calling and return arguments as quad.

Type `quaddemo` for a demonstration.

■ **Example 11.1**

Let us compute the following integral with different methods:

$$\int_0^1 e^{-x^2} \, dx$$

(a) Using the `trapz` command we first have to create a vector with x values. We try 5 and 10 values:

```
x5 = linspace(0,1,5); x10 = linspace(0,1,10);
```

Then we create the vector **y** as a function of **x**:

```
y5 = exp(-x5.^2); y10 = exp(-x10.^2);
```

Now the integral can be computed:

```
format long;
integral5  = trapz(x5,y5), ...
integral10 = trapz(x10,y10)
```

return:

```
integral5 =
   0.74298409780038

integral10 =
   0.74606686791267
```

(b) Using the quad command, we first have to create the function in an M-file. The file **integrand.m** contains the function and looks like:

```
function y = integrand(x)

y = exp(-x.^2);
```

The integral is computed, first with standard tolerance and then with the tolerance specified:

```
format long;
integralStd = quad('integrand',0,1)
integralTol = quad('integrand',0,1,0.00001)
```

give:

```
integralStd =
   0.74682612052747

integralTol =
   0.74682414517798
```

(c) Using the quad8 command: we can use the **M-file** created in (b), and type:

```
integral8Std = quad8('integrand',0,1)

integral8Std =
   0.74682413281243
```

This is the most accurate result MATLAB can give.

(d) With the `cumtrapz` command it is easy to calculate the integral for different intervals.

```
x = 0:5;
cumtrapz(x)

ans =
         0    0.5000    2.0000    4.5000    8.0000   12.5000
```

(e) We want to compute the double integral:

$$\int_0^1 \int_0^1 e^{-x^2-y^2}\,dy\,dx$$

see Figure 11.1. First, an M-file containing the function must be created, **integrand2.m:**

```
function y = integrand2(x,y)

y = exp(-x.^2-y.^2);
```

Then we compute a number of integrals in the y direction for fixed x values with quad:

```
x = linspace(0,1,15);

for i = 1:15
   integral(i) = quad('integrand2',0,1,[],[],x(i));
end
```

Now we have computed 15 integrals in the y direction. The result from these can now be used together with the `trapz` command to obtain the double integral:

```
format short;
dIntegral = trapz(x,integral)


dIntegral =
    0.5575
```

To get a picture of the area of integration we type:

```
[X,Y] = meshgrid(0:.1:1,0:.1:1);
Z     = integrand2(X,Y);

mesh(X,Y,Z); view(30,30);
```

which results in the picture shown in Figure 11.1. The commands `mesh` and `view` are defined in Section 13.5.

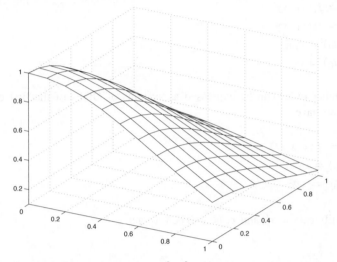

Figure 11.1 *The function $e^{-x^2-y^2}$ in the region $[0, 1] \times [0, 1]$.*

■

Indefinite integrals, $\int_a^x f(t)\,dt$, cannot be computed by the commands above. The MATLAB Symbolic Math Toolbox and the Student Edition of MATLAB provide commands for treating such integrals.

11.2 Ordinary differential equations

Let us now study systems of ordinary differential equations, ODEs, of first order where the initial values are known. In this section we mostly discuss this type of differential equation, but we also have two examples with so called **boundary value problems** for ODE that are solved numerically by creating a sparse linear system of equations.

In Symbolic Math Toolbox there are commands that may give symbolic solutions to some ordinary differential equations, i.e., the solution is given as a mathematical expression.

In the **initial value problem** below, we have two unknown functions, $x_1(t)$ and $x_2(t)$ and denote the derivative by:

$$\frac{dx_i}{dt} = x_i'$$

In many applications the independent variable t is the time.

$$\begin{cases} x_1' = f_1(x_1, x_2, t) \\ x_2' = f_2(x_1, x_2, t) \\ x_1(t_0) = x_{1,0} \\ x_2(t_0) = x_{2,0} \end{cases}$$

ODEs of higher order can be expressed as systems of ODEs of the first order. For instance, if we have:

$$\begin{cases} x'' = f(x, x', t) \\ x(t_0) = x_0 \\ x'(t_0) = xp_0 \end{cases}$$

we can substitute $x_2 = x'$, and $x_1 = x$. Then we get:

$$\begin{cases} x_1' = x_2 \\ x_2' = f(x_1, x_2, t) \\ x_1(t_0) = x_0 \\ x_2(t_0) = xp_0 \end{cases}$$

which is a system of ODEs of the first order.

Numerical solution of an initial value problem for a certain time interval $0 \leq t \leq T$ means dividing the time into a finite set of discrete time points, e.g., with intervals of the same size Δt:

$$t_i = i \Delta t, \quad i = 0, \dots, N$$

where the time step $\Delta t = T/N$ for some integer N. The derivatives are replaced by **differential quotients** resulting in **difference equations** that describe the solution at the different time levels. See Example 11.2 on the numerical solution of initial value problems for more information on finite difference quotients. The stability of the method depends on the size of Δt and the numerical method, i.e., in which way the ODE has been approximated.

In many applications there are **stiff differential equations**, that in some areas demand a very small time step Δt. The difficulty in solving these problems is due to the different time scales involved in the problem, i.e., the derivatives of the solutions may have large variations.

MATLAB uses **Runge–Kutta–Fehlberg methods** to solve ODE problems. The solution is computed in a finite number of points where the spacing depends on the solution itself.

Fewer points are used in intervals where the solution is smooth and more points where the solution varies rapidly.

For more information on when to use which solver and which algorithms are used, we recommend you to use `helpdesk`. The syntax is the same for all solvers and is given on the first two rows in Commands 108 where `solver` represents the ODE solver to be used. The time interval is given as a vector `t = [t0 tt]`.

The command `ode23` solves a system of ordinary differential equations with an order of accuracy (2, 3), and the function `ode45` uses a Runge–Kutta–Fehlberg method with an order of accuracy (4, 5). Note that in this case, $\mathbf{x}'$ has the meaning of the derivative of $\mathbf{x}$, not the conjugate of $\mathbf{x}$.

In Commands 108 *solver* is to be replaced by the method, e.g. `ode45`, one wishes to use.

| Commands 108 | RUNGE–KUTTA–FEHLBERG METHODS |

`[time,X] =` `solver(str,t,x0)`	computes the solution of the ODE, or the system of ODEs given by the string **str**. The solution is given partly in the vectors **time**, which contains the time values, and partly in the matrix **X**, whose columns are the solutions of each equation in these values. For a scalar problem the solution is given in the vector **X**. Solutions are computed from the time $\mathbf{t}(1)$ to $\mathbf{t}(2)$, and the initial value is $\mathbf{x0}$, i.e., $\mathbf{x}(\mathbf{t}(1))$. The system is described by the function in the M-file given by **str**. This function should take two arguments, the scalar t and the vector $\mathbf{x}$, and should return the vector $\mathbf{x}'$ (the derivative of $\mathbf{x}$). For a scalar ODE $\mathbf{x}$ and $\mathbf{x}'$ are scalars. Type `odefile` for more information on the M-files. See also the `numjac` command which computes the Jacobian of a function numerically.

`[t,X] =`
`solver(str,t,`
`x0,val)`
	works like above. The struct **val** contains instructions from the user to the solver. See odeset and Table 11.1 for more information.

`ode45`	is recommended as a first method to try.
`ode23`	is a method of lower order than `ode45`.
`ode113`	is used for higher order of accuracy or large scale computations.
`ode23t`	solves moderately stiff problems.
`ode23s`	solves stiff differential equations. It is also useful when there is a constant mass matrix in the system.
`ode15s`	as `ode23s` but with a higher accuracy.
`ode23tb`	solves stiff problems. It is also useful when there is a constant mass matrix in the system.

Commands 108   (CONTINUED)

set = odeset(set1,val1, set2,val2, ...)	returns the struct **set** with settings that can be used for the ODE solvers. See Table 11.1 for information on which settings that are available.
odeget(set, 'set1')	returns the value of the setting *set1* in the struct **set**.

There are a lot of settings available for the ODE solvers that are controlled by odeset, see Table 11.1. For example if one wants the solution plotted during the computation one gives inst = odeset('OutputFcn','odeplot');.

Table 11.1   SETTINGS FOR THE ODE SOLVERS

RelTol	gives the relative error tolerance for the solvers.
AbsTol	gives the absolute error tolerance for the solvers.
Refine	gives a factor with which the number of output points are multiplied.
OutputFcn	is a string with the name of a output function called by the solver after each time step: odephas2 (plot phase plane 2D), odephas3 (plot phase plane 3D), odeplot (plot solution), odeprint (print intermediate results).
OutputSel	is an integer vector that tells which elements of the answer that should be sent to the function specified by OutputFnc.
Stats	if Stats is on statistics are shown on the cost of the computations.
Jacobian	sets Jacobian on if the ODE-file is coded so that F(t,y,'jacobian') returns dF/dy.
JConstant	sets JConstant on if the Jacobian df/dy is constant.
JPattern	sets JPattern on if the ODE-file is coded so that F([],[],'jpattern') returns a sparse matrix with zeros showing non-zero elements dF/dy.
Vectorized	sets Vectorized on if the ODE-file is coded so that F(t,[y1 y2 ...]) returns [F(t,y1) F(t,y2) ...].
Events	sets Events on if the ODE-file has functions with 'events' in the argument.
Mass	sets Mass to on if the ODE-file is coded so that F(t,[],'mass') returns M or $M(t)$.
MassConstant	sets MassConstant to on if the mass matrix $M(t)$ is constant.
MaxStep	is a scalar for the upper limit of the step length the solver may use.

Table 11.1	(CONTINUED)
`InitialStep`	is a scalar that gives the initial step length. If this gives too large an error the solver uses a smaller step.
`MaxOrder`	is only used by `ode15s`. Should be an integer from one to five giving the highest order of `ode15s`.
`BDF`	is only used by `ode15s`. Sets BDF on if the backward difference formulas are to be used instead of the numerical difference formulas normally used.
`NormControl`	sets `NormControl` on if the solver should control the error in every integration step according to `norm(e) <= max(RelTol*norm(y),AbsTol)`.

Try also the command `odedemo`.

■ Example 11.2

(a) To solve the following ODE:

$$\begin{cases} x' = -x^2 \\ x(0) = 1 \end{cases}$$

we create the function *xprim1*, stored in the M-file **xprim1.m:**

```
function xprim = xprim1(t,x)

xprim = -x.^2;
```

Then we call MATLAB's ODE solver and finally we plot the solution:

```
[t,x] = ode45('xprim1',[0 1],1);

plot(t,x,'-',t,x,'o');
xlabel('time t0 = 0, tt = 1');
ylabel('x values x(0) = 1');
```

and get Figure 11.2. MATLAB has computed the solution marked with circles. The `plot` command is presented in Section 13.1.

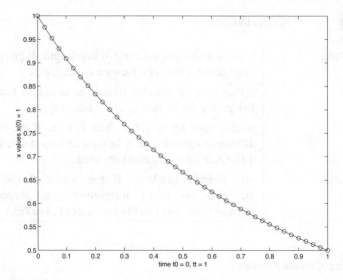

Figure 11.2 *The solution of the ODE defined by the function* ***xprim1***.

(b) The procedure for solving the following ODE is equivalent:

$$\begin{cases} x' = x^2 \\ x(0) = 1 \end{cases}$$

First we create the function *xprim2* stored in the M-file **xprim2.m:**

```
function xprim = xprim2(t,x)


xprim = x.^2;
```

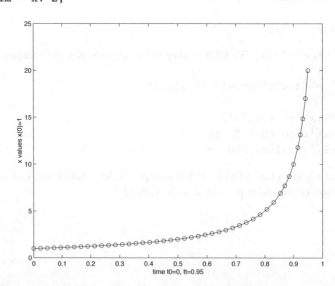

Figure 11.3 *The solution of the ODE defined by the function* ***xprim2***.

Then we call the ODE solver and plot the result:

```
[t,x] = ode45('xprim2',[0 0.95],1);
```

```
plot(t,x,'o',t,x,'-');
xlabel('time t0=0, tt=0.95');
ylabel('x values x(0)=1');
```

and obtain Figure 11.3.

Note that the points where MATLAB computes the solution are denser in the area where the absolute value of the derivative is large.

(c) To solve

$$\begin{cases} x' = x^2 \\ x(0) = -1 \end{cases}$$

the same function as in (b) above can be used. We only have to change the initial data:

```
[t,x] = ode45('xprim2',[0 1],-1);
```

```
plot(t,x);
xlabel('time t0 = 0, tt = 1');
ylabel('x values x(0) = -1');
```

This gives Figure 11.4.

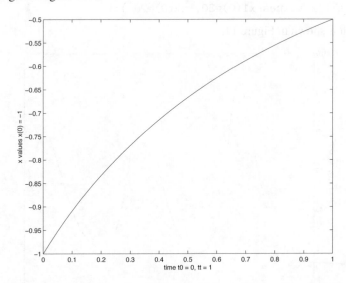

Figure 11.4 *The solution to the ODE defined by* **xprim2**, *with new initial data.*

(d) To solve the following system is not much harder:

$$\begin{cases} x_1' = x_1 - 0.1x_1x_2 + 0.01t \\ x_2' = -x_2 + 0.02x_1x_2 + 0.04t \\ x_1(0) = 30 \\ x_2(0) = 20 \end{cases}$$

This system occurs in population dynamics and can be regarded as a simplified prey–predator model, e.g., for foxes and rabbits. The prey is represented by x_1 and the predators by x_2. If the prey have unlimited amount of food and no predators are present, we have $x_1' = x_1$, that is exponential growth. A large amount of prey increases the amount of predators and few predators increase the amount of prey. Moreover, both populations are considered to increase in time. These non-linear differential equations were developed by Lotka and Volterra during the 1920s.

We create the function *xprim3*, stored in the M-file **xprim3.m**:

```
function xprim = xprim3(t,x)

xprim   = [ x(1) - 0.1*x(1)*x(2)  + 0.01*t; ...
            -x(2) + 0.02*x(1)*x(2)  + 0.04*t];
```

then we make a call to the ODE-solver and plot the result:

```
[t,x] = ode45('xprim3',[0 20],[30; 20]);
```

```
plot(t,x);
xlabel('time t0=0, tt=20');
ylabel('x values x1(0)=30, x2(0)=20');
```

which is shown in Figure 11.5.

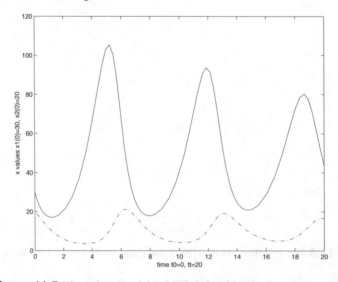

Figure 11.5 *The solution of the ODE defined by the function* ***xprim3***.

It is also possible to plot x_1 as a function of x_2 in MATLAB. The command plot(x(:,2),x(:,1)) displays the phase–plane plot shown in Figure 11.6.

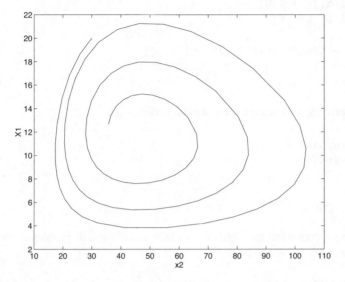

Figure 11.6 *The solution x_1 of the ODE defined by* **xprim3** *as a function of* x_2

■

■ **Example 11.3**

The following system is stiff for some values of a and b:

$$\begin{cases} x_1' = a - (b+1)x_1 + x_1^2 x_2 \\ x_2' = bx_1 - x_1^2 x_2 \\ x_1^0 = 1 \\ x_2^0 = 3 \end{cases}$$

The equations are defined by an M-file **stiff1.m** which looks like this:

```
function stiff = stiff1(t, x)

global a;               % Variables cannot be sent in the
global b;               % argument list.
stiff = [0;0];          % Stiff must be a colon vector

stiff(1) = a - (b+1)*x(1) + x(1)^2*x(2);
stiff(2) = b*x(1) - x(1)^2*x(2);
```

The following M-file gives us a stiff problem:

```
global a; a = 100;
global b; b = 1;
tic;
[t,X] = ode23('stiff1',[0 10],[1 3]);
toc
size(t)
```

A run gave the following computational performance:

```
elapsed_time =
   72.1647


ans =
      34009                1
```

With the solver ode23s, which is specially made for stiff problems, we get better performance:

```
elapsed_time =
    1.0098


ans =
    103        1
```

For **boundary value problems** we have, besides the differential equation, values prescibed at the boundaries. In one dimension this means at least two conditions. We show two examples below:

- Suppose we want to study the temperature distribution in a rod with the temperature T_0 in one end and T_1 in the other end; see Figure 11.7.

  Let $y(x)$ represent the temperature in the rod and let the function $f(x)$ be an external source of heat warming the rod.

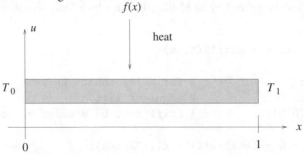

Figure 11.7 *Temperature distribution in a rod.*

We start at time $t = 0$ and let the heat spread in the rod for a long time. After some time an equilibrium that does not depend on time is reached. This is called a stationary solution or steady state. This stationary solution may be represented by the following model equation:

$$\begin{cases} -y''(x) = f(x), & 0 < x < 1 \\ y(0) = T_0 \\ y(1) = T_1 \end{cases}$$

where we suppose that the ends of the rod are at $x = 0$ and $x = 1$.

- Suppose that we have a beam firmly fastened at its ends (or a bridge connecting two islands); see Figure 11.8.

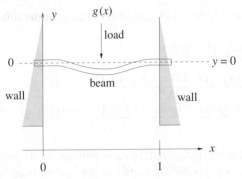

Figure 11.8 *Load on a beam or heavy traffic on a bridge.*

Let $y(x)$ represent the bending of the beam when under a load of the function $g(x)$. The problem demands two boundary conditions to be given at each end of the beam. We suppose that the beam extends a good bit into the wall and is firmly fastened, i.e., the derivative of y at the wall is zero. We get an ODE of the following kind, where we have introduced a natural coordinate system:

$$\begin{cases} y''''(x) = g(x), & 0 < x < 1 \\ y(0) = y'(0) = y(1) = y'(1) = 0 \end{cases}$$

Since the solution of the boundary value problem already exists on the boundary it is not possible to solve the problem by taking one step at a time, as with initial value problems. One therefore has to solve a system of equations that give us all of the unknown variables simultaneously.

Suppose that we have an ODE to which the function $y(x)$ is the solution. This ODE problem is solved numerically by replacing the differential equation with a **difference approximation**. To do this one divides the interval into a finite number of points $x_0, x_1, \ldots, x_M$, where $x_{j+1} = x_j + \Delta x$, and then tries to compute the approximations $y_j \approx y(x_j)$ in the interior points of the area, given certain boundary values, e.g., y_0 and y_M, or more; see Figure 11.9.

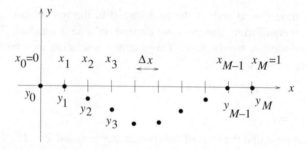

Figure 11.9 *Dividing the area of computation* $[0, 1]$ *into M intervals.*

The derivatives of the solution $y(x)$ may be replaced by **finite differences**, e.g.,

$$
\begin{cases}
y'(x_j) \approx \dfrac{y(x_{j+1}) - y(x_j)}{\Delta x} \\[2mm]
y''(x_j) \approx \dfrac{y(x_{j+1}) - 2y(x_j) + y(x_{j-1})}{\Delta x^2} \\[2mm]
y''''(x_j) \approx \dfrac{y(x_{j+2}) - 4y(x_{j+1}) + 6y(x_j) - 4y(x_{j-1}) + y(x_{j-2})}{\Delta x^4}
\end{cases}
$$

If we replace the derivatives in the ODE by these differences, we get a system of equations for all unknown y_j. The coefficient matrix of the system is of band form, where the width of the band depends on how many derivatives the differential equation has.

■ **Example 11.4**

Let's study the temperature distribution in a rod according to the equation on page 225. We replace the derivatives with divided differences and get:

$$
\begin{cases}
-\dfrac{y_{j+1} - 2y_j + y_{j-1}}{\Delta x^2} = f_j, \quad j = 1, \ldots, M \\[2mm]
y_0 = T_0 \\[1mm]
y_M = T_1
\end{cases}
$$

where $f_j = f(x_j)$. Suppose that, for simplicity, $M = 6$, i.e., y_0 and y_6 are given and $y_1, y_2, \ldots, y_5$ are the unknown variables. We now get:

$$
\begin{cases}
-y_0 + 2y_1 - y_2 = \Delta x^2 f_1 \\
-y_1 + 2y_2 - y_3 = \Delta x^2 f_2 \\
-y_2 + 2y_3 - y_4 = \Delta x^2 f_3 \\
-y_3 + 2y_4 - y_5 = \Delta x^2 f_4 \\
-y_4 + 2y_5 - y_6 = \Delta x^2 f_5
\end{cases}
$$

Note that $y_0 = T_0$ and $y_M = T_1$ have to be moved to the right side of the system. On matrix form we have a tridiagonal system with diagonal elements equal to 2 and the elements on the upper and lower bidiagonals are equal to 1.

$$\begin{pmatrix} 2 & -1 & 0 & 0 & 0 \\ -1 & 2 & -1 & 0 & 0 \\ 0 & -1 & 2 & -1 & 0 \\ 0 & 0 & -1 & 2 & -1 \\ 0 & 0 & 0 & -1 & 2 \end{pmatrix} \begin{pmatrix} y_1 \\ y_2 \\ y_3 \\ y_4 \\ y_5 \end{pmatrix} = \begin{pmatrix} \Delta x^2 f_1 + T_0 \\ \Delta x^2 f_2 \\ \Delta x^2 f_3 \\ \Delta x^2 f_4 \\ \Delta x^2 f_5 + T_1 \end{pmatrix}$$

Below we show the file **temperature.m** that solves the problem. The user must first give the number of intervals, then $f(x)$ (using point notation) and finally T_0 and T_1. See Chapter 9 for more information on sparse matrices.

```
% Temperature distribution in a rod with teperature T0 and T1
% at the left and right end point respectively.
% The rod, located between 0 and 1 on the x-axis,
% is divided into M subintervals, each of length 1/M.
% The sparse system Ax=b is created and solved.
% The matrix A is tridiagonal and stored as a sparse matrix.

clear;

M = input('Give the number of subintervals (M): ');
deltax = 1/M;
xx = 0:deltax:1;

funcStr = input('Give f(x),
            the extra heat source (e.g., x.^3): ', 's' );

T0 = input('Give y(0) (left):  ');
T1 = input('Give y(1) (right): ');

% Build the tridiagonal matrix A and the right hand side b.

vectorOnes = ones(M-1,1);
A = spdiags([-vectorOnes, 2*vectorOnes, -vectorOnes],
            [-1 0 1],M-1,M-1);

x = xx(2:end-1);      % x-values in inner part of the region.
f = eval(funcStr);    % Corresponding f(x)-values.

b = deltax^2*f;
```

```
b(1)    = b(1)    + T0; % Special treatment at boundaries x=0, x=1.
b(end) = b(end) + T1;
b = b';
```

```
% Solve the linear equation.
```

```
y = A\b;              % y in the inner region: j = 1, 2, ..., M-1.
y = [T0;y;T1];        % y in the entire region 0 <= x <=1.
```

```
clf;
```

```
% Upper plot: The external heat source.
% Lower plot: The heat distribution in the rod.
```

```
subplot(2,1,1);
plot(x,f);
grid on;
title('External heat source f(x).', 'FontSize', 14 );
```

```
subplot(2,1,2);
plot(xx,y,'r');
grid on;
title('Temperature distribution in a rod.', 'FontSize', 14);
```

With 100 intervals and $f(x) = x^2 + sin(10\pi x)$ we get the result in Figure 11.10.

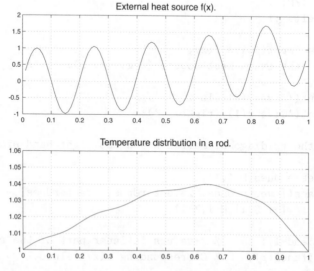

Figure 11.10 *The result of the boundary value problem: temperature distribution of a rod.*

■ Example 11.5

If we replace the derivatives in the beam example on page 225, i.e., where the solution is approximated with y_j, we get:

$$\begin{cases} \dfrac{y_{j+2} - 4y_{j+1} + 6y_j - 4y_{j-1} + y_{j-2}}{\Delta x^4} = g_j, & j = 2, \ldots, M - 2 \\ y_0 = \dfrac{y_1 - y_0}{\Delta x} = y_M = \dfrac{y_M - y_{M-1}}{\Delta x} = 0, \end{cases}$$

which we rewrite as:

$$\begin{cases} y_{j+2} - 4y_{j+1} + 6y_j - 4y_{j-1} + y_{j-2} = \Delta x^4 g_j, & j = 2, \ldots, M - 2 \\ y_0 = y_1 = y_{M-1} = y_M = 0 \end{cases}$$

This is really a linear system of equations with $M - 3$ equations to solve for $M - 3$ unknown $y_2, y_3, \ldots, y_{M-2}$. If $M = 10$ we get:

$$\begin{pmatrix} 6 & -4 & 1 & 0 & 0 & 0 & 0 \\ -4 & 6 & -4 & 1 & 0 & 0 & 0 \\ 1 & -4 & 6 & -4 & 1 & 0 & 0 \\ 0 & 1 & -4 & 6 & -4 & 1 & 0 \\ 0 & 0 & 1 & -4 & 6 & -4 & 1 \\ 0 & 0 & 0 & 1 & -4 & 6 & -4 \\ 0 & 0 & 0 & 0 & 1 & -4 & 6 \end{pmatrix} \begin{pmatrix} y_2 \\ y_3 \\ y_4 \\ y_5 \\ y_6 \\ y_7 \\ y_8 \end{pmatrix} = \Delta x^4 \begin{pmatrix} g_2 \\ g_3 \\ g_4 \\ g_5 \\ g_6 \\ g_7 \\ g_8 \end{pmatrix}$$

The result is a five-diagonal band matrix and the system is solved fast and efficiently with the \ operator.

■

Programming in MATLAB

12

MATLAB contains several commands to control the execution of MATLAB statements, such as conditional statements, loops, and commands supporting user interaction. In this chapter we describe these facilities. MATLAB can be seen as a high-level programming language, enabling the user to solve matrix problems and other problems. Users who are acquainted with other programming languages, such as Pascal, C++, or FORTRAN, have an advantage, but we feel confident that the material can be understood by all readers.

12.1 Conditional statements

Decisions in MATLAB are made with `if`. The basic form of an `if` statement is:

```
if logical expression
    statements
end
```

Note that a space is required between `if` and *logical expression*. The *statements* refer to one single command or several commands separated by commas, semicolons, or 'returns'. These commands are only executed if the logical expression is **true**. A logical expression can be a scalar, a vector or a matrix, and a logical expression is **true** if all its elements are non-zero.

An `if` statement can be written in a single line:

```
    if logical expression, statements, end
```

However, the former formulation is usually preferable, making the MATLAB program more structured and easy to read.

■ **Example 12.1**

Suppose an $m \times n$ matrix **A** is defined. The following statements remove the first column of **A** if all the elements of the first column are zero:

```
if A(:,1) == 0
  A = A(1:m,2:n)
end
```

or written in a single row:

```
if A(:,1) == 0, A = A(1:m,2:n), end
```

∎

The `if` statement can be used in more complex contexts in combination with `elseif` and `else`. There are many structures possible:

> if *logical expression*
>   *statements 1*
> else
>   *statements 2*
> end

The commands of *statements 1* are executed if the *logical expression* is **true**, and the commands of *statements 2* if it is **false**.

Consider the following `if` statement

> if *logical expression 1*
>   *statements 1*
> elseif *logical expression 2*
>   *statements 2*
> end

The *statements 1* are executed if *logical expression 1* is **true**, while the *statements 2* are executed if *logical expression 1* is **false** and *logical expression 2* is **true**.

Note that `elseif` must be written as a single word, since it is interpreted differently if written `else if`. The command `elseif` does not require an extra end, as the command `else if` does.

Another example of how `if` statements can be nested is as follows:

> if *logical expression 1*
>   *statements 1*
> elseif *logical expression 2*
>   *statements 2*
> else
>   *statements 3*
> end

and an even more complex construction:

```
if logical expression 1
    statements 1
    if logical expression 2
        statements 2
    else
        statements 3
    end
else
    statements 4
end
```

■ Example 12.2

(a) Solve the system $\mathbf{Ax} = \mathbf{b}$ if $\mathbf{A}$ is non-singular, otherwise determine the reduced row echelon form of the enlarged matrix $(\mathbf{A} \quad \mathbf{b})$. Hint: a matrix is non-singular if it is square and has full rank.

```
% Given some matrix A and right-hand side b.

s = size(A)

if (s(1) == s(2)) & (rank(A) == s(1))
    x = A\b
else
    rref([A b])
end
```

(b) If the determinant of the matrix $\mathbf{A}$ is zero, compute how many eigenvalues are zero:

```
if det(A) == 0
    length(find(eig(A) == 0))
end
```

■

Another kind of conditional statement is the `switch-case` statement, as follows:

```
switch logical expression (scalar or string)
case value 1
    expression 1
case value 2
    expression 2
...
otherwise
    expression
end
```

The *logical expression* is calculated and gives a scalar or string as a result. This result is then compared to *value 1, value 2, ...* and if they match the corresponding *expression* under case is performed. If no match is found the statement under otherwise is performed.

If the result of *expression* is a scalar, then the test: *expression* == *value* is performed to decide which expression to execute. If the result is a string, then the test: strcmp(*expression, value*) is performed. If a test is true the corresponding expression is executed and the following cases are ignored.

One may let the case testing be a comparison between different values by placing the different values in a cell matrix; see Example 12.3.

■ **Example 12.3**

We perform a test to see whether the number of eyes on a dice is odd or even:

```
function dicetest(result)

switch result
case {1,3,5}
  disp('odd number of eyes')
case {2,4,6}
  disp('even number of eyes')
otherwise
  disp('What kind of dice do you have?')

end
```

When we run this function we may get the following:

```
dicetest(1)

odd number of eyes

dicetest(4)

even number of eyes

dicetest(7)

What kind of dice do you have?
```

■

If there is a risk that a statement will malfunction, one may use the combination try/catch which has the following form:

```
try
    expression 1
catch
    expression 2
end
```

MATLAB starts to execute *expression 1*, but if there is an error, the error message is stored in lasterr and *expression 2* is executed.

12.2 Loops

MATLAB has two commands, **for** and **while**, for repeated execution of statements. These add the flexibility to execute statements once or several times under logical control.

The command for is like do or for commands in most programming languages, which means repeating a statement or group of statements a predefined number of times. An end finishes the group of statements.

The general syntax of a for loop is:

```
for variable = expression
    statements
end
```

Just like the if statement, a for statement can be written in a single line:

```
for variable = expression, statements, end
```

A blank is required between for and *variable*. Here, *variable* is the name of the loop variable. The expression assigns an initial value, an incremental value, and a final value of the loop variable. The incremental value can be negative or left out. If left out, the loop variable is increased by 1 in each iteration. Usually, the colon notation is used to define the *expression*, for instance i:j:k or i:j; see Section 4.3.

The columns of the expression are stored in the loop variable one by one. Thus it is possible to have a matrix as the expression. For instance, the following statement:

```
for v = A, ..., end
```

is equivalent to:

```
for j = 1:n, v = A(:,j); ..., end
```

When the expression is written with colon notation the columns are scalars, for example in the MATLAB statement for `v = i:j:k`.

Loops can be nested:

```
for variable I = expression A
    statements 1
    for variable II = expression B
        statements 2
    end
    statements 3
end
```

■ Example 12.4

(a) The following matrix with three non-zero diagonals (a tridiagonal matrix):

$$A = \begin{pmatrix} 5 & 1 & 0 & 0 & 0 \\ 1 & 5 & 1 & 0 & 0 \\ 0 & 1 & 5 & 1 & 0 \\ 0 & 0 & 1 & 5 & 1 \\ 0 & 0 & 0 & 1 & 5 \end{pmatrix}$$

can be created using the command `for` repeatedly, which looks much like it would in any standard programming language:

```
A = [];

for k = 1:5
  for j = 1:5

    if k == j
       A(k,k) = 5;
    elseif abs(k-j) == 1
       A(k,j) = 1;
    else
       A(k,j) = 0;
    end

  end
end
```

The semicolon, ';', is vital here. If we write these assignments without the semicolon, the matrix **A** is written on the screen 25 times, every time an element of **A** is assigned a value.

This is also an example of how inefficient careless use of for loops can be. With the help of timing one may see how much of the calculation time is spent on, e.g., for loops; see Example 12.21. The following commands accomplish the same thing as above, but are much more efficient:

```
A = zeros(5);

for k = 1:4
  A(k,k) = 5;
  A(k,k+1) = 1;
  A(k+1,k) = 1;
end

A(5,5) = 5;
```

This matrix can be obtained in an even more compact and efficient way, yet much clearer, using the command diag:

```
A = [];

A = diag(5*ones(5,1)) + diag(ones(4,1),1) + ...
       diag(ones(4,1),-1);
```

It should be added that a large matrix with this type of structure should be created as a sparse matrix; see Chapter 9.

(b) Let us generate a table of the function $y = f(x) = 1 + 1/x$ evaluated in the interval $[-2, -0.75]$ in steps of 0.25. Store the x and y values in the vectors **r** and **s**, respectively, and display the results in a table:

```
r = []; s = [];

for x = -2.0:0.25:-0.75
  y = 1 + 1/x;
  r = [r x];
  s = [s y];
end

[r; s]'
```

Again this table could, and probably should, be generated without using a for loop. The result is:

```
ans =
    -2.0000      0.5000
    -1.7500      0.4286
    -1.5000      0.3333
    -1.2500      0.2000
    -1.0000           0
    -0.7500     -0.3333
```

(c) The MATLAB command sum(A) gives a row vector containing the sum of elements of the columns of the matrix **A**. A similar result can be obtained with the
following program:

```
A = [1 2 3;4 5 6]

sum_v = [];

for v = A
   sum_v = [sum_v sum(v)]
end

disp('Compare w/ sum(A):');
disp(sum(A));
```

which results in:

```
A =
    1     2     3
    4     5     6


sum_v =
    5


sum_v =
    5     7


sum_v =
    5     7     9


Compare w/ sum(A):
    5     7     9
```

(d) Let us store the following MATLAB commands in the file **qrmethod.m**:

```
% The matrix A, the integers m and n, should be
% defined prior to calling this file.
% The QR-method is applied after transformation
% to upper Hessenberg. Stop after n steps.
% Display the result every m:th step.
```

```
A = hess(A);

for i = 1:n
  [Q,R] = qr(A);
  A = R*Q;
  nd = norm(diag(A,-1));

  if rem(i,m) == 0
    A, i, nd
  end

end
```

The following commands now perform the unshifted QR method (see Section 8.2) with 30 iterations, presenting the result every 15th iteration:

```
A0 = [-9 -3 -16;13 7 16;3 3 10 ];
m = 15; n = 30;
format long;
A = A0;
qrmethod;

A =
   9.98997467074377   22.62301237506363  -15.53274662438004
   0.00708686385759   -5.98568512552925    5.77401643542405
                  0    0.00741470005235    3.99571045478546

i =
    15

nd =
   0.01025677416162

A =
  10.00000471624660   22.62743993744967   15.51339551121122
  -0.00000333488655   -6.00001449452640   -5.77348898879412
                  0    0.00001693654612    4.00000977827978

i =
    30

nd =
    1.726175143943722e-05
```

(e) In Section 7.5 the command `planerot` is defined. This algorithm uses that command to return a matrix that zeros all elements below the main diagonal of any matrix of size $m \times n$ given as an input argument.

```
function B = Givens(A)
%
% A of size m x n will be reduced to an upper triangular
% matrix if we multiply with B, the matrix that this
% function returns. That is, this function can be used to
% QR-factorize A according to Q = B' and R = B * A
% so that Q * R = A.

[m,n] = size(A);
B     = eye(m);

for j = 1:n
  for i = j:m
    for k = (i+1):m
        G      = eye(m);
        Plan   = planerot([A(j,j) A(k,j)]');
                                    % Find 2x2 matrix.
        G(j,j) = Plan(1,1); G(k,j) = Plan(2,1);
        G(j,k) = Plan(1,2); G(k,k) = Plan(2,2);
                              % Place correctly in mxm matrix.

        B = G*B;
        A = G*A ;        % <- To see the step-by-step reduction
                         % of AA remove this semicolon.
    end
  end
end
```

The algorithm zeros one element below the main diagonal for each step of the inner loop by making a 2×2 matrix out of two elements in **A**. The resulting matrix can be used to create a QR factorization.

Let us define a test matrix **Atest** as:

$$\textbf{Atest} = \begin{pmatrix} 1 & 2 & 3 & 1 & 2 & 3 \\ 4 & 4 & 1 & 2 & 2 & 1 \\ 7 & 6 & 3 & 2 & 1 & 1 \\ 1 & 2 & 1 & 0 & 0 & 2 \end{pmatrix}$$

The following commands:

```
Atest = [1 2 3 1 2 3;4 4 1 2 2 1;
         7 6 3 2 1 1;1 2 1 0 0 2];

Giv = Givens(Atest);
Q   = Giv', R = Giv*Atest
QR = Q*R                        % Just checking!
```

will give the MATLAB output:

Q =

0.1222	0.6630	0.6674	0.3162
0.4887	0.1842	-0.5721	0.6325
0.8552	-0.2947	0.2860	-0.3162
0.1222	0.6630	-0.3814	-0.6325

R =

8.1854	7.5745	3.5429	2.8099	2.0769	1.9547
0.0000	1.6208	1.9523	0.4420	1.3997	3.2047
-0.0000	-0.0000	1.9069	0.0953	0.4767	0.9535
0.0000	0.0000	0.0000	0.9487	1.5811	0.0000

QR =

1.0000	2.0000	3.0000	1.0000	2.0000	3.0000
4.0000	4.0000	1.0000	2.0000	2.0000	1.0000
7.0000	6.0000	3.0000	2.0000	1.0000	1.0000
1.0000	2.0000	1.0000	0	0	2.0000

Note that by multiplying Q and R we get the original matrix **Atest** back, hence **QR = Atest**.

(f) The following program builds a snowflake by using two `for` loops and the complex plane. The algorithm generates Helge von Koch's curve, which is an example of a fractal. The program contains some graphical commands that are defined in Chapter 13 but the comments explain briefly what happens. The algorithm divides each side of the current geometrical figure in three equal parts. The first and the last part are sides to the new geometry. The middle part is replaced by two sides of an equilateral triangle; see Figure 12.1.

Figure 12.1 *Two iterations on a line with the von Koch algorithm.*

If we let the iteration go on forever almost every part of a plane would be covered; in fact the fractal has the dimension 1.2619, a little more than just one but less than two.

```
% File: Koch.m
% This program plots Helge von Koch's snowflake, a fractal.

clear;                    % Deletes old variables.

% Vector new defines a triangle in the
% complex plane. That is the start geometry.

new = [0.5+(sqrt(3)/2)*i,-0.5+(sqrt(3)/2)*i,...
       0,0.5+(sqrt(3)/2)*i];

plot(new);                % Plots the triangle and
pause(0.5);               % waits 0.5 seconds.

% Iterates five times: Vector old is the previous iteration.

for k = 1:5;
  old = new;
  [m,n] = size(old);
  n = n - 1;

  % There are n-1 sides in the figure defined by old.
  % For each side: Define 4 new points (one is 'old').

  for j = 0:n-1;
    diff = (old(j+2)-old(j+1))/3;
    new(4*j+1) = old(j+1);
    new(4*j+2) = old(j+1) + diff;
    new(4*j+3) = new(4*j+2) + diff*((1-sqrt(3)*i)/2);
    new(4*j+4) = old(j+1) + 2*diff;
  end;

  % Last element of vector new is same as last element in old.

  new(4*n+1) = old(n+1);

  plot(new);              % Plots the new figure
  pause(0.5);             % and waits 0.5 seconds.
end;

% The last line makes the plot more 'neat' by removing
% the axis and making them equal.

axis off; axis square;
```

Executing this program will result in a figure that gradually becomes more complex.

In Figure 12.2 we see the final plot.

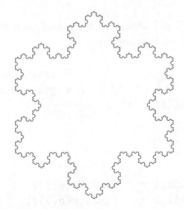

Figure 12.2 *Helge von Koch's fractal after* 5 *iterations. The original geometry was a triangle.*

■

The command `while` repeats statements as long as a logical expression is true. The construction is terminated with an `end`, just like the `for` statement. We use the term `while` loop to denote the whole `while` statement, that is:

> `while`, *statements*, `end`

The general `while` loop has the form:

> `while` *logical expression*
> > *statements*
>
> `end`

and a single line `while` loop looks like:

> `while` *logical expression, statements*, `end`

While loops can be nested like `for` loops:

> `while` *logical expression A*
> > *statements 1*
> > `while` *logical expression B*
> > > *statements 2*
> >
> > `end`
> > *statements 3*
>
> `end`

■ Example 12.5

(a) Construct a random 2×2 matrix with eigenvalues between -1 and 1. This can be carried out with the following iterations:

```
A = rand(2);                    % Constructs a matrix with
                                % eigenvalues in [-1,1].
while max(abs(eig(A))) >= 1
  A = rand(2);
end

e = eig(A);
TheText = ['lambda_1 = ',num2str(e(1)), ...
           ', lambda_2 = ',num2str(e(2))];

A                               % Shows the resulting matrix
disp(TheText)                   % and eigenvalues.
```

When the program is executed, we get:

```
A =
    0.1517    0.6628
    0.2098    0.5295

lambda_1 = -0.077395, lambda_2 = 0.7586
```

where the variables `lambda_1` and `lambda_2` are the eigenvalues of the resulting matrix **A**.

A variable can be added to count the number of iterations. Note that a different result will be recieved if the program is executed once more.

```
A = rand(2); niter = 1;

while max(abs(eig(A))) >= 1
  disp(['Step ' num2str(niter)]);
  disp(['Eigenvalues: ' num2str(eig(A)', 5)]);
  A = rand(2);
  niter = niter + 1;
end

disp(['Final result - step ' num2str(niter)]);
disp(['Eigenvalues: ' num2str(eig(A)', 5)]);
```

resulting in:

```
Step 1
Eigenvalues: 1.3871    -0.41031
Step 2
Eigenvalues: -0.18924     1.2166
Step 3
Eigenvalues: 1.0151    -0.11415
Final result - step 4
Eigenvalues: 0.054835     0.95675
```

(b) The MacLaurin series of the function $\ln(1 + x)$ is

$$\ln(1 + x) = \sum_{k=1}^{\infty} \frac{(-1)^{k+1} x^k}{k}$$

Estimate $\ln(1 + x)$, with $x = 0.5$ by adding terms in the MacLaurin series until the next term to be added is smaller than the built-in variable *eps*. Count the number of terms. This can be carried out in the following way:

```
lnsum = 0; x = 0.5; k = 1;

while abs((x^k)/k) >= eps
  lnsum = lnsum + ((-1)^(k+1))*((x^k)/k);
  k = k + 1;
end

disp(['The sum = ',num2str(lnsum),...
      ', number of iter = ',num2str(k) ]);
```

which gives the result:

```
The sum = 0.40547, number of iter = 47
```

We verify this result with:

```
ln = log(1.5)

ln =
    0.4055
```

■

Sometimes it is useful to quit a loop prior to its natural termination. This can be accomplished with the command break. If break is applied to an inner loop of nested loops, only the inner loop is terminated, and the outer loop or loops continue.

The use of break should be avoided, since a program using the command break is usually difficult to understand and maintain. Such a program can always be rewritten without break:

■ **Example 12.6**

Determine the machine epsilon through iterations.

(a) For loop with the command break:

```
macheps = 1;

for i = 1:1000
  macheps = macheps/2;

  if macheps + 1 <= 1
    break
  end

end

macheps = macheps*2
```

The result on a Sun SPARC station is:

```
macheps =
    2.2204e-16
```

(b) While loop without break:

```
macheps = 1;

while macheps + 1 > 1
  macheps = macheps/2;
end

macheps = macheps*2
```

■

12.3 More about M-files

We introduced M-files in Section 2.9. In this section we cover some additional aspects of M-files.

The inline command makes it possible to create functions without using M-files; see Section 5.1.4.

MATLAB can handle recursive functions. Such a function makes a call to itself possible, but with some criterion changed so that the program does not enter an eternal loop.

■ **Example 12.7**

We have the following M-file named **sqpulse.m** defined:

```
function f = sqpulse(n,x)

% Recursive function for the sum
% 1/2 + 2/pi cos(x pi) + ... + 2sin(n pi/2)cos(n x pi).
% For n --> inf this will be equal to a square pulse.

if (n == 1)
  f = 1/2 + 2/pi*cos(x*pi);             % stop criterion
else
  f = 2*sin(n*pi/2)/n/pi*cos(n*x*pi) + ...
      sqpulse(n-1,x);
end
```

This function will return, if n is large enough, the value 1 for $x \in [-0.5, 0.5]$ and for x that can be made a part of that set by adding an even number, that is $x = -1.75$ will give sqpulse(n,x) = 1 since $-1.75 + 2$ equals 0.25. For all other numbers the function **sqpulse** is zero; see Figure 12.3.

If n is chosen too small the square pulse will be sinusoidal due to the cosine functions that our square pulse is built of.

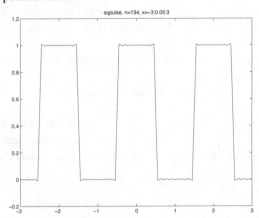

Figure 12.3 *The result of* plot(x, sqpulse(n,x)) *with x and n as in the title.*

■

Comments have been added to many M-files already. They are written after a percentage sign %:

```
% Comment.
```

It's good practice always to add comments to programs, enabling future understanding of what the programs do, and preferably how they do it.

The lookfor command (see Section 2.7) looks through the first comment line in all M-files for a specified text. Thus it can be a good idea to include keywords in the first comments line.

■ **Example 12.8**

```
% Course:      Applied Linear Algebra; Uppsala Univ.
% Assignment: homework #7 - LU-decomposition
% Date:         980505
% Author:       Tomas P.
% File name:    assignment7.m
%------------------------------------------------------------
% diary assignment        % Stores output in file "assignment".

txt1 = ...
    sprintf('\nAssignment #7, Syst. of Eq., T.P. 980505.\n');
txt2 = ...
    sprintf('Ax=b <==> (LU)x=b <==> (i) Ly=b + (ii) Ux=y.\n');

disp([txt1 txt2]);

A = [4 3;1 2];          % Creates system matrix A
b = [5;10];             % and right-hand side vector b.

[L,U] = lu(A);          % LU-decomposition of matrix A.

%L, U                    % Shows L and U.

y = L\b;                % (i) Forward elimination.
x = U\y;                % (ii) Back substutution.
disp('Solution of Ax=b:');   % Writes the resulting vector.
disp(x);

%x2 = A\b                % Check solution.

%diary off
```

gives the result:

```
Assignment #7, Syst. of Eq., T.P. 980505.
Ax=b <==> (LU)x=b <==> (i) Ly=b + (ii) Ux=y.
```

```
Solution of Ax=b:
    -4
     7
```

■

The comment sign, %, may be useful when debugging. By 'commenting away' key commands it is often possible to track down the error; see also Section 12.7.

When MATLAB first executes a function, a compiled version is created that is used the next time the function is called. It is now possible to save this compiled variant on a file, a so called P-file. This P-file can be used in the same way as the M-file, but it is not possible to list it. This may be useful if one wants to hide code:

Commands 109   P-FILES

`pcode fun1 fun2 ...` `-inplace`	compiles the functions **fun1**, **fun2**, ... , and saves these with the same name as **fun1**, **fun2**, ... , but with the suffix '.p'. If -inplace is given the P-files are saved in the same directory as the M-files.
`[M,MEX] = inmem`	returns a cell matrix **M** with strings with the names of the compiled M-files available in the memory. If **MEX** is given a list of loaded MEX-files is also returned; see Section 15.2.1 and Section 15.3.1.

The command echo toggles between echoing or not echoing the commands as they are executed from a command file. When the echo is turned on, all commands and comments are echoed to the screen, which is also very useful in the process of killing bugs. The command echo can also be given explicitly as echo on and echo off.

Function files are not affected by the above. Instead the following holds for function files:

Commands 110   ECHO FROM FUNCTION FILES

`echo fname on`	turns on the echo of the function **fname.m**.
`echo fname off`	turns off the echo of **fname.m**.
`echo fname`	toggles the echo between on and off in the function **fname.m**.
`echo on all`	turns on the echo of all functions.
`echo off all`	turns off the echo of all functions.

Usually all M-files are cleared from the memory with the clear command. The clearing may be controlled with the following commands:

Commands 111   LOCKING OF M-FILES

`mlock`	locks the currently running M-file so that it is not affected by `clear`.
`mlock filename`	locks the M-file **filename**.
`munlock`	unlocks the currently running M-file so that it is cleared if `clear` is called.
`munlock filename`	unlocks the M-file **filename**.
`mislocked` *filename*	returns 1 if the M-file currently running, or, if **filename** is given, the file **filename**, is locked. Else 0 is returned.

A function can have zero, one, or several arguments (parameters), and the same function can also be called with a varied number of arguments. For instance, the function `triu(A)` returns an upper triangular matrix, while `triu(A,1)` returns a strictly upper triangular matrix.

Commands 112   NUMBER OF ARGUMENTS

`nargin`	is a variable containing the number of arguments the function was called with.
`nargout`	is a variable containing the number of return arguments the function was called with.
`inputname(x)`	returns the name of the variable of the input argument in place number x on the inputlist. If instead of a named variable there is an expression an empty string is returned.
`errorstr = nargchk(min, max,number)`	is used to control the number of input arguments of a function. The parameter *number* is the number of input arguments given by `nargin`. If *number* is outside the interval between *min* and *max* an error string **errorstr** is returned, otherwise an empty matrix is returned.
`varargin`	is a cell matrix with an arbitrary number of input arguments to a function.
`varargout`	is a cell matrix with an arbitrary number of output arguments to a function.

■ **Example 12.9**

A variable number of arguments can be used to define default values, that is values to use if nothing else is specified. The function **random** stored in the function **random.m** generates an $m \times n$ matrix with random values of normal distribution. If the expectation value v is not specified then $v = 0$ is used.

```
function A = Random(m,n,v)

% Returns a matrix of size m x n
% with variance 0 and expectation v.
% If v is not specified, use v=0.

if nargin == 2, v = 0; end
A = randn(m,n) + v;
```

The calls

```
A = Random(2,2,4); B = Random(2,2);
```

give the elements of **A** the expectation value 4, and the elements of **B** the expectation value 0.   ∎

Because the cells in a cell matrix do not need to have the same data type the input and output arguments of different types can be packed in the cell matrices **varargin** and **varargout**. An example of this is shown below:

■ Example 12.10

We want to have a function that for an arbitrary number of vectors computes the mean, the median, and the standard deviation for each vector. This can be done in the following way:

```
function [varargout] = stat(varargin)

for i = 1:length(varargin)
  x = varargin{i};     % Pick out the input arguments.
  y.medel = mean(x);   % Save the results in a structure.
  y.median = median(x);
  y.std = std(x);
  varargout{i} = y;    % Put the results in the output arguments.
end
```

In the program above we start with picking one input argument from the cell matrix **varargin**. Then we compute the mean, the median and the standard deviation for this input argument and put these results in the struct **y**. This struct is now put in a cell in the cell matrix **varargout**. When we try this function we may get the following result:

```
a = [1 6 8 9];
b = [42 12 56 72 5 34];
[ares,bres] = stat(a,b)

ares =
    medel: 6
   median: 7
      std: 3.5590

bres =
    medel: 36.8333
   median: 38
      std: 25.5689
```

■

One may mix ordinary input and output arguments with **varargin** and **varargout** but then **varargin** and **varargout** have to be last in each list of arguments. Below follow a couple of examples of different kinds of function heads.

■ **Example 12.11**

The function **test1** takes one argument x and then an arbitrary number of extra arguments. Only one output argument is returned:

```
function y = test1(x,varargin)
```

The function **test2** only takes one input argument. One required output argument and an arbitrary number of extra output arguments are returned:

```
function [y,varargout] = test2(x)
```

■

A function can also have an optional return argument. For instance bar(x,y) plots the elements of the vector **y** at the locations of vector **x** while [xx,yy] = bar(x,y) does not plot anything but returns the vectors **xx** and **yy** such that the command plot(xx,yy) will give the same graph as bar(x,y). More about bar can be found in Section 6.5.

■ **Example 12.12**

We have the M-file **ngon.m** written below. It computes the roots of $c^n = 1$ as default but as an optional input argument the complex number z can be defined and then the roots of $c^n = z$ are computed.

These roots define an *n*-gon in the complex plane. If we do not give any output arguments the polygon will be plotted. If we give one output argument we get a complex vector that defines the corners of the polygon in the complex plane. If we give two output arguments, two real vectors that define the polygon in a plane are returned.

```
function [aa,bb] = ngon(n,z)

% File: ngon.m
% The n roots of c^n = z are the corners
% of an n-gon in the complex plane.
% Then check the number of return values and
% act differently for the case of: none, 1, 2.

% If only one input argument, set z = 1 (default)

if nargin == 1
   z = 1;
end

% The roots are c=re+i*im , k=1:n

k = 1:n;
re = abs(z)*cos((angle(z)+(k-1)*2*pi)/n);
im = abs(z)*sin((angle(z)+(k-1)*2*pi)/n);
xx = [re re(1)]; yy = [im im(1)];

% Check the number of output arguments requested.
% nargout == 0:
%    plot n-gon in a shade of gray depending
%    on the phase angle of z.
% nargout == 1:
%    return complex vector such that plot(cc)
%    draws the outlines of the polygons in the complex plane.
% nargout == 2:
%    return real xx and yy vectors such that
%    plot(xx,yy) draws the outline of the polygon.

if nargout == 0
   patch(xx,yy,[abs(angle(z)/pi) abs(angle(z)/pi)...
                                 abs(angle(z)/pi)])
   axis('equal')
elseif nargout == 1
   aa = xx + yy*i;
else
   aa = xx;
```

```
   bb = yy;
end
```

The command `angle` is introduced in Section 2.4 and `patch` in Section 14.2.11. To see what **ngon** does let us give the following commands:

```
subplot(2,2,1); ngon(5);
```

The upper left corner will be plotted by **ngon**. The equation solved is $c^n = 1$, $n = 5$:

```
subplot(2,2,2); cv = ngon(5,i); plot(cv); axis('equal')
```

The upper right corner is the complex plane with the solutions to $c^n = i$, $n = 5$, as corners of the polygon:

```
subplot(2,2,3); [rv1,rv2] = ngon(5,-1);
plot(rv1,rv2); axis('equal')
```

The lower left corner is a polygon with the solutions to $c^n = -1$, $n = 5$, equal to `rv1+i*rv2`:

```
subplot(2,2,4); ngon(5,-i);
```

The lower right corner shows a polygon whose corners are the solutions of $c^n = -i$, $n = 5$.

The polygons are shown in Figure 12.4. To find the definitions of `subplot` and `plot` see Chapter 13.

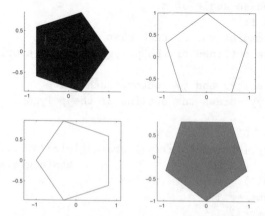

Figure 12.4 *Pentagons created with the user-defined function **ngon**.*

All variables in function files are **local**. Thus, a variable in a function file with the same name as a variable in the MATLAB workspace is a completely different variable, stored at a different memory location. Like all rules, this rule has an exception: global variables can be used in MATLAB.

A **global** variable is accessible in all function files where it is declared global. It is possible to see which variables are declared global with the commands who or whos. To clear global variables; see Section 2.3.

Usually a variable is not persistent between function calls. To make a variable keep its value it has to be declared persistent. How persistent may be used is demonstrated in Example 12.13.

■ **Example 12.13**

We create a function **persdemo**.

```
function persdemo(x)

if x
  persistent TIMESUSED;
  TIMESUSED
end;
if (exist('TIMESUSED','var') & ~isempty(TIMESUSED))
    TIMESUSED = TIMESUSED + 1;
 else
    TIMESUSED = 1;
end;

TIMESUSED

if TIMESUSED < 3
  disp('Keep on calling');
else
  disp('Type clear persdemo to clear persistent value');
end;
```

If we try this function we get:

```
persdemo(1)

TIMESUSED =
    []
TIMESUSED =
    1
Keep on calling
```

```
persdemo(1)
```

TIMESUSED =
 1
TIMESUSED =
 2
Keep on calling

```
persdemo(1)
```

TIMESUSED =
 2
TIMESUSED =
 3
Type clear persdemo to clear persistent value

A call with a 0 as the argument makes **TIMEUSED** to be interpreted as not being persistent.

```
persdemo(0)
```

TIMESUSED =
 1
Keep on calling

```
persdemo(0)
```

TIMESUSED =
 1
Keep on calling

If **persdemo** again is called with **TIMEUSED** as persistent we get:

```
persdemo(1)
```

TIMESUSED =
 3
TIMESUSED =
 4
Type clear persdemo to clear persistent value

To zero the variable it has to be cleared from the memory.

```
clear persdemo,persdemo(1)
```

TIMESUSED =
     []
TIMESUSED =
     1
Keep on calling

■

There are a number of commands which help control M-files.

Commands 113   CONTROL OF M-FILES

`run filename`	runs the command file **filename** where **filename** is the complete search path and the name of the file.
`pause`	pauses the execution of an M-file. The execution is resumed as soon as an arbitrary key is pressed (see Example 13.19(c)).
`pause(n)`	pauses the execution during *n* seconds before resuming the execution. The pause command can for instance be useful when a lot of graphics is to be presented.
`pause off`	instructs MATLAB to skip subsequent pauses.
`pause on`	instructs MATLAB to take pauses when a `pause` is given.
`break`	terminates the `for` and `while` loops. If this command is given in a nested loop, only the innermost loop is terminated, see Section 12.2.
`return`	terminates an M-file. MATLAB immediately returns to the place where the function was called.
`error(str)`	terminates the execution of an M-file and writes both an error message and the string **str** on the screen.
`errortrap state`	controls whether the execution should stop when errors occur. The value of **state** may be either on, which catches the errors and continues the execution, or `off`, which stops the execution when errors occur.
`global`	declares variables as global. Global variables can be accessed in function files without being included in the parameter list. The command `global` is followed by a list of variables separated by spaces. Variables declared as global remain global until the complete workspace is cleared, or the command `clear global` is used.
`isglobal(name)`	returns 1 if the variable **name** is declared global, 0 otherwise.

Commands 113	(CONTINUED)

keyboard	calls the keyboard as if it was a command file. When given inside an M-file, the execution is paused, and commands can be given in the MATLAB command window. The prompt is now *K >>* to indicate this special status. This is a way to check or change variables when an M-file is executed, and all MATLAB commands are allowed. The execution of the M-file is resumed as soon as the keyword return is written. If keyboard is called in a function file, the workspace of this function and its global variables are accessible. The command keyboard is useful when debugging.
mfilename	returns a string with the name of the M-file currently running. With this function a function may get its own name.
warning(message)	shows a warning message in the string **message** but does not stop the execution.
warning val	controls the warning messages. Valid values on val are:

	off	stops the following warning messages.
	on	turns on the warning messages again.
	backtrace	shows the line where the command causing the warning is found.
	debug	activates the debugger when a warning is found.
	once	displays Handle Graphics backwards compatibility warnings only once per session.
	always	displays all warnings messages.

[vt,f] = warning	returns the current warning state **vt** and warning frequency **f** as strings.

It is possible to have subfunctions to user-defined functions. These subfunctions can only be called by its main function, which is the same as the name of the M-file, and by other functions in the M-file. It is not possible to have more than one main function in the same M-file. One example of the structure of a function and its subfunctions is in the file **main.m**:

```
function y = main(x)          % Main function
...                           % Statements
z1 = under1(x);               % Call to first underfunction
...                           % Statements
y = under2(a);                % Call to second underfunction
...                           % Statements
```

```
function y = under1(x)        % First underfunction
...                           % Statements

function y = under2(x)        % Second underfunction
...                           % Statements
[b1, b2] = under3(a1, a2);    % Call to third underfunction
...                           % Statements

function y = under3(x1, x2)   % Third underfunction
...                           % Statements
```

It is also possible to have so called private functions. This kind of function is an M-file put in a subdirectory called **private**. The private functions may only be called from functions in the directory directly above **private**.

When MATLAB finds a call to a function in an M-file it first looks for a subfunction, second for a private function and last for a function in MATLAB's search path; see Commands 22. This means one may write one's own private functions, with the same name as a function in MATLAB, and put them in a **private** subdirectory to the program that will use these. At the same time, other programs in other directories are able to call M-files with the same name as the private functions, but now MATLAB's function will be executed.

12.4 Functions as parameters to other functions

In most high-level languages, like Pascal or FORTRAN, it is possible to write a general function **F** by including another function **f** as a parameter. This can also be done in MATLAB, by including a string **f** containing the expression describing the function or a name of a function. Inside **F**, the function **f** can be evaluated using eval or feval.

The command eval(see Section 5.1.4) evaluates a MATLAB expression given as a string. This string can for instance contain mathematical expressions:

```
a = eval('sin(2*pi)') or
x = 2*pi; b = eval('sin(x)')
```

The variables used in the string **f** must have the same names as the variables in **F** if eval is used.

The command feval evaluates functions, either built-in functions like sin or functions stored as M-files. A call to feval can look like this:

```
a = feval('sin',2*pi)
```

Commands 114   EVALUATING FUNCTIONS

feval(fcn,x1,..., xn)	evaluates the function given by the string **fcn**. The parameters $x1, \ldots, xn$ are passed to the function in the order of appearance. The feval command is usually used inside functions that have other functions as parameters.
[y1,y2,...] = feval(fcn,x1,..., xn)	is the same as the previous, but now returns multiple variables.

Suppose a function **fcn** is written with the elementwise operators, that is +, -, .*, ./, .\, .^. Then the command feval(fcn,x) returns a vector if **x** is a vector, and there is no problem passing a vector valued function as parameter to **F** if feval is used in **F**. If the command eval is used inside **F**, and is applied directly to vectors, the elementwise operators must be used in the parameter string function **f**.

■ **Example 12.14**

We now want to write a MATLAB function returning a table of $f(x)$, with x in the interval $[a, b]$, in steps of k. We assume that the function **f** is defined with elementwise operators.

(a) With feval:

> Input arguments: A string with the name of a function, limits a and b and the step length k.
> Output arguments: A matrix with two columns, the x values and $f(x)$ for these values.

The following function is stored in the file **Functab1.m**.

```
function Y = Functab1(f,a,b,k)

% Evaluates a scalar function in [a,b]
% at the values x(j) = a + j*k.
% The result is a table containing
% x values and f(x) for those x values.

x = a:k:b;
z = feval(f,x);
Y = [x;z]';
```

(b) With eval. The same result can be obtained by using a command string as input argument to the function. This command string is evaluated with the command eval; see Section 5.1.4.

Input arguments: A command string containing an expression defining the
function, limits *a* and *b*, and the step length *k*.

Output arguments: A matrix with two columns, containing the *x* values and
$f(x)$ for these values.

The following function is stored on the file **Functab2.m**.

```
function Y = Functab2(f,a,b,k)

% Evaluates a scalar function in [a,b]
% at the values x(j) = a + j*k.
% The result is a table containing
% x values and f(x) for those x values.

x = a:k:b;
z = eval(f);  % f must be a function of x
Y = [x;z]';
```

Suppose we want a table of the function $oneplusx(x) = 1+x$ for *x* in $[-1, 1]$. The
function **oneplusx** is stored in the file **oneplusx.m**. The following are examples
of how the functions **Functab1** and **Functab2** can be called to generate such a
table. They all give the same result.

```
Tab = Functab1('oneplusx',-1,1,0.25)
```

```
Tab =
    -1.0000         0
    -0.7500    0.2500
    -0.5000    0.5000
    -0.2500    0.7500
          0    1.0000
     0.2500    1.2500
     0.5000    1.5000
     0.7500    1.7500
     1.0000    2.0000
```

Other ways of creating the table are:

```
Tab = Functab2('oneplusx(x)',-1,1,0.25)
```

or

```
Tab = Functab2('1+x',-1,1,0.25)
```

∎

12.5 Structs

MATLAB can create **structs** where a variable has more than one field. Structs are available in most modern programming languages, e.g., struct in C/C++ and record in Pascal, but there are some differences. To create a struct one can use direct assignment or the `struct` command. The struct is freely typed so a vector of a struct does not need to, but should, have the same data type in a certain field; see Example 12.15. The only restriction is that the fields can only contain scalars or cell matrices of a fixed dimension for the whole struct.

To get the data from the fields, a period notation, '.', is used where one types the name of the struct and the name of the field with a period in between, see Example 12.15.

The following functions working on structs are available:

Commands 115	FUNCTIONS ON STRUCTS
`struct(f1,V1, f2,V2, ... )`	returns a struct with the fields *f1*, *f2* , ... having the corresponding values **V1**, **V2**, ... The parameters **V1**, **V2**, ... , may be cell matrices of the same size or scalars.
`fieldnames(S)`	returns a column vector with the names of the fields in **S**.
`getfield(S,f)`	returns the values in the field *f* in the struct **S**. This is the same as `S.f`.
`isstruct(S)`	returns 1 if **S** is a struct, 0 otherwise.
`isfield(x)`	returns 1 if **S** is a field of a struct, 0 otherwise.
`setfield(S,f,v)`	gives the field *f* of the struct **S** the value *v*. This is the same as `S.f = v`.
`rmfield(S,fvect)`	returns the struct **S** without the fields in the vector **fvect**.
`struct2cell(S)`	returns a cell matrix with the values in the struct **S**.
`handle2struct`	converts handle graphics hierarchy to struct with the field **type** (object type, e.g., **line**, **handle**, **properties**, **children** or **special**). Advanced graphics and handles are discussed in Chapter 14.
`struct2handle`	converts a struct to a handle graphics hierarchy. The fields are as in `handle2struct`.
`[out1,out2,...]= deal(in1,in2,...)`	copies input to output, i.e., the same as `out1 = in1; out2 = in2;`. See `helpdesk` for examples.

■ **Example 12.15**

A struct for storing equations with a name and description may look like this:

```
curve(1).name = 'Circle';
curve(1).function = '(x-a)^2 + y(-b)^2 = r^2';
curve(1).description =
'Circle with radius r centered in x = a, y=b';
```

To create other elements in the vector **curve** we use struct:

```
curve(2) =
struct('name','line','function',2,'description','A two?')'
```

This works although the value in the field *function* is a string in the first case and an integer in the second. Note that **curve** is a vector of two structs. ■

12.6 Objects

Objects in MATLAB differ from structs in that there is the possibility of connecting functions with the object and that the object may be created according to a class. These functions are often called **methods** in object oriented contexts. It is possible to protect the variables of a class and only let the class methods get access to them, which gives some control of the type.

Commands 116	OBJECT RELATED FUNCTIONS
`class(object)`	returns the class name of the object **object**.
`class(object,class, parent1, parent2,...)`	returns **object** as a variable of the type **class**. The parameters **parent1**, **parent2**, ... , are given if the object returned should inherit properties.
`isa(object,class)`	returns 1 if **object** is of the type **class**, otherwise 0.
`isobject(x)`	returns 1 if **x** is an object, otherwise 0.
`superiorto(class1, class2,...)`	controls the order of priority when calling methods. If a class is defined as `superiorto` this method is primarily used.
`inferiorto(class1, class2,...)`	controls the order of priority when calling methods. If a class is defined as `inferiorto` this method is used last.
`methods class`	returns the names of the methods defined for the class **class**.

To create an object of a class the class **properties** has to be defined, i.e., one creates a pattern for how objects of this class should be. Primarily a directory must be created. It must have the same name as the class but beginning with an @ sign (on VAX/VMS systems a $ is used instead). Next a **constructor** is needed to be able to create objects according to the class pattern. This is a function (in an M-file) that will return a variable according to the class pattern.

■ **Example 12.16**

If we want to create an object named **curve** we first create the directory **@curve**. Then we create the constructor in the file **@curve/curve.m**. It might look like this:

```
function l = curve(a)

% Constructor for the curve class.
% l = curve creates and initalizes a curve object.
% The parameter a can be a cell array with the mathematical
% function in one cell and the description in another cell, or
% another curve object. The mathematical formula must be
% on the same form that FPLOT requires, see FPLOT.
% An object containing the x axis is returned if no
% argument is passed.

if nargin == 0  % Default constructor in the case that
        l.fcn = '0';
        l.descr = 'x axis';
        l = class(l, 'curve');
% A copy of the object should be returned if
% the argument passed is a curve-object.
elseif isa(a,'curve')
        l = a;
elseif (ischar(a{1}) & ischar(a{2}))
        l.fcn = a{1};
        l.descr = a{2};
        l = class(l, 'curve');
% An error message is passed if the argument
% passed was of the wrong type.

else
        disp('Curve class error #1: Invalid argument.')
end
```

■

The line `l = class(l,'curve')` in Example 12.16 gives the variable its class connection. If this is left out only a struct is returned that has no access to the class methods.

To use the values of the object we use methods, i.e., the functions connected to the class and created in separate M-files put in the class directory. Note that the object is one of the arguments which differs from some other object oriented languages, where the syntax usually is `object.method(argument)`.

■ **Example 12.17**

It might be interesting to plot the curve in Example 12.16 according to the description:

```
function p = plot(l,area)

% curve.plot plots the function of the curve l in the area which
% must be a 1x4 matrix with the elements XMIN XMAX YMIN YMAX
% or a 1x2 vector with the elements XMIN XMAX.

% Generates the stepvalues and a vector with x values

step = (limits(2)-limits(1))/40;
x = limits(1):step:limits(2);

% Plots the function and the description

fplot(l.function, limits);
title(desciption)
```

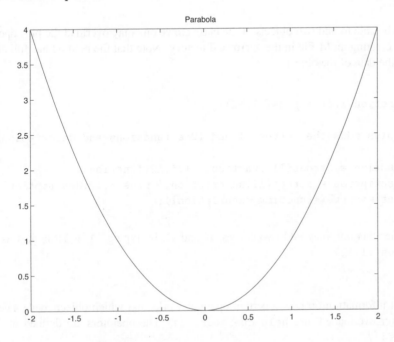

Figure 12.5 *Plot of the object parabola.*

Running the class **curve** may look like this:

```
parabola = curve({'x*x' 'A parabola'})

parabola=
curve=object: 1-by-1

plot(parabola,[-2 2])
```

This gives us Figure 12.5.

∎

The data of the object are only available from the methods. This gives the programmer a chance to check the typing of the variables in a way that is not possible with the structs. Hence, there need to be special methods for the class such that the user is able to change the fields of the object.

In MATLAB different operators mean different things for different classes. To create a so called **overloaded operator** a method with the name of the operator is created with the code for how the operator works.

∎ **Example 12.18**

To be able to add two objects of the class **curve** one may overload the plus operator by creating an M-file in the **@curve** directory. Note that the method has full access to the data of the objects.

```
function ltot = plus(l1,l2)

% plus adds the curves l1 and l2:s functions and descriptions.

function = strcat(l1.function,' + ',l2.function);
description = strcat(l1.description,' plus ',l2.description);
ltot = curve({function description});
```

After this one may add two curves, **l1** and **l2**, by typing l1 + l2 or just as well plus(l1,l2).

∎

To get information on how a certain operator works and which objects have a certain operator overloaded, use help operatorname. The operators are defined in Commands 117.

Commands 117   OVERLOADED OBJECT OPERATORS

`plus(a,b)`	is the function representing $\mathbf{a} + \mathbf{b}$.
`minus(a,b)`	is the function representing $\mathbf{a} - \mathbf{b}$.
`uplus(a)`	is the function representing $+\mathbf{a}$.
`uminus(a)`	is the function representing $-\mathbf{a}$.
`times(a,b)`	is the function representing $\mathbf{a}.*\mathbf{b}$.
`mtimes(a,b)`	is the function representing $\mathbf{a}*\mathbf{b}$.
`rdivide(a,b)`	is the function representing $\mathbf{a}./\mathbf{b}$.
`ldivide(a,b)`	is the function representing $\mathbf{a}.\backslash\mathbf{b}$.
`mrdivide(a,b)`	is the function representing $\mathbf{a}/\mathbf{b}$.
`mldivide(a,b)`	is the function representing $\mathbf{a}\backslash\mathbf{b}$.
`power(a,b)`	is the function representing $\mathbf{a}.^{\mathbf{b}}$.
`mpower(a,b)`	is the function representing $\mathbf{a}^{\mathbf{b}}$.
`lt(a,b)`	is the function representing $\mathbf{a} < \mathbf{b}$.
`gt(a,b)`	is the function representing $\mathbf{a} > \mathbf{b}$.
`le(a,b)`	is the function representing $\mathbf{a} <= \mathbf{b}$.
`ge(a,b)`	is the function representing $\mathbf{a} >= \mathbf{b}$.
`ne(a,b)`	is the function representing $\mathbf{a} = \mathbf{b}$.
`eq(a,b)`	is the function representing $\mathbf{a} == \mathbf{b}$.
`and(a,b)`	is the function representing $\mathbf{a}\&\mathbf{b}$.
`or(a,b)`	is the function representing $\mathbf{a} \mid \mathbf{b}$.
`not(a)`	is the function representing $\tilde{}\mathbf{a}$.
`colon(a,b)`	is the function representing $\mathbf{a} : \mathbf{b}$.
`colon(a,s,b)`	is the function representing $\mathbf{a} : \mathbf{s} : \mathbf{b}$.
`transpose(a)`	is the function representing $\mathbf{a}'$.
`ctranspose(a)`	is the function representing $\mathbf{a}.'$.
`display(a)`	is the function representing $\mathbf{a}$.
`horzcat(a,b,...)`	is the function representing $[\mathbf{a}\,\mathbf{b}\,...]$.
`vertcat(a,b,...)`	is the function representing $[\mathbf{a};\,\mathbf{b};\,...]$.
`subsref(a,i)`	is the function representing $\mathbf{a}(\mathbf{i}_1, \mathbf{i}_2, \ldots, \mathbf{i}_n)$. The `substruct` command is very useful when redefining this function.
`subsasgn(a,i,b)`	is the function representing $\mathbf{a}(\mathbf{i}_1, \mathbf{i}_2, \ldots, \mathbf{i}_n) = \mathbf{b}$.
`subsindex(a,b)`	is the function representing $\mathbf{b}(\mathbf{a})$.

When a function has an overloaded operator and one wishes to use the ordinary operator the `builtin` command is used.

Commands 118	SKIPPING OVERLOADED OPERATORS
`builtin(fcn,x1, x2,...)`	evaluates the built-in function **fcn** for the arguments *x1*, *x2*, ... , instead of using the overloaded operator.

Classes in MATLAB may inherit properties from other classes. The use of this is beyond the scope of this book and for information on this we recommend a book in C++. To create an object that inherits properties the parents are set in the `class` command.

12.7 Debugging and timing

There are commands in MATLAB that can be useful when debugging M-files, that is looking for errors in them. These commands can be used to set and clear breakpoints, execute M-files line by line, and check variables in different workspaces. The debug commands all start with the letters db, and we have already encountered dbtype (see Section 2.9) which produces a program list with line numbers.

The commands to set, clear, and list all breakpoints are given in Commands 119 below.

Commands 119	BREAKPOINTS
`dbstop in fname`	places a breakpoint at the first executable line in the M-file **fname**.
`dbstop at r in fname`	places a breakpoint at line *r* in the M-file **fname**. If *r* is not an executable line, the execution is stopped at the first executable line after *r*.
`dbstop if v`	stops the execution when the condition *v* is met. The condition *v* can be either `error` if an error occurs, or `naninf/infnan` if a NaN or inf occurs.
`dstop if warning`	stops the execution if there is a warning.
`dbclear at r in fname`	removes the breakpoint at line *r* in the file **fname**.
`dbclear all in fname`	removes all breakpoints in the file **fname**.
`dbclear all`	removes all breakpoints in all M-files.
`dbclear in fname`	removes the breakpoint at the first executable line in the file **fname**.
`dbclear if v`	removes the breakpoint at line *v* set with `dbstop if v`.
`dbstatus fname`	produces a list of all breakpoints in the file **fname**.
`mdbstatus`	displays the information from `dbstatus` with the row numbers separated with semicolons.

These commands, together with the commands listed below, give us good tools to follow and control the execution of M-files. Constructions with try/catch are useful when debugging; see Section 12.1. One would, for example, get a more general solution to the problem in Example 5.8(a) with try/catch instead of eval.

Commands 120   CONTROL OF THE EXECUTION

dbstep	executes the next line of the M-file.
dbstep n	executes the next *n* lines and then stops.
dbstep in	stops the execution at the first executable line in the next function called.
dbcont	executes all lines until the next breakpoint or the end of the file is reached.
dbmex	is a command for debugging of MEX-files, see Section 15.2.1 and Section 15.3.1. Is not available in Windows or on a Macintosh.
dbquit	quits the debugging mode.

To start debugging, a function with a breakpoint is called. MATLAB now enters the debugging mode, which is indicated by a K in the MATLAB-prompt: *K>>*. The most important difference is that we can now access the local variables of the function, but not the variables in the MATLAB workspace. We illustrate this with the function **Factab.m** that produces a table of the factorials 1!, ... , *n*!.

■ **Example 12.19**

First we list the function **Factab.m** with line numbers:

```
dbtype Factab
```

```
1    function Tab = Factab(n)
2    %
3    % Generates a table of 1!, ..., n!
4
5    numbers = 1:n; facts = [];
6
7    for i = numbers
8       facts = [facts factorial(i)]
9    end
10
11   Tab = [numbers' facts'];
```

This function calls the function **factorial**, which is also listed:

```
dbtype factorial

1    function p = factorial(nn)
2    %
3    % Computes the factorial of nn.
4
5    if ( nn == 0 )
6      p = 1;
7    else
8      p = nn*factorial(nn-1);
9    end
```

To start debugging, we set a breakpoint at the first executable line of the function and then make a call to it. Notice the letter K that appears in the prompt.

```
dbstop in Factab            % Sets breakpoint in Factab.
Table = Factab(5);          % Calls Factab to debug it.
5   numbers = 1:n;
K>> dbstep                  % Executes one line.
6   facts = [];
K>> numbers                 % Returns value of numbers.

numbers =

      1     2     3     4     5

K>> numbers = [numbers 6]   % Enlarge the vector with number 6.

numbers =

      1     2     3     4     5     6

K>> dbstop 12               % Breakpoint at line 12.
K>> dbcont                  % Continues to the next breakpoint.
12  Tab = [numbers' facts'];
K>> dbquit                  % Quits the debugging.

dbstatus Factab             % Lists all breakpoints used.
Breakpoints for Factab are on lines 5, 12.
```

A function which is calling another function is referred to as a nested function call. MATLAB uses a stack to keep track of workspaces and variables in the functions, and the following commands can be used to switch between workspaces of the nested functions.

Commands 121	CHANGE WORKSPACE
dbstep in	steps into the function if the next executable line is a function call.
dbup	switches to the workspace of the calling function, allowing its variables to be examined.
dbdown	switches back down to the workspace of the called function.
dbstack	shows the stack of nested function calls.

■ **Example 12.20**

We again use the function **Factab**; see Example 12.19. We start by placing breakpoints in both **Factab** and **factorial**:

```
dbstop Factab            % Sets breakpoint in Factab.
dbstop factorial         % Sets breakpoint in factorial.
Factab(3);               % Calls Factab.
5    numbers = 1:n;
K>> dbcont               % Steps to next break point.
5    if ( nn == 0 )
K>> dbstack              % Now we are in function factorial.
In /home/aw/BOOK/factorial.m at line 5
In /home/aw/BOOK/Factab.m at line 8
K>> who                  % Shows the current values.

Your variables are:

nn         p

K>> dbup                 % Switches to calling work space.
In workspace belonging to /home/aw/BOOK/Factab.m.
K>> who                  % Which variables are current now?

Your variables are:

Tab      facts      i        n        numbers

K>> dbdown               % Back to work space of factorial.
In workspace belonging to /home/aw/BOOK/factorial.m.
K>> dbquit               % Quits the debugging.
```

To debug command files, use the command keyboard. MATLAB's special debugging commands can only be used to debug function files.

■

To make efficient programs you need a tool to tell you which parts of the program use the most time. The `profile` command is such a tool:

Commands 122   TIMING OF M-FILES

`profile choice`	is a command for timing of M-files. The variable **choice** may be one of the following:

filename	timing of the M-file **filename**; only one file may be analyzed at a time.
`on, off`	turns on or off the timing for the M-file specified.
`reset`	clears the timing data of the profile tool.
`report`	shows a timing report.
`report n`	shows the n rows in the program that use the most time.
`report frac`	shows the rows that use at least the fraction *frac* of the time. The value of *frac* has to be in the interval $0 < frac < 1$.
`done`	ends the timing.

`info = profile`	returns a struct **info** that may be used for graphic representation of the data from the timing. It contains the following fields:

info.file	contains the name, including a complete pathway, of the M-file timed.
info.function	contains the name of the function.
info.interval	contains timing intervals in seconds.
info.count	contains a vector with timing data.
info.state	contains the status of the timing tool, which is `on` or `off`.

`profsumm choice`	creates a summary of the profile of the M-file. Valid values for **choice** are:

`n`	shown the n rows in the program that use the most time.
`frac`	shows the rows in the program that use at least the fraction *frac* of the time. The value of *frac* has to be in the interval $0 < frac < 1$.
`str`	reports if there are rows containing the string **str**.

The `profsumm` command can also use information stored on the struct **info** shown above.

■ **Example 12.21**

We will now time two different programs that perform exactly the same task to decide
which program is the more efficient. The first program,which is on the file **particle.m**,
looks like this:

```
% Random walk. A particle starts at the origin, and is
% moved randomly up to a half unit in either direction
% in every step.

%disp('Give the number of steps')    % The number of steps.
%n = input('>>>');
n = 500;

x = cumsum(rand(n,1)-0.5);           % Random x values.
y = cumsum(rand(n,1)-0.5);           % Random y values.

clf;                                 % Clear graphics window.
plot(x,y);                           % Plots the walk.
hold on;                             % Holds the plot.
plot(x(1),y(1),'o',x(n),y(n),'o');   % Marks start/finish.
axs   = axis;                        % Gets min and max.
scale = axs(2) - axs(1);             % Calculates a scale.

text(x(1)+scale/30,y(1),'Start');    % Writes text to the right
text(x(n)+scale/30,y(n),'Finish');   % of Start and Finish.

hold off;                            % Resets hold to standard.

xlabel('x'); ylabel('y');
title('Random walk')
```

The other program is on the file **particleBad.m**:

```
% Random walk. A particle starts at the origin, and is
% moved randomly up to a half unit in either direction
% in every step.

%disp('Give the number of steps')    % The number of steps.
%n = input('>>>');
n = 500;
%x = cumsum(rand(n,1)-0.5);           % Random x values.
%y = cumsum(rand(n,1)-0.5);           % Random y values.
```

```
x(1) = rand(1,1)-0.5;
y(1) = rand(1,1)-0.5;

for i = 2:n
  x(i) = rand(1,1)-0.5 + x(i-1);
  y(i) = rand(1,1)-0.5 + y(i-1);
end

clf;                          % Clear graphics window.
plot(x,y);                    % Plots the walk.
hold on;                      % Holds the plot.
plot(x(1),y(1),'o',x(n),y(n),'o'); % Marks start/finish.

axs   = axis;                 % Gets min and max.
scale = axs(2) - axs(1);      % Calculates a scale.

text(x(1)+scale/30,y(1),'Start');  % Writes text to the right
text(x(n)+scale/30,y(n),'Finish'); % of Start and Finish.

hold off;                     % Resets hold to standard.

xlabel('x'); ylabel('y');
title('Random walk')
```

We give the following commands:

```
profile particle; particle; profile report; profile off;
profile particleBad; particleBad; profile report; profile off;
```

The result is:

```
Total time in "particle.m": 0.22 seconds
100% of the total time was spent on lines:
        [13 25 12 26 17 15]


             11:
0.03s, 14%   12: clf;
                 % Clear graphics window.
0.11s, 50%   13: plot(x,y);
                 % Plots the walk.
             14: hold on;
                 % Holds the plot.
0.01s,  5%   15: plot(x(1),y(1),'o',x(n),y(n),'o');
                 % Marks start/finish.
```

```
             16:
0.02s,  9%   17: axs   = axis;
                 % Gets min and max.
             18: scale = axs(2) - axs(1);
                 % Calculates a scale.
             24:
0.03s, 14%   25: xlabel('x'); ylabel('y');
0.02s,  9%   26: title('Random walk')
```

Total time in "particleBad.m": 0.57 seconds

98% of the total time was spent on lines:
      [16 15 21 20 33 34 31 25 23 22]

```
             14: for i = 2:n
0.15s, 26%   15:   x(i) = rand(1,1)-0.5 + x(i-1);
0.18s, 32%   16:   y(i) = rand(1,1)-0.5 + y(i-1);
             17: end

             19:
0.04s,  7%   20: clf;
                 % Clear graphics window.
0.10s, 18%   21: plot(x,y);
                 % Plots the walk.
0.01s,  2%   22: hold on;
                 % Holds the plot.
0.01s,  2%   23: plot(x(1),y(1),'o',x(n),y(n),'o');
                 % Marks start/finish.
             24:
0.01s,  2%   25: axs   = axis;
                 % Gets min and max.
             26: scale = axs(2) - axs(1);
                 % Calculates a scale.
             30:
0.01s,  2%   31: hold off;
                 % Resets hold to standard.
             32:
0.03s,  5%   33: xlabel('x'); ylabel('y');
0.02s,  4%   34: title('Random walk')
```

We can see how much time the program used, and which rows used the most time. If we want a plot to present the result of the latest profile run, we can simply type:

```
t = profile
```

```
t =

        file: '/home/matlab/VER5/kapitel12/particleBad.m'
    interval: 0.0100
       count: [33x1  double]
       state: 'off'
```

```
pareto(t.count)
```

The pareto command is introduced in Section 6.5 and in Section 13.1. We get the plot in Figure 12.6 where the bars show the execution time for the row on the *x* axis. On the left *y* axis is the execution time in hundredths of seconds and on the right *y* axis is the fraction, in per cent, of the total execution time. The line shows the total execution time.

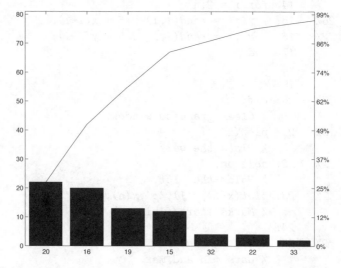

Figure 12.6 *Graphical representation of the timing of **particleBad.m***

Graphics and Sound

13

MATLAB has a wide range of two- and three-dimensional graphics commands which are flexible and easy to use. It is also possible to include sound effects in MATLAB programs. Many graphics commands are shown in the demonstration programs included in MATLAB. Those who still have not tried the demo *command are strongly recommended to do so now!*

The graphics commands are presented in two chapters. This chapter covers the basic high-level commands, while Chapter 14 is devoted to advanced graphics and focuses on the low-level control of details.

13.1 Two-dimensional graphics

ordered pairs, and one way to do it is to use the plot command. This command can be given with different numbers of arguments. The simplest form is just to pass the data to plot, but line types and colors can also be specified by using a string, here denoted **str**. The types and colors allowed in this string are listed in Table 13.1. If the line type is not specified a solid line is used. Note that **A** is an $m \times n$ matrix in the Command table below.

Commands 123	THE PLOT COMMAND

plot(x,y)	plots the vector **y** versus the vector **x**. The ordered set of coordinates (x_j, y_j) are drawn, with the horizontal axis as the x axis, and the vertical axis as the y axis.
plot(y)	plots the ordered set of coordinates (j, y_j). The horizontal axis is the j axis, and the vertical axis is the y axis.
plot(z)	plots the ordered set of coordinates $(\text{real}(z_k), \text{imag}(z_k))$. The horizontal axis is the real axis, and the vertical axis is the imaginary axis. Thus, the complex numbers z_k are drawn in the complex plane.
plot(A)	plots the columns of **A** versus their indices. For an $m \times n$ matrix **A**, n sets of m pairs, or n curves with m points are plotted. The different curves are drawn in different colors on a color monitor, and with different line types on a black-and-white monitor.
plot(x,A)	plots the matrix **A** versus the vector **x**. For an $m \times n$ matrix **A** and a vector **x** of length m, the columns of **A** are plotted versus **x**. If **x** is of length n, the rows of **A** are plotted versus **x**. The vector **x** can be either a row or a column vector.

Commands 123 (CONTINUED)

`plot(A,x)`	plots the vector **x** versus the matrix **A**. For an $m \times n$ matrix **A** and a vector **x** of length m, the vector **x** is plotted versus the columns of **A**. If **x** is of length n, the vector **x** is plotted versus the rows of **A**. The vector **x** can be either a row or column vector.
`plot(A,B)`	plots the columns of **B** versus the columns of **A**. Thus if **A** and **B** are both $m \times n$ matrices, n sets of curves with m coordinates are plotted.
`plot(...,str)`	draws a plot according to the arguments, but using the color and style given by the string **str**. The values allowed in **str** are listed in Table 13.1 below.
`plot(x1,y1,str1,` `x2,y2,str2,...)`	plots **x1** versus **y1** with color and style according to **str1**, then plots **x2** versus **y2** according to **str2** and so on. Each pair of entries can have any of the forms above, but real and complex data cannot be mixed. If the strings **str1**, **str2**, ... are left out, MATLAB chooses the color and style of each plot.
`[l,f,p,errorm] =` `colstyle(str)`	returns the different parts of the line type specified in **str**. Here **l** is the line type, **f** is the color and **p** is the point type. If something went wrong an error message is returned in **errorm**.

Table 13.1   POINT TYPES, LINE TYPES AND COLORS.

Point types		Line types	
.	period, dot	–	solid line
*	star	– –	dashed line
square	square	–.	dashed–dotted line
diamond	diamond	:	dotted line
pentagram	pentagram	none	no line
hexagram	hexagram	**Colors**	
none	no dots	g	green
o	lower-case letter o	m	magenta
+	plus sign	b	blue
x	cross	c	cyan
<	triangle pointing left	w	white
>	triangle pointing right	r	red
^	triangle pointing up	k	black
v	triangle pointing down	y	yellow

By passing the string **str** as an argument to `plot`, the color and style in the plots can be specified. The values allowed, and their meaning, are listed in Table 13.1. Style and color can be combined. For instance, 'y+' gives a plot drawn with yellow plus signs, and 'b--' a blue dashed line. If several series of data are to be drawn, but no styles are specified, they are given different colors from yellow to black following Table 13.1. On a black-and-white monitor, the series are given different line types.

The size of the symbols, the widths of the lines, and so on, can also be changed; see Example 13.1(g) or Section 14.2.

The axes are automatically scaled, using the minima and maxima of the data to be plotted. To manually set the scaling, see the command `axis` in Section 13.3.

■ **Example 13.1**

   (a) Let us make a plot of the following data:

```
x = [-4 -2 0 1 3 5];
y = [16 4 0 1 9 25];
```

    The command `plot(x,y)` gives Figure 13.1.

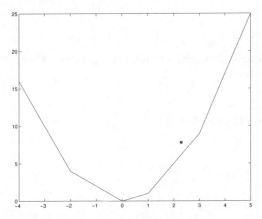

Figure 13.1 *The vector* **y** *plotted against the vector* **x**.

   (b) Points can be plotted as easily in MATLAB:

```
x = -pi:0.05:pi;
plot(x,sin(x).*cos(x),'o')
```

    gives us Figure 13.2.

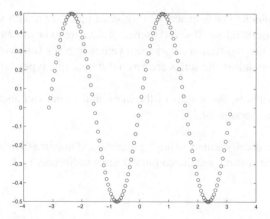

Figure 13.2 *The function* $\sin x \times \cos x$ *plotted with small circles.*

(c) Several functions can be drawn on the same graph:

```
x = 0:0.1:2;
A = [sin(pi*x);0.5+0.5*x];
plot(x,A);
```

gives us Figure 13.3.

(d) The axes can be switched by shifting the arguments. Compare Figure 13.3 with Figure 13.4 given by:

```
x = 0:0.1:2;
A = [sin(pi*x);0.5+0.5*x];
plot(A,x);
```

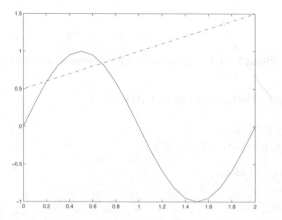

Figure 13.3 *The matrix* **A** *plotted against the vector* **x**.

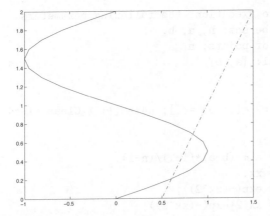

Figure 13.4 *The vector* **x** *plotted against the matrix* **A**.

(e) The command `plot` can also handle complex matrices.

```
clear i;                    % Assure that i is complex.

r = linspace(0,2);         % Creates a vector r.
theta = linspace(0,10*pi); % Creates a vector of angles.

[x,y] = pol2cart(theta,r); % Transforms polar coordinates
z = x + i*y;               % to a complex vector.

plot(z)                    % Plots z.
```

This gives us Figure 13.5. Notice that complex data can also be plotted with the commands `polar`, `quiver`, `feather`, `compass`, and `rose`; see Section 13.2.

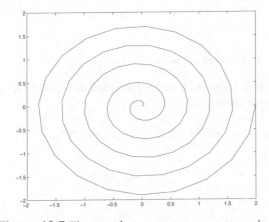

Figure 13.5 *The complex vector* **z** *represents a spiral.*

(f) The following commands form the file **expotest.m**:

```
% Prior to execution, the following parameters
% should be set: n, a, b.
% Number of points: n.
% Interval: [a, b].

x = [];
e1 = []; e2 =[]; e3 = []; e4 = []; % Clear e1-e4

for i = 1:n
    xx     = a + (b-a)*(i-1)/(n-1);
    x(i)   = xx;
    e1(i) = exp(-(xx^2));
    e2(i) = xx^2*exp(-(xx^2));
    e3(i) = xx*exp(-(xx^2));
    e4(i) = exp(-xx);
end
```

However, the following code, with the same result, is much more efficient, easier
to read and less prone to entry errors:

```
x = linspace(a,b,n);

e1 = exp(-x.^2);
e2 = (x.^2).*exp(-x.^2);
e3 = x.*exp(-x.^2);
e4 = exp(-x);
```

Now the following statements:

```
n = 50;
a = 0;
b = 3;
expotest
plot(x,e1,x,e2,x,e3,x,e4);
```

give the graph in Figure 13.6 (left). The graph in Figure 13.6 (right) is the result
of the following command:

```
plot(x,e1,'+',x,e2,'*',x,e3,'o',x,e4,'x');
```

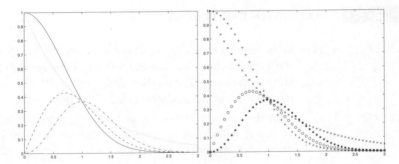

Figure 13.6 *Some exponential functions plotted with standard symbols (left) and user-chosen symbols (right).*

(g) Suppose we have the same variables as in (f). Now we want to change the thickness of the lines:

```
hold on;
plot(x,e1,'LineWidth',1);
plot(x,e2,'LineWidth',2);
plot(x,e3,'LineWidth',3);
plot(x,e4,'LineWidth',4);
hold off;
```

The command `hold on` holds the plot so that we may plot more than one graph in the same picture, while `hold off` turns it off; see Commands 130. The curve **e1** gets the thinnest line, **e4** the thickest. This gives us Figure 13.7.

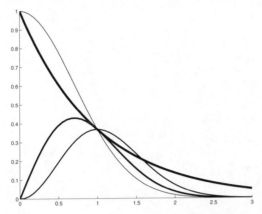

Figure 13.7 *Exponential function plotted with different thicknesses.*

The command `errorbar` can be used in MATLAB to plot data with error bars. This command is used just like the command `plot` but now error bounds are supplied to each point.

Commands 124	PLOT WITH ERROR BARS
errorbar(x,y,e,*str*)	plots the vector **y** versus the vector **x**, and draws error bars of size e_i symmetrically above and below y_i. The optional string **str** determines the style and the color, see Table 13.1. See also the plot command in Commands 123 for more options.
errorbar(x,y,l,u,*str*)	plots the vector **y** versus the vector **x**, and draws error bars of size l_i below and u_i above y_i. The optional string **str** determines the style and the color.

■ **Example 13.2**

We now generate a series of numbers, and suppose that the error bounds are 15%. Then we generate a graph showing the data and the error bars:

```
x = linspace(0,10,50);      % Creates a series of values.
y = exp(sin(x));            % Creates the data.

delta = 0.15*y;             % Calculates 15 % error bounds.
errorbar(x,y,delta);        % Plots graph with error bars.
```

These commands give us Figure 13.8.

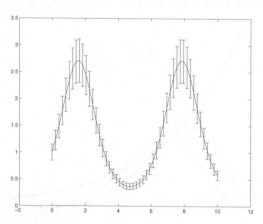

Figure 13.8 *The function $e^{\sin x}$ with error bars.*

■

Comet plots can be drawn with the command comet. A comet plot is an animation of the drawing process. The comet3 command plots comet plots in three dimensions; see Section 13.5.

Commands 125 COMET PLOT

`comet(x,y)`	draws a comet plot of the vector **y** versus the vector **x**. If only one vector is given, it is plotted versus its indices.
`comet(x,y,l)`	draws a comet plot with a comet tail of length l, given as a relative length of the vector **y**. The default is, if no length is given, $l = 0.1$.
`comet`	draws an example of a comet plot.

Type `doc comet` for more information.

There are some functions in MATLAB which change the look of the graph.

Commands 126 OTHER PLOT COMMANDS

`area(x,y)`	works like `plot` but colors the space under the line.
`area(x,A)`	plots the first row of the matrix **A** versus the vector **x**, then the sum of the next row and the previous rows versus **x**. Each field gets its own color.
`area(y)`	uses `x = 1:size(y,1)`.

`area(...,`
`'Property',`
`Value,...)`
	sets the specified properties of the underlying patch object that area creates; see Chapter 14.

`barh(x,A,`*format*`)`	plots the $m \times n$ matrix **A** as m groups with n bars. The string **format** may be color types or the string `'stacked'` that stacks the values on one another.
`barh(A)`	works like barh but uses `x = 1:m`.
`ezplot(f,` *xmin, xmax*`)`	plots the function **f** from *xmin* to *xmax*. If these are not specified the function is plotted approximately between -2π and 2π. The ezplot command uses an algorithm to decide where the function has significant changes and this is why the boundaries are not completely known.
`pareto(y,`*x*`)`	plots the bars for the elements in **y** in descending order. The vector **x** may be given and should contain the index for the **x** axis; if not given the elements index from the vector **y** are used. The pareto command also plots a line with the cumulative sum of the elements.
`pie(x,`*explode*`)`	plots a pie diagram of the vector **x**. If `sum(x) <= 1` an incomplete pie diagram is produced. The vector **explode** is of the same size as **x** and for the non-zero elements in **explode** the corresponding slices will be pulled out.

Commands 126   (CONTINUED)

scatter(x,y,*size, color*)	plots colored circles in the points specified by **x** and **y**, which has to be of the same size. The size of the circles (in points) is set with *size*, which may be a vector. The color of the circles is set with **color** which may be a vector, a matrix or a color string, see helpdesk for more information.
plotmatrix(X,Y)	plots a matrix of scatter plots with the columns of **X** plotted versus the columns of **Y**.
plotmatrix(X)	works like plotmatrix(X,X), but plots histograms on the diagonal.
[H, AX, BigAx, P]= plotmatrix(...)	returns a matrix of handles **H** to the whole graph. The matrix **AX** contains handles to the individual subaxes and the matrix **BigAx** contains handles to a big axis which frames the subaxes. The handle for the histogram plots is stored in **P**. **BigAx** is left as the current handle (used by, e.g., axes).
plotyy(x1,y1,x2, y2,*fun1,fun2*)	plots **y1** versus **x1** with the scale on the left *y* axis and **y2** versus **x2** with the scale on the right *y* axis. If the parameters **fun1** and **fun2** are not given the plots are drawn as if plot had been used. The parameters **fun1** and **fun2** may be strings like 'semilogx', 'loglog' and so on, i.e., different functions drawing plots; see Section 13.2.

■ **Example 13.3**

If one wants to plot information with different scales in the same graph one may do so like this:

```
% plotyy demonstration
% Definition of data
x = 0:0.25:4;
y = exp(x);

clf reset;      % Plotyy is sensitive to what is defined in
                % the axes and a clf reset minimizes bugs
                % related to this problem.

plotyy(x,y,x,y,'plot','semilogy')
hold on;
title('Plotyy')
ylabel('Linear scale')
```

This gives us Figure 13.9. Unfortunately `plotyy` has problems with other commands, e.g., `legend`, suited for only one defined axis. An other **plotyy.m** is available from `ftp://ftp.mathworks.com/pub/tech-support/library/graphics /plotyy.m`.

It gives us the possibility of defining labels for all axes.

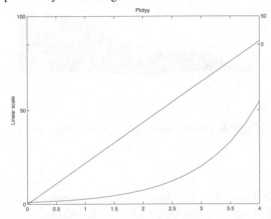

Figure 13.9 *Data plotted with* `plot` *and* `semilogy` *in the same graph with the help of the* `plotyy` *command.*

■

■ **Example 13.4**

MATLAB can plot cumulative plots using the `area` command.

```
% Demonstration of the area command
x = 0:10;
A = [ sin(x);x;(x/3).^2 ]';

clf;
areahandle = area(x,A)
hold on
title('Area plot')
legend(areahandle,'sin(x)','sin(x)+x','sin(x)+x+(x/3)^2',2)
```

The result is shown in Figure 13.10.

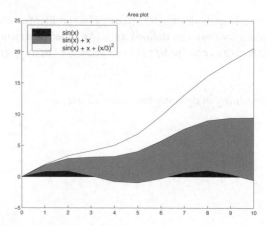

Figure 13.10 *Three curves plotted with* `area`.

Standard MATLAB and user-defined functions can be plotted with the command `fplot`. Interval limits and names of functions are given as parameters.

Commands 127   **GRAPHS OF FUNCTIONS**

`fplot(fcn,lim,str)`	plots the function specified in the string **fcn**. This can be either a standard function, or a user-defined function in the M-file **fcn.m**, inline functions are not allowed. The vector **lim**= [x_{min} x_{max}] determines the plotting interval. The vector can also include four components, where the third and fourth arguments are limits on the *y* axis, **lim**= [x_{min} x_{max} y_{min} y_{max}]. If the string **str** is passed to `fplot`, the style and color of the plot can be changed according to Table 13.1.
`fplot(fcn,lim,str, tol)`	plots as above, but with a relative error that is less than *tol*.

Note that it is not possible to plot a so called inline function using the `fplot` command.

■ **Example 13.5**

We write the following to plot $\sin x^2$;

```
fplot('sin(x.^2)',[0 10]);
```

and we get Figure 13.11.

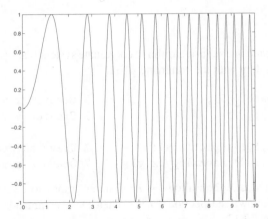

Figure 13.11 *The function* $\sin x^2$ *plotted with the command* fplot.

■

13.2 Plots in other coordinate systems and in the complex plane

The command plot uses Cartesian coordinates. However, it is also possible to use other coordinate systems. A string argument **str** can be passed to all the following commands, specifying the style and color of the plot. Values allowed are listed in Table 13.1.

| Commands 128 | TO PLOT IN OTHER COORDINATE SYSTEMS |

polar(theta,r)	plots in polar coordinates. The elements of the vector **theta** are the arguments in radians, and the elements of the vector **r** are the distances from the origin.
semilogx(x,y)	plots in a semi-logarithmic coordinate system, a $\log_{10}$ scale is used for the x axis. This is the same as plot(log10(x),y), but no warning message is given for $\log_{10}(0)$.
semilogy(x,y)	plots in a semi-logarithmic coordinate system, a $\log_{10}$ scale is used for the y axis. This is the same as plot(x,log10(y)), but no warning message is given for $\log_{10}(0)$.
loglog(x,y)	plots in a logarithmic coordinate system. Both axes are scaled with a $\log_{10}$ scale. This is the same as plot(log10(x), log10(y)), but no warning message is given for $\log_{10}(0)$.

See also Section 2.4 on commands for changing coordinate system.

■ **Example 13.6**

(a) To draw a graph in a semi-logarithmic coordinate system is as easy as in the normal Cartesian system with the command `plot`.

```
x = linspace(0,7);              % Creates x values.
y = exp(x);                     % Creates y values.

subplot(2,1,1); plot(x,y);      % Draws an ordinary plot.
subplot(2,1,2); semilogy(x,y);  % Draws a semi-logarithmic.
```

The command `subplot` allows several small graphs to be drawn in the same graphics window; see Section 13.3. When these commands are executed, we obtain Figure 13.12.

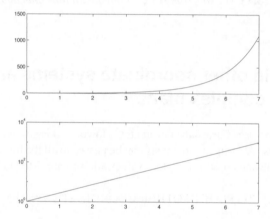

Figure 13.12 *The exponential function drawn with normal axes (upper) and with logarithmic scale on the y axis (lower).*

(b) To plot a graph when the coordinates are polar one uses the command `polar`. The function

$$r = e^{\cos t} - 2\cos 4t + \left(\sin \frac{t}{12}\right)^5$$

describes a curve in the complex plane. Here we describe two ways of plotting it.

```
% Define functions.

t = linspace(0,22*pi,1100);
r = exp(cos(t)) - 2*cos(4*t) + (sin(t./12)).^5;

subplot(2,1,1)
p = polar(t,r);                 % Plot in polar coordinates.

subplot(2,1,2)
```

```
[x,y] = pol2cart(t,r);   % Find the cartesian coordinates.

plot(x,y);               % Plot in x-y plane.
```

The two different plots can be seen in Figure 13.13 (upper) and (lower).

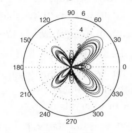

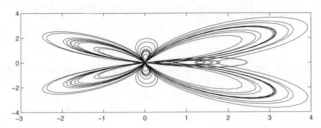

Figure 13.13 *Plots in polar (upper) and Cartesian (lower) coordinates.*

■

Complex numbers can be plotted with the commands quiver, feather, compass, and rose. These can also be used for real matrices; see Example 13.16 (b).

| Commands 129 | COMPLEX PLANE GRAPHICS |

quiver(X,Y)	draws an arrow for each pair of coordinates given by X_{ij} and Y_{ij}. The command quiver(real(Z),imag(Z)) can be interpreted as a plot of the argument and magnitude of the complex numbers in the matrix **Z**.
quiver(x,y,dx,dy)	draws an arrow at the coordinates (x_i, y_i), with argument and magnitude given by (dx_i, dy_i).
quiver(X,Y,Dx,Dy)	draws an arrow at the coordinates (X_{ij}, Y_{ij}), with argument and magnitude given by (Dx_{ij}, Dy_{ij}).
quiver(X,Y,...,s)	draws arrows as above, but now scaled with a factor s. If left out, the default value is $s = 1$.
quiver(X,Y,...,str)	draws the arrows using the line type **str**; see Table 13.1.
feather(Z)	draws arrows showing the magnitudes and arguments of the elements of the complex matrix **Z**, originating from equidistant points on the x axis.

Commands 129 (CONTINUED)

feather(X,Y)	is equivalent to feather(X+Y*i).
feather(Z,str)	draws the arrows using the line type **str**; see Table 13.1.
compass(Z)	draws arrows originating from the origin, showing the magnitudes and arguments of the elements of the complex matrix **Z**.
compass(X,Y)	is equivalent to compass(X+Y*i).
compass(Z,str)	draws the arrows using the line type **str**; see Table 13.1.
rose(v)	draws an argument histogram, that is a circular histogram showing the frequency of the arguments in the vector **v**. The number of intervals is 36.
rose(v,n)	is the same as the above, but now *n* intervals are used.
rose(v,x)	draws an argument histogram, using the intervals specified in the vector **x**.

Figure P.5 in the color plate section shows the quiver-plot for a function $z = f(x, y)$ with four extrema.

■ **Example 13.7**

Let **Z** be defined as:

$$\mathbf{Z} = \begin{pmatrix} 1+i & 2-i & 3-5i \\ -4+3i & 5-3i & i \\ -1-i & 3+3i & -1 \end{pmatrix}$$

The following commands give Figure 13.14.

```
clear i;      % Assure that i is complex number.

Z = [1+i 2-i 3-5i; -4+3i 5-3i i; -1-i 3+3i -1];

clf;
subplot(2,2,1);  quiver(real(Z),imag(Z)); title('quiver');
subplot(2,2,2);  feather(Z);              title('feather');
subplot(2,2,3);  compass(Z);              title('compass');
subplot(2,2,4);  rose(angle(Z(:)));       title('rose');
```

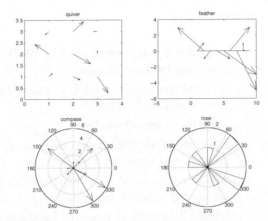

Figure 13.14 *Complex numbers represented by graphics.*

The command `subplot` makes it possible to draw several plots in the same graphics window, see Section 13.3. The commands give us Figure 13.14.

■

13.3 Controlling the graphics

The graphics in MATLAB are object oriented. The commands listed in this chapter are used to set and create the necessary objects to draw and change graphics. In this section we discuss a few commands which on a high level change these objects, many by a single command. It is also possible to manipulate the attributes of a single graphics object. This is discussed in detail in Chapter 14, which describes commands for advanced graphics.

MATLAB has two kinds of window: **command windows** and **graphics windows**. The command window is used when the MATLAB commands are given. A graphics window is the window in which graphics are shown. The graphics windows may be controlled with the commands in this section, but also controlled in a more direct way; see Chapter 14.

The hardware determines if it is possible to have graphics windows as well as the command window on the screen simultaneously. There are commands to switch between the windows, to clear the windows, and to hold the current plot.

Commands 130	WINDOW COMMANDS

`figure(gcf)`	shows the current graphics window. The command `figure` can also be used to switch between graphics windows, and to create new graphics windows; see Section 14.2.
`shg`	displays the current graphics window, the same as `figure(gcf)`.

Commands 130 (CONTINUED)

`clf`	clears the current graphics window. Warning: the window is also cleared if `hold on` is set.
`clg`	is an old command equivalent to `clf`. May be removed in later versions of MATLAB.
`clc`	clears the command window.
`home`	moves the cursor to its 'home', that is the upper left corner of the command window.
`hold on`	holds the current plot, enabling graphics to be added to the current plot using the same scaling.
`hold off`	releases the graphics window, so the next plot will replace the current graphics. This is the default status.
`hold`	toggles between `hold on` and `hold off`.
`ishold`	returns 1 if the current plot is held, otherwise 0.

The command `subplot` is used to draw several plots in the same graphics window. It does not draw anything, but it defines how the graphics window is to be divided, and in which subwindow the next plot is to be drawn.

Commands 131 SUBPLOTS

`subplot(m,n,p)`	splits the graphics window into m rows, and n columns, and sets subwindow p as the current. The subwindows are numbered by row from left to right, top to bottom. This command can in the current version of MATLAB also be written `subplot(mnp)`.
`subplot`	sets the graphics window to the default mode, that is a single window. The same as `subplot(1,1,1)`.

■ **Example 13.8**

(a) Show a matrix with running random numbers in the top left corner of the command window:

```
clc                    % Clears the command window.

for i = 1:10
  home                 % Sends the cursor "home".
  A = rand(5)          % Creates and prints the matrix.
  pause(1);            % Waits 1 second.
end
```

(b) The following MATLAB commands plot the function $f(x) = -x \sin x$ in the top left subwindow, its derivative $f'(x) = -x \cos x - \sin x$ in the top right subwindow, an approximate derivative in the bottom left, and the relative error in the exact derivative and approximate derivative in the bottom right subwindow.

```
% Creates x-values. Generates f-values, y11,
% and the derivative, y12. Approximates
% derivative, y21, and its error, y22.
n = 1000;
x = linspace(-10,10,n);

y11 = (-x).*sin(x);
y12 = (-x).*cos(x) - sin(x);
y21 = diff(y11)./(x(2)-x(1));
y22 = (y21 - y12(1:n-1));

% Plots in upper left-hand corner.

subplot(2,2,1); plot(x,y11);
title('The function')

% Plots in upper right-hand corner.

subplot(2,2,2); plot(x,y12);
title('The derivative')

% Plots in lower left-hand corner.

subplot(2,2,3); plot(x(1:n-1),y21);
title('The approximated derivative')

% Plots in lower right-hand corner.

subplot(2,2,4); plot(x(1:n-1),y22);
title('The difference')
```

These commands give Figure 13.15.

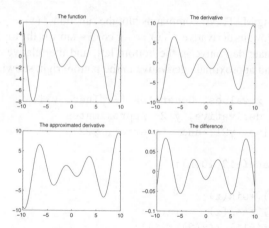

Figure 13.15 *The function* x sin x, *its derivative, an approximate derivative, and the difference.*

The command subplot can also be used for three-dimensional graphics and the subplots can be of different sizes in the same window, as the following example shows.

■ **Example 13.9**

This example contains an M-file that computes the Mandelbrot fractal and visualizes it in three different ways. The program takes points in a grid defined by the user in the complex plane and iterates each number c that belongs to the defined grid according to this algorithm:

$$z_0 = 0$$
$$z_{i+1} = z_i^2 + c$$

If z_i is divergent then the current c is not a part of the Mandelbrot set. The number of iterations in each point c of the complex plane is saved in a matrix **Mandelbrot** with the same size as the grid in the complex plane. The algorithm will only iterate 100 times so divergent points will get the value 100 in the matrix **Mandelbrot**.

```
% Mandelbrot program. MandelbrotProg.m.

clear;
renum = input('renum: ');    % Reads number of real points.
imnum = input('imnum: ');    % Reads number of imaginary points.

remin = -2;    remax = 1;    % Defines which numbers to compute.
immin = -1.5; immax = 1.5;
```

```
% Vectors of correct size.
reval1 = linspace(remin,remax,renum);
imval1 = linspace(immin,immax,imnum);

% Grid in imaginary plane.
[Reval, Imval] = meshgrid(reval1,imval1);

Imvalreal = Imval; Imval = Imval*i;
Cgrid = Reval + Imval;

for reind = 1:renum
  disp(['reind = ',int2str(reind)]);         % Writes loopstatus.

  % Iteration loop z(i+1) = (z(i))^2 + c.
  for imind = 1:imnum
    c = Cgrid(reind,imind);
    numc = 0;                                 % Initiations.
    zold = 0.0 + i*0.0;
    z    = zold^2 + c;                        % z(0) = c.

    while (abs(z) <= 2) & ...
          (numc < 100)
      numc = numc + 1;
      zold = z;
      z = zold^2 + c;                         % New z!
    end

    % Let the matrix mandelbrot have the number
    % of iterations for the point Cgrid(n,m) in
    % position mandelbrot(n,m).
    Mandelbrot(reind,imind) = numc;
  end
end

% Graphics, displays the matrix mandelbrot in
% three different ways:

clf;                                          % Clears the figure.

subplot(2,2,1);                               % Upper left corner.
mesh(reval1,imval1,Mandelbrot);               % Plots mesh grid.
axis([-2 1 -1.5 1.5 0 100])                   % Change axis limits.

subplot(2,2,2);                               % Upper right corner.
contour(reval1,imval1,Mandelbrot,100); % Contour plot.
```

```
grid;                                   % Adds grid.

subplot(2,1,2);                         % Lower figure (only one)!
surf(Reval,Imvalreal,Mandelbrot);      % Surface plot of Mandelbrot

view(2);                                % Viewpoint directly above.

% Each cell has only one color and
% use the inverse jet color bar.
shading flat;
colormap(flipud(jet));

% Show colour bar. Change axis.
colorbar; axis([-2 1 -1.5 1.5]);
```

This program results in Figure 13.16.

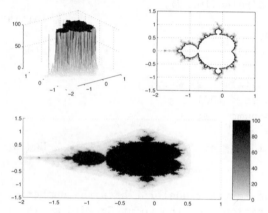

Figure 13.16 *The Mandelbrot fractal visualized in three different ways: upper left: a mesh plot; upper right: a contour plot; lower: a surface plot viewed from directly above.*

Graphics can be placed almost anywhere in the graphics windows, with more control than allowed by `subplot`; see Chapter 14.

The axes of each plot are usually automatically scaled to fit all the points in the window. Thus the corners of the plot are defined by:

$$(\min(\mathbf{x}), \min(\mathbf{y})), (\max(\mathbf{x}), \min(\mathbf{y})), (\min(\mathbf{x}), \max(\mathbf{y})), (\max(\mathbf{x}), \max(\mathbf{y})).$$

Sometimes it can be hard to see some of the points, since they might coincide with the axes due to the scaling. Fortunately, the command `axis` in MATLAB can be used to change the scaling.

It is also possible to use the mouse to change the scaling. This is possible by the command zoom.

Commands 132   AXES, SCALING, AND ZOOMING

axis	returns the limits of the current plot to a row vector. For two-dimensional graphics, it has the elements: $[x_{min}, x_{max}, y_{min}, y_{max}]$. For three-dimensional graphics (see Section 13.5) it is $[x_{min}, x_{max}, y_{min}, y_{max}, z_{min}, z_{max}]$.
axis(str)	gives different results depending on the string **str**:

'manual'	freezes the scaling of the axes. If the current graphics window is held with hold the following plots will use the same scale.
'auto'	resets the scaling to MATLAB's automatic scaling.
'equal'	sets the same scale to both the x and the y axes.
'tight'	gives the axes the same scale in both the x and the y direction and plots only the part of the coordinate system where the data is.
'fill'	sets the boundaries of the axes so they match the range of the data set.
'ij'	flips the y axis, so that positive y is down, and negative is up.
'xy'	resets the y axis, making positive y up.
'image'	resizes the graphics window, to make the pixels have the same height as width, adapting to the computer.
'square'	resizes the graphics window to make the window square.
'vis3d'	locks the relation between the axes. This is for example used when rotating 3D objects.
'normal'	resets the graphics window to standard size.
'off'	tells MATLAB not to show the axes or the scale.
'on'	tells MATLAB to show the axis and the scale again.

This command can also be given in the form axis normal, and so on.

axis(v)	sets the scales according to the vector **v**, making $x_{min} = v_1$, $x_{max} = v_2$, $y_{min} = v_3$, $y_{max} = v_4$. For three-dimensional graphics also $z_{min} = v_5$ and $z_{max} = v_6$ are set. For logarithmic plots, discussed earlier in this chapter, use the actual values, not logarithmic values. It is also possible to set the scales using axlimdlg; see Commands 169.

(CONTINUED)

axis(axis)	locks the scaling. Keeps MATLAB from changing the scale when plots are added to existing plots. See the command hold in Section13.3.
xlim([xmin xmax])	sets $x_{min} = xmin$ and $x_{max} = xmax$.
xlim	returns $[x_{min}, x_{max}]$.
ylim([ymin ymax])	sets $y_{min} = ymin$ and $y_{max} = ymax$.
ylim	returns $[y_{min}, y_{max}]$.
zlim([zmin zmax])	sets $z_{min} = zmin$ and $z_{max} = zmax$.
zlim	returns $[z_{min}, z_{max}]$.
box	controls whether the graphics should be enclosed by axes from all sides. The command box on turns the function on, and box off turns it off. Just box changes between on and off. This works also with 3D pictures.
datetick(axis, format)	formats the text at the coordinate axis **axis** according to the date format *format*. The parameter **axis** can be $'x'$ (default), $'y'$ or $'z'$. See Section 2.5 for more information on date formats.
dragrect(X, *step*)	allows the user to pull rectangles over the screen. The rectangles are specified by the matrix **X** which must be of the size $n \times 4$, where each row specifies a rectangle. If *step* is given the rectangles can only be pulled in even steps of that size.
grid on	draws a grid in the graphics window. If the previous plot is plotted with, e.g., polar (see Section 13.2), the grid is plotted in polar coordinates.
grid off	removes the grid from the graphics window.
grid	toggles between grid on and grid off.
zoom on	enables the user to zoom in on two-dimensional graphics by clicking the left mouse button in the graphics window. The right mouse button can be used to zoom out. It is also possible to select an area by 'click and drag'. The scale is adjusted to make the selected area fill the graphics window.
zoom off	disables the zoom.
zoom out	resets the full scale.
zoom	toggles between zoom on and zoom off.
zoom(factor)	zooms the current axis by *factor*.
zoom axis	scales the axes. If *axis* is xon or yon only that axis is scaled.

The axes and the grid can be controlled in more detail; see Chapter 14. Closely related to the command axis are the commands caxis and saxis, setting the scales for the colors and sounds, respectively; see Sections 13.6 and 13.8.

As described in Section 2.3, commands can be considered to be functions with string arguments. Hence, `axis('square')` can also be written as `axis square`, and `grid off` is equivalent to `grid('off')`.

■ **Example 13.10**

(a) Let us define a set of values representing the unit circle:

```
t = 0:0.2:2*pi + 0.2;    % A parameter for the angle.
x = sin(t);              % x-values.
y = cos(t);              % y-values.
```

The following command gives us Figure 13.17:

```
plot(x,y,'-')
```

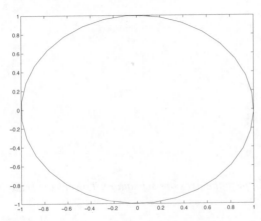

Figure 13.17 *A circle might look oval if the scaling is not adjusted.*

(b) The axes can be rescaled to make the circles look like circles. We also draw a grid this time.

```
axis('square');          % Adjusts the scale.
grid on;                 % Draws a grid.
```

These commands give us the plot in the upper part of Figure 13.18. The plot in the lower part of the same figure is obtained with:

```
axis('normal');          % Reset the axes.
grid off;                % Turns off the grid.
axis([-2 2 -3 3]);       % Changes the axes, scaling.
```

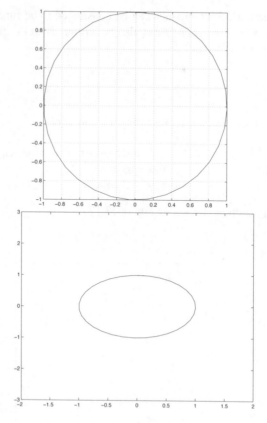

Figure 13.18 *Upper: the axes are set square. Lower: the scale is set manually.*

There are several commands to write text in a graphics window. The commands `title`, `xlabel`, `ylabel`, `zlabel` write standard text items. MATLAB has a large number of special symbols and a few formatting functions, which are well described in the section on text in MATLAB Help Desk. The command `text` can be used to write text anywhere in the graphics window. All these commands are applied to the current `subplot`, and should usually be given after the graphics are drawn in the window. To change fonts and other properties, see Section 14.2.

| Commands 133 | TEXT IN GRAPHICS WINDOWS |

`title(txt)`	writes the string **txt** as a title centered in the top of the graphics window.
`xlabel(txt)`	writes the string **txt** as a label centered below the x axis.
`ylabel(txt)`	writes the string **txt** as a label centered beside the y axis.
`zlabel(txt)`	writes the string **txt** as a label centered beside the z axis.

Commands 133	(CONTINUED)

`text(x,y,txt)`	writes the string **txt** in the graphics window at position (x, y). The coordinates x and y are given in the same scale in which the plot is drawn. For **x** and **y** vectors, the string **txt** is written at positions (x_i, y_i). If **txt** is a vector of strings, that is a matrix of characters, with the same number of rows as **x** and **y**, the string on the ith row is written at position (x_i, y_i) in the graphics window.
`text(x,y,txt,'sc')`	writes the string **txt** at position (x, y) in the graphics window. The coordinates are given with $(0.0, 0.0)$ as the lower left-hand corner, and $(1.0, 1.0)$ as the top right-hand corner.
`gtext(txt)`	lets the user place the string **txt** in the graphics window. A cross is moved in the graphics window, with the arrow keys or a mouse. When the cross is at the desired location, the user presses any key, or any button on the mouse, and the string is written to the window.
`legend(str1,str2, ...  pos )`	writes a legend in the current plot with the specified strings **str1**, **str2** and so on as labels. If *pos* is given the legend is placed as follows:

-1	places the legend box outside the axes to the right.
0	places the box inside the axis so that a minimum of points are covered.
1	places the box in the top right corner.
2	places the box in the top left corner.
3	places the box in the lower left corner.
4	places the box in the lower right corner.
$[x\ y]$	forces the lower left corner of the box to the coordinates (x, y).

`legend(H,str1, str2,...)`	returns the handle **H** to get the right string to the right curve. Necessary for plots using a matrix as input.
`legend off`	removes legend from current plot.

The commands converting numbers to strings, that is `num2str`, `int2str`, `sprintf`, and so on (see Section 5.1.2) can be useful and sometimes even necessary to use together with these text commands.

■ Example 13.11

(a) Let us write a simple program that performs a random walk. This can be a simulation of the movement of a particle in air.

The program is stored as **particle.m**:

```
% Random walk. A particle starts at the origin, and is
% moved randomly up to a half unit in either direction
% in every step.

disp('Give the number of steps')    % The number of steps.
n = input('>>>');

x = cumsum(rand(n,1)-0.5);           % Random x-values.
y = cumsum(rand(n,1)-0.5);           % Random y-values.

clf;                                 % Clear graphics window.
plot(x,y);                           % Plots the walk.
hold on;                             % Holds the plot.
plot(x(1),y(1),'o',x(n),y(n),'o');   % Marks start/finish.

axs   = axis;                        % Gets min and max.
scale = axs(2) - axs(1);             % Calculates a scale.

text(x(1)+scale/30,y(1),'Start');    % Writes text to the right
text(x(n)+scale/30,y(n),'Finish');   % of Start and Finish.

hold off;                            % Resets hold to standard.

xlabel('x'); ylabel('y');
title('Random walk')
```

When this program is run, with the command `particle`, we get:

Give the number of steps
>>> 100

We now obtain Figure 13.19.

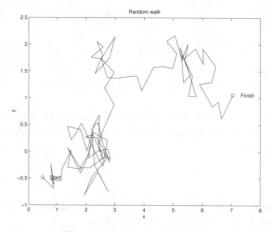

Figure 13.19 *Random walk.*

(b) If we change a few things on the lines that write text in the graph, e.g., to:

```
text(x(1)+scale/30,y(1),'Start','FontSize',20,'FontName',...
                                              'Times');
text(x(n)+scale/30,y(n),'Finish','FontSize',20,'FontName',...
                                              'Times');
xlabel('x','FontSize',18,'FontWeight','bold');
ylabel('y','FontSize',18,'FontWeight','bold');
title('Random walk','FontSize',18,'FontWeight','bold');
```

we get Figure 13.20 instead.

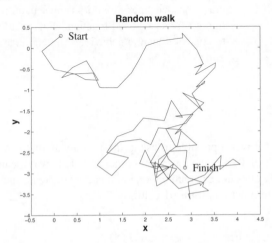

Figure 13.20 *A random walk with changed text format.*

The command ginput is used to get information from a graphics window. This command places a cursor in the graphics window, and this cursor can be moved by the user, either with the keyboard or with the mouse. By moving it to the desired position, and pressing a key or a mouse button, the coordinates are passed to MATLAB. If the number of coordinates to be read is not specified, MATLAB keeps reading coordinates for each key or mouse button pressed until the key 'return' is pressed.

<table>
<tr><td>Commands 134</td><td>READING DATA FROM A GRAPHICS WINDOW</td></tr>
</table>

[x,y] = ginput	reads coordinates from a graphics window. A cursor which can be positioned with the mouse, or with the arrow keys, is placed in the graphics window, and by pressing a mouse button or any key, the coordinates are sent to MATLAB. These coordinates are stored in the vectors **x** and **y**. The process is terminated with the 'return' key.
[x,y] = ginput(n)	reads *n* coordinates from the graphics window.

> ### Commands 134   (CONTINUED)
>
> | | |
> |---|---|
> | `[x,y,t] = ginput(...)` | also returns a vector **t** with integers specifying which mouse buttons were pressed. The left button returns 1, the middle button 2, and the right button returns 3. If the keyboard was used, the ASCII codes of the keys pressed are returned. |
> | `waitforbuttonpress` | stops MATLAB until a mouse button or a key is pressed in current figure. If a mouse button is pressed, `waitforbuttonpress` returns 0, if a key on the keyboard is pressed, 1 is returned. |
> | `rbbox` | draws dashed lines around a rubber band box in the current figure. It can be used together with `waitforbuttonpress` to control dynamic behavior. The command is used in, e.g., `zoom`. |

■ Example 13.12

In MATLAB 4 it was a possible to use `ginput` in a way that rescaled the graphics window so that $(0, 0)$ was the lower left corner and $(1, 1)$ was the upper right corner. This possibility does not exist any more, but it is easy to create such a window using the user-defined function **ginput01** below:

```
function [x,y,button] = ginput01(N);

if (nargin == 0), N = inf; end

[x,y,button] = ginput(N);
xylim = get(gca,{'xlim','ylim'}); % Gets the limits of the axes.
x = (x-xylim{1}(1))/diff(xylim{1}); % Rescales x and y using
y = (y-xylim{2}(1))/diff(xylim{2}); % the limits of the axes.
```

The get command is described in Chapter 14.

■

■ Example 13.13

The `ginput` and `waitforbuttonpress` commands provide the MATLAB programmer with tools to create simple interactive programs. The M-file below uses both commands for drawing a picture out of points specified by the user. When the plot is drawn the program waits for the user to click in the figure before deleting it.

```
% M-file for interactive drawing.

n = figure;                % New figure.

disp('To draw a line in the figure:')
disp('Press the left mouse button in the figure for start,')
disp('each bend and stop of the line. ')
disp('Press right mouse button when finished.')

[x,y,t] = ginput(1);       % Read first mouse button press coord.
plot(x,y,'o')              % Marks it with a circle.
xx = x; yy = y;            % Save coordinates.
hold on; axis([0 1 0 1]);% Holds the figure and lock the axis.

while t ~= 3               % While not the right button pressed
  [x,y,t] = ginput(1);     % read new coordinates and
  plot(x,y,'o')            % marks it with a circle.
  xx = [xx x];             % Saves coordinates.
  yy = [yy y];
end

clf; line(xx,yy);          % Clears the figure and draw a line.

disp('Click on the figure when you are done')

waitforbuttonpress;        % Wait until button press in figure.
delete(n);                 % Remove figure.
```

The commands figure, delete and line are introduced in Section 14.2. Other interactive commands are presented in Section 14.3. Figure 13.21 is produced from the M-file above

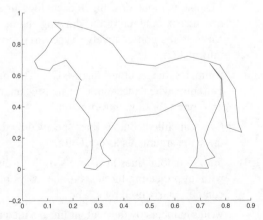

Figure 13.21 *A result of the interactive program in Example 13.13.*

13.4 Generating grids and drawing contour plots

Contour plots of a function of two variables, such as $z = \mathbf{f}(x, y)$, can be drawn in both two and three dimensions. The former is accomplished with the command contour, and the latter with contour3. Note that MATLAB 5 can handle non-uniform grids.

Commands 135	CONTOUR PLOTS

contour(Z)	draws a contour plot of the values in the matrix **Z**. The elements are interpreted as representing levels over the (x, y) plane. If **Z** is an $m \times n$ matrix, the scale on the horizontal axis is set as 1 to n and the vertical scale is set as 1 to m.
	The command C = contour(Z) returns a contour matrix **C** to be used by, for example, the command clabel. See also contourc.
contour(Z,n)	draws contour lines for n levels. If not specified, 10 levels are drawn.
contour(Z,v)	draws contour lines for the levels specified in the vector **v**.
contour(x,y,Z)	draws contour lines for the matrix **Z**, using the vectors **x** and **y** as the coordinates to **Z**, that is **x** and **y** set the scale on the axes.
contour(x,y,Z,n)	draws n levels, using the vectors **x** and **y** as the scale of the axes.
contour(x,y,Z,v)	draws contour lines at the levels specified by the vector **v** using the vectors **x** and **y** as the scale of the axes.
contour(...,str)	draws contour lines using the line types and colors defined by the string **str**. See the plot command and Table 13.1 in Section 13.1.
C = contourc(...)	computes the contour matrix **C** for use by contour and clabel without drawing the contour lines. **C** is a two-row matrix containing the drawing segments for each level curve stored consecutively. Type help contourc for more information.
C = contours(...)	computes the contour matrix **C**. The matrix is used by contour when the region is non-rectangular. Type help contours for more information.
contourf(Z)	draws the filled contour lines specified by the matrix **Z**. Uses the same arguments as contour.
contour3(x,y,Z,n)	draws contour lines at n levels in three dimensions, that is without projecting the lines to the (x, y) plane. Returns the contour matrix used by clabel.
clabel(C)	writes numbers by the contour lines to indicate the levels they represent. The positions are random. The matrix **C** is the contour matrix returned by the commands contour or contourc.

Commands 135   (CONTINUED)

`clabel(C,v)`	writes numbers indicating the levels specified in the vector **v**. The matrix **C** is the contour matrix returned by the commands `contour` or `contourc`.
`clabel(C,'manual')`	lets the user place numbers indicating the levels at that position. A cursor is placed in the contour plot, and the user moves this cursor either with the mouse, or the arrow keys. Pressing a mouse button or any key places the number. The process is terminated by pressing the key 'return'.

If a matrix **Z** is defined and we wish to see a contour plot of it, the command `contour(Z)` or `contour3(Z)` can be used.

Figure P.4 in the color plate section shows the result of `contourf` for a function $z = f(x, y)$ with four extrema.

■ **Example 13.14**

(a) Suppose we have defined a matrix **Z** which describes the surface of the two-dimensional function shown in Figure 13.35. Then the following program gives the plots in Figure 13.22:

```
[X,Y] = meshgrid(-3:1/8:3);
Z      = peaks(X,Y).*sin(X);

v1 = -4:-1;
v2 = 0:4;

clf;

subplot(2,1,1);        % Upper subplot.
contour(Z,v1,'k-');    % Draws solid lines for Z negative.
hold on;

contour(Z,v2,'k--');   % Draws dashed lines for Z nonnegative.
hold off;

subplot(2,1,2);        % Lower subplot.
C = contour(Z);        % Draws the contour lines.
clabel(C);             % Writes the contour labels.
```

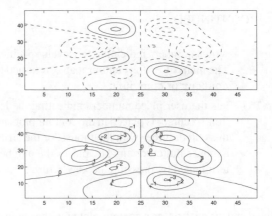

Figure 13.22 *Contour plots.*

(b) We may also use `contour` for non-rectangular grids. Figure 13.23 is plotted with the program in Example 13.23. In Figure 13.23 we have reset the text font to show that each contour line has its own graphics handle. See Chapter 14 for more information on graphical objects and handles.

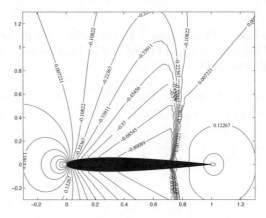

Figure 13.23 *Contour lines of the air pressure, isobars, of a wing profile in 15 levels.*

The `contourf` command fills the areas between the lines; see Figure 13.24. The graph is plotted with white lines instead of black; see Example 13.23.

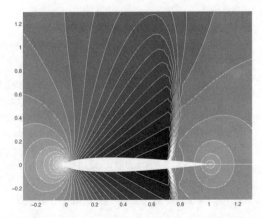

Figure 13.24 *Contour lines for a wing profile created with* contourf. *The number of levels is 30 and they are uniformly spaced between* −1 *and* 1.

However, it might be necessary to compute **Z**. This is accomplished in two steps. First, we define a grid in the domain where we wish to draw the contour lines. The domain is defined by two vectors **x** and **y** with length n and m respectively, for the x and y values in the grid. Note that the elements of **x** and **y** do not have to be equidistant. We then form the grid with the command [U,V] = meshgrid(x,y). The actual grid is the two matrices **U** and **V**, containing its x and y coordinates. The matrix **U** consists of the vector **x** copied to m rows, and **V** of the vector **y** copied to n columns. This is shown in Figure 13.25, where the y axis is drawn downwards to emphasize the correspondence between the grid points and the elements of the matrices.

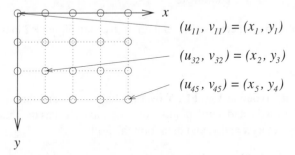

Figure 13.25 *A grid with five values of* **x** *and four values of* **y** *defines two* 4×5 *matrices* **U** *and* **V** *with elements from the vectors* **x** *and* **y**.

The meshgrid command has equivalents for generating cylindrical grids and spherical grids.

Commands 136	GENERATION OF GRID

`[U,V] =` `meshgrid(x,y)`	gives matrices forming a grid with the x coordinates and y coordinates from the vectors **x** and **y**. A vector **x** of length n containing the x coordinates in ascending order, and a vector **y** of length m in ascending order, are copied m and n times respectively, to form the two $m \times n$-matrices **U** and **V**. These matrices represent the x and y coordinates in the whole rectangular domain. The coordinate pairs (u_{ij}, v_{ij}), $i = 1, \ldots, m$, $j = 1, \ldots, n$, can be used to calculate $z_{ij} = f(u_{ij}, v_{ij})$, with the command Z = f(U,V), see Figure 13.25.
`[U,V] = meshgrid(x)`	is the same as `[U,V] = meshgrid(x,x)`.
`[U,V,W] =` `meshgrid(x,y,z)`	gives a three-dimensional grid in the same manner, and can be used to evaluate functions of three variables.
`[X,Y,Z] =` `cylinder(r,n)`	returns coordinate matrices like meshgrid, but the generated coordinates form the surface of a cylinder or cone. The radius of the cylinder is taken from the vector **r**, containing the radii in n equidistant points along the cylinder axis. If n is not specified, $n = 20$ is used. If neither **r** nor n is specified, $\mathbf{r} = (1 \quad 1)$ and $n = 20$ are used.
`cylinder(r,n)`	plots the cylinder according to the above instead of returning the coordinates.
`[X,Y,Z] = sphere(n)`	returns n equally spaced coordinates on a unit sphere in the matrices **X**, **Y** and **Z**, all $(n+1) \times (n+1)$ matrices.
`sphere(n)`	plots the sphere according to the above instead of returning the coordinates.

The command sphere has been used several times to create Figure P.2 in the color plate section.

■ Example 13.15

Suppose we want to define a grid **U**, **V** over the unit square and that we want 5 grid points along the x axis, and 4 grid points along the y axis, just as in Figure 13.25. We first define the vectors **x** and **y**, and then form the grid:

```
x = linspace(0,1,5);   % Defines the x values.
y = linspace(0,1,4);   % Defines the y values.

[U,V] = meshgrid(x,y)   % Forms the grid.

U =
         0     0.2500     0.5000     0.7500     1.0000
         0     0.2500     0.5000     0.7500     1.0000
         0     0.2500     0.5000     0.7500     1.0000
         0     0.2500     0.5000     0.7500     1.0000
```

$V =$

0	0	0	0	0
0.3333	0.3333	0.3333	0.3333	0.3333
0.6667	0.6667	0.6667	0.6667	0.6667
1.0000	1.0000	1.0000	1.0000	1.0000

The second step is to evaluate the function $z = f(x, y)$ over the domain. With the grid defined, this is just $Z = f(U, V)$. This requires the function f to be defined with elementwise operators; see Section 3.5.

■ **Example 13.16**

(a) Let us draw contour plots for the following three functions:

$$\begin{cases} Z_1 = f_1(x, y) = \sin x \cdot \sin y & x, y \in [0, \pi] \times [0, \pi] \\ Z_2 = f_2(x, y) = x - 0.5x^3 + 0.2y^2 + 1 & x, y \in [-3, 3] \times [-3, 3] \\ Z_3 = f_3(x, y) = \sin(\sqrt{x^2 + y^2})/\sqrt{x^2 + y^2} & x, y \in [-8, 8] \times [-8, 8] \end{cases}$$

The first part of the program generates the grids and evaluates the functions. The final part of the program draws the plots. This is the program **contours.m**:

```
x = 0:0.2:3*pi;            % Generates coordinates.
y = 0:0.25:5*pi;
[XX,YY] = meshgrid(x,y);
Z1 = sin(XX).*sin(YY);     % Evaluates Z1.


x = -3:0.25:3;             % Generates coordinates.
y = x;
[XX,YY] = meshgrid(x,y);
Z2 = XX - 0.5*XX.^3 + 0.2*YY.^2 + 1;   % Evaluates Z2.


x = -8:0.5:8;              % Generates coordinates.
y = x;
[XX,YY] = meshgrid(x,y);
r = sqrt(XX.^2+YY.^2) + eps;
Z3 = sin(r)./r;            % Evaluates Z3.

clf;

subplot(2,2,1); contour(Z1);
title('sin(x)*sin(y)');

subplot(2,2,2); contour(x,y,Z3);
title('sin(r)/r');
```

```
subplot(2,2,3); contour3(Z2,15);
title('x-0.5x^3 + 0.2y^2 + 1');

subplot(2,2,4); contour3(x,y,Z3);
title('sin(r)/r');

subplot(2,2,3); rotate3d;
```

The last line allows us to rotate the lower left graph to get a better view using the mouse; rotate3d is described in Section 13.5. When we execute this program, we get, after some rotating, Figure 13.26.

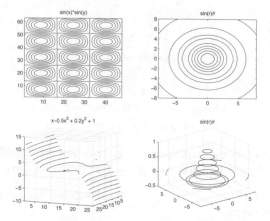

Figure 13.26 *Contour plots of some functions.*

(b) To get a really revealing plot of a function, we draw contour lines in the same plot as we plot gradients. The gradients can be computed with the command gradient (see Section 6.2) and they can be plotted with the command quiver (see Section 13.2). This interesting plot can be obtained with the following statements:

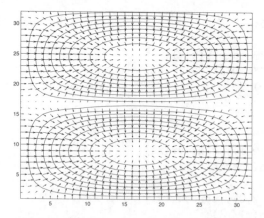

Figure 13.27 *Contour plot with gradients.*

```
[X,Y]        = meshgrid(-pi/2:0.1:pi/2,-pi:0.2:pi);
Z            = abs(sin(Y).*cos(X));
[DZDX,DZDY]  = gradient(Z,.1,0.2);

contour(Z);          hold on;
quiver(DZDX,DZDY);   hold off;
```

and we get Figure 13.27.

■

13.5 Three-dimensional graphics

A three-dimensional plot can be drawn with the command plot3. This command is almost the same as plot, but plot3 needs a third vector or matrix argument. Style and color can be specified with a string in the same way as for plot; see Table 13.1.

Commands 137	THREE-DIMENSIONAL PLOTS
plot3(x,y,z)	plots a graph through the points defined by (x_i, y_i, z_i). The vectors **x**, **y** and **z** must be of equal length.
plot3(X,Y,Z)	plots graphs for each column of the matrices **X**, **Y** and **Z**. These matrices must be of equal size. Alternatively, some of the matrices can be vectors of the same length as the columns of the matrices.
plot3(x,y,z,str)	plots a graph according to the above, and uses the style and color specified by the string **str**. See Table 13.1 for allowed values.
plot3(x1,y1,z1, str1,x2,y2,z2, str2,...)	plots the graph (**x1**, **y1**, **z1**) with style and color according to **str1**, and (**x2**, **y2**, **z2**) with style according to **str2**, etc. If **str1**, **str2**, and so on are left out, MATLAB chooses colors and styles.

■ **Example 13.17**

Inspired by Example 13.11 we now write a program simulating a random walk in three dimensions. The program called **particle3.m** looks like this:

```
% Random walk in 3D.
% Create the x, y, z vectors using
% random numbers. Plot the "walk".

n = input('Give the number of steps : ');
```

```
x = cumsum(rand(1,n)-0.5);
y = cumsum(rand(1,n)-0.5);
z = cumsum(rand(1,n)-0.5);

plot3(x,y,z);                                  % Plots the walk.
grid on;                                       % Shows the grid
text(x(1),y(1),z(1),'Start','FontSize',20);    % Writes Start.
text(x(n),y(n),z(n),'Finish','FontSize',20);   % Writes Finish.
```

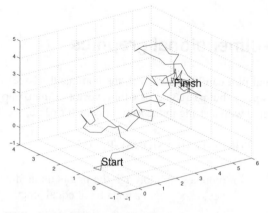

Figure 13.28 *Random walk in three dimensions.*

We get Figure 13.28 when this program is executed.

■

Text in three-dimensional figures is written with the same commands as for two-dimensional figures, that is `title`, `text`, `xlabel`, `ylabel`, and `zlabel`; see Section 13.3.

| Commands 138 | FUNCTIONS FOR THREE-DIMENSIONAL PLOTS |

`bar3(x,A,width,` `format)`	plots the columns of the matrix **A** as vertical bars, with the width *width*, if given, versus the vector **x**. The string **format**, if given, may be one of the following strings: `'detached'` gives the default detached bar chart. `'grouped'` gives a grouped bar chart. `'stacked'` gives a stacked bar chart. `linespec` uses the line color specified; see Table 13.1.
`bar3(A)`	is the same as `bar3(1:size(A,1),A)`.
`bar3h(x,A,width,` `format)`	plots the columns in the matrix **A** as horizontal bars, with the width *width*, if given, versus the vector **x**. The string **format**, if given, is the same as for `bar3`; see above.

Commands 138 (CONTINUED)

pie3(x,*explode*)	works like pie but the pie is three-dimensional.
quiver3(x,y,z,u, v,w,*s*,*format*)	plots arrows from coordinates from the three vectors **x**, **y** and **z**. The arrows have length and direction specified by the vectors **u**, **v** and **w**, scaled according to the factor *s* which is 1 if not given. The string **format**, if given, specifies the line format.
ribbon(x,y,*width*)	plots **y** versus **x** as a three-dimensional ribbon instead of the usual curve. If *width* is given the ribbon gets that width instead of the standard 0.75.
scatter3(x,y,z, *size*,*color*)	plots colored circles at the points specified by **x**, **y** and **z**, which must be of the same size. See scatter for more information.
stem3(x,y,A)	plots a stem chart from the matrix **A** versus the axes **x** and **y**.
stem3(A)	plots a stem chart from the matrix **A** versus a normalized xy plane.
stem3(...,format)	plots a stem chart formatted according to **format**. The string 'filled', which fills the top circle, may be given apart from the standard line formats.
trimesh(Tri,x,y,z)	plots triangular mesh plots according to the matrix **Tri**. The vectors **x**, **y** and **z** defines the triangles. See Chapter 6 for information on triangulation.
trisurf(Tri,x,y,z)	plots triangle areas according to the matrix **Tri** as a surface. The vectors **x**, **y** and **z** defines the corners of the triangles.

The commands bar3 and pie3 are demonstrated in Figure P.6 in the color plate section.

■ **Example 13.18**

We have the vector x = [1 2 3 4 5] and want to plot a three-dimensional pie chart with the largest section exploded. To do this we need the vector explode = [0 0 0 0 1], where all elements are zero except the one corresponding to the largest value of **x**. If we now type pie3(x,explode) we get Figure 13.29.

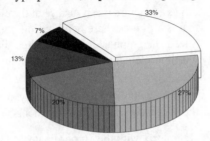

Figure 13.29 *A three-dimensional pie chart with the largest section exploded.*

■

In the same way as a two-dimensional plot can be animated with the command comet, a three-dimensional plot can be animated with the command comet3.

COMET PLOT IN THREE DIMENSIONS

comet3(x,y,z)	draws an animated three-dimensional plot of the function $z = $ $\mathbf{f}(x, y)$, that is a plot with a comet tail between the coordinates (x_i, y_i, z_i).
comet3(x,y,z,p)	gives the same animated plot as above, but the tail is of length p. The length of the tail is given as relative part of the vector **y**, and p is set to 0.1 if not specified.

A surface graph of the function $z = \mathbf{f}(x, y)$ can be obtained in the following way in MATLAB:

1. form the grid as described in Section 13.4;

2. evaluate Z = f(U,V), where the matrices **U** and **V** are the coordinates for the x and y values respectively;

3. draw the surface with one of the surface graphics commands available in MATLAB. Note that the grid does not need to be rectangular, but if not, the grid coordinates must be included in the function call.

The commands in Commands 140 are used to draw a mesh surface of functions in three dimensions.

THREE-DIMENSIONAL MESH PLOTS

mesh(Z)	plots the values in the matrix **Z** as height values above a rectangular grid, and connects neighboring points into a mesh surface. The color is given by the height, i.e., the elements in **Z**.
mesh(Z,C)	plots the values in the matrix **Z** as height values above a rectangular grid, in the color specified for each point by the elements of the matrix **C**.
mesh(U,V,Z,C)	draws a function mesh surface of the elements in the matrix **Z**, that is a figure where neighboring points are connected with lines. The graph is drawn in a three-dimensional perspective, with the elements z_{ij} as height values over the grid points (u_{ij}, v_{ij}).

The viewpoint is set automatically, and can be changed with the command view. The arguments are:

U matrix with the x coordinates
V matrix with the y coordinates
Z matrix with the z coordinates, usually $z_{ij} = \mathbf{f}(u_{ij}, v_{ij})$
C matrix with the color for each point. If **C** is left out, $\mathbf{C} = \mathbf{Z}$ is used.

Commands 140 (CONTINUED)

`meshc(...)`	draws a mesh surface like the command `mesh`, but also draws a contour plot below the graph.
`meshz(...)`	draws a mesh surface like the command `mesh`, but also draws a reference grid down to the (x, y) plane.
`waterfall(...)`	is like `meshz`, but the reference grid is only drawn in one direction.
`hidden` *val*	toggles between drawing and not drawing lines that are hidden behind the mesh surface drawn by the command `mesh`. The variable *val* may be on, which means do not plot hidden lines, or `off`, which means plot hidden lines. This command is only applicable to the command `mesh`.

The graph can be rotated using the command `rot90` on the defining matrix. Also, see the command `view` later in this section. It is easy to decide a view with the `rotate3d` command.

Commands 141 MATRIX ROTATION

`rotate3d` *val*	allows the user to rotate a three-dimensional plot with the mouse. If *val* is given it may be on, which turns on the function, or `off`, which turns off the function.
`rot90(A)`	returns the matrix **A** rotated 90 degrees counter-clockwise. Often used together with the command `mesh`.
`rot90(A,k)`	returns the matrix **A** rotated $k \times 90$ degrees counter-clockwise.

We would also like to stress that the command `mesh` can be very useful to get an image of a matrix. This can be useful in understanding for instance how numerical methods work.

■ **Example 13.19**

(a) We now want to write a MATLAB program to draw a mesh grid of the same functions as in Example 13.16, and we assume that the same matrices **Z1**, **Z2**, and **Z3** are already defined. The following statements are given:

```
% The matrices Z1, Z2, and Z3 will be defined in
% in contours.m.
% Draws the graphs of four functions.

clear;
contoursProg;                    % Runs contours.m.
```

```
disp('Matrices defined!');
clf;

subplot(2,2,1), mesh(Z1)
title('sin(x)*sin(y)');

subplot(2,2,2), meshz(Z2)
title('x - 0.5*x^3 + 0.2*y^2 + 1');

subplot(2,2,3), waterfall(Z2)
title('x - 0.5*x^3 + 0.2*y^2 + 1')

subplot(2,2,4), meshc(Z3)
title('sin(r)/r')
```

When this is executed, we obtain Figure 13.30.

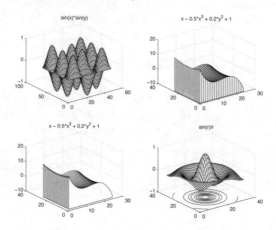

Figure 13.30 *Some functions plotted with various mesh commands.*

(b) The following MATLAB program performs the LU and the QR factorization of a given matrix **A**, and also plots the matrices **L**, **U**, **Q**, **R** in four subplots in the graphics window. These commands are stored in **luqrmesh.m**:

```
if ~exist('A')
  A = input('Give a matrix A: ');
else
  disp('The following matrix exists:');
  A
end

[L,U] = lu(A);
[Q,R] = qr(A);
```

```
subplot; mesh(A); title('The matrix A');
disp('Press any key when you are ready!');
pause; clf;

subplot(221); mesh(L); title('The matrix L');
subplot(222); mesh(U); title('The matrix U');
subplot(223); mesh(Q); title('The matrix Q');
subplot(224); mesh(R); title('The matrix R');
```

The program runs, if we suppose **A** is defined, with the command:

luqrmesh

The following matrix exists:
A =

30	1	7	2	6	5
4	24	9	4	0	1
9	9	21	6	1	7
8	3	7	21	3	9
4	9	1	6	27	9
1	6	4	2	3	9

Press any key when you are ready!

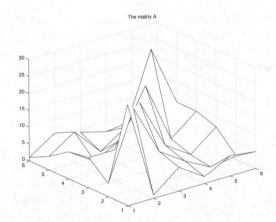

Figure 13.31 *The matrix* **A** *drawn with mesh.*

First we get Figure 13.31 and after another key is pressed, we get Figure 13.32.

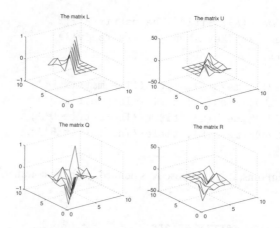

Figure 13.32 *The matrices* **L**, **U**, **Q** *and* **R**.

■

There are a number of special three-dimensional plot functions in MATLAB.

Earlier in this section we discussed how to draw a mesh surface graph. A shaded surface graph is drawn in the same way: create two matrices with the x and y coordinates of each point, evaluate the function, and draw the graph with a suitable command.

Surface graphs can be produced with the commands `fill`, `fill3`, `surf`, `surfc` and `surfl`. The command `surfl` shows a shaded surface plot with lighting. It is based on a combination of diffuse, specular, and ambient lighting models. These kind of surfaces are viewed with a gray scale and by the use of the command `shading interp`, defined in Commands 146. It is also possible to create the normal vector components of a surface and obtain diffusive or specular reflectance using these data.

Commands 142	SURFACE GRAPHS AND LIGHTING

`surf(X,Y,Z,C)`	draws a surface graph of the surface specified by the coordinates (X_{ij}, Y_{ij}, Z_{ij}). If **X** and **Y** are vectors of length m and n respectively, **Z** has to be a matrix of size $m \times n$, and the surface is defined by (X_j, Y_i, Z_{ij}). If **X** and **Y** are left out, MATLAB uses a uniform rectangular grid. The colors are defined by the elements in the matrix **C**, and if left out **C** = **Z** is used.
`surfc(X,Y,Z,C)`	does the same as `surf(...)`, except that MATLAB also draws a contour plot beneath the surface.
`surfl(X,Y,Z,ls)`	does the same as `surf(...)`, but also places a light in the direction **ls** = $[v, h]$ or **ls** = $[X, Y, Z]$, where the parameters are the same as for the command `view`.

Commands 142 (CONTINUED)

`surfl(X,Y,Z,ls,r)`	does the same as above, but the user may give the relative contributions due to ambient light, diffuse reflection, specular reflection, and the specular spread coefficient using the vector **r** = [*ambient, diffuse, specular, spread*].
`surfnorm(X,Y,Z)`	is the same as `surf`, but also draws normals.
`[Nx,Ny,Nz] =` `surfnorm(X,Y,Z)`	gives the normals to the surface defined by the matrices **X**, **Y**, **Z**, but does not draw the graph. Thus $(nx_{ij}, ny_{ij}, nz_{ij})$ is a vector defining the normal in the point (X_{ij}, Y_{ij}, Z_{ij}). The normals have length $= 1$.
`diffuse(Nx,Ny,Nz,` `ls)`	returns the reflectance of a diffuse surface with normal components given by **Nx**, **Ny**, **Nz**, using Lambert's law. **ls** is the three-component vector defining the light source position.
`specular(Nx,Ny,Nz,` `ls,v)`	returns specular reflectance of a surface with normal components **Nx**, **Ny**, **Nz**, using the positions of the light source **ls** and the viewer **v**.
`light`	creates a source of light with standard values.
`light(`*propstr,val,* `...)`	creates a light object with the properties **propstr** set to *val*. More than one property may be set at a time. Setting the properties demands some knowledge of graphical objects; see Chapter 14, especially Table 14.26 on lighting objects.
`lightangle(azimuth,` `hight)`	creates a lighting object 'infinitely' far away. For positioning a spherical coordinate system is used, where *azimuth* is the horizontal rotation in degrees and *height* is the 'height' in degrees.
`camlight(azimuth,` `height)`	creates a source of light in the coordinate system of the camera; see Commands 144. For positioning a spherical coordinate system is used, where *azimuth* is the horizontal rotation in degrees and *height* is the 'height' in degrees.
`camlight headlight`	creates a source of light at the position of the camera.
`camlight right`	creates a source of light to the right and above the camera.
`camlight left`	creates a source of light to the left and above the camera.
`camlight(...,type)`	sets the type of source of light. The string **type** may be `'local'` (default) or `'infinite'`.
`lighting mode`	changes the lighting of polygon and surface objects, i.e., graphs plotted with, e.g., `surf` or `patch`. Valid values of *mode* are: `flat`, `gourand`, `phong` and `none`. More on these modes are found in `helpdesk`.

Commands 142 (CONTINUED)

`material mode`	changes the reflectance of polygon and surface objects, i.e., graphs plotted with, e.g., `surf` or `patch`. Valid values of *mode* are: `skiny`, `dull` and `metal`. See `helpdesk` for more information.
`material([ka kd kn n sc])`	sets different values for the reflectance of the surface. See `helpdesk` on the meaning of the different attributes. ka changes the attribute `AmbientStrength` kd changes the attribute `DiffuseStrength` kn changes the attribute `SpecularStrength` n changes the attribute `SpecularExponent` sc changes the attribute `SpecularColorReflectance`
`pcolor(Z)`	draws a pseudocolor plot of the matrix **Z** as a rectangular array of cells with colors determined by the values of the elements of **Z**.
`pcolor(X,Y,Z)`	the same as `surf(X,Y,Z)`; `view(2)`, see Commands 143.
`fill(x,y,c)`	draws the polygon with the corners specified by the coordinate vectors **x** and **y**. The polygon is filled with the color specified in the string **c** (see Table 13.1) or by the values in a vector **c** of the same length as **x** and **y**. If **x** or **y** are matrices, a polygon is drawn for each column.
`fill3(x,y,z,c)`	draws the polygon specified by **x**, **y**, and **z**. The polygon is filled with the color in the string **c**, or in the values in the vector **c**; see Section 13.6. If the arguments are matrices, a polygon is drawn for each column.

The color scales used by these commands can be adjusted; see Section 13.6.

The command `light` has been used to create a light source for Figure P.2 in the color plate section.

■ **Example 13.20**

(a) Let us draw $(\sin r)/r$ with a contour plot shown beneath:

```
x       = -8:0.5:8;
[Xx Yy] = meshgrid(x);

R = sqrt(Xx.^2+Yy.^2) + eps;
Z = sin(R)./R;
```

```
clf;
surfc(Xx,Yy,Z); title('(sin r)/r');
```

and we get Figure 13.33.

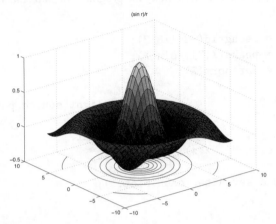

Figure 13.33 *A bell-shaped surface, with contour lines beneath.*

(b) We now draw the same function with normals plotted. We assume that **Xx, Yy** and **Z** have been computed as in (a). The following statement gives us Figure 13.34:

```
surfnorm(Xx,Yy,Z)
```

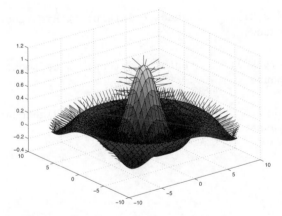

Figure 13.34 *A bell-shaped function with normals.*

■ **Example 13.21**

Let us study the commands surfl and surf using different weights for the ambient light, diffuse reflection and specular reflection. We will use a built-in function peaks, which is commonly used for demonstration of the three-dimensional graphics commands. For better visualization, we have manipulated the axes, according to Chapter 14, but these specific commands are omitted here, and we will only show some parts of the program. Let us now study the program which results in Figure 13.35:

```
[X,Y]      = meshgrid(-3:1/8:3);
Z          = peaks(X,Y).*sin(X);
[Nx,Ny,Nz] = surfnorm(Z);

s  = [-3 -3 2];             % The light source position.
k1 = [0,1,0,0];            % Diffuse.
k2 = [0,0,1,1];            % Specular.
DD = diffuse(Nx,Ny,Nz,s);

disp('Press a key after each plot.');

clf;

colormap(gray);
axis([-3 3 -3 3 min(min(Z)) max(max(Z))]);

surfl(X,Y,Z,s);            shading interp;  % Leftmost  upper.
axis off; pause;

surfl(X,Y,Z,s,k1);         shading interp;  % Rightmost upper.
axis off; pause;

surfl(X,Y,Z,s,k2);         shading interp;  % Leftmost  lower.
axis off; pause;

surf(X,Y,Z,DD);            shading interp;  % Rightmost lower.
axis off; pause;
```

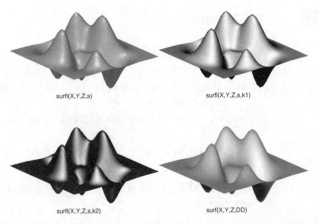

surfl(X,Y,Z,s) surfl(X,Y,Z,s,k1)

surfl(X,Y,Z,s,k2) surf(X,Y,Z,DD)

Figure 13.35 *Three-dimensional shaded surface graphs with different lighting models.*

A graph might be easier to grasp if it is viewed from a different angle. The command `view` is used to change the view of the graph. It is possible both to specify a viewpoint, and to specify the angles of azimuth and elevation; see Figure 13.36. It is also possible to change the perspective with the command `viewmtx`.

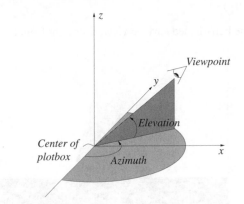

Figure 13.36 *How the view command works.*

| Commands 143 | VIEWPOINT AND PERSPECTIVE |

`view(v,h)`	sets the view angle. The scalar v is the azimuth angle, that is the angle in the xy plane counter-clockwise. The elevation above the plane is set by the scalar h. Both v and h are in degrees.
`[v,h] = view`	returns the angles v in the xy plane and h above the xy plane, currently in use by `view`.
`view(r)`	places the viewer in position $\mathbf{r} = (x \quad y \quad z)$.

Commands 143   (CONTINUED)

`view(n)`	sets the view angles according to
	n=2 the standard two-dimensional viewpoint, that is straight down from above.
	n=3 the standard three-dimensional viewpoint.
`view`	gives the 4×4 matrix used to transform the data when drawing the graphics.
`view(T)`	makes MATLAB use **T**, a 4×4 matrix, when drawing the graphics.
`viewmtx(v,h,s,r)`	returns a 4×4 matrix that defines a viewpoint and a view direction. Type `help viewmtx` to obtain more information.

■ **Example 13.22**

(a) Suppose Figure 13.33 is in the graphics window. The command:

`view([1 0 0]);`

gives the same bell-shaped surface viewed straight from the side in Figure 13.37.

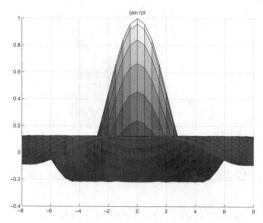

Figure 13.37 *A bell-shaped surface seen from the side.*

(b) The matrix **Matlabmatrix** consists of ones and zeros, where the ones form the letters MATLAB. Unfortunately, the matrix is too big to be shown here. The following commands draw a mesh surface of the matrix, and also draw a spy plot; see Section 9.3 of the matrix. The commands are stored in the file **meshplot.m**:

```
% Matlabmatrix.m creates a matrix, Matlabmatrix, which
% represents the word MATLAB, using ones and zeros.

Matlabmatrix;                        % Run Matlabmatrix.m.

clf;                                 % Clears figure.

subplot(2,2,1); mesh(Matlabmatrix);  % Draws standard mesh.
title('Standard view');              % Writes title.

subplot(2,2,2); mesh(Matlabmatrix);  % Draws mesh surface.
view([1 -4 2]);
axis([0 200 0 20 0 3]);              % Adjusts the view.
title('Viewed from position [1,-4,2]');

subplot(2,2,3); mesh(Matlabmatrix);  % and so on...
view([-1 -2 -7]);
title('Viewed from beneath');

subplot(2,2,4); spy(Matlabmatrix);   % The command spy shows
title('This is the matrix structure'); % the non-zero
                                     % elements.
```

Running the program with meshplot; gives us Figure 13.38.

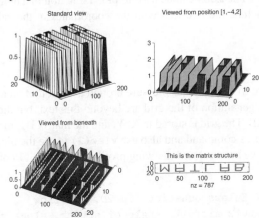

Figure 13.38 *MATLAB matrix drawn in different ways.*

When we use the command spy (see Section 9.3) we notice that the origin is placed in the upper left hand corner. This is the best way to illustrate a matrix, since we write and define matrices in this way.

(c) Although the command view is mostly useful in connection with three-dimensional graphics, it is possible to apply view to two-dimensional graphics. If we have

Figure 13.17 in the graphics window, which is created with the two-dimensional command plot, then the command:

```
view([1 0.6 0.35])
```

shows the same circle drawn in three dimensions, seen from position $(1, 0.6, 0.35)$ in Figure 13.39.

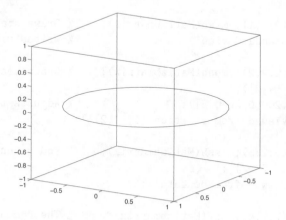

Figure 13.39 *A circle in space.*

◼

The commands surf and mesh can be used to plot a function in a non-rectangular grid. We now have to include the matrices with the coordinates in the call to the graphics routine.

◼ **Example 13.23**

Suppose we want to study the air pressure around a section of an aircraft wing. The calculations and generation of the grid are beyond this text, but the figure is easy to draw in MATLAB. The grid is stored in **X**, **Y**, and the matrix **P** is the air pressure. We zoom with the axis command and also use view(2) to see the pictures from above. In some figures we have colored the wing profile with the fill command.

```
% Solution of Eulers equations in 2D, for flow
% around NACA0012 airfoil. Angle of attack, alpha = 0.
% Mach number = 0.85. Roe's second order method.
% Grid = 200*80 points, stored as X, Y on FoilXY.mat.
% Computed solution stored in matrix P on FoilPressure.mat.

if ~exist('X')
    disp('X does not exist.');
    load FoilPressure;             % Loads data for solution.
    load FoilXY;                   % Loads data for grid.
```

```
else
   disp('X exists');
end;


BodyX = X(:,1);
BodyY = Y(:,1);                          % Defines the airfoil.
BodyU = P(:,1);


maxP = max(max(P)); minP = min(min(P));  % Max and min pressure.


% Grid around the airfoil.
clf;
mesh(X,Y,P,ones(size(X))); view(2);      % Draws the grid.
axis([-0.3 1.3 -0.3 1.3]);               % Sets the view.
pause;


% Surface plot of the pressure distribution.
clf;
surf(X,Y,P); shading interp; view(2);    % Draws the surface.
axis([-0.3 1.3 -0.3 1.3]);               % Sets the view.
pause;


% Contour plot using black contour lines and labels.
clf;
fill(BodyX,BodyY,'k'); hold on;          % Draws filled airfoil.
axis([-0.3 1.3 -0.3 1.3]);               % Sets the view.
[C,H] =  contour(X,Y,P,15,'k');          % Draws contour lines.
h = clabel(C,H);                         % Contour elevation
                                         % labels.


for lev = 1:length(h)                    % Changes font of labels.
    set(h(lev),'fontname','times');
end;
pause;


% Filled contour plot, using contourf and white contour lines.
% Label every second line.
clf;
DrawLevel = linspace(-1,1,30);           % Defines which lines
                                         % to draw.

[C,H] = contourf(X,Y,P,DrawLevel,'w');   % Draws contour lines.
axis([-0.3 1.3 -0.3 1.3]);               % Sets the view.
pause;
```

The result is shown in Figures 13.40, 13.41, 13.23 and 13.24. The grid (see Figure 13.40) is plotted using a constant matrix of the same size as **P**.

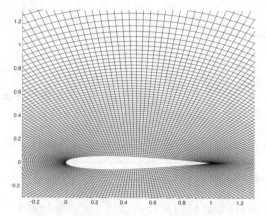

Figure 13.40 *Grid around a wing profile.*

Figure 13.41 *Air pressure around a wing profile.*

The camera is another, more detailed, way to control the viewpoint. The properties of the camera are shown in Figure 13.42.

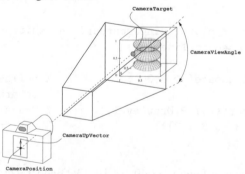

Figure 13.42 *The camera and its properties.*

The following commands may be used to control the camera.

Commands 144   CAMERA

`camdolly(dx,dy,dz,` `dirval,coordsys)`	moves the camera with the vector (dx, dy, dz). The string **dirval** tells whether the point the camera is directed towards, the target, should be moved with the camera. There are two alternatives:

'movetarget' moves the target with the camera (default).
'fixtarget' does not move the target with the camera.

The string **coordsys** tells which coordinate system is to be used. There are three alternatives:

'camera'	is a normalized coordinate system in the camera with the x axis pointing right and the y axis pointing upwards (default). Example: `camdolly(1,-1,0)` moves the camera to the right and downwards so that the old target is moved to the upper left corner.
'pixels'	is a pixel based coordinate system in the camera with the x axis pointing right and the y axis pointing upwards. The variable dz is ignored.
'data'	is the coordinate system of the picture object.

`camlookat`	moves the camera to look at a specific part of the drawing area. Demands knowledge of how the different parts (graphical objects) are related; see Chapter 14, specially Table 14.12.
`camorbit(dteta,dfi,` `coordsys,dirval)`	rotates the camera around the target. It rotates $dteta$ degrees horizontally and dfi degrees vertically. The string **coordsys** gives the coordinate system and may be 'camera' (default) or 'data' (see `camdolly`). If coordsys is 'data' the rotation is around the line from the target to the direction $dirval$.
`campan(dteta,dfi,` `coordsys,dirval)`	rotates the target around the camera. It rotates $dteta$ degrees horizontally and dfi degrees vertically. The string **coordsys** gives the coordinate system and may be 'camera' (default) or 'data' (see `camdolly`). If coordsys is 'data' the rotation is around the line from the target to the direction $dirval$.
`campos`	returns the position of the camera.
`campos([x y z])`	sets the position of the camera. The position of the camera will from now on not be computed by MATLAB; see below.
`campos('pos')`	decides whether MATLAB will compute the position of the camera automatically or not. The string **pos** may be 'auto' or 'manual'.

Commands 144   (CONTINUED)

`campos('mode')`	shows whether MATLAB computes the position of the camera or not.
`camproj`	returns the current projectory.
`camproj(projec)`	sets the current projectory. The string **projec** may be either `'ortographic'` (default) or `'perspective'`.
`camroll(dteta)`	rotates the camera *dteta* degrees counter-clockwise around the line from the target and the position of the camera.
`camtarget`	returns the target.
`camtarget([x y z])`	sets the target. The target will from now on not be computed automatically; see below.
`camtarget('pos')`	decides whether MATLAB will compute the target or not. The string **pos** may be either `'auto'` or `'manual'`.
`camtarget('mode')`	shows whether MATLAB computes the target or not.
`camup`	returns the up vector.
`camup(up)`	sets the up vector of the camera, i.e., the upward direction in the picture, to the vector *up*. The up vector will from now on not be computed automatically; see below.
`camup('pos')`	decides whether MATLAB will compute the up vector or not. The string **pos** may be either `'auto'` or `'manual'`.
`camup('mode')`	shows whether MATLAB computes the up vector or not.
`camva`	returns the camera view angle.
`camva(val)`	sets the camera view angle to `val`. The camera view angle will from now on not be computed automatically; see below.
`camva('pos')`	decides whether MATLAB will compute the camera view angle automatically or not. The string **pos** may be either `'auto'` or `'manual'`.
`camva('mode')`	shows whether MATLAB computes the camera view angle or not.
`camzoom(zoom)`	zooms the picture. With *zoom* greater than 1 the picture becomes larger, and between 0 and 1 it becomes smaller.
`daspect`	returns the current scaling.
`daspect('pos')`	decides whether MATLAB will compute the scale automatically or not. The string **pos** may be either `'auto'` or `'manual'`.
`daspect('mode')`	shows whether MATLAB computes the scaling or not.
`daspect([x y z])`	decides how the plot area should be scaled in the x, y and z directions. The scaling will from now on not be computed automatically; see below.

Commands 144   (CONTINUED)

pbaspect	returns the current scaling.
pbaspect('pos')	decides whether MATLAB will compute the scale automatically or not. The string **pos** may be either 'auto' or 'manual'.
pbaspect('mode')	shows whether MATLAB computes the scaling or not.

■ **Example 13.24**

We look once more at Figure 13.33. We now type:

```
axis vis3d off    % No axis plotted.
for x = 1:10
  camorbit(5,10); % Orbits the camera ten times.
  drawnow         % Forces the plot to be drawn now.
end
for x = 1:10
  camroll(5);     % Rolls the camera ten times.
  drawnow
end
```

First the camera orbits the plot, and then the plot rolls. The final result is shown in Figure 13.43. The command drawnow forces the plot to be drawn immediately instead of after finishing the loop.

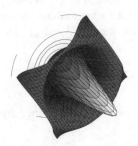

(sin r)/r

Figure 13.43 *The bell-shaped surface orbited and rolled.*

■

To investigate functions of three variables graphically, MATLAB has the command slice. This command draws surfaces in three dimensions, and the colors in points on the surfaces are proportional to the values of the function in these points.

Commands 145	SLICES IN THREE DIMENSIONS
slice(V,xs,ys,zs, nx)	draws slices of the functions in three variables defined by the matrix **V**. The matrix **V** is in itself a set of *nx* layers, evaluated over three matrices obtained from meshgrid with three arguments. The vectors **xs**, **ys**, and **zs** specify which slices to plot.
slice(x,y,z,V,xs, ys,zs)	plots planes in three dimensions with the colors specified in the matrix **V**. The old syntax for slice is still available; this is an extension. The vectors **x**, **y** and **z** are used as axes. The parameters **xs**, **ys** and **zs** give the planes to plot.

■ **Example 13.25**

Let us try to get an idea of what the function $f(x, y, z) = x^2 + y^2 + z^2$ looks like in the cube:

$$[-1 \ 1] \times [-1 \ 1] \times [-1 \ 1]$$

We first define a three-dimensional grid with meshgrid and evaluate the function over the grid:

```
[X,Y,Z] = meshgrid(-1:0.1:1,-1:0.1:1,-1:0.1:1);
V = X.^2 + Y.^2 + Z.^2;
```

Notice that the function is evaluated at 21^3 points. We can now decide which of the slices parallel to the axes we want to draw. A vector (1 3 21), for instance, indicates that we want to draw slices 1, 3 and 21. The command:

```
slice(V,[11],[11],[1 11]);
```

gives Figure 13.44, where the slices are defined by the planes x = 11, y = 11, z = 1, and z = 11.

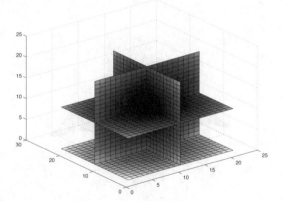

Figure 13.44 *A function of three variables illustrated with the command* `slice`.

As expected, this function is constant along spheres. This is more obvious in color than it is in black and white.

■

13.6 Color control

In MATLAB the user can control colors and illumination of the three-dimensional surface graphs.

The command `shading` configures how the surfaces are plotted. The surface can be drawn with or without the mesh, and with flat or interpolated color scales.

Commands 146	SURFACE PROPERTIES

shading type	redraws the surface with the following properties according to type:
	faceted draws the mesh in the surface; this is the default.
	interp uses interpolated colors on the surface.
	flat draws all facets in constant colors from the corners of the facets.

Two different shading types are shown for a Riemann surface in Figure P.3 in the color plate section.

■ **Example 13.26**

In Example 13.20 we plotted a bell-shaped surface with the mesh visible. If we want Figure 13.33 with the colors interpolated, we give the following command with Figure 13.33 in the graphics window:

```
shading interp
```

and now we obtain Figure 13.45.

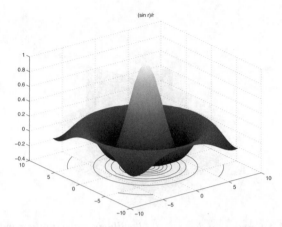

Figure 13.45 *The bell-shaped surface with interpolated colors.*

MATLAB uses color maps to draw surface plots. A color map is an $m \times 3$ matrix in which the rows form the colors, specified by the amount of red in the first column, the amount of green in the second column, and the amount of blue in the last column. Thus the map specifies m colors.

The color on the surface is specified by an index to the color map. This index is usually calculated relative to the minimum and maximum of the surface. The command colormap is used to set which color map MATLAB uses.

| Commands 147 | COLOR MAPS |

colordef definition	changes the color settings for graphs. Valid values of **definition** are:

white	gives a light background and dark axes.
black	gives dark background and light axes.
none	gives MATLAB 4's color settings.

colormap(Cm)	sets the current color table to **Cm**. The matrix **Cm** can be one of MATLAB's own tables, or a user-defined table.
colormap	returns the current graphics table in an $m \times 3$ matrix.
colorbar	draws a vertical color scale in a bar in the current graphics window. See also help colorbar.
colorbar('horiz')	draws a horizontal color scale in a bar in the current graphics window.

To use a predefined color map one may, e.g., give the command `colormap(winter(m))` where *m* is the number of color in the color map. There are 17 predefined color maps in MATLAB (see Table 13.2 and Figure P.1 in the color plate section.).

Table 13.2	COLOR MAPS IN MATLAB
colorcube	returns regularly spaced colors in the RGB colorspace.
lines	returns a color map according to axes ColorOrder.
autumn	returns a red and yellow color map.
spring	returns a magenta and yellow color map.
summer	returns a green and yellow color map.
winter	returns a blue and green color map.
gray	returns a linear gray color scale.
hsv	returns bright saturated colors from red over blue to red again.
hot	returns a hot color mix of black, over red, to yellow and white.
cool	returns cold colors of cyan and magenta.
bone	returns a bluish gray color scale.
copper	returns a copper color scale.
pink	returns variations of pink colors.
flag	returns the colors of the UK and US flags, red, white, and blue, but also black, repeated cyclically.
prism	returns the six colors red, orange, yellow, green, blue, and violet, cyclically repeated.
jet	returns an alternative hsv color table from red to blue, that is from hot to cold.
white	returns an all white color map.

■ **Example 13.27**

Suppose we have Figure 13.37 in the graphics window. The command:

```
colorbar
```

gives Figure 13.46.

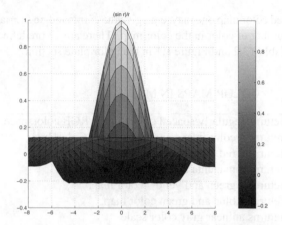

Figure 13.46 *The bell-shaped curve with a color bar.*

■

There are a few additional commands to manipulate the color maps.

Commands 148	MANIPULATION OF COLORS

`rgb2hsv(Cm)`	returns an hsv-map from the $m \times 3$ rgb color map **Cm**. The hsv map contains the same colors as the rgb map, but they are now saturated.
`hsv2rgb(Cm)`	returns an $m \times 3$ rgb color map from the hsv color map **Cm**.
`rgbplot(Cm)`	draws a graph of the columns of the color map **Cm**. The lines are drawn in red, green, and blue respectively.
`caxis(v)`	sets the current interval of the color map to be $\mathbf{v} = [v_{min}, v_{max}]$ where the components v_{min} and v_{max} are the lower and upper index bounds of the color map.
`caxis`	returns the current interval of the color map.
`caxis('auto')`	resets the scaling to the MATLAB automatic scaling.
`spinmap(t,s)`	rotates the colormap for t seconds using the step s. If s is not specified, $s = 2$ is used, and if t is not specified, $t \approx 3$ is used.
`spinmap(inf)`	rotates the color map forever.
`brighten(s)`	brightens the current colormap if $0 < s < 1$ and darkens the color map if $-1 < s < 0$. The figure is redrawn.
`nt = brighten(Cm,s)`	returns a brighter/darker color map of **Cm**, but does not redraw the current plot.
`contrast(Cm,m)`	returns a color table of length m from the color table **Cm**, with increased contrasts on a black-and-white monitor. If m is omitted, a table of the same size as **Cm** is returned.

Commands 148 (CONTINUED)

whitebg	toggles the background color in the graphics window between black and white. The colors of scales and so on are changed if necessary to remain visible.
whitebg(str)	sets the background color according to **str**, which is either a string (see Table 13.1) or an rgb vector.
graymon	sets parameters for black-and-white monitors.

■ **Example 13.28**

We study the hsv color map with the command rgbplot:

```
clf;
rgbplot(hsv);
title('rgbplot of hsv');
axis([0 70 -0.1 1.1]);
```

and obtain Figure 13.47.

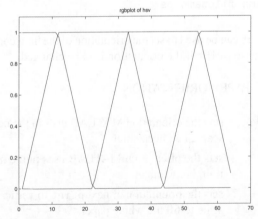

Figure 13.47 *An rgbplot over the hsv color map.*

■

13.7 Hard copy of the graphics window

Assuming that necessary hardware and software are installed, it is possible to get hard copies from the MATLAB graphics window. The command print can be used to get a hard copy either to a file or to a printer, and is applied to the current figure.

On a PC or Macintosh system, the print alternative under the file menu is the easiest way to print graphics.

Commands 149	PRINT HARD COPIES
`print`	sends a high-resolution copy of the current graphics window to a printer. This requires that the print command is assigned to a printer, type `help print` for more information.
`print filename`	sends a copy of the current graphics window to the file **filename**.
`print filename -deps`	sends a copy in eps-format, encapsulated PostScript, to the file named **filename**. This file can later be imported to a document. To see more options, type `help print`.
`[str,dev] = printopt`	gives the command string and device used by `print`. It is possible to modify this M-file; type `help printopt`.

If no printer is specified to MATLAB when it is installed, then print the graphics to a file and send this file to the printer using a system command. On a SUN Solaris 2.x, e.g., one types:

```
!lp -dskrivarnamn filename.ps
```

The command `orient` can be used to set the orientation of the hard copy. This command should be given prior to `print` if the orientation is to be changed.

Commands 150	PAPER ORIENTATION
`orient landscape`	sets the orientation MATLAB uses in the next `print` to landscape, i.e., horizontal.
`orient portrait`	sets the orientation MATLAB uses in the next `print` to portrait, i.e., vertical.
`orient tall`	sets the orientation of next `print` to vertical, but also sets the scale to fill the whole paper.
`orient`	returns the current orientation in a string.

■ **Example 13.29**

This book includes many figures from MATLAB. They were created with various MATLAB commands and printed to hard copies with a statement like:

```
print -deps fig10
```

The pictures were imported directly into this book. This is an example of MATLAB working in cooperation with other programs, in this case LATEX.

■

The command `orient` sets attributes of the current figure. The use of graphical objects (see Chapter 14) gives more detailed control of the properties of hard copies. Paper size, position on the paper, background colors, and lots of other properties can be set.

13.8 Sound

MATLAB can make a vector sound with the command sound.

| Commands 151 | SOUND |

`sound(y)`	sends the vector **y** to the speaker. The vector is scaled to maximize the amplitude.
`sound(y,f)`	same as the previous but with sample frequency f Hz. The command is not available on a Sun SPARC station.
`soundsc(x,f,slim)`	plays the vector **x** in the same way as sound except that soundsc scales the sound vector so that the sound is as loud as possible. If f is given it is used as the sample frequency. Here **slim** sets the full sound range, the default is $[min(x) \ max(x)]$.

■ **Example 13.30**

(a) A sine wave might sound like this:

```
x = sin(linspace(0,10000,10000));   % A pure sine wave.
sound(x);                           % Make the sound.
```

(b) There are a few predefined sounds, which can be loaded with the command load. Here we try two of them:

```
load train;           % Load sound data for train whistle.
whos;                 % Shows variables y, Fs:
                      % vector y: the created signal.
                      % scalar Fs: frequency in Hz.
sound(y);             % Make the sound.

load chirp;           % Load sound data for bird chirps.
sound(y);             % Make the new sound.
```

■

There are additional sound commands on some systems; type help sounds to check for specific systems.

Sun SPARC stations use sound files with the sound vector stored as mu-law encoded data.

Commands 152   SOUND COMMANDS ON SPARC STATIONS

auread(fstr)	reads and returns a vector from the file named **fstr**.
auwrite(sv,fstr)	writes the vector **sv** to a Sun audio file named **fstr**.
lin2mu(sv)	converts the linear sound vector **sv** to a mu-law encoded vector.
mu2lin(sv)	converts the mu-law encoded sound vector **sv** to a linear vector.

Microsoft Windows use sound files in .wav format.

Commands 153   SOUND COMMANDS SPECIFIC TO MICROSOFT
WINDOWS

wavread(fstr)	returns the sampled data in the file named **fstr**. Type help wavread for more information.
wavwrite(sv,f,fstr)	writes the sampled sound vector **sv** with the sampling rate f to a file named **fstr**.

Advanced Graphics

14

The graphics system in MATLAB is object oriented, which means that a graphical output, such as a curve, is built of graphical objects. The high-level MATLAB commands are usually sufficiently advanced that users do not have to concern themselves about including objects. However, it is possible to use low-level MATLAB commands in order to adjust the objects.

In MATLAB it is possible to introduce a graphical user interface (GUI) to the applications, for instance radio buttons, slide bars and menus. With these an application can easily be controlled by the user.

Movies can be created in MATLAB by joining a sequence of pictures. These movies can be used to make interesting demonstrations.

14.1 Construction of a figure

A picture consists of a number of **graphical objects** which are stored in hierarchical order. To understand the connections we use an example.

■ **Example 14.1**

Graphical example with plot regions:

```
clear;

x  = 0.1:0.1:4*pi;      % Creates the vector x.
y1 = sin(x);            % Creates y1 values.
y2 = sin(x)./x;         % Creates y2 values.

figure;                 % Creates a new window.

subplot(1,2,1);         % Defines the first subplot area.
plot(x,y1);             % Plots the curve with a line.

subplot(1,2,2);         % Defines the second subplot area.
plot(x,y2,'*');         % Plots the curve with symbols.
```

The commands given above plot the two vectors **y1** and **y2** as functions of **x** in two subregions of the graphics window. The result is illustrated in Figure 14.1.

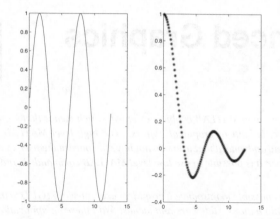

Figure 14.1 *Figures plotted in different plot regions.*

A picture is composed of five graphical objects arranged in a hierarchical structure. First, there is the window, which is a **figure object**. Then there are two objects defining plot regions with corresponding axes, called **axes objects**. These were created with the subplot command. Finally, there are two **line objects** created with the plot command. The hierarchical structure of the objects in Example 14.1 is shown in Figure 14.2.

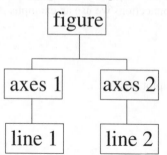

Figure 14.2 *The hierarchical structure of the objects.*

For each of the objects, some properties can be modified. For instance, we can change the position of the graphical window and the background color for the figure object. For an axes object we can, for example, change the scale and the position in the plot region. The line object can be made thicker, in another color, in another style and so on.

As a result of the hierarchical structure, changes made to an object affect all underlying objects in the structure as well. If we change the screen position of the figure object, for instance by using the mouse, the line and axes objects follow. However, if we change the axis scale of the right axes object only the line in this axes object is affected.

There is one object missing in Figure 14.2: the **root object**. The purpose of this root is to be the root of all graphical objects, that is the root of the entire hierarchy.

Some of the properties can be modified directly when the object is created. When **y2** was plotted, the '*' sign indicated that stars were to be used instead of a line for the curve. The calls to subplot specify which position of the window the plot region has. However, most of the properties can be changed only by the set command described below. In the following example we modify some of the properties of the figure from the previous example.

■ **Example 14.2**

```
% As in the previous example, but the position of the left
% subplot area and the x-axis of the second subplot area
% are changed.

clear;

x  = 0.1:0.1:4*pi;
y1 = sin(x);
y2 = sin(x)./x;

fg = figure;                  % Creates window and figure handle.

r1 = subplot(1,2,1);      % Creates subplot and axis handle.
l1 = plot(x,y1);          % Creates line and line handle.

r2 = subplot(1,2,2);
l2 = plot(x,y2,'*');

disp('The previous example');
pause;

set(r1,'Position',[0.1 0.1 0.3 0.3]);  % Changes position.
set(l1,'LineWidth',5);                  % Thickens line width.

set(r2,'XTick',[1 4 11]);              % Changes x axis.
set(l2,'LineStyle','+');               % Changes marks.

pause;
delete(fg);                            % Deletes window.
```

By specifying a variable name when the commands figure, subplot and plot are used, we create a **handle** or **identifier** to the object. By using this handle we can modify the object using the set command. In the example each object has one property changed. The position of the first plot region is changed and the second plot region gets a different *x* axis scale. Our window now looks like Figure 14.3.

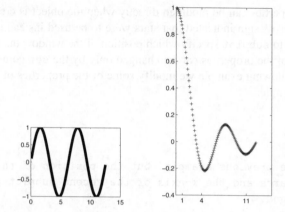

Figure 14.3 *The example from Figure 14.1 but with some properties changed.*

14.2 Graphical objects

The various objects existing in MATLAB 5.2 are listed in Table 14.1.

Graphically, the object hierarchy is shown in Figure 14.4.

Examples of the different types of graphical objects are shown in Figure 14.5.

A **parent** influences all its **children**, and these children influence their children, and so on. Consequently, an axes object influences an image, but does not affect a uicontrol.

According to Table 14.1, the object handle of the root is zero and the handle of figure objects are integers. The other objects use floating points as object handles.

To plot an object, the low-level command of the same name as the object is used, for example the command `line` to draw a line.

The objects have two types of properties:

- Attributes, which determine the appearance of the objects and store data.
- Methods, which determine what function is called when something happens to the objects, for example, when they are created or deleted, or when the user clicks on them.

Some properties have default values. These values hold if nothing else is stated.

Some attributes are used to indicate the color of the object. These can be given as RGB triplets, that is, a vector with three elements $[r\ g\ b]$ $(0 \leq r, g, b \leq 1)$ indicating the amount of red, green and blue in the color. Red is, for example, represented by $[1, 0, 0]$.

Instead of RGB triplets, it is possible to give a string containing one of the predefined colors in MATLAB, for example 'black' and 'blue'.

The different types of objects can be examined in helpdesk under Handle Graphics Objects, where a detailed description of the properties is given. Information can also be obtained in the MATLAB manuals *Using MATLAB Graphics* and *Building GUIs with MATLAB*.

Table 14.1　　　　　GRAPHICAL OBJECTS

Object	Parent	Description
root	–	The screen is the root object. All other graphical objects are children to the root. The object handle is zero.
figure	root	A window on the screen is a figure object. The object handle is an integer, which is indicated in the window title.
axes	figure	An axes object defines a plot region in the window. It also describes the position and orientation of the children.
uicontrol	figure	User interface controls. When the user clicks with the mouse on a control object, MATLAB performs a task specified by the chosen control.
uimenu	figure	Menus on top of the window are created. The user can control the program with these menus.
uicontext-menu	figure	Creates context menus to graphical objects, that is menus that are shown when the user clicks on graphical objects.
image	axes	An image is defined by a matrix which uses the current color map. Images can also have their own color map.
line	axes	Graphical primitive that is created by, for example, plot, plot3, contour and contour3.
patch	axes	Polygons filled in solid or interpolated colors.
surface	axes	A surface with four corners defined by input. Can be drawn with solid or interpolated colors or as a mesh.
text	axes	Character string whose position is defined by its parent, the axes object.
light	axes	Defines the illumination of a polygon or a surface.

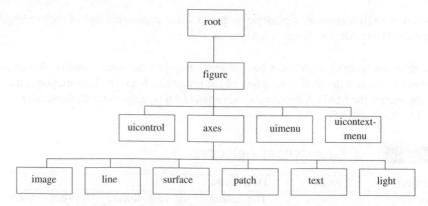

Figure 14.4 *The hierarchy of the graphical objects.*

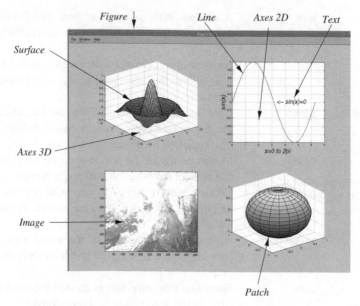

Figure 14.5 *Examples of different types of graphical objects.*

14.2.1 General functions

To handle graphical objects, MATLAB has two basic commands, get and set. By using these the properties of all objects can be inspected and manipulated.

■ **Example 14.3**

(a) We create a graphical window and its handle gfp:

```
gfp = figure;
```

First we control what unit the window uses:

```
get(gfp,'units')
```

```
ans =
      pixels
```

Now we change the size and position of the window:

```
set(gfp,'Position',[100 500 400 400])
```

The lower left corner of the window is moved to position $(100, 500)$ and the size of the window is set to 400×400 pixels.

(b) In some high-level commands, for example `plot`, one can change these properties directly. For instance, the curves drawn in Example 14.1 could have been made by:

```
plot(x,y1,'LineWidth',5);
plot(x,y2,'LineStyle','+'); or plot(x,y2,'+');
```

(c) If we want to know what kind of pointers there are to choose between, `set` and `gcf` can be used; see Commands 155.

```
set(gcf,'Pointer')
```

```
[ crosshair | fullcrosshair | {arrow} | ibeam | watch | topl |
topr | botl | botr | left | top | right | bottom | circle |
cross | fleur | custom ]
```

■

Commands 154	GENERAL OBJECT FUNCTIONS
`set(h,prstr,alt, ...)`	sets the property **prstr** to the value *alt* for the objects that vector **h** points at. Several properties can be written after each other.
`set(h,a)`	sets properties for the objects that vector **h** points at. The parameter **a** is a structure whose field names are the names of the properties to be changed, and whose field values are the new values of the corresponding properties.
`set(h,pn,pv,...)`	sets properties for the objects that vector **h** points at. The parameter **pn** is a cell vector containing the names of the properties to be changed and **pv** is a cell vector containing the new values. Several cell vectors with properties can be written after each other.
`set(h,pn,pv)`	sets the property, whose name is **pn**(j), for the object that **h**(i) points at to the value **pv**(i, j). The parameter **h** is a vector containing pointers to objects, **pn** is a cell vector containing property names and **pv** is an $m \times n$ cell matrix, where m is the length of **h** and n the length of **pn**, containing values. This variant makes it possible to set the properties of the objects individually.

Commands 154   (CONTINUED)

`set(h)`	returns all changeable properties for the object with handle h. The properties are returned in a structure whose field names are the names of the properties, and whose field values are the values of the corresponding properties.
`set(0,'Default')`	checks which object properties have default values. It returns a structure whose field names are `'ObjectNamePropertyName'` and whose field values are the default values of the corresponding properties. Note: only properties whose values are strings are returned.
`set(0, 'DefaultObject NamePropertyName')`	returns a cell vector containing the default value of property `PropertyName` of object type `ObjectName`. Note: only properties whose values are strings are returned.
`set(h,prstr)`	returns a cell vector containing all accepted values of property **prstr** of the object type with handle h.
`get(h)`	lists all properties and their values for the object with handle h. The information is returned in a structure whose field names are the names of the properties, and whose field values are the values of the corresponding properties.
`get(h,prstr)`	returns the current value of property **prstr** of the object with handle h.
`get(h,pn)`	returns a cell matrix where element (i, j) is the value of property **pn**(j) of the object with handle **h**(i). The parameter **pn** is a cell vector and **h** is a vector containing handles.
`get(0,'Factory')`	returns for all object types the factory values of all properties whose default values the user can change. The factory values are returned in a structure whose field names are `'ObjectNamePropertyName'`, and whose field values are the factory values of the corresponding properties.
`get(0, 'FactoryObject NamePropertyName')`	returns the factory value of property `PropertyName` of the object `ObjectName`.
`get(0,'Default')`	checks which object properties have default values. The properties are returned in a structure whose field names are `'ObjectNamePropertyName'`, and whose field values are the default values of the corresponding properties.
`get(0, 'DefaultObject NamePropertyName')`	returns the default value of property `PropertyName` of an object of type `ObjectName`.

Commands 154 (CONTINUED)

`allchild(h)`	returns handles to the children of the object with handle **h**(i). Hidden handles are also returned; see `'HandleVisibility'` in Table 14.2. If **h** is a scalar handle a vector is returned, and if **h** is a vector of handles a cell matrix is returned.
`findobj`	returns a vector of handles to the root object and all its children.
`findobj(`*h*`,`*prstr*`,`*alt*`, ...)`	if the parameters **prstr** and *alt* are given, a vector is returned containing handles to all objects having the property **prstr** set to *alt*. Several properties can be written after each other. If **h** is given, the search is restricted to the objects with handles in **h** and the children of these objects. If **prstr** and *alt* are not given, a vector is returned containing the handles of the children of the objects with handles in vector **h**.
`findobj(`*h*`,'flat', prstr,alt,...)`	does the same as the above, but the children of the objects are not examined.
`findall(h)`	is similar to `findobj(h)`, but here hidden handles to children are returned; see `'HandleVisibility'` in Table 14.2.
`copyobj(h,p)`	copies objects and their children. The vector **h** contains handles to the objects to be copied, and **p** is a vector containing handles to their new parents. These parents must be of the same type as the old. The function returns a vector containing handles to the new objects.
`ishandle(h)`	checks if the the elements in vector **h** are handles to objects. The function returns a vector whose elements are 1 if the corresponding elements in **h** are handles, and 0 otherwise.
`setuprop(h,prstr, val)`	makes it possible for the user to define new properties in objects of the figure and axes types. The new property of the object with handle *h* is specified in the string **prstr** and is set to the value **val**, which can be anything. Unless property **prstr** already exists, it is created.
`getuprop(h,prstr)`	returns the value of the user-defined property **prstr** in a figure or axes object with handle *h*.
`clruprop(h,prstr)`	deletes the user-defined property **prstr** in a figure or axes object with handle *h*.

Commands 154   (CONTINUED)

`handle2struct(h)`	translates the object hierarchies with handles in vector **h** to a structure. The structure has the following fields:

	.type	the type of the objects.
	.properties	a structure containing the values of the properties.
	.children	a structure matrix, having one element for each child of the objects with handles in vector **h**.
	.handle	the handles of the objects.
	.special	undocumented field.

`struct2handle(s)`	is the inverse of the command `handle2struct`: the structure s is translated to hierarchies of objects, which are returned.

MATLAB 5 also has a tool, `propedit`, which is a property editor. This editor is much easier to use than the low-level commands `set` and `get`. The tool `propedit` is especially useful when building graphical user interfaces; see Commands 170.

Furthermore, there are three functions which return the handle of the current graphical object.

Commands 155   CURRENT OBJECT

`gcf`	returns the handle of the current figure object.
`gca`	returns the handle of the current axes object.
`gco(h)`	returns the handle of the current object, that is the object last clicked on with the mouse. If *h* is given, a handle is returned to the current object in the window with handle *h*.

■ **Example 14.4**

The following commands return the properties of the current window and axes:

```
get(gcf);    % Get properties for current figure.
get(gca);    % Get properties for current axes.
```

■

■ **Example 14.5**

It is also possible to move the objects made by the `subplot` command. Suppose that we have these two subplots, a toothbrush and toothpaste:

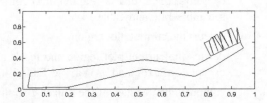

Figure 14.6 *Two axes objects made by* `subplot`.

We can get the positions of the lower subplot by typing:

```
subplot(2,1,2);
get(gca,'Position')
```

```
ans =
    0.1300  0.1100  0.7750  0.3400
```

To move the object we type:

```
 set(gca,'Position',[0.15 0.49 0.775 0.34])
```

Figure 14.7. Thus axes objects can be positioned on top of each other.

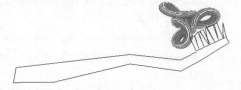

Figure 14.7 *Manipulation puts the toothpaste on the toothbrush.*

There are also functions for deleting objects, restoring the default values and saving objects on files.

OTHER GENERAL FUNCTIONS

`clf`	clears the current window.
`clf reset`	clears the current window and resets all figure properties except `Position`, `Units`, `PaperPosition` and `PaperUnits`; see Table 14.6 and Table 14.6.
`cla`	deletes the current plot region.
`cla reset`	deletes the current plot region and resets all axes properties except `Position` and `Units`, see Table 14.10.
`rotate(h,ax,a,`*`o`*`)`	computes new values of the object *h* so that it is rotated by angle *a* around axis **ax**. The optional parameter **o** gives the start position of the rotation. The default is [0 0 0].
`remapfig(pos,` `newpos,` *`fig`*`,h)`	moves children to the figure object with handle *fig*. Every child object inside the area specified by **pos** is moved to the area specified by **newos**. The parameters **pos** and **newpos** have the form [*left bottom width height*]. The whole area of an axes object is [0 0 1 1]. If *fig* is not given, the default figure is used. Also, if **h** is given, only those children with handles in vector **h** are moved.
`reset(h)`	resets the window (figure object) or plot region (axes object) with handle *h* to the default values.
`delete(h)`	deletes the object with handle *h*.
`close(`*`h`*`)`	closes current window. If **h** is given, the windows with handles in **h** are closed. The parameter **h** can be a scalar, vector or matrix containing handles to axes objects.
`close name`	closes window named **name**.
`close all`	closes all windows whose handles are not hidden. Hidden handles are managed by the property `HandleVisibility`; see Table 14.2.
`close all hidden`	closes all windows, including those with hidden handles.
`status = close(...)`	sets **status** to 1 if the corresponding window was closed, otherwise 0.
`hgsave(h,filename)`	saves the object with handle *h* and its children to the file **filename**. If **filename** lacks a suffix, `.fig` is added.
`hgload(filename)`	reads an object and its children (if any), from the file **filename**. If **filename** lacks a suffix, `.fig` is added. It returns a handle to the read object.

14.2.2 Common attributes and methods

Some attributes and methods are common for all types of objects due to inheritance. However, some of these are meaningless to some objects; see the tables of attributes and methods for each type of object.

Table 14.2	COMMON ATTRIBUTES AND METHODS
ButtonDownFcn	is a string indicating what callback function is called, that is what M-file or MATLAB command is executed when the pointer is over the object (but not over one of its children) and the mouse button is pressed down.
Children	is a vector containing handles to the object's children.
Clipping	determines if clipping is used or not. If Clipping is set to 'on' (default), the part of a graphical object shown is limitted by the size of the axes object. If Clipping is set to 'off', parts outside the axes object are also shown.
CreateFcn	determines what M-file or what MATLAB commands should be executed when the object is created. This must be specified as Default, as in this example for a figure object: set(0,'DefaultFigureCreateFcn',function), where the string function is the desired M-file or MATLAB commands.
DeleteFcn	determines what M-file or what MATLAB commands should be executed when the object is deleted.
BusyAction	determines how MATLAB handles interrupts of the callback functions of the object. If Interruptible, see below, is 'off', BusyAction will determine what happens:
	'queue' (default) puts the callback function responsible for the interrupt in a queue where it is put on hold until the callback function of the object has finished.
	'cancel' ignores all possible interrupts from other callback functions, that is, they are never executed.
HandleVisibility	determines if the handle of the object is accessible from the parent's list of children; see Children.
	'on' (default) makes it always accessible.
	'callback' makes it only accessible from callback functions and from functions called from callback functions. This makes it possible to protect the object from being changed by a user from the command line.
	'off' makes it never accessible.

Table 14.2	(CONTINUED)
HitTest	determines if the object can be selected by the mouse, that is if the object can be current object. HitTest can either be 'on' (default) or 'off'. See also the command gco in Commands 155 and axes object property CurrentObject in Table 14.7.
Interruptible	determines how MATLAB handles interrupts of the callback functions of the object. If Interruptible is 'on' (default), the callback function responsible for the interrupt can be executed before the callback function of the object has finished. If Interruptible is 'off', the callback function responsible for the interrupt is put in a queue where it is put on hold until the callback function of the object has finished.
Parent	is the handle of the parent of the object.
Selected	indicates if an object is selected or not. Selected can either be 'on' or 'off'.
SelectionHighlight	determines if a selected object is indicated on the screen by four edge handles and four vertex handles. SelectionHighlight can either be 'on' (default) or 'off'.
Tag	is a string the user sets to identify objects. Very useful when building graphical interfaces.
Type	is a read-only string indicating the type of the object.
UserData	is a matrix containing data the user wants to store in the object. The matrix is not used by the object itself.
UIContextMenu	is a handle of a context menu connected to the object. MATLAB shows the context menu when the right mouse button is pressed (Macintosh Control-click) over the object. See Section 14.2.8.
Visible	determines whether the object is visible on the screen. Visible can be either 'on' (default) or 'off'.

14.2.3 Root object

As mentioned above, the screen is the root object. Its sole task is to be the parent of all other objects. In MATLAB one can examine and alter some of its properties with set and get. The root object has the following attributes and methods.

Table 14.3	ROOT OBJECT COMMON ATTRIBUTES AND METHODS
Automatic-FileUpdates	is either 'on' or 'off', but its use is undocumented.
CallbackObject	is a handle to the object whose callback function is currently executing. If no callback function is executing [] is returned. See also the command gcob in Commands 171.
Language	is a system environment variable, but its use is undocumented.
CurrentFigure	is a handle to the current figure object. If no figure object exists [] is returned. See also the command gcf in Commands 155.
Diary	is a string indicating whether MATLAB saves input and output in the command window to a file. Diary can either be 'on' or 'off' (default).
DiaryFile	is a string indicating on what file input and output saved, see Diary.
Echo	is a string indicating whether MATLAB shows program lines in M-files when they are executed. Echo can either be 'on' or 'off' (default).
ErrorMessage	is a string holding the latest error message from MATLAB.
Format	is a string indicating how MATLAB presents numbers. The following possibilities exist: 'short', 'shortE' (default), 'shortG', 'long', 'longE', 'longG', 'bank', 'hex', '+' and 'rational'.
FormatSpacing	is a string indicating whether MATLAB puts empty lines at output in the command window. FormatSpacing can either be 'loose' (default) or 'compact'.
PointerLocation	is a vector holding the current position of the mouse pointer counted from the lower left corner of the screen.
PointerWindow	is a read-only handle of the MATLAB window having the mouse pointer. The handle is 0 if the mouse pointer is not over any MATLAB window.
Profile	is a string indicating whether MATLAB should use the profile tool. This tool measures, during execution of a program, the time taken by the different parts of the program. Profile can either be 'on' or 'off' (default). See Section 12.7.
ProfileFile	is a string indicating in what file any profile data is saved (see above).
ProfileCount	is an $n \times 1$ vector containing profile data. Element k in the vector indicates how many times the profile tool found line k in the M-file during execution.

Table 14.3   (CONTINUED)

ProfileInterVal	is a scalar indicating by what time interval the profile tool checks on which line an executing M-file is.
RecursionLimit	is the limit of the number of nested recursive calls MATLAB can do to an M-file. If this number is exceeded MATLAB returns an error message.
ScreenDepth	is a scalar indicating screen depth, that is the number of bits used per pixel.
ScreenSize	is a read-only vector containing four elements indicating the screen size. The vector has the form [*left bottom width height*].
ShowHidden-Handles	is a string indicating whether all handles of all objects are accessible, overruling their individual HandleVisibilty attributes; see Table 14.2. ShowHiddenHandles can either be 'on' or 'off' (default).
Units	is a string indicating what unit MATLAB uses to measure size and position. The following units are available: 'pixels' (standard), 'normalized', 'inches', 'centimeters', 'points' and 'characters'. The choice of unit affects the attributes PointerLocation and ScreenSize.
Parent	is always [], that is the root object has no parent.

When MATLAB is used in an X Windows environment, the root object has a few extra attributes and methods.

Table 14.4   EXTRA ATTRIBUTES AND METHODS FOR THE ROOT OBJECT IN AN X WINDOWS ENVIRONMENT

TerminalHideGraph-Command	is a string indicating the command sequence to hide graphical windows when switching from graphic to command mode.
TerminalShowGraph-Command	is a string indicating the command sequence to show graphical windows when switching from command to graphic mode.
TerminalOneWindow	is a string indicating whether the terminal just has one window, in which case TerminalOneWindow is 'on' (default). Otherwise it is 'off'.
TerminalDimensions	is a vector indicating in pixels the size of the terminal.
TerminalProtocol	is a string indicating what type of terminal emulation is used. The following alternatives exists: 'none', 'x', 'tek401x' and 'tek410x'. When this attribute is set, one must restart MATLAB to change it.

Some of the common attributes and methods are meaningless to the root object.

Table 14.5   ATTRIBUTES AND METHODS MEANINGLESS TO THE
              ROOT OBJECT

BusyAction	ButtonDownFcn	Clipping	CreateFcn
DeleteFcn	HandleVisibility	HitTest	Interruptible
Selected	SelectionHighLight	UIContextMenu	Visible

■ **Example 14.6**

The root object has handle 0, thus a call looks like:

```
scrsize = get(0,'ScreenSize')
```

Scrsize =
        0   0   1152   900

The command returns the screen size in pixels.

■

14.2.4 Figure object

A figure object is a graphical window. The parent is the screen, the root object, and the figure inherits a lot of the root's properties. Properties can be changed either when the figure is created or with the set command.

A figure object can be created in several ways.

Commands 157   FIGURE OBJECT

figure(*prstr*,*alt*, ...)	sets the property **prstr** to the value *alt* and returns the handle of the figure. Several properties can be written after each other.
figure(fp)	sets the current figure object to the window with handle *fp*. All graphics commands are applied to the current figure.
refresh(*fp*)	forces MATLAB to redraw the figure object with handle *fp*. If just refresh is written, the current figure object is redrawn.
drawnow	forces MATLAB to draw an object. For instance, MATLAB will not draw objects from plot commands in a loop until the loop is finished unless drawnow is given after each plot command.

Commands 157   (CONTINUED)

`newplot`	opens a new figure or axes; alternatively clears the current figure or axes depending on the value of the `NextPlot` property. Write `help newplot` for more information.
`fignamer(str)`	returns a string with the next free figure name beginning with the string **str**. It can, for example, be used to set the property Name below.
`setptr(h,cursor)`	sets the shape of the cursor in figure with handle *h*. The shape is specified by the string **cursor**, try `help setptr` to see the alternatives available. It returns a cell matrix indicating the shape of the cursor. See also the various `Pointer` attributes below.
`p = getptr(h)`	returns a cell matrix **p** indicating the form of the cursor in the figure object with handle *h*. This cell matrix can be used to set the shape of the cursor: `setptr(h,p{:})`. See also the various `Pointer` attributes below.

The figure object has the following common attributes and methods.

Table 14.6   COMMON ATTRIBUTES AND METHODS OF FIGURE
OBJECTS

`BackingStore`	is a string indicating whether MATLAB saves a copy of the figure window for fast update of the screen when it is moved to the foreground. `BackingStore` can either be `'on'` (default) or `'off'`.
`IntegerHandle`	is a string indicating whether handles are reusable integers or non-reusable floating point numbers. If they are integers, `IntegerHandle` is set to `'on'` (default), otherwise `IntegerHandle` is set to `'off'`.
`MenuBar`	is a string indicating whether MATLAB shows or hides its menus in the upper border of the window. `MenuBar` can either be `'figure'` (shows menus, default) or `'none'` (hides menus). The command `menubar` returns a string with the alternative most suitable for the operating system used.
`Name`	is a string indicating the title of the figure window. Default is an empty string.

Table 14.6	(CONTINUED)
NextPlot	is a string indicating how MATLAB plots new graphs in the figure window. 'add' (default) means the current figure window is used. 'replace' means the window is cleared, all properties but Position are restored, and all children are removed. Equivalent to the command clf reset. 'replace children' means all children are removed, but the properties are not restored. Equivalent to the command clf.
NumberTitle	is a string indicating whether the figure windows are numbered. If NumberTitle is 'on' (default) the window gets the title "Figure No. N: Name" where Name (see above) is a string. If NumberTitle is 'off' the window only gets the title "Name".
Pointer	is a string indicating what type of mouse pointer is used. The following alternatives are available: 'crosshair', 'arrow' (default), 'watch', 'topl', 'topr', 'botl', 'botr', 'circle', 'cross', 'fleur', 'left', 'right', 'top', 'bottom', 'fullcrosshair', 'ibeam', and 'custom'.
PointerShapeCData	is a 16×16 matrix indicating a user-defined mouse pointer. PointerShapeCData is only used if Pointer is set to 'custom'. In the matrix 1 represents black, 2 white and NaN transparency.
PointerShapeHot-Spot	is a two element vector indicating a point (row and column) in PointerShapeCData. This point will be used to determine the position of the mouse pointer. Default is [1, 1].
Position	is a four element vector [*left bottom width height*] indicating where on the screen the figure window is, and how big it is.
Renderer	is a string indicating how the graphics are drawn. The following methods are available: 'painters' is fast if the graphics are simple. 'zbuffer' is faster and more exact than 'painters' when the graphics are complex, but needs more memory. 'OpenGL' is superior to both 'painters' and 'zbuffer', but it needs support in software or hardware.

Table 14.6	(CONTINUED)
RendererMode	is a string indicating which method of the above is used. If RendererMode is set to 'auto' (default) MATLAB chooses a method depending on the complexity of the graphics. If RendererMode is set to 'manual' MATLAB does not change method.
Units	is a string indicating what unit MATLAB uses to measure size and position. The following units are available: 'pixels' (standard), 'normalized', 'inches', 'centimeters', 'points' and 'characters'. The choice of unit affects the attributes CurrentPoint and Position.
WindowStyle	is a string indicating in which mode the figure window is. WindowStyle can either be 'normal' (default) or 'modal'. In the latter case all input (buttons pressed on the mouse and keys pressed on the keyboard) is restricted to the window until it is set to 'normal', removed or Visible is set to 'off'. Modal windows do not show any menus or uimenu children. Control-C at the MATLAB prompter turns all modal windows to normal windows.
Clipping	has no effect.
Parent	is always 0 (the handle of the root).
SelectionHighLight	has no effect.

Events related to figure objects are handled with the following attributes and methods.

Table 14.7	EVENT DRIVEN ATTRIBUTES AND METHODS IN FIGURE OBJECTS
CloseRequestFcn	is a string indicating what function is executed when a figure window is closed (default is 'closereq').
CurrentCharacter	is a read-only character indicating the last key pressed on the keyboard.
CurrentAxes	is a handle to the current axes object; see also the command gca in Commands 155.
CurrentObject	is a handle to the current object; that is the object last clicked on, see CurrentPoint below. See also the command gco in Commands 155.
CurrentPoint	is a vector indicating the coordinates of the last mouse button pressed.

Table 14.7 (CONTINUED)

KeyPressFcn	is a string indicating what callback function, that is what M-file or MATLAB command, that is executed when a key is pressed in the figure window.
Resize	is a string indicating whether the user can resize the figure window with the mouse. Resize can either be 'on' (default) or 'off'.
ResizeFcn	is a string indicating what function is executed when the figure window is resized.
SelectionType	is a read-only string indicating the most recent type of selection done by the mouse. UNIX has the following alternatives: 'normal' (left button, default), 'extended' (shift-left button or middle button), 'alternate' (control-left button or right button) and 'open' (double click).
WindowButtonDown-Fcn	is a string indicating what function is executed when a mouse button is pressed in a figure window.
WindowButton-Motion Fcn	is a string indicating what function is executed when the mouse pointer is moved into a figure window.
WindowButtonUpFcn	is a string indicating what function is executed when a mouse button is released in a figure window.

The following attributes and methods are used to control the coloring of figure objects and their children.

Table 14.8 ATTRIBUTES AND METHODS FOR COLORING OF FIGURE OBJECTS AND THEIR CHILDREN

Color	is an RGB triplet or one of the predefined colors in MATLAB, indicating the background color of the figure window.
Colormap	is an $m \times 3$ matrix indicating m different RGB triplets (colors) that constitute the color table used by polygon, surface and image objects. Default is a matrix that contains 64 colors. See also Section 13.6.
Dithermap	is an $m \times 3$ matrix (color table) used when viewing 'true color' data on 'pseudo color' (8 bits or lower) screens. A default color table of 64 colors is available.

Table 14.8	(CONTINUED)
DithermapMode	is a string indicating whether manual or automatic translation of colors is used when viewing 'true color' data on 'pseudo color' screens. If DithermapMode is set to 'manual' (default) the color table Dithermap is used (see above). If DithermapMode is set to 'auto', MATLAB generates a color table based on the current colors. The 'auto' mode produces better approximations than 'manual', but takes more time.
FixedColors	is a read-only $m \times 3$ matrix (color table) indicating the colors not given by Colormap, for example the colors of the line, text and unicontrol objects.
MinColorMap	is a scalar showing the lowest number of system colors used by MATLAB to store the color table Colormap (see above). Should equal the number of rows in Colormap, default is 64.
ShareColors	is a string indicating how MATLAB stores Colormap (see above). ShareColors can either be 'on' (default) or 'off'. The alternative 'off' is suitable when the possibility of a fast change of Colormap is desired. See helpdesk for more information.

The attributes below are used to control the appearance of printouts of figure objects.

Table 14.9	PRINTOUT ATTRIBUTES OF FIGURE OBJECTS
InvertHardCopy	is a string indicating whether printouts of the figure object are inverted. Default, 'on', produces dark objects on a light background; 'off' the opposite.
PaperUnits	is a string indicating what unit MATLAB uses in printouts. The following units are available: 'normalized', 'inches' (default), 'centimeters' and 'points'. The choice of unit affects the attributes PaperSize and PaperPosition.
PaperOrientation	is a string indicating the paper orientation in printouts of the figure. PaperOrientation can either be 'portrait' (vertical orientation, default) or 'landscape' (horizontal orientation).
PaperPosition	is a four element vector [*left bottom width height*] indicating where on the paper the figure is printed.

Table 14.9	(CONTINUED)
PaperPositionMode	is a string indicating whether manual or automatic positioning of the figure on the paper is used. If PaperPositionMode is set to 'manual' (default) MATLAB uses PaperPosition (see above). If PaperPositionMode is set to 'auto' it is printed as it looks on the screen.
PaperSize	is a read-only two element vector [*width height*] indicating the size of the paper.
PaperType	is a string indicating what type of paper is used. The following alternatives are available: 'usletter' (default), 'uslegal', 'A0', 'A1', 'A2', 'A3', 'A4', 'A5', 'B0', 'B1', 'B2', 'B3', 'B4', 'B5', 'arch-A', 'arch-B', 'arch-C', 'arch-D', 'arch-E', 'A', 'B', 'C', 'D', 'E' and 'tabloid'.

■ **Example 14.7**

(a) To replace the numbered title of the window with a name of your own, the following commands can be used:

```
fp = figure;
set(fp,'NumberTitle','off');
set(fp,'Name','ExampleWindow');
```

(b) To change the position and size of the window:

```
set(fp,'Position',[100 100 400 400]);
```

■

14.2.5 Axes objects

An axes object defines a plot region within a figure window. The parent is therefore the figure object, and its children are the line, image, patch, surface, and text objects.

The properties of the axes object define not only the position, but also orientation and size of the figure to be plotted.

AXES OBJECTS

axes(*prstr*,*alt*,...)	creates an axes object that covers all of the window with properties according to default values. The optional property **prstr** is set to *alt*. Several properties can be written after each other. Returns the handle to the plot region.
axes(h)	sets the current axes object to *h*.

Since it is possible to define the size of the axes object, it is also possible to have several axes objects in the same figure object; compare with the subplot command. When a graphical command is used it works in the current axes object.

Axes objects have the following common attributes and methods.

Table 14.10   AXES OBJECT COMMON ATTRIBUTES AND METHODS

Box	is a string indicating whether the plot region is surrounded by a border. Box can either be 'on' or 'off' (default).
CurrentPoint	is a 2×3 matrix $\begin{pmatrix} x_b & y_b & z_b \\ x_f & y_f & z_f \end{pmatrix}$ in axes object coordinates holding the points indicating the position of the most recent mouse button pressed. The points lie on the line perpendicular to the screen and crossing the mouse pointer. The point having subindex b (f) lies in the back (front) plane of the bounding box of the plot region.
DataAspectRatio	is a vector [dx dy dz] indicating how graphical data is scaled in the x, y and z directions, respectively.
DataAspectRatio-Mode	is a string indicating whether MATLAB calculates data aspect ratios automatically. If DataAspectRatioMode is set to 'auto' (default) MATLAB generates DataAspectRatio. If DataAspectRatioMode is set to 'manual' DataAspectRatio is used directly. DataAspectRatioMode is automatically set to 'manual' if DataAspectRatio is set.
DrawMode	is a string indicating which method is used to draw the image. DrawMode can either be 'normal' (default) or 'fast'. The latter is faster, but can cause non-correct graphs. This attribute is meaningless when the parent (a figure object) has Renderer set to 'zbuffer'.
LineStyleOrder	is a string indicating the line and point types used when plotting several lines. For example, '-*|:|o' indicates three different types of lines that will be used cyclically. Default is '-', that is all lines are solid.

Table 14.10	(CONTINUED)
LineWidth	is a scalar indicating the thickness in points of the coordinate axes. Default is 0.5 points.
NextPlot	is a string indicating how MATLAB plots new graphs in the plot region.

	'add'	(default) means the current plot region is used.
	'replace'	means the window is cleared, all properties (except Position) are restored, and all children are removed. Equivalent to the command cla reset.
	'replace children'	means all children are removed, but the properties are not restored. Equivalent to the command cla.

PlotBoxAspectRatio	is a vector [*px py pz*] indicating how the plot box, defined by *Lim (see Table 14.13), is scaled in the *x*, *y* and *z* directions, respectively.
PlotBoxAspect-RatioMode	is a string indicating whether MATLAB calculates plot box aspect ratios automatically. If PlotAspectRatioMode is set to 'auto' (default) MATLAB generates PlotAspectRatio. If PlotAspectRatioMode is set to 'manual' PlotAspectRatio is used directly. PlotAspectRatioMode is automatically set to 'manual' if PlotAspectRatio is set.
Projection	is a string indicating which projection model is used. If Projection is set to 'orthographic' (default) all parallel lines in the data set are drawn parallel on the screen. This model is good for numerical data. In the other model, 'perspective', objects further away from the viewer become smaller on the screen. This model is therefore good for 'real' objects, for example, in solid models.
Position	is a four element vector [*left bottom width height*] indicating the position and size of the plot region in the figure window.
Title	is a handle to a text object that contains the title of the plot region.
Units	is a string indicating what unit MATLAB uses to measure size and position. The following units are available: 'inches', 'centimeters', 'normalized' (default), 'points', 'pixels' and 'characters'. The choice of unit affects the attribute Position, see above.
View	is an obsolete attribute, use CameraPosition, CameraUpVector and CameraViewAngle instead; see Table 14.12. See also the command view.

■ **Example 14.8**

Suppose we want to construct a picture which cannot be displayed with the limited options of the subplot command. Here we create five plot regions by using the axes command.

```
[X,Y]  = meshgrid(-2:0.3:2,-2:0.3:2);
ZS     = cos(X).*cos(Y);
                                      % Position:
a(1) = axes('Position',[0.1 0.1 0.2 0.2]); % Lower left.
a(2) = axes('Position',[0.8 0.1 0.2 0.2]); % Lower right.
a(3) = axes('Position',[0.8 0.8 0.2 0.2]); % Upper right.
a(4) = axes('Position',[0.1 0.8 0.2 0.2]); % Upper left.
a(5) = axes('Position',[0.3 0.3 0.5 0.5]); % Middle.

for i = 1:5,
  axes(a(i));              % Plots the picture in the different
  surf(ZS);               % plot areas.

  if i == 1               % Changes the viewpoint of the
     view(37.5,30);       % different plot areas.
  elseif i == 2           % The middle plot
     view(-37.5,70);      % keeps the default angle
  elseif i == 3           % (-37.5,30)
     view(10,30);
  elseif i == 4
     view(0,-20);
  end;
end;
```

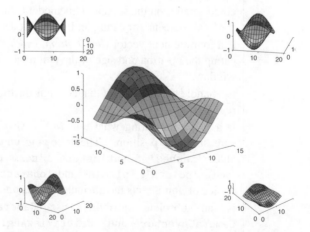

Figure 14.8 *Positioning of the plot regions made by* axes.

Note that the first two numbers define the position of the lower left-hand corner and the last two the width and height of the plot region. Within the current window the position is normalized in the interval [0,1]. The result is displayed in Figure 14.8. We see the same surface in all plot regions but from different angles.

∎

The attributes below are used to control the coloring of axes objects and their children.

Table 14.11	ATTRIBUTES AND METHODS FOR COLORING OF AXES OBJECTS AND THEIR CHILDREN
`AmbientLightColor`	is an RGB triplet or one of the predefined colors in MATLAB indicating the color of the background light. This light affects all objects by the same amount, and is only in effect if there is a light source object in the axes object.
`CLim`	is a vector [*cmin cmax*] indicating how MATLAB translates color data (`CData`) for polygon and surface objects to the color table `Colormap` of the figure object. The scalar *cmin* is mapped to the first color in the color table, and *cmax* is mapped to the last color. Values in `CData` between *cmin* and *cmax* are mapped linearly, and values less than *cmin* or greater than *cmax* are mapped to the first or last color respectively.
`CLimMode`	is a string indicating whether MATLAB calculates `CLim` automatically. If `CLimMode` is set to `'auto'` (default) MATLAB searches for the minimum and maximum value in `CData` in all visible graphical objects. These values are then stored in `CLim`. If `CLimMode` is set to `'manual'` `CLim` is used directly. `CLimMode` is automatically set to `'manual'` if `CLim` is set.
`Color`	indicates the background color of the plot region; `'none'` (default) means the region is transparent. The color is specified by either an RGB triplet or one of the predefined colors in MATLAB.
`ColorOrder`	is an *m* × 3 matrix of RGB values that is used by `plot` and `plot3`. These functions will pick colors cyclically from this matrix when the color is not specified by the user.

MATLAB uses a 'camera' to determine how objects in the axes object are viewed. To control the 'camera', the following attributes are used.

Table 14.12   CAMERA ATTRIBUTES IN AXES OBJECTS

`CameraPosition`	is a vector [*x y z*], in axes object coordinates, indicating the position of the camera.
`CameraPositionMode`	is a string indicating whether MATLAB calculates the camera position automatically. If `CameraPositionMode` is set to 'auto' (default) MATLAB generates Camera-Position. If `CameraPositionMode` is set to 'manual' `CameraPosition` is used directly. `CameraPosition-Mode` is automatically set to 'manual' if Camera-Position is set.
`CameraTarget`	is a vector [*x y z*], in axes object coordinates, indicating the target point in the axes object for the camera.
`CameraTargetMode`	is a string indicating whether MATLAB calculates the target point for the camera automatically. If `CameraTargetMode` is set to 'auto' (default) MATLAB sets `CameraTarget` to the center point of the axes object. If `CameraTargetMode` is set to 'manual' `CameraTarget` is used directly. `CameraTargetMode` is automatically set to 'manual' if `CameraTarget` is set.
`CameraUpVector`	is a vector [*x y z*], in axes object coordinates, indicating the rotation of the camera along the line of sight. Default in 3D is [0 0 1], which means the positive *z* axis points upwards.
`CameraUpVectorMode`	is a string indicating whether MATLAB automatically sets the `CameraUpVector`. If `CameraUpVectorMode` is 'auto' (default) MATLAB sets `CameraUpVector` to [0 0 1] in 3D and [0 1 0] in 2D. If `CameraUpVectorMode` is 'manual' `CameraUpVector` is used directly. `CameraUpVectorMode` is automatically set to 'manual' if `CameraUpVector` is set.
`CameraViewAngle`	is a scalar indicating the view angle in degrees (0 to 180). The wider the view angle the smaller the objects will look. Note that this attribute does not affect perspective distortion.
`CameraViewAngle-Mode`	is a string indicating whether MATLAB automatically calculates the view angle. If `CameraViewAngleMode` is set to 'auto' (default) MATLAB sets `CameraViewAngle` to the smallest possible angle where all objects are visible. If `CameraViewAngleMode` is set to 'manual' `Camera-ViewAngle` is used directly. `CameraViewAngleMode` is automatically set to 'manual' if `CameraViewAngle` is set.

Axes, scale markers, legends and grids in axes objects and their children are controlled by the following attributes, where the character ∗ stands for either X, Y or Z.

Table 14.13	AXES OBJECT ATTRIBUTES AND METHODS TO CONTROL AXES
`GridLineStyle`	is a string indicating which line type is used by a grid in the axes object. The following alternatives are available: `'-'`, `'--'`, `':'` (default), `'-.'` and `'none'`. Compare this with the command `grid` in Commands 132.
`Layer`	is a string indicating where the axes are placed on children to the axes object. The children must be 2D, or 3D with `View` set to [0 90] and `DrawMode` set to `'fast'`; see Table 14.10. `Layer` can either be `'bottom'` (default) or `'top'`, which places the axes below or above the plot region respectively.
`TickLength`	is a vector [2*Dlen* 3*Dlen*] indicating the length of the scale markers on the axes, for 2D and 3D graphs respectively. The values in `TickLength` are in per cent of the longest axis.
`TickDir`	is a string indicating whether the scale markers on axes are pointing inwards or outwards. Default is `'in'` for 2D graphs, and `'out'` for 3D graphs.
`TickDirMode`	is a string indicating whether MATLAB sets `TickDir` automatically. If `TickDirMode` is set to `'auto'` (default) MATLAB sets `TickDir`. If `TickDirMode` is set to `'manual'` `TickDir` is used directly. `TickDirMode` is automatically set to `'manual'` if `TickDir` is set.
`XAxisLocation`	is a string indicating where scale markers and text (numbering) are placed on the x axis. `XAxisLocation` can either be `'bottom'` (default) or `'top'`, which places markers and text below or above the graph respectively.
`YAxisLocation`	is a string indicating where scale markers and text (numbering) are placed on the y axis. `YAxisLocation` can either be `'left'` (default) or `'right'`, which places markers and text to the left or to the right of the graph respectively.
`*Color`	is an RGB triplet or one of the predefined colors in MATLAB indicating the color of the ∗ axis. Scale markers, text (numbering) and grids in the ∗ direction gets this color. Default is `'white'`.
`*Dir`	is a string indicating the direction of the ∗ axis. `*Dir` can either be `'normal'` (default) or `'reverse'` which reverse the direction.

Table 14.13   (CONTINUED)

*Grid	is a string indicating whether a grid should be drawn in the * direction. *Grid can be either 'on' or 'off' (default). Use the command grid to place/remove a grid in all directions; see Commands 132.
*Label	is a handle to a text object that contains the label used under the * axis.
*Lim	is a vector [*min max*] indicating the minimum and maximum value on the * axis.
*LimMode	is a string indicating whether MATLAB calculates *Lim automatically. If *LimMode is set to 'auto' (default) MATLAB sets *Lim depending on plot data. If *LimMode is set to 'manual' *Lim is used directly. *LimMode is automatically set to 'manual' if *Lim is set.
*Scale	is a string indicating whether a linear or logarithmic scale is used on the * axis. *Scale can either be 'linear' or 'log'.
*Tick	is a vector having monotonically increasing values, indicating where the scale markers are placed on the * axis.
*TickLabel	is a string matrix indicating the text (numbering) used on the * axis. The strings in the matrix are reused if there are not enough of them.
*TickLabelMode	is a string indicating whether MATLAB sets *TickLabel automatically. If *TickLabelMode is set to 'auto' (default) MATLAB sets *TickLabel. If *TickLabelMode is set to 'manual' *TickLabel is used directly. *TickLabelMode is automatically set to 'manual' if *TickLabel is set.
*TickMode	is a string indicating whether MATLAB sets *Tick automatically. If *TickMode is set to 'auto' (default) MATLAB sets *Tick. If *TickMode is set to 'manual' *Tick is used directly. *Tick is automatically set to 'manual' if *Tick is set.

The appearance of both text on axes and numbering of axes, if any, in an axes object is controlled by the following attributes.

Table 14.14	AXES OBJECT ATTRIBUTES TO CONTROL AXES TEXT
FontAngle	is a string indicating the angle of the font. The following alternatives are available: 'normal' (default), 'italic' and 'oblique'.
FontName	is a string indicating the font used.
FontSize	is a scalar indicating the size of the font. FontSize is in units FontUnits, see below.
FontUnits	is a string indicating the unit used for FontSize. The following alternatives are available: 'inches', 'centimeters', 'normalized', 'points' (default) and 'pixels'.
FontWeight	is a string indicating the thickness of the font. The following alternatives are available: 'light', 'normal' (default), 'demi' and 'bold'.

The axes are scaled by using the maximum and minimum of the given data with 1, 2 or 5 units between each mark as default. If we want to manipulate the marks and the grid lines, this can be done through the properties 'XTick' and 'YTick'.

■ **Example 14.9**

The following program shows how the scale marks and grid lines can be changed:

```
x = [1 3 7];               % Creates x-vector
y = [6 9 2];               % and y-vector.

s1 = subplot(2,2,1);       % Upper left-hand corner.
plot(x,y);
grid;                      % Uses default grid lines.
title('Default');

s2 = subplot(2,2,2);       % Upper right-hand corner.
plot(x,y);
set(s2,'XTick',x);         % Changes x axis marks.
set(s2,'XGrid','on');      % Plots x axis grid lines.
title('X scale manipulated');

s3 = subplot(2,2,3);       % Lower left-hand corner.
plot(x,y);
set(s3,'YTick',[2 6 9]);   % Changes y axis marks.
set(s3,'YGrid','on');      % Plots y axis grid lines.
set(s3,'GridLineStyle','-.'); % Use dash-dot grid lines.
title('Y scale manipulated');
```

```
s4 = subplot(2,2,4);          % Lower right-hand corner.
plot(x,y);
set(s4,'XTick',x);            % Changes both axes marks.
set(s4,'YTick',[2 6 9]);
grid;                         % Plots grid lines, both axes.
title('Both scales manipulated');
```

This returns Figure 14.9.

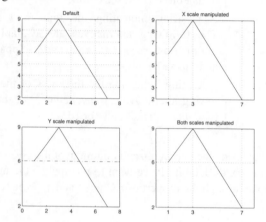

Figure 14.9 *Example of different scale marks and grid lines.*

■

14.2.6 Uicontrol objects

Uicontrol objects are used to build graphical user interfaces, GUIs. These objects can create all the control objects usually found in graphical user interfaces, that is buttons, slide bars, radio buttons, etc. For this reason, the inclusion of uicontrol objects in a program makes it much easier to handle.

For more information about GUIs see Section 14.3.

<table>
<tr><td>Commands 159</td><td>UICONTROL OBJECTS</td></tr>
</table>

| uicontrol(*fp,prstr,* *val,...*) | returns a handle to the created control window in figure window with handle *fp*. If *fp* is not given the current figure window is used. With **prstr** and *alt* the properties are manipulated: what kind (buttons, slide bars, etc.), size, position, and so on. Several properties can be written after each other. The property 'CallBack' controls the consequence of the choice of the user. |

Commands 159 (CONTINUED)

[outstr,pos] = textwrap(h,instr)	wraps the text **instr** to fit in the üicontrol object with handle *h*. The parameter **instr** is a cell vector that contains one row of text per cell, and **outstr** is a cell vector that contains the wrapped text. The vector **pos** contains recommended position and size for the uicontrol object.
popupstr(h)	is a string that contains the current selected item (text) in the pop-up menu with handle *h*. A pop-up menu is a uicontrol object with Style set to 'popupmenu'; see below.

Uicontrol objects have the following attributes and methods.

Table 14.15 UICONTROL OBJECTS ATTRIBUTES AND METHODS

BackgroundColor	is an RGB triplet or one of the predefined colors in MAT-LAB indicating the background color of the object.
Callback	is a string indicating what callback function is executed when the user, for example, clicks on a object. The uicontrol objects of type 'frames' and 'text' (see Style below) have callback functions that cannot be chosen interactively.
CData	is an $m \times n \times 3$ matrix with RGB values representing a true color image that is shown on the 'pushbutton' or 'togglebutton', see 'Style' below.
Enable	is a string indicating what the uicontrol object does when it is clicked on with the mouse. The following alternatives are available:
	'on' (default) means that 'Callback' is executed.
	'inactive' means that 'ButtonDownFcn' is executed.
	'off' means that 'ButtonDownFcn' is executed, and the title of the object (see String) becomes 'blurred'.
Extent	is a read-only vector [0 0 *width height*] indicating the size of the text String.
ForegroundColor	is an RGB triplet or one of the predefined colors in MAT-LAB indicating the color of the text String, see below, default is 'black'.
Horizontal Alignment	is a string indicating the horizontal alignment of the text String (see below). The following alternatives are available: 'left', 'center' (default) and 'right'.

Table 14.15	(CONTINUED)

`ListboxTop`	is a scalar used by uicontrol objects of type `'listbox'`. The scalar is an index indicating which string in the cell vector `String` (see below) is in the top of the list box.
`Max`	is a scalar indicating the maximum value for `Value` (see below). This attribute is interpreted differently according to the type of uicontrol object: • For `'radiobutton'`, `'checkbox'` and `'togglebutton'` it is `Value` when they are "on". • For `'slider'` it is the largest value that can be chosen. • For `'edit'` `Max`, `Min` > 1 indicates that the object accepts several lines of input. • For `'listbox'` `Max`, `Min` > 1 indicates that several items can be selected. • For objects `'frame'`, `'popupmenu'` and `'text'` this attribute is meaningless.
`Min`	is a scalar indicating the minimum value for `Value` (see below). This attribute is interpreted differently according to the type of uicontrol object: • For `'radiobutton'`, `'checkbox'` and `'togglebutton'` it is `Value` when they are "off". • For `'slider'` it is the smallest value that can be chosen. • For objects `'edit'` and `'listbox'` see `Max` above. • For objects `'frame'`, `'popupmenu'` and `'text'` this attribute is meaningless.
`Position`	is a four element vector [*left bottom width height*] indicating the position and size of the object on the screen.
`String`	is a string that sets text in the object. For `'popupmenu'`, `'listbox'`, `'edit'` and `'text'` several options and lines of text can be specified if `String` is a cell vector, a string matrix or a string with its lines separated by `'|'` (`'popupmenu'`, `'listbox'`) or `'\n'` (`'edit'`, `'text'`).
`Style`	is a string indicating the type of object. The following alternatives are available: `'pushbutton'` (default), `'radiobutton'`, `'checkbox'`, `'edit'` (editable text), `'text'`, `'slider'`, `'frame'`, `'listbox'`, `'popupmenu'` and `'togglebutton'` (on/off button).

Table 14.15	(CONTINUED)
SliderStep	is a vector [*minstep maxstep*] indicating the change, in per cent, a click on the arrows and slide bar respectively gives. Default is [0.01 0.1].
TooltipString	is a string that is shown when the user has moved the mouse pointer onto the uicontrol object.
Units	is a string indicating what unit is used. The following alternatives are available: 'inches', 'centimeters', 'normalized', 'points', 'pixels' (default) and 'characters'. The choice of unit affects the attributes Extent and Position, see above.
Value	is an attribute that is interpreted differently depending on the type of unicontrol object: • For 'radiobutton', 'checkbox' and 'togglebutton' see Max and Min above, respectively. • For 'slider' it is the current value. • For 'popupmenu' it is the number of the current selected alternative. • For 'listbox' it is a vector that contains the numbers of the current selected alternatives. • For all other unicontrol objects this attribute is meaningless.
Children	is always [], that is a unicontrol object never has children.
Clipping	has no effect.
HitTest	has no effect.

To control the appearance of any text in unicontrol objects, these attributes are used.

Table 14.16	ATTRIBUTES FOR CONTROL OF TEXT IN UICONTROL OBJECTS			
FontAngle	FontName	FontSize	FontUnits	FontWeight

For a complete description see Table 14.13.

14.2.7 Uimenu objects

Uimenu objects are, like uicontrol objects, used to build graphical user interfaces. The purpose of uimenu objects is to build pull-down menus, and these are placed in the top of figure windows.

Commands 160   UIMENU OBJECTS

`uimenu(p,prstr,alt,` `...)`	creates a pull-down menu at the top of the figure window with handle p, and returns the handle of the new uimenu object. If p is not specified, the current figure window is used. If p is instead a handle to a menu, a submenu is created. It is therefore possible to create a hierarchy of menus. The properties of the menu, and its name, what to do in case of a choice, and so on are given as property **prstr** with value *alt*. Several properties can be written after each other.
`makemenu(h,mencho,` `calls,tags)`	creates a menu structure in the figure object with handle h. The parameter **mencho** is a string matrix that contains the name of the menu choices and **calls** is a string matrix that contains the MATLAB commands that are executed when the user has made a choice from the menu. If the string matrix **tags** is given, the corresponding Tag attribute (see Table 14.2) is set in the uimenu objects that are part of the menu. The command makemenu returns a vector with handles to the created uimenu objects. Try `help makemenu` for more information. It is also possible to use the tool `menuedit` to create menus; see Section 14.3.5.
`umtoggle(h)`	swaps status for the uimenu object with handle h from selected to unselected and vice versa. It returns 1 if the uimenu object is selected and 0 if it is unselected. See also the uimenu attribute Checked below.
`winmenu(h)`	creates a submenu to the menu Window in the figure window with handle h. If h is not given the current figure window is used. The menu Window must have its Tag attribute set to 'winmenu'; see Table 14.2. Try `help winmenu` for more information.

Uimenu objects have the following attributes and methods.

Table 14.17   UIMENU OBJECTS ATTRIBUTES AND METHODS

`Accelerator`	is a character that makes it possible for the user to choose the menu item from the keyboard by pressing `Control-Accelerator` or, on the Macintosh, `Command-Accelerator`. This short-cut works only for menu items that have callback functions but have no children.
`Callback`	is a string indicating what callback function is executed when the user has chosen the menu item.
`Checked`	is a string indicating whether the menu item is selected. Checked can either be 'on' or 'off' (default).

Table 14.17	(CONTINUED)
Enable	is a string indicating whether the menu item is selectable. Enable can either be 'on' (default) or 'off'. In the latter case the menu item becomes 'blurred'.
ForegroundColor	is an RGB triplet or one of the predefined colors in MAT-LAB, indicating the color of the text Label. Note: this attribute is only used in X Windows.
Label	is a string indicating the name of the menu item. It is possible to underline a character in the name by preceding it with an '&'. The menu item will then be chosen if the user presses the key on the keyboard corresponding to the underlined character.
Position	is a scalar indicating the relative position on the menu row. The value 1 means the leftmost position, or in a menu, the uppermost.
Separator	is a string indicating whether a separation line is drawn above the menu item. Separator can either be 'on' or 'off' (default).
ButtonDownFcn	has no effect.
Children	is a vector that contains handles to submenus, if any.
Clipping	has no effect.
Selected	has no effect.
SelectionHighLight	has no effect.
UIContextMenu	has no effect.

14.2.8 Uicontextmenu objects

The Uicontextmenu objects are used to create context menus, which are a new type of menu introduced in MATLAB 5.2. These menus are shown when the user presses down the right mouse button (on the Macintosh Control-click) when the mouse pointer is over an object. From this menu the user can then make a choice. The context menus are accordingly always connected to another object; see property UIContextMenu in Table 14.2.

Commands 161	UICONTEXTMENU OBJECTS
uicontextmenu(*prstr*, *alt*, ...)	creates a uicontextmenu object with property **prstr** set to *alt* and returns the handle to the new object. Several properties can be written after each other.

Uicontextmenu objects have the following attributes and methods.

Table 14.18	UICONTEXTMENU OBJECT ATTRIBUTES AND METHODS
Callback	is a string indicating what callback function is executed when the right mouse button (Macintosh Control-click) is pressed down on the object.
Children	is a vector that contains handles to the uimenu objects, that is menu items, that are defined for the uicontextmenu object.
ButtonDownFcn	has no effect.
Clipping	has no effect.
HitTest	has no effect.
Selected	has no effect.
SelectionHighlight	has no effect.
UIContextMenu	has no effect.

■ **Example 14.10**

In this example we will create a context menu connected to a surface object. From the menu the user will be able to change the line type that the surface object is drawn with.

```
% Draw a sphere-surface.
figure(1)
sphere;
sp = findobj(1,'Type','surface');      % Get a pointer to it.

% Define menu-choices, i.e. callback functions.
cb1 = ['set(sp,''LineStyle'',''none'')'];
cb2 = ['set(sp,''LineStyle'',''--'')'];
cb3 = ['set(sp,''LineStyle'','':'')'];
cb4 = ['set(sp,''LineStyle'',''-'')'];

% Define the context-menu.
cmenu = uicontextmenu;
set(sp,'UIContextMenu',cmenu)
menp  = uimenu(cmenu,'Label','Linetypes');
item1 = uimenu(menp, 'Label','none',  'Callback',cb1);
item2 = uimenu(menp, 'Label','dashed','Callback',cb2);
item3 = uimenu(menp, 'Label','dotted','Callback',cb3);
item4 = uimenu(menp, 'Label','solid', 'Callback',cb4);
```

When the user presses down the right mouse button (Macintosh Control-click) the menus in Figure 14.10 become visible.

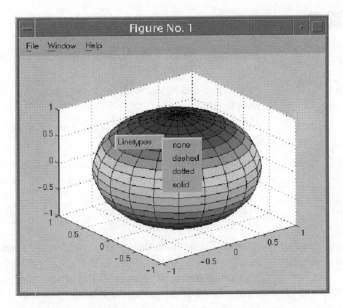

Figure 14.10 *A surface object with a context menu.*

∎

14.2.9 Image objects

It is also possible to display images in MATLAB. An image in MATLAB is defined as a matrix whose elements correspond to points in the picture and the element values correspond to the colors of the points. The images in MATLAB are therefore of the 'bitmapped' type.

The command `image`, which is both a high-level and low-level command, plots a matrix as a picture on the screen. The corresponding function to capture the image of a graphical window is the command `capture`. Note, however, that `capture` and `image` often give a lower resolution than MATLAB's internal representation, and that they also require more memory.

Commands 162	IMAGE OBJECTS

`image(C)`	plots the matrix **C** as an image. Each element of **C** is a point of the image and the value defines the color. If **C** is not given, a default image is plotted. The handle of the image is returned.
`image(x,y,C)`	plots the matrix **C** as an image. The vectors **x** and **y** contain minima and maxima values of the x and y axis, respectively.
`image(`*prstr*`,`*alt*`, ...)`	creates an image whose appearance and properties are defined by **prstr** and *alt*. Several properties can be written after each other. These can later be changed with the `set` command.

Commands 162 (CONTINUED)

imagesc(...)	is the same as image but the data is scaled to use the full color map.
capture(h)	creates a new window with the same contents as the window with handle *h*.
[C,Cm] = capture	returns an image matrix **C** with corresponding color map **Cm** without displaying the image.
imfinfo(filename, *fmt*)	returns a structure that contains information about an image file. The string **filename** is the name of the file and **fmt** is its file format. The format can be 'bmp', 'hdf', 'jpg', 'jpeg', 'pcx', 'tif', 'tiff' or 'xwd'. See helpdesk for more information.
[A,Ftab] = imread (filename,*fmt*,*idx*)	reads an image from an image file with name **filename** to the matrix **A**. The matrix **Ftab** is the color table of the image. The string **fmt** is the format of the image, see above. If the format is not specified MATLAB tries to guess it. The scalar *idx* indicates the number of the image to be read if there is more than one image in the file (only for 'tiff' and 'hdf' format images). See helpdesk for more information.
imwrite(A,*Ftab*, filename,*fmt*,*prstr*, *alt*)	as above, but instead writes an image to a file. If the file format **fmt** is not specified, the filename must have **fmt** as suffix. For 'hdf', 'jpeg' and 'tiff' images it is possible to set certain properties; the property **prstr** is set to *alt*. See helpdesk for more information.

Figure P.7 in the color plate section shows an image of the earth, displayed with the image-command. The command colormap(map) gives the correct colors.

Image objects have the following attributes and methods.

Table 14.19 IMAGE OBJECT ATTRIBUTES AND METHODS

Cdata	indicates the color of the elements in the image matrix. The data has the same format as the color of the vertices in patch object; see Table 14.21.
CDataMapping	see Table 14.21.
EraseMode	see Table 14.20.
Xdata	is a vector of size 1×size(CData,2) that contains the *x* coordinates of the image.
YData	is a vector of size 1×size(CData,2) that contains the *y* coordinates of the image.
Children	is always [], that is an image object never has children.

■ **Example 14.11**

The command image without any parameters produces a predefined upside down image as in Figure 14.11.

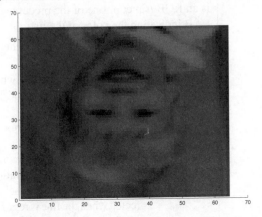

Figure 14.11 *What MATLAB shows when no parameters are given to the command image.*

■

14.2.10 Line objects

Normally, the low-level command line is not used directly to create a line object. Instead a high-level command is used, for example plot. It is possible, however, both to manipulate existing lines and to draw new lines with the line command. In contrast to high-level plot commands, which perform many things besides the actual plotting, for example replace axes, the only thing a line command does is to draw a line.

Commands 163	LINE OBJECTS
line(x,y)	draws the line defined by the vectors **x** and **y** in the current figure. If **x** and **y** are two matrices of the same size, a line is drawn for each column. The handle to the new line object is returned.
line(x,y,z)	plots a line in three dimensions analogously to the preceding command.
line(*prstr*,*alt*,...)	plots a line with property **prstr** set to value *alt*. Several properties can be written after each other.

Line objects have the following attributes and methods.

Table 14.20	LINE OBJECT ATTRIBUTES AND METHODS
`Color`	is an RGB triplet or one of the predefined colors in MAT-LAB indicating the color of the line.
`EraseMode`	is a string indicating what happens when a line object is destroyed:
	`'normal'` (default) means that the whole area affected is redrawn. This method is exact, but can sometimes take time.
	`'none'` means that the line is not removed if it is moved or destroyed.
	`'xor'` means that lines are drawn and removed by performing an XOR operation with the background graphics. The background is not affected when the line is removed, but the color of the line is depending on the underlying graphics.
	`'back-ground'` means that a line is removed by replacing it with the background color. The background is affected, but the line always get the right color.
`LineStyle`	is a string indicating the line type. The following alternatives are available: `'-'` (default), `'--'`, `':'`, `'-.'` and `'none'`.
`LineWidth`	is a scalar indicating the thickness of the line in points, default is 0.5 points.
`Marker`	is a string indicating what marker type is used to plot data. The following alternatives are available: `'+'`, `'o'`, `'*'`, `'.'`, `'x'`, `'square'`, `'diamond'`, `'∧'`, `'v'`, `'>'`, `'<'`, `'pentagram'`, `'hexagram'` and `'none'` (default).
`MarkerSize`	is a scalar indicating the size, in points, of the markers. Default is 6 points. Note that MATLAB plots markers at 1/3 of the specified size.
`MarkerEdgeColor`	indicates the color of an unfilled point type or the edge color of a filled point type. `MarkerEdgeColor` can be an RGB triplet, one of the predefined colors in MATLAB, `'none'` or `'auto'` (default, gives the color `Color`; see above).
`MarkerFaceColor`	indicates the face color of a filled point type. `MarkerFaceColor` can be an RGB triplet, one of the predefined colors in MATLAB, `'none'` or `'auto'` (default, gives the color `Color`; see above).

Table 14.20	(CONTINUED)
XData	is a vector with x coordinates.
YData	is a vector with y coordinates.
ZData	is a vector with z coordinates.
Children	is always [], that is the line object has not any children.

14.2.11 Patch objects

A patch object is an area defined by a filled polygon. The corners of the polygon are defined by two or three vectors, **x**, **y** and **z**, depending on the number of dimensions. The corners are defined in the order of the vector elements. The polygon is filled with the color specified by the patch command.

Commands 164	PATCH OBJECTS
patch(x,y,c)	creates a polygon, defined by the vectors **x** and **y** in the current plot region. The parameter **c** is the color of the polygon and can be a scalar, vector or matrix, see CData and FaceVertexCData below. If **x** and **y** are matrices, a polygon for each column is drawn. The command patch returns the handle to the patch object.
patch(x,y,z,c)	creates a polygon in three dimensions, analogously to the 2D case.
patch(*prstr*,*alt*,...)	creates a polygon with property **prstr** set to *alt*. Several properties can be written after each other.

■ **Example 14.12**

An example with a sphere and its own patch object:

```
sphere(10);            % Plots a sphere with 121 "corners".

x = [-2 -2  2  2];     % Defines x-positions of our polygon.
y = [-2  2  2 -2];     % Defines y-positions of our polygon.
z = [-2 -2 -2 -2];     % Defines z-positions of our polygon.
c = [-2 -1  1  2];     % Defines colors of our polygon.

p1 = patch(x,y,z,c);   % Plots the polygon and keeps a handle.
```

The commands result in Figure 14.12.

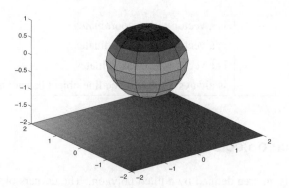

Figure 14.12 *A sphere and polygon drawn with* patch.

The appearance and properties of a patch object can be redefined with set and read by get. Patch objects have the following attributes and methods.

Table 14.21	PATCH OBJECT ATTRIBUTES AND METHODS
Cdata	indicates the color of the polygon. Also see CData Mapping • An RGB triplet, one of the predefined colors in MATLAB, or a scalar that works as an index to the colormap of the parent indicates the color of the polygon. • An $m \times 3$ matrix with RGB values or a vector with indices gives one color per surface in the polygon. • An $m \times n \times 3$ matrix with RGB values or a matrix with indices gives one color per vertex in the polygon. On pseudo color screens dithering of the RGB triplets is necessary, and this is done with the help of the Colormap and Dithermap attributes in the parent figure object; see Table 14.8. If CData contains NaNs MATLAB will not color the surfaces of the polygon. See also FaceVertexCData.

Table 14.21	(CONTINUED)

CDataMapping

is a string indicating the interpretation of a possible 'color index' in `Cdata` or `FaceVertexCData`. The index is an integer indicating a position, directly or indirectly, in the color table `ColorMap` (see Table 14.8) of the parent figure object:

`'scaled'`	(default) means that MATLAB transforms the color data linearly to cover the interval indicated by `CLim` in the parent figure object; see Table 14.11.
`'direct'`	means that an index directly indicates the color in table `ColorMap` of the parent figure object. Indices outside the color table are mapped to the first (if index < 1) or last index.

FaceVertexCData

indicates the color of the surfaces or vertices of the polygon.

- An RGB triplet or a scalar that works as an index to the colormap of the parent (see `CDataMapping`) means that the polygon gets one color.

- An $m \times 3$ matrix, where m is the number of rows in `Faces`, with RGB values or an $m \times 1$ vector with indices (see `CDataMapping`) gives one color per surface in the polygon.

- An $m \times 3$ matrix, where m now is the number of rows in `Vertices`, with RGB values or an $m \times 1$ vector with indices (see `CDataMapping`) gives one color per vertex in the polygon.

See also `CData`.

EdgeColor

indicates how the edges of the polygon are colored.

- An RGB triplet or one of the predefined colors in MATLAB means that all edges get one color; default is `'black'`.

- The alternative `'none'` means that the edges are not drawn.

- The alternative `'flat'` means that an edge gets the same color as the preceding vertex.

- The alternative `'interp'` means that a linear interpolation of data in `Cdata` or `FaceVertexCData` gives the color of the edge.

EraseMode

see Table 14.20.

Table 14.21	(CONTINUED)
FaceColor	indicates how the surfaces of the polygon are colored. • An RGB triplet (default). • The alternative 'none' means that the surfaces are not drawn. • The alternative 'flat' means that a surface gets the same color as the first vertex. • The alternative 'interp' means that a bilinear interpolation of the colors of the vertices gives the color of the surface.
Faces	is an $m \times n$ matrix indicating how the vertices are connected. Defines m surfaces with up to n vertices each. Each row in the matrix indicates how each surface is connected, and the number of elements in the row different from NaN indicates the number of vertices. See helpdesk for more information.
LineStyle	is a string indicating the line type of the edges; see Table 14.20.
LineWidth	is a scalar indicating the thickness of the edges; see Table 14.20.
Marker	is a string indicating the marker type in the vertices of the polygon; see Table 14.20.
MarkerEdgeColor	see Table 14.20. The alternative 'auto' (default) gives the color EdgeColor. Moreover, there is the undocumented alternative 'flat'.
MarkerFaceColor	see Table 14.20. The alternative 'auto' means that the face color is the color Color of the parent axes object. The alternative 'none' means that the face color is the color Color of the parent figure object instead. Moreover, there is the undocumented alternative 'flat'.
MarkerSize	see Table 14.20.
Vertices	is an $m \times 3$ matrix that contains the x, y, and z coordinates for the vertices of the polygon; see also Faces.
XData	is a vector or a matrix with the x coordinates of the vertices. If XData is a matrix each column represents the x coordinates for a separate surface in the polygon. In this case, XData, YData and ZData must have the same dimension.
YData	is like XData, but for the y coordinates.
ZData	is like XData, but for the z coordinates.
Children	is always [], that is a patch object never has children.

In MATLAB it is possible to illuminate polygons by creating a so called light object; see Table 14.26. How this illumination affects the patch object is described by the following attributes and methods.

Table 14.22   ATTRIBUTES AND METHODS TO INDICATE
ILLUMINATION EFFECTS OF PATCH OBJECTS

`FaceLighting`	is a string indicating what algorithm is used to calculate the effect of light objects on surfaces of the polygon. `'none'` (default) means that the light has no effect. `'flat'` means that the light affects the whole surface in the same way. This method is, for example, used when studying facet surfaces. `'gourand'` means that the illumination effect is interpolated over the whole surface. This method is, for example, used on curved surfaces. `'phong'` is similar to `'gourand'`, produces a better result, but takes more time.
`EdgeLighting`	is like `FaceLighting` but for the vertices of the polygon.
`BackFaceLighting`	indicates how light affects the surface of the polygon when its surface normals in the vertices point away from the camera; see Table 14.12. `'unlit'` means the surface is not illuminated. `'lit'` means the surface is illuminated in the usual way. `'reverse lit'` (default) means the surface is illuminated as if the surface normals pointed towards the camera. Useful for separation of inner and outer surfaces of an object.
`AmbientStrength`	is a scalar, between 0 and 1, indicating the strength of the background illumination (the so called ambient light) of the polygon. See also axes object attribute `AmbientColor`.
`DiffuseStrength`	is a scalar, between 0 and 1, indicating the intensity of the 'diffuse' light reflected from the polygon. Dull objects have a large `DiffuseStrength`.
`SpecularStrength`	is a scalar, between 0 and 1, indicating the intensity of the 'specular' light reflected from the polygon. Shiny objects have a large `SpecularStrength`.
`SpecularExponent`	is a scalar ≥ 1 indicating the 'mirror-likeness' of the polygon. The scalar is usually between 1 and 500, most materials have values between 5 and 20.

Table 14.22	(CONTINUED)
`SpecularColor-` `Reflectance`	is a scalar, between 0 and 1, indicating how the color of the 'specular' light depends on the color of the light object and polygon. If it is 0 it depends on both, and if it is 1 it only depends on the color of the light object. See also axes object attribute `AmbientLightColor`; Table 14.11.
`VertexNormals`	is an $m \times 3$ matrix that contains the surface normals in the m vertices of the polygon. The matrix is created by MATLAB to help calculating the effect of light objects on the polygon, but can be set by the user to give interesting illumination properties.
`NormalMode`	is a string indicating whether MATLAB automatically sets `VertexNormals`. If `NormalMode` is set to `'auto'` (default) MATLAB calculates `VertexNormals`. If `NormalMode` is set to `'manual'` `VertexNormals` is used directly. `NormalMode` is automatically set to `'manual'` if the user sets `VertexNormals`.

14.2.12 Surface objects

Surface objects create 'flying carpets' in three dimensions.

Commands 165	SURFACE OBJECTS
`surface(x,y,Z,c)`	creates a filled surface defined by **x**, **y** and **Z** in the current plot region. The vectors or matrices **x** and **y** are optional. **Z** is a matrix, see XData, YData and ZData in Table 14.23. The parameter **c** is a scalar or a matrix indicating the color used, see CData in Table 14.23. If **c** is not given, the matrix **Z** is also used as **c**. The command `surface` returns the handle to the created surface object.
`surface(prstr,alt,` `...)`	creates a surface with property **prstr** set to *alt*. Several properties can be written after each other. The handle to the created surface object is returned.

The surface objects have the following attributes and methods, of which many are the same as the one in Table 14.21.

Table 14.23	SURFACE OBJECT ATTRIBUTES AND METHODS
CData	indicates the color of each vertex on the surface, that is it specifies the color of each point in ZData. If FaceColor is set to 'texturemap', CData does not need to have the same size as ZData. In this case MATLAB maps CData to the surface indicated by ZData. See Table 14.21 for how the colors of the vertices are specified.
CDataMapping	see Table 14.21.
EdgeColor	see Table 14.21.
EraseMode	see Table 14.20.
FaceColor	see Table 14.21. Moreover, FaceColor can be set to 'texturemap', see CData.
LineStyle	see Table 14.21.
LineWidth	see Table 14.21.
Marker	see Table 14.21.
MarkerEdgeColor	see Table 14.21.
MarkerFaceColor	see Table 14.21.
MarkerSize	see Table 14.21.
MeshStyle	is a string indicating which edges of the grid that are drawn: 'both' (default), 'row' or 'column'.
XData	is an $m \times n$ matrix or an $m \times 1$ vector (the column vector is repeated to form an $m \times n$ matrix) indicating the x coordinates of the surface.
YData	is an $m \times n$ matrix or an $m \times 1$ vector (the column vector is repeated to form an $m \times n$ matrix) indicating the y coordinates of the surface.
ZData	is an $m \times n$ matrix indicating the z coordinates of the surface, that is its height.
Children	is always [], that is a surface object never has children.

It is possible to illuminate surface objects in the same way as polygons. The attributes and methods are summarized below (Table 14.24); for a complete description see Table 14.22.

Table 14.24	ATTRIBUTES AND METHODS TO INDICATE ILLUMINATION EFFECTS OF SURFACE OBJECTS

FaceLighting	EdgeLighting	BackFaceLighting
AmbientStrength	DiffuseStrength	SpecularStrength
SpecularExponent	SpecularColorReflectance	VertexNormals
NormalMode		

■ **Example 14.13**

(a) In Example 14.12 we could have created the sphere in the following way:

```
[X,Y,Z] = sphere;          % Get sphere-coordinates.
ss = surface(X,Y,Z);       % Creates surface-object and plot it.
view(3);
```

The object property 'FaceColor' can be changed from 'flat' to 'interp' using the set command:

```
 set(ss,'FaceColor','interp')
```

To see the alternatives, type:

```
set(ss,'FaceColor')
```

[none | {flat} | interp | texturemap] -or-a ColorSpec.

The property FaceColor is in effect, for example, when the command patch, surface or mesh is given, and the value 'texturemap' can then be used instead of 'interp' or 'flat'. The alternative 'none' is used in the example below.

(b) The command mesh is a high-level command that uses surface. We can get a handle to a plot that mesh has made in the same way as from the command surface. The following program uses both patch and mesh and changes properties in the obtained objects.

```
% The vectors x1,y1 and z1 represent a cube
% in three dimensions.

z1 = [1 1 -1 -1 1 1 -1 -1 -1 -1 1 1 1 1 -1 -1];
y1 = [1 -1 -1 1 1 1 1 1 1 -1 -1 1 -1 -1 -1 -1];
x1 = [1 1 1 1 1 -1 -1 1 -1 -1 -1 -1 -1 1 1 -1];

clf                                 % Clears current figure.
p = plot3(x1,y1,z1);                % Draws lines of a cube,
                                    % keeps a handle.
set(p,'LineWidth',3,'Color','b')    % Changes line properties.

[XX,YY,ZZ] = sphere(15);            % The matrices XX,YY,ZZ
hold on;                            % defines unit sphere.

h1 = mesh(XX,YY,ZZ);                % Draws unit sphere,
                                    % keeps handle.

% Changes sphere properties.
set(h1,'EdgeColor','b','FaceColor','c')
```

```
h2 = mesh(2.*XX,2.*YY,2.*ZZ);        % Draws sphere (radius 2),
                                     % keeps handle.
% Changes sphere properties.
set(h2,'EdgeColor','r','FaceColor','none')

set(gca,'Visible','off')             % Changes property visible
                                     % for current axes.

axis square                          % Makes spheres round.
```

The result is the plot shown in Figure 14.13.

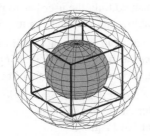

Figure 14.13 *A unit sphere inscribed in a cube that is inscribed in a larger sphere.*

■

14.2.13 Text objects

When text is displayed in a figure window, a text object is created. This is done by the `text` command. One specifies where the text is to be written, and it is also possible to change the properties of the object.

Commands 166	TEXT OBJECTS
`text(x,y,txt)`	returns the handle to the text object. Writes the string **txt** to the current two-dimensional plot region starting at (x, y). The coordinates are specified in the scale of the current axes.
`text(x,y,z,txt)`	writes the string **txt** to the current three-dimensional plot region like the previous command.
`text(prstr,alt,...)`	creates a text object with the property **prstr** set to *alt*. Several properties can be written after each other.

Text objects have the following attributes and methods.

Table 14.25	TEXT OBJECT ATTRIBUTES AND METHODS
Color	is an RGB triplet or one of the predefined colors in MAT-LAB indicating the color of the text; default is 'white'.
EraseMode	see Table 14.20.
Editing	indicates whether the text is editable. The alternative 'off' (default) means that the text cannot be edited. If Editing is set to 'on' MATLAB places a cursor in the beginning of the text, and the text can now be edited. To finish editing, the user has to press ESC, click on a figure window and set Editing to 'off'.
Extent	is a four element read-only vector [*left bottom width height*] indicating the position (in the plot region) and size of the text String.
FontAngle	is a string indicating the angle of the font. The following alternatives are available: 'normal' (default), 'italic' and 'oblique'.
FontName	see Table 14.14.
FontSize	see Table 14.14.
FontUnits	see Table 14.14.
FontWeight	see Table 14.14.
Horizontal Alignment	is a string indicating the horizontal alignment of the text. The following alternatives are available: 'left' (default), 'center' and 'right'.
Position	is a vector [*x y*] or [*x y z*] indicating the position of the text in two or three dimensions.
Rotation	is a scalar indicating the rotation of the text in degrees, default is 0.
String	is a cell vector, string matrix or string that contains the text that is displayed.
Units	is a string indicating what unit is used. The following units are available: 'inches', 'centimeters', 'normalized', 'points', 'pixels', 'characters', and 'data' (default). The alternative 'data' means that the same unit as in the parent axes object is used. The choice of unit affects the attributes Position and Extent, see above.
Interpreter	is a string indicating whether String contains LaTeX text formating commands ('tex', default) or not ('none'). See helpdesk for more information.

Table 14.25	(CONTINUED)
`VerticalAlignment`	is a string indicating the vertical alignment of the text. The following alternatives are available: `'top'`, `'cap'` (like `'top'` but with space for capital letters), `'middle'` (default), `'baseline'` (places the baseline of the font at indicated *y* position) and `'bottom'`.
`Children`	is always `[]`, that is a text object never has children.

■ **Example 14.14**

In this example we want the line and the corresponding text in the same color. In addition, the line width and the text font are changed.

```
clear; clf;

x   = linspace(2,10,100);
y1  = sin(x);
y2  = bessel(1,x);
ha  = axes('Position',[0.1 0.1 0.6 0.8]);

l1 = line(x,y1);
t1 = text(x(100),y1(100),'Sine');

l2 = line(x,y2);
t2 = text(x(100),y2(100),'Bessel');

set(l1,'Color'      ,'Blue'  );      % Line 1: sets color
set(l1,'LineWidth' ,3        );      % and width.

set(t1,'Color'      ,'Blue'  );      % Text 1: Sets color,
set(t1,'FontWeight','bold'   );      % weight, and size.
set(t1,'FontSize'  ,18       );

set(l2,'Color'      ,'Red'   );      % Line 2: color and width.
set(l2,'LineWidth' ,10       );

set(t2,'Color'      ,'Red'   );      % Text 2: color, angle,
set(t2,'FontAngle' ,'italic' );      % font, and size.
set(t2,'FontName'  ,'palatino');
set(t2,'FontSize'  ,30       );

set(ha,'Box','off');                 % Do not draw the box,
                                     % draw only the axes.
```

The result is displayed in Figure 14.14, but unfortunately without the colors.

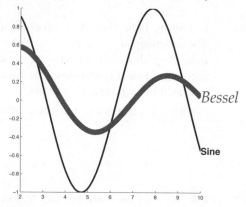

Figure 14.14 *Lines with corresponding text.*

14.2.14 Light objects

The light objects, which create light sources, are a new type of objects introduced in MAT-LAB 5. The light sources are not explicitly visible, but their effect on patch and surface objects is. How the light affects these objects is determined by the following properties of theirs: `AmbientStrength`, `DiffuseStrength`, `EdgeLighting`, `FaceLighting`, `BackFaceLighting`, `SpecularStrength`, `SpecularExponent`, `SpecularColor-Reflectance`, and `VertexNormals`. For a description of these properties see Table 14.22 and Table 14.24.

It is also possible to define background light filling the whole plot region, see the attribute `AmbientLightColor` in Table 14.11.

Commands 167	LIGHT OBJECTS

`light(`*prstr*`,`*alt*`,...)` creates a light object with property **prstr** set to *alt*. Several properties can be written after each other. The handle to the created light object is returned.

Figure P.2 and Figure P.8 in the color plate section have been created with the `light`-command. Object properties have been set using handles.

Light objects have the following attributes and methods.

Table 14.26	LIGHT OBJECT ATTRIBUTES AND METHODS

`Position`	is a vector [*x* *y* *z*], in the unit of the parent axes object, indicating the position or direction of the light; see `Style`.
`Color`	is an RGB triplet or one of the predefined colors in MATLAB indicating the color of the light.
`Style`	is a string indicating what type of light source it is: `'infinite'` (default) means that the light source transmits parallel rays of light in the direction `Position`. `'local'` means that the light source is placed at the position `Position` and transmits rays of light in all directions.
`ButtonDwnFcn`	has no effect.
`Children`	is always `[]`, that is a light object never has children.
`Clipping`	has no effect.
`HitTest`	has no effect.
`Interruptibel`	does not affect the callback function `DeleteFcn`.
`Selected`	has no effect.
`SelectionHighlight`	has no effect.
`UIContextMenu`	has no effect.

■ **Example 14.15**

We will in this example create a surface object and watch the difference in appearance with and without a light source. Consider the following program:

```
% Create a surface-object and plot it 'as usual'.

subplot(2,1,1)
surf(peaks);
axis('off')
title('unlit surface')

subplot(2,1,2)
sp = surf(peaks);

% Surface-color red, no mesh and lighting-algorithm 'phong'.

set(sp,'FaceColor','red')
set(sp,'EdgeColor','none')
```

```
set(sp,'FaceLighting','phong')

% Use parallel beams along the x-axis.

light('Position',[1 0 0],'Style','infinite')
axis('off')
title('lit surface')
```

When the program is run we get Figure 14.15.

unlit surface

lit surface

Figure 14.15 *Surface with and without illumination.*

14.3 Graphical user interfaces

MATLAB has powerful tools to build graphical user interfaces. Moreover, it has a number of predefined windows, as follows:

| Commands 168 | PREDEFINED WINDOWS |

dialog(*prstr*,*alt* ,...)

creates a figure object with settings suitable for a dialog box. The optional property **prstr** is set to the value *alt*. Several properties can be written after each other. The window is modal; see msgbox. The handle to the created figure object is returned.

msgbox(message, *title*,*icon*,*icondata*, *iconclr*,*mode*)

creates a window with a message and returns a handle to the window, that is to the figure object.

- The parameter **message** is a string, a string matrix, or a cell vector and **title** is a string that sets a title for the window.

- The string **icon** indicates what type of icon that will be shown in the window. The following alternatives are available: 'none', 'error', 'help', 'warn' or 'custom'.

- Only if the icon type is 'custom', data for the user-defined icon should be given in **icondata** and used color table in **iconclr**.

- The parameter **mode** indicates what type of window it is, the following types are available: 'modal' needs user feedback before the program continues, 'nonmodal' does not need feedback before the program continues, and 'replace' is non-modal and replaces a possible window with the same **title**.

helpdlg(*hlpstr*,*title*)

creates a dialog box with the help text **hlpstr** in a window with the name **title**. The window disappears when a button is chosen with the mouse. It returns a handle to the window, that is to the figure object.

helpwin topic

displays a help window about the MATLAB commando topic. It can also be a user-defined command in an M-file. Links are created to other relevant commands that are indicated on the line 'See Also' in the help section of the command.

helpwin(hlpstr, heading,*title*,*prstr*, *alt*,...)

displays a help text in the help window **title** under the heading **heading**. Here, **hlpstr** is a help text that can be a cell vector, a string matrix or a string with each row separated with a '\n', that is a 'return' character. The string **prstr** is a property of a text object that is set to *alt*, and it will affect the appearance of the help text. Several properties can be written after each other.

helpwin(r1 t1; r2 t2;...,*page*, *title*,*prstr*,*alt*,...)	is as above (**r1, r2**... headings and **t1, t2**... help texts), but gives the possibility of creating several pages of help under different headings. The string **page** must be equal to one of the headings and means that the corresponding help text is displayed first; default is **r1**.
warndlg(*warn*,*title*)	creates a dialog box with a warning message. The text **warn** is displayed in a window with the name **title**. The window disappears when a button is chosen with the mouse. It returns a handle to the window, that is to the figure object.
errordlg(*errstr*, *title*,'*on*')	creates a dialog box with the error message **errstr** in a window with name **title**. If '*on*' is given, the window, if it exists, with the name **title** will be moved to the foreground. If the window does not exist, a new window is created with the name **title**. The window disappears when a button is chosen with the mouse. It returns a handle to the window, that is to the figure object.
questdlg(qst, *title*,*alt*1,*alt*2,*alt*3, *default*)	creates a dialog box with the question **qst** and the name **title**. If the optional parameters are not given, a window is created with the three buttons 'Yes', 'No' and 'Cancel'. It is possible though to define your own buttons with the texts **alt1**, **alt2** and **alt3** (at least two must be given). The string **default** indicates what happens if the user presses return: if the standard buttons are used, the string must be equal to 'Yes', 'No' or 'Cancel', otherwise it must be equal to **alt1**, **alt2** or **alt3**. The window disappears when a button is chosen, and the chosen alternative is returned.
inputdlg(legend, *title*,*lineNr*,*dfltAns*)	creates a window for input of data. The cell vector **legend** contains a legend for the answers. The string **title** indicates the name of the window, and **lineNr** is a vector that contains the number of rows for each answer (or a scalar that applies for all rows). The cell vector **dfltAns** contains default answers. The command inputdlg returns a cell vector that contains the answers given by the user.
menu(title,alt1, alt2,...)	creates a menu with the title **title** and the alternatives **alt1**, **alt2** etc., and waits for input from the keyboard or the mouse. It returns an integer indicating the choice of the user. Note: if menu is called from another graphical object, the property 'Interruptible' must be set to 'yes' in that object.

Commands 168   (CONTINUED)

`[selection,ok] =`
`listdlg(`
`'ListString',`
`S,`*`prstr`*`,`*`alt`*`,...)`
	creates a window where the user can choose items from a list. The parameter **S** is a cell vector that contains the list. The string **prstr** is a property of the window that is set to *alt*. Several properties can be written after each other. See `helpdesk` for more information about the properties available. If the vector **selection** is given, then it indicates indices in the list **S** for the chosen items. If *ok* is given, it is 1 if the user pressed the **OK** button, otherwise 0 (**selection** is in this case []).

`[`*`fname`*`,`*`path`*`] =`
`uigetfile(filter,`
`title``,`*`x`*`,`*`y`*`)`
	creates a window to open a file. The string **filter** is used to indicate what files are listed; the string can include "wildcards" or just be a single filename. For example, the filer '*.m' displays a list only including M-files. The string **title** sets the name of the window. The parameters *x* and *y* indicate where the window (the upper left corner) is placed on the screen; this option is, however, not available on all operating systems. If **fname** and **path** are given, the chosen filename and its path are returned as strings. If the user chose `cancel` or any error occurred, 0 is returned.

`[`*`fname`*`,`*`path`*`] =`
`uiputfile(filter,`
`title``,`*`x`*`,`*`y`*`)`
	does the same as the above, but for output to a file.

`pagedlg(`*`fig`*`)`	creates a dialog box where the user chooses the paper format used for printout of the current figure. The optional parameter *fig* indicates that the paper format applies to figure number *fig* instead of the current.

`printdlg(`
`'`*`−crossplatform`*`',`
`fig``)`
	creates a dialog box from which the user can print a figure. The optional parameter *fig* indicates that figure number *fig* is printed instead of the default current figure. If '-crossplatform' is given, a MATLAB dialog box is used instead of the standard window of the operating system.

`uisetcolor(`*`x`*`,`*`title`*`)`	creates a window from which the user can select a color. The optional parameter **x** can either be a handle to a graphical object or an RGB triplet. This color is used as the default color and black is used if **x** is not given. The string **title** sets the name of the window. The command `uisetcolor` returns an RGB triplet unless the user chose `cancel` or any error occurred, in which case 0 is returned.

Commands 168 (CONTINUED)

uisetfont(*pr*,*title*)	creates a window from which the user can select a font. The string **title** sets the name of the window. The optional parameter **pr** must be a handle to an axes object or a text object. After the selection, the font selected is applied to the object with handle **pr**. If **pr** is not given, a handle to a new text object with the chosen font is returned, unless the user chose cancel in which case 0 is returned.
btngroup(*h*,prstr, val,...)	is used to create a row of tools, that is, a row of buttons, in the figure window with handle *h*. If *h* is not given the current window is used. The appearance of the row of tools is controlled by setting different properties: property **prstr** is set to value *alt*, and several properties can be written after each other. Use help btngroup for more information about what properties are available. To control the row of tools there are also the commands btndown, btnup, btnicon, btnpress and btnstate. Use help for more information.
tabdlg	is used to create a dialog box with flaps. Use help tabdlg for more information.
waitbar(x,*title*)	creates a wait bar. The parameter *x* indicates the portion of work done. The string **title** sets the name of the window. This function should be called repeatedly with increasing *x* (from 0 to 1) to show the progress of work. A handle to the window, that is the figure object, is returned. The window is closed with close when the work is done.

To change properties interactively in graphical objects there are a few tools supplied:

Commands 169 TOOLS FOR INTERACTIVE CONTROL OF PROPERTIES

axlimdlg	is a graphical user interface for defining the scale limits of the axes in an axes object. Use help axlimdlg for more information.
edtext	is a graphical user interface for interactive editing of text objects in an axes object. Use help edtext for more information.
plotedit	is a graphical user interface that is used to add text and arrows to an axes object. It is also possible to change a few attributes of the axes object. Use help plotedit for more information.

■ **Example 14.16**

We create a simple menu with three alternatives:

```
choice = menu('Choose:','Enter','Wait','Leave')
```

This gives the window in Figure 14.16 in an X Windows environment.

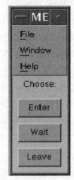

Figure 14.16 *A menu created by the command* menu. *Since the menu is so narrow in this example, only the first two letters of the window title 'MENU' are visible.*

A choice is made by a click on one of the buttons 'Enter', 'Wait', or 'Leave'. If the middle button is chosen, that is wait, MATLAB returns:

```
choice =
        2
```

because we chose the second alternative.

The menus look different depending on the operating system used. If there are no graphics available, MATLAB writes the menu alternatives in the command window and waits for input from the keyboard.

■

Sometimes one wants to create advanced graphical user interfaces, and then the pre-defined windows are often not sufficient and new windows must be defined. For this purpose there is the **Guide** (Graphical User Interface Development Environment) package of tools. This package consists of five programs for the creation of windows, menus etc. Although it is possible to just use the set and get commands (see Commands 154) the Guide package makes the development of graphical user interfaces considerably more productive.

| **Commands 170** | THE GUIDE PACKAGE |

ctpanel(*h*)	displays a control panel with links to the other programs in the Guide package. The figure objects with handles in the optional vector **h** are put under the control of the program. If **h** is not given, the current figure is controlled instead. In this program it is also possible to add uicontrol objects, for example buttons and text boxes, to the figure objects.
guide(*h*)	works as above but in addition all tools in the Guide package are updated to work with the figure objects with handles in the optional vector **h**. If **h** is not given the current figure is used.
propedit(*h*)	opens the property editor. This tool is used to set all the object properties listed in the preceding section. The parameter **h** is a handle or a vector with handles to objects. If **h** is not given the current object is used. If the objects with handles in a vector **h** are of different types, only their common properties are listed.
align	opens the alignment tool. This tool is used to align uicontrols and plot regions, so that they are laying in straight lines, and their distance between themselves. The alignment tool can be used separately; see helpdesk for more information.
cbedit(*h*)	opens the callback editor. This tool is used to decide what happens when the user presses a button, writes text in a text box, etc. The parameter **h** is a handle or a vector with handles to objects. If **h** is not given the current object is used.
menuedit(*h*)	opens the menu editor. This tool is used to change some of the properties in user-defined menus. The parameter **h** is a handle or a vector with handles to figure objects. If **h** is not given the current figure object is used.

When designing a graphical user interface, the first thing to do is to carefully think through the look and behavior of the interface. Thereafter it is easy to implement your ideas using the tools supplied in the Guide package.

The layout of the program is implemented first, and the package works in this respect much like an object oriented drawing program. It is just a matter of drawing the windows with buttons, pop-up menus, etc.

Next, after the interface is drawn, the function of the interface is added. When the user presses a button we want something 'to happen'. The function of the interface is carried out by the callback functions, and these are easily put into the graphical objects by the callback editor in the Guide package.

The above summarizes the development of a graphical user interface. The remainder of this section deals with the individual tools in the Guide package (see Commands 170), and their uses are illustrated in a running example.

In this example all screen shots of windows are taken from an X Windows environment, but the principles are the same in Windows and Macintosh. Actually, a user interface created in one operating system can be moved to another without the need to rewrite anything.

More information about building a graphical user interface is found in the MATLAB manual *Building GUIs with MATLAB*. This manual also has some general advice about what to think about when creating a graphical user interface.

14.3.1 The control panel

By writing guide at the MATLAB prompt, the control panel is started and a figure window is opened which is under the control of the Guide tools. This is indicated by a grid in the figure; see Figure 14.18. If figure windows are already open, the current figure object will be taken under control.

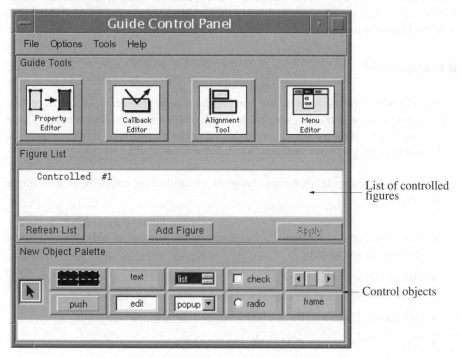

Figure 14.17 *The control panel.*

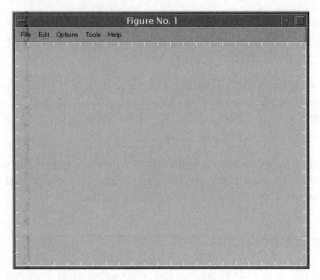

Figure 14.18 *A figure window under the control of the Guide tools.*

From Figure 14.17 we can see that there are links to the other tools in the Guide package. Furthermore, there are 10 different types of control objects that can be added to a figure window to build a user interface.

■ **Example 14.17**

We will now demonstrate how one can build a simple graphical user interface. As an example we will create a window from which the user can select a color. There is actually already a predefined window that performs this task, uisetcolor (see Commands 168), and our ambition is to build something similar.

Firstly, we must decide what control objects are needed; the following objects might be suitable:

- Three slide bars ('slider') which indicate the amount of red, green and blue respectively in the color.
- Three fields with editable text ('edit') where the user can give exact numbers of the desired amount of red, green and blue respectively in the color.
- One frame ('frame') that is filled with the currently selected color.
- Seven explanation strings ('text') to the above.
- Two buttons ('pushbutton'): CANCEL and OK.

When this is done we use the control panel to design our window. We select the objects we want in the control panel and drag them to our figure object. In this stage we just give a rough layout of the window; the objects do not need to have the exact size and position wanted. Note also that it is possible to cut, paste and copy control objects in the figure window.

After the placement of control objects the window looks something like the one shown in Figure 14.19.

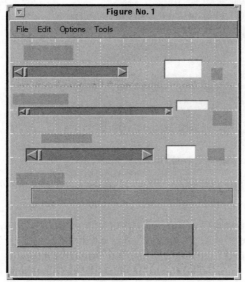

Figure 14.19 *The placement of control objects.*

Now this does not look too good, but we will adjust the window using the next two tools.

■

14.3.2 The property editor

By pressing the button for the property editor in the control panel, the following window is displayed (Figure 14.20):

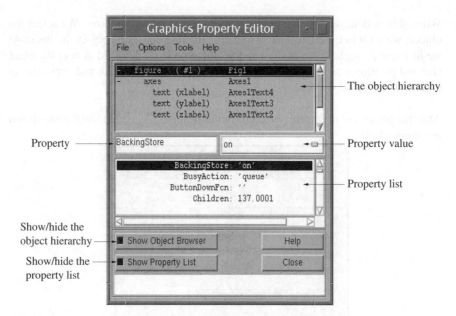

Figure 14.20 *The property editor showing the object hierarchy and the property list.*

As can be seen, the property editor consists of four parts. The first, from the top, is the object hierarchy (see Figure 14.4), indicating what objects are included and how they relate to each other. In the left column there are characters indicating whether the objects have children: A '+' sign means the object has children and can be expanded, that is the children are shown if the name is clicked on. A '−' sign means the object has children and already is expanded. No character means the object does not have any children. By selecting objects, one or several (with shift-click), their properties are displayed in the property list in the middle of the window. Objects can either be selected in the hierarchy list or directly in the figure.

In the property list all properties of the objects are listed. If objects of different types are selected, only their common attributes are shown. If selected objects have different values for some property, this is indicated as 'Multiple Values' in the list. By selecting a property, its name and value can be seen in the boxes 'Property' and 'Property value' just above the property list. Instead of selecting it, it is also possible to enter its name in the 'Property' box. The whole name does not have to be written, only as many characters as make it unique. For example, by writing col and pressing return, the property editor understands that Color is the property intended.

In the boxes 'Property' and 'Property value' it is, obviously, possible to change a property and its value. The latter box is either a pop-up menu, if the property only can be assigned a limited number of values, or a text field. In a text field the property editor ignores all values after the first space, so if one writes a new value at the beginning of the line and presses Return, the old value is discarded.

■ **Example 14.18**

Continuation of Example 14.17. With the help of the property editor we can improve the design of our interface. We change the following properties:

All objects
HandleVisibility: 'callback'

The window ('figure')
MenuBar: 'none'
NumberTitle: 'off'
Name: 'Color Picker'
Resize: 'off'
Tag: 'ColPick'

The slide bars ('slider')
Position: [? ? 200 20]
Max: 100
Value: 0
Tag: 'RedSl', 'GreenSl', and 'BlueSl', respectively

The text above the slide bars ('text')
Position: [? ? 50 16]
FontSize: 12
HorizontalAlignment: left
BackgroundColor: [0.8 0.8 0.8]
ForegroundColor: 'red', 'green', and 'blue', respectively
String: 'Red', 'Green', and 'Blue', respectively

The text fields to the right of the slide bars ('edit')
Position: [? ? 50 25]
String: '0'
UserData: 0
FontSize: 12
HorizontalAlignment: left
Tag: 'RedTxt', 'GreenTxt', and 'BlueTxt', respectively

The text to the right of the above text fields ('text')
Position: [? ? 16 16]
FontSize: 12
HorizontalAlignment: left
BackgroundColor: [0.8 0.8 0.8]
String: '%'

The color frame ('frame')
Tag: 'col'
BackgroundColor: 'black'

The text above the color frame ('text')

Position:	[? ? 50 16]
FontSize:	12
HorizontalAlignment:	left
BackgroundColor:	[0.8 0.8 0.8]
String:	'Color'

The buttons ('pushbutton')

Position:	[? ? 70 30]
FontSize:	14
FontWeight:	'bold'
String:	'CANCEL' and 'OK' respectively
Tag:	'cancel' and 'OK' respectively

After these adjustments, the window looks like the one in Figure 14.21.

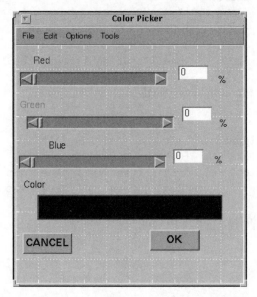

Figure 14.21 *After property editor adjustments.* ■

14.3.3 The alignment tool

By pressing the button for the alignment tool in the control panel, the window in Figure 14.22 is displayed.

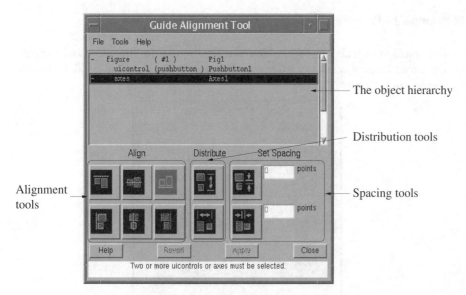

The object hierarchy

Distribution tools

Alignment tools

Spacing tools

Figure 14.22 *The alignment tool.*

The alignment tool has the object hierarchy displayed in the top of the window. This works just as in the property editor: objects can either be selected in the hierarchy list or directly in the figure. A difference, however, is that here at least two objects must be selected.

When some objects have been selected they can be adjusted relative to each other. This is done by choosing an adjustment tool, that is pressing the appropriate button below the object hierarchy, and then applying the adjustments by pressing 'Apply'. If the adjustments do not turn out as intended, they can be undone by pressing 'Revert'.

There are three groups of adjustment tools. The first is the group of alignment tools. These tools align the selected objects with an axis; each of the six tools specifies a unique axis.

The next group of adjustment tools is the group of distribution tools. These tools distribute the objects horizontally or vertically so that the distance between each pair of selected objects is constant. The two outermost objects are always kept in place while the objects in between are adjusted.

The third group of adjustment tools is the group of spacing tools. By specifying a distance, these tools set a fixed horizontal or vertical space between each pair of selected objects. The adjustment of the selected objects starts from the bottom left corner and continues upwards and to the right. Note that it might happen that some objects end up outside the figure window.

■ **Example 14.19**

Continuation of Example 14.17. Now it is time to use the alignment tool to finally get a nice looking window. After the adjustments, our color picker looks like the window in Figure 14.23.

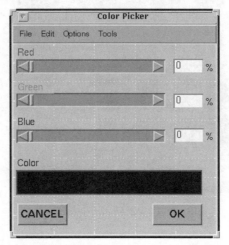

Figure 14.23 *After alignment tool adjustments.*

The interface can now be activated by a double click on the text 'Controlled #1: Color Picker' in the control panel. Just before the interface is activated MATLAB asks if we want to save the interface, and we do that in the file **ColorPicker.m**, which is an ordinary M-file. A look at that file in a text editor is worthwhile. In addition a data MAT-file is saved under the name **ColorPicker.mat**. When the files are saved the interface is activated and we can drag the slides, press the buttons etc., but nothing happens! This is because we have not yet worked on the function of the interface. For this, we need the next tool: the callback editor.

■

14.3.4 The callback editor

By pressing the button for the callback editor in the control panel, the window in Figure 14.24 is displayed.

At the top of the callback editor is the object hierarchy, and it works in the same way as in the property editor. The objects we want to write callback functions for can either be selected in the hierarchy list or directly in the figure.

Objects have different types of callback functions connected to different types of events. An event is, for example, when the object is created or destroyed, or when the user clicks on it with the mouse. The type of callback function desired is selected from the callback function menu; see Figure 14.24.

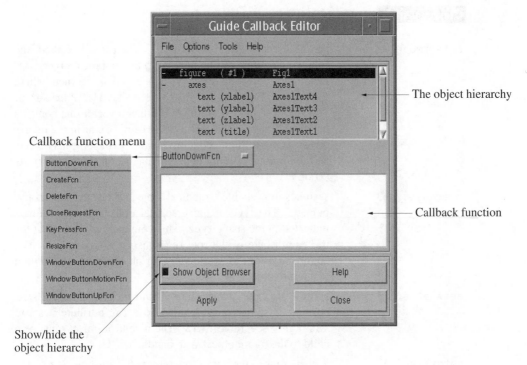

Figure 14.24 *The callback editor.*

When the type of callback function is chosen, it can be written in the text field in the middle of the callback editor. The callback function is written just as one would have done in a MATLAB command window. However, unless the function is very short, it is more convenient to call an M-file that contains the callback function code. Note that if one makes changes in this M-file, for example in a debugging session, these changes will not take effect before the command `clear functions` is entered at the MATLAB prompter.

There are a number of commands in MATLAB that are useful when writing callback functions:

Commands 171   CALLBACK FUNCTION COMMANDS

[h, *fig*] = gcbo	returns a handle *h* to the object whose callback function is currently executing. If no function is executing then [] is returned. An optional handle *fig* to the parent figure object can also be returned.
gcbf	returns a handle to the parent figure object of the object whose callback function is currently executing. If no function is executing then [] is returned. If the callback function belongs to a figure object, a handle to this is returned.

selectmoversize	can be used as ButtonDownFcn. When it is executed, the following actions can be applied to the graphical object: select, move, copy and resize. A structure **A** is returned, where the field **A.Type** can be 'Select', 'Move', 'Resize' or 'Copy'. The field **A.Handles** is either a vector that contains handles to the selected objects ('Select') or an $m \times 2$ matrix where the first column contains handles to the original objects and the second column contains handles to the new objects ('Copy').
overobj(type)	searches for visible graphical objects beneath the mouse pointer. The type of the graphical objects searched for is indicated in the string **type**. This command assumes that the Units attribute of the root object is set to 'pixels'. The command overobj works only for objects who are children to a figure object.
setstatus(h,str)	sets the attribute String in a uicontrol object whose Style attribute is set to 'text' and whose Tag attribute is set to 'Status'; see Table 14.15. The uicontrol object must be a child to the figure object with handle h.
getstatus(h)	is analogous to the above, but returns the attribute String.
hidegui(*h*,*status*)	sets the property HandleVisibility of the figure object with handle h; see Table 14.2. If h is not given the current figure object is used. The parameter **status** is an optional string that can either be 'on' (default), 'off' or 'callback'. The purpose of this command is to protect a user interface from being destroyed by its user via commands from the command window.
status = hidegui(*h*)	returns the property HandleVisibility of the figure object with handle h. If h is not given the current figure object is used.
waitfor(h,*prstr*,*alt*)	blocks the calling function until the graphical object with handle h is destroyed or the user presses Control-C. If the optional property **prstr** is given, this property must be altered in addition to break the blockage. Furthermore, if *alt* is given, **prstr** must be assigned this specific value to break the blockage. Nothing happens if h is not a handle, **prstr** is not a valid property or *alt* is not a valid value.
uiwait(*h*)	blocks the calling function. A callback function must exist in one of the control objects of the figure object with handle h, that either destroy the figure object or calls uiresume. If h is not given the current figure object is used.

Commands 171 (CONTINUED)

uiresume(h)	is called to resume the execution of a function that has been blocked by uiwait, see above.
status = uisuspend(h)	suspends all user interaction with control objects of the figure object with handle *h*. For example, clicks on buttons do not have any function any more. A structure **status** is returned that contains information about the properties of the figure object. The interaction with the user is resumed by uirestore.
uirestore(status)	resumes the interaction with the user that was suspended by uisuspend. The parameter **status** is the structure that was returned by uisuspend.

■ **Example 14.20**

Continuation of Example 14.17. We continue the development of our color picker by setting the figure window under the control of the Guide tools again by a double click on the text 'Active #1: Color Picker' in the control panel. After that we write the following callback functions of type 'Callback' in the callback editor:

Red slide bar:	CbColPic redsl;
Red text field:	CbColPic redtxt;
Green slide bar:	CbColPic greensl;
Green text field:	CbColPic greentxt;
Blue slide bar:	CbColPic bluesl;
Blue text field:	CbColPic bluetxt;
Cancel button:	CbColPic cancel;
OK button:	CbColPic ok;

We then write the M-file **CbColPic.m**:

```
function CbColPic(action)

switch(action)

  case 'redsl'                    % Red slider.
                                  % Gets pointer to red textframe.
    RedTxtPtr = findobj(gcbf,'Tag','RedTxt');
                                  % Reads slidervalue.
    Val = get(gcbo,'Value');
                                  % Sets red textframe to slidervalue.
    set(RedTxtPtr,'String',num2str(Val,3));
                                  % Updates framecolor.
    LocalUpdateCol;

  case 'greensl'                  % Green slider...
```

```
      GreenTxtPtr = findobj(gcbf,'Tag','GreenTxt');
      Val = get(gcbo,'Value');
      set(GreenTxtPtr,'String',num2str(Val,3));
      LocalUpdateCol;

   case 'bluesl'                    % Blue slider...
      BlueTxtPtr = findobj(gcbf,'Tag','BlueTxt');
      Val = get(gcbo,'Value');
      set(BlueTxtPtr,'String',num2str(Val,3));
      LocalUpdateCol;

   case 'redtxt'                    % Red textframe.
                                    % Gets pointer to red slider.
      RedSlPtr = findobj(gcbf,'Tag','RedSl');
                                    % Gets string in textframe.
      Str = get(gcbo,'String');
                                    % Converts the string.
      Val = LocalChStr(Str);
                                    % Sets slidervalue.
      set(RedSlPtr,'Value',Val);
                                    % Sets the string in the textframe.
      set(gcbo,'String',num2str(Val,3));
                                    % Stores the value in UserData.
      set(gcbo,'UserData',Val);
                                    % Updates the colorframe.
      LocalUpdateCol;

   case 'greentxt'                  % Green textframe...
      GreenSlPtr = findobj(gcbf,'Tag','GreenSl');
      Str = get(gcbo,'String');
      Val = LocalChStr(Str);
      set(GreenSlPtr,'Value',Val);
      set(gcbo,'String',num2str(Val,3));
      set(gcbo,'UserData',Val);
      LocalUpdateCol;

   case 'bluetxt'                   % Blue textframe...
      BlueSlPtr = findobj(gcbf,'Tag','BlueSl');
      Str = get(gcbo,'String');
      Val = LocalChStr(Str);
      set(BlueSlPtr,'Value',Val);
      set(gcbo,'String',num2str(Val,3));
      set(gcbo,'UserData',Val);
      LocalUpdateCol;

end
```

```
function OutVal = LocalChStr(InStr)     % Converts strings.

temp = str2num(InStr);                  % Conv. string to number.

if (isempty(temp))                      % String not a number,
  OutVal = get(gcbo,'UserData');        % use previous value.
elseif (temp > 100)                     % Number greater than 100.
  OutVal = 100;
elseif (temp < 0)                       % Number less than 0.
  OutVal = 0;
else
  OutVal = temp;
end


function Col = LocalUpdateCol           % Updates colorframe.

% Pointers to the sliders.
RedPtr   = findobj(gcbf,'Tag','RedSl');
GreenPtr = findobj(gcbf,'Tag','GreenSl');
BluePtr  = findobj(gcbf,'Tag','BlueSl');

% Get slider-values.
RedVal   = get(RedPtr,  'Value')/100;
GreenVal = get(GreenPtr,'Value')/100;
BlueVal  = get(BluePtr, 'Value')/100;
Col = [RedVal,GreenVal,BlueVal];

% Get pointer to the color-frame.
FrPtr = findobj(gcbf,'Tag','col');
% Set its color.
set(FrPtr,'BackgroundColor',Col);
```

In the color picker window, we obviously want a slide bar and its corresponding text field to indicate the same amount of the color, for example red. Therefore, we have connected these two so that when a slide bar for a color is updated the corresponding text field is updated too, and vice versa.

Two functions have also been written:

- LocalChStr(InStr) tries to translate the string InStr to a number. This function is used when reading a string entered by the user in one of the text fields.

- LocalUpdateCol sets the color in the color frame.

We activate the user interface by a double click on the text 'Controlled #1: Color Picker' in the control panel and save the interface. The color picker can now be tried out, slide bars can be dragged and values can be written in the text fields. Also, the color frame will show the chosen color! See Figure 14.25.

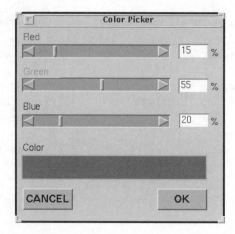

Figure 14.25 *After the callback functions have been written and the window has been activated.*

We have not yet specified what will happen when the buttons are pressed, but we will do that in the next subsection.

■

14.3.5 The menu editor

By pressing the button for the menu editor in the control panel, the following window is displayed (Figure 14.26):

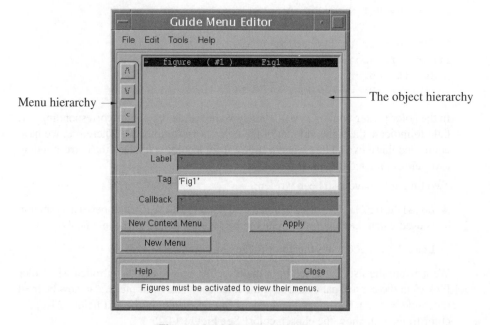

Figure 14.26 *The menu editor.*

At the top of the menu editor is the object hierarchy, and it works in the same way as in the other Guide tools. A difference, however, is that here only figure and menu objects are shown.

The other parts of the menu editor and their use are:

- The button 'New Menu', which is used to add new menus to a figure object or new menu items to an already existing menu.

- The button 'New Context Menu', which is used to create context menus for an object; see Section 14.2.8.

- The text field 'Label', where the label of a menu or menu item is entered. This string is what is displayed in the user interface.

- The text field 'Tag', where a tag is entered, and which is assigned to a menu. This tag can be used when writing callback functions.

- The text field 'Callback', where the callback function of a menu is entered, that is the commands or M-files that will be executed when the user chooses the menu. The callback function must, unlike in the property editor (see the preceding subsection), be a string.

- The four buttons to the left of the object hierarchy, marked 'Menu hierarchy' in the figure above, which are used to move menus on the menu row, or move menu items within a menu.

■ Example 14.21

Continuation of Example 14.17. With the help of the menu editor we will soon define callback functions for the 'CANCEL' and 'OK' buttons, but first we will add a menu that might be useful: a menu with predefined colors.

We start as usual by a double click on the text 'Active #1: Color Picker' in the control panel to put our color picker window under the control of the Guide tools again. A new menu is created, and we assign to it the following data:

```
Label: 'Color'            Tag: ''    Callback: ''
Label: 'Pink'             Tag: ''    Callback: 'CbColPic menpink;'
Label: 'Military Green'   Tag: ''    Callback: 'CbColPic menmilgreen;'
Label: 'Beige'            Tag: ''    Callback: 'CbColPic menbeg;'
```

Then we must add the callback functions to the menu items in the M-file **CbColPic.m**:

```
function CbColPic(action)

switch(action)

...
```

```
       case 'menpink';                          % Menu-choice pink.
          LocalUpdateAll([1 0.4 0.7]);

       case 'menmilgreen'                        % Menu-choice green.
          LocalUpdateAll([0.15 0.55 0.2]);

       case 'menbeg'                             % Menu-choice beige.
          LocalUpdateAll([1 0.9 0.8]);

   end

   ...

   function LocalUpdateAll(Color)               % Update all.

   Color = 100.*Color;

   % Get pointers to the sliders and update them.

   RedSlPtr   = findobj(gcbf,'Tag','RedSl');
   GreenSlPtr = findobj(gcbf,'Tag','GreenSl');
   BlueSlPtr  = findobj(gcbf,'Tag','BlueSl');
   set(RedSlPtr,'Value',Color(1));
   set(GreenSlPtr,'Value',Color(2));
   set(BlueSlPtr,'Value',Color(3));

   % Get pointers to the textframes and change those.

   RedTxtPtr   = findobj(gcbf,'Tag','RedTxt');
   GreenTxtPtr = findobj(gcbf,'Tag','GreenTxt');
   BlueTxtPtr  = findobj(gcbf,'Tag','BlueTxt');
   set(RedTxtPtr,'String',num2str(Color(1),3));
   set(GreenTxtPtr,'String',num2str(Color(2),3));
   set(BlueTxtPtr,'String',num2str(Color(3),3));

   % Get pointer to the colorframe and set its color.

   FrPtr = findobj(gcbf,'Tag','col');
   set(FrPtr,'BackgroundColor',Color./100);
```

Note that we have written a function that updates all slide bars, text fields and the color frame.

We activate our user interface by a double click on the text 'Controlled #1: Color Picker' in the control panel and thereafter save it. Now the new menu works too; see Figure 14.27.

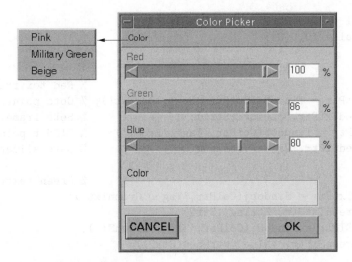

Figure 14.27 *After the addition of a new menu.*

At last we take care of the 'CANCEL' and 'OK' buttons. When the user presses the 'OK' button we clearly want the color picker to return the chosen color, therefore we need such a routine in our program. Furthermore, we add the possibility to start the color picker with an initial color. The initial color will also be returned if the user presses the 'CANCEL' button. We write a new function which we put in an M-file called **uicolor.m**:

```
function rgbout = uicolor(rgbin)

ColorPicker;                          % Loads colormixer.
set(0,'ShowHiddenHandles','on');      % Gets pointer.
ColPtr = findobj(0,'Tag','ColPick');
ColPtr = ColPtr(1);                   % Latest created.

if (nargin >= 1)                      % Checks input (if any).
   if ((length(rgbin) ~= 3) | (min(rgbin) < 0) | ...
            (max(rgbin) > 1))         % Warning: invalid input.
     warndlg('Invalid Colorspecific.','Warning');
     Str1 = '0'; Str2 = '0'; Str3 = '0';% Standard values instead.
     InCol = [0,0,0];
   else                               % Input.
     Str1 = num2str(rgbin(1) * 100,3);
     Str2 = num2str(rgbin(2) * 100,3);
     Str3 = num2str(rgbin(3) * 100,3);
     InCol = rgbin;
   end
else                                  % Standard values if
                                      % no input.
```

```
   Str1 = '0'; Str2 = '0'; Str3 = '0';
   InCol = [0,0,0];
end


                                         % Red textframe.
RedTxtPtr = findobj(ColPtr,'Tag','RedTxt'); % Gets pointer.
set(RedTxtPtr,'String',Str1);             % Sets frame.
RedSlPtr = findobj(ColPtr,'Tag','RedSl');  % Slider pointer.
set(RedSlPtr,'Value',str2num(Str1));      % Sets slider.


                                         % Green textframe...
GreenTxtPtr = findobj(ColPtr,'Tag','GreenTxt');
set(GreenTxtPtr,'String',Str2);
GreenSlPtr = findobj(ColPtr,'Tag','GreenSl');
set(GreenSlPtr,'Value',str2num(Str2));


                                         % Blue textframe...
BlueTxtPtr = findobj(ColPtr,'Tag','BlueTxt');
set(BlueTxtPtr,'String',Str3)
BlueSlPtr = findobj(ColPtr,'Tag','BlueSl');
set(BlueSlPtr,'Value',str2num(Str3));


FrPtr = findobj(ColPtr,'Tag','col');    % Pointer to colorframe.
set(FrPtr,'BackgroundColor',InCol);     % Sets colorframe.


% Input stored in colormixer's UserData.
set(ColPtr,'UserData',InCol);

uiwait(ColPtr);                          % Waits for answer.
rgbout = get(ColPtr,'UserData');         % Gets choosen color..
close(ColPtr);                           % Closes colormixer.
set(0,'ShowHiddenHandles','on');         % Hiddes pointer.
```

The program above stops to wait for the user to pick a color. The initial color, an RGB triplet, is stored in the UserData of the color picker, and when the user has made a choice the color is also read from there. Therefore, we only need to overwrite this color in the callback function for the 'OK' button, since we wanted to return the initial color if the user presses 'CANCEL'. The two callback functions are added to the file **CbColPic.m**:

```
function CbColPic(action)


switch(action)


   ...
```

```
  case 'cancel'
    uiresume(gcbf);

  case 'ok'
    Col = LocalUpdateCol;
    set(gcbf,'UserData',Col)
    uiresume(gcbf);

end

...
```

Our color picker application is now completed. To use it we call **uicolor** (but not **ColorPicker**, since it only defines the window itself). Below is an example showing how it can be used to change the foreground and background color in a figure window with a plot region:

```
function change

fp = figure;                % Create a figure-window.
ap = axes;                  % Create plotarea.

InCol = get(fp,'Color');    % Set background color in the
OutCol = uicolor(InCol);    % window.
set(fp,'Color',OutCol);

InCol = get(ap,'Color');    % Set foregroundcolor in plotarea.
OutCol = uicolor(InCol);
```

∎

14.4 Movies

14.4.1 Introductory example

We start this section on movies with an example. A short movie is made by letting the bell-shaped curve in Example 13.8 oscillate.

∎ **Example 14.22**

```
x        = -8:0.5:8;        % Defines surface.
[XX,YY] = meshgrid(x);

r = sqrt(XX.^2+YY.^2) + eps;
Z = sin(r)./r;
```

```
surf(Z);                              % Plots frame.


% Saves values of axes. Later used to make all
% frames in same scale.
% Create matrix storing the movie. It takes 20 frames.

theAxes = axis;
fmat = moviein(20);


% Loops the snapshots. Creates movie data.

for j = 1:20
   surf(sin(2*pi*j/20)*Z,Z)   % Plots surface of each step.
   axis(theAxes)              % Uses same axes all the time.
   fmat(:,j) = getframe;      % Copies frame to matrix.
end

movie(fmat,10);               % Shows movie 10 times.
                              % This is fun!
```

As can be seen, the movie is saved frame by frame in the column direction in a matrix, and thereafter it is shown. Before the recording of the movie, though, we save the minimum and maximum values of the axes so that every frame has the same axes. ∎

14.4.2 Copying a figure window

The command getframe is used to copy a figure window to a column vector.

Commands 172	COPYING GRAPHICS
getframe(*p*,*r*)	copies the image in the object with handle *p*. The object can be the screen, a figure or a plot region. If *p* is not given then the current figure window is used. The optional parameter **r** indicates that a rectangle in the object is copied instead. **r** is a vector of the form [*left bottom width height*].
[X,Ftab] = getframe(...)	returns an image matrix **X** and a color table **Ftab**.
[X,Ftab] = frame2im(F)	translates a movie frame **F** to an image matrix **X** whose elements are indices in the color table **Ftab**.

14.4.3 Creating a movie

Before a movie can be recorded, space must be allocated to its frames. These frames are stored in the column direction in a matrix, and such a matrix is created by the command `moviein`.

Commands 173   CREATING A MOVIE

`moviein(n)`	creates a matrix that can store n frames. The size of the frames is decided by the size of the current figure window, and consequently one of the frames must first be plotted; see Example 14.22.
`F = im2frame(X,Ftab)`	translates an image matrix **X**, whose elements are indices in the color table **Ftab**, to a frame **F**. This command can be used to create movies from a sequence of images.

14.4.4 Showing a movie

A movie is shown with the help of the `movie` command, which takes parameters indicating how and where the movie is played.

Commands 174   SHOWING A MOVIE

`movie(`p`,Mat,`$n, fps,$ `pos)`	shows the movie matrix **Mat** n times with fps frames per second. If **n** is a vector of integers, the frames are shown in the order indicated by the vector. The optional parameter p is a handle to a figure or axes object where the movie is shown. If the optional parameter **pos** $= (x, y)$ is given, the movie is shown in the indicated position. x and y are in the unit `Units`, and relative to the bottom left corner of object p.

MATLAB in Combination with Other Programs

MATLAB can be used together with other programs. FORTRAN or C routines can be called from MATLAB, and the opposite is also possible, that is MATLAB can be called from FORTRAN or C. Thus fast compiled programs can utilize the powerful matrix or graphical commands of MATLAB, and bottlenecks in MATLAB programs can be avoided by writing these parts in C or FORTRAN and compiling them.

MATLAB can also cooperate with other applications, for instance Microsoft Word for Windows. This is briefly discussed in the last section of this chapter. What can be done depends on the computer system and installation.

15.1 MATLAB and FORTRAN or C, an introduction

MATLAB can be called from FORTRAN or C programs, and C or FORTRAN programs can be called from MATLAB. The latter can be useful if a MATLAB program is too slow. Since MATLAB is an interpreting language, the commands are interpreted as they are executed. The result of this is, for instance, that for-loops sometimes might be slow.

The libraries included with MATLAB are written in FORTRAN 77 and C, but it is possible to link them with FORTRAN 90 or C++ as well.

It is not recommended to write FORTRAN or C routines unless it is really necessary. The advantage of MATLAB is the possibility of expressing the operations at a high level, relieving the programmer of worries about index loops and other unimportant trouble makers.

A compiled routine that can be called from MATLAB is termed a MEX-file. MATLAB keeps track of how they are called. They can, when compiled, be used like an M-file.

In Section 2.8 we encountered the binary files MATLAB creates. These are called MAT-files, and there are routines in the libraries to read and write them in C or FORTRAN programs. Note that these files can be transferred between different platforms, for example one can read a MAT-file created in a Windows environment into a UNIX environment. In Section 15.4 we also show how to read or write other binary files or text files in MATLAB. This can be useful when a specific format is required by another program.

A MATLAB compiler, a C Math Library and a C++ Math Library are also commercially available from The MathWorks, Inc. The first can be used either as an automatic MEX-file generator or as a C source code generator for stand-alone applications together with the C Math Library.

MATLAB is written in C, and data are referenced by **pointers**. Thus using MATLAB together with other programming languages requires the use of pointers.

All types of variables, for example scalars, vectors, matrices, strings, cell matrices and structs, are saved in the MATLAB 5 environment as so called mxArrays, and all data manipulation is performed on these mxArrays.

The new data types in MATLAB 5, that is multidimensional matrices, cell matrices and structs, are only possible to manipulate in C, unfortunately not in FORTRAN.

There are four main categories of routines to use in C or FORTRAN programs communicating with MATLAB.

mx	manipulating mxArrays.
mat	MAT-file routines.
eng	MATLAB engine routines.
mex	MEX routines, that is routines that perform some operation in the MATLAB environment.

Some examples are presented in the following sections. These examples, which are the same in both programming languages, should give a basic understanding of how MATLAB and C or FORTRAN can interact. They have been compiled on a workstation running Sun OS 5.5.1 and the window system Solaris CDE version 1.0.2, but the basic idea is the same for any system. Some important details may, however, vary between platforms. This is why the examples shipped together with MATLAB can be of great interest. They can be found in the library:

```
.../matlab52/extern/examples
```

where the three dots, . . . , in the search path indicate that this part of the path is system dependent.

Extensive documentation with examples can be obtained with the MATLAB command helpdesk. Choose Application Program Interface there. Furthermore there is the MATLAB 5 manual *Application Program Interface Guide*.

15.2 MATLAB and C

In order to mix C and MATLAB it is important that the C compiler used complies with the ANSI C standard.

15.2.1 Manipulating mxArrays in C

Manipulation of mxArrays is done by the routines described below. In order to use these routines the header file **matrix.h** must be included in the program, that is, the program header must contain the following line:

```
#include "matrix.h"
```

The routines in the table below are used to allocate and free memory. It is good programming practice to free memory that is no longer needed. It is unnecessary to use MATLAB routines to create data structures because this is done automatically by MATLAB after the program terminates (however, see the routines `mexMakeArrayPersistent` and `mexMakeMemoryPersistent` in Commands 195), but if one is careful this should be done anyway.

Commands 175	MEMORY MANAGEMENT IN C

`void *mxCalloc(size_t n,size_t size);`
allocates memory. The parameter *n* is the number of elements being allocated and *size* is the number of bytes per element. It returns a pointer to the beginning of the allocated memory if the allocation was successful, otherwise NULL. The library `<stdlib.h>` must be included in the program. Use `mxFree` to free the memory when it is no longer in use.

`void mxSetAllocFcns(calloc_proc callocfcn,free_proc`
`freefcn,realloc_proc reallocfcn,malloc_proc mallocfcn);`
is used to free memory in a non-MEX program. Use `helpdesk` to get more information.

`void mxFree(void *ptr);`
frees the memory that *ptr* points to.

`void *mxRealloc(void *ptr,size_t size);`
reallocates memory that has been previously allocated using `mxCalloc`. The parameter *ptr* is a pointer to the beginning of the memory and *size* is the number of elements being allocated. It returns a pointer to the beginning of the allocated memory if the allocation was successful, otherwise NULL. The library `<stdlib.h>` must be included in the program. Use `mxFree` to free the memory when it is no longer in use.

`void mxDestroyArray(mxArray *array_ptr);`
frees the memory to the mxArray that *array_ptr* points to.

The common routines below are used to manage and examine mxArrays, for example naming them, reshaping them and examine to which category they belong.

| Commands 176 | COMMON ROUTINES USED TO HANDLE MXARRAYS IN C |

mxComplexity
is an enum-data type used to indicate if an mxArray has imaginary components. It can
have the value mxCOMPLEX (complex mxArrays) or mxREAL (other).

mxClassID
is an enum-data type used to indicate to which category an mxArray belong to. It can
have the following values:

mxCELL_CLASS,	cell type.
mxSTRUCT_CLASS,	struct type.
mxOBJECT_CLASS,	user-defined type.
mxCHAR_CLASS,	string type.
mxSPARSE_CLASS,	stores sparse matrices.
mxDOUBLE_CLASS,	data is double precision floating point numbers.
mxSINGLE_CLASS,	data is single precision floating point numbers.
mxINT8_CLASS,	data is 8 bit integer.
mxUINT8_CLASS,	data is 8 bit unsigned integer.
mxINT16_CLASS,	data is 16 bit integer.
mxUINT16_CLASS,	data is 16 bit unsigned integer.
mxINT32_CLASS,	data is 32 bit integer.
mxUINT32_CLASS,	data is 32 bit unsigned integer.
mxUNKNOWN_CLAS,	the category cannot be determined.

mxClassID mxGetClassID(const mxArray *array_ptr);
returns the category of the mxArray that *array_ptr* points to; see above.

const char *mxGetClassName(const mxArray *array_ptr);
is used as above but returns the category in a string.

bool mxIsClass(const mxArray *array_ptr,const char *name);
returns true if the mxArray that *array_ptr* points to has the category in the string **name**.
The following values of name correspond to the categories above (see mxClassID):
"cell", "struct", "char", "sparse", "double", "single", "int8", "uint8",
"int16", "uint16", "int32", and "uint32". It is also possible to define your own
category names.

const char *mxGetName(const mxArray *array_ptr);
returns a string that contains the name of the mxArray that *array_ptr* points to.

void mxSetName(mxArray *array_ptr,const char *name);
assigns the name **name** to the mxArray that *array_ptr* points to.

double mxGetScalar(const mxArray *array_ptr);
returns the value of the first real element of the mxArray that *array_ptr* points to. It
always returns the value as a double. If the mxArray is of struct or cell type 0.0 is
returned, if the mxArray is of sparse type the value of the first non-zero real element is
returned and if the mxArray is empty an undetermined value is returned.

Commands 176 (CONTINUED)

`mxArray *mxDuplicateArray(const mxArray *in);`
copies the mxArray that *in* points to. It returns a pointer to the copy. Free the memory used by the copy using `mxDestroyArray` when it is no longer needed; see Commands 175.

`int mxGetNumberOfElements(const mxArray *array_ptr);`
returns the number of elements in the mxArray that *array_ptr* points to. Use `mxGetClassID` to find out the elements type.

`int mxGetElementSize(const mxArray *array_ptr);`
returns the number of bytes that is required to store one element of the mxArray that *array_ptr* points to. If one has a cell or struct mxArray the size of a pointer to these is returned. It returns 0 if the operation failed.

`int mxGetNumberOfDimensions(const mxArray *array_ptr);`
returns the number of dimensions in the mxArray that *array_ptr* points to and is always greater than or equal to 2.

`const int *mxGetDimensions(const mxArray *array_ptr);`
returns a pointer to an integer vector that contains the number of elements in each dimension of the mxArray that *array_ptr* points to.

`int mxSetDimensions(mxArray *array_ptr,const int *size,int ndims);`
is used to reshape or increase/decrease the number of elements in the mxArray that *array_ptr* points to. The parameter *ndims* is the number of dimensions desired and *size* is a pointer to an integer vector that contains the desired number of elements in each dimension. It returns 0 if the operation was successful, 1 otherwise. If one wishes to increase/decrease then memory has to be allocated/freed; use `helpdesk` to get more information.

`int mxGetM(const mxArray *array_ptr);`
returns the number of 'rows', that is the number of elements in the first dimension of the mxArray that *array_ptr* points to.

`void mxSetM(mxArray *array_ptr,int m);`
is used to reshape or increase/decrease the number of 'rows' in the mxArray that *array_ptr* points to. The parameter *m* is the number of 'rows' desired, see `mxSetDimensions`.

`int mxGetN(const mxArray *array_ptr);`
returns the number of 'columns', that is, the number of elements in the second dimension of the mxArray that *array_ptr* points to.

`void mxSetN(mxArray *array_ptr,int n);`
is used to reshape or increase/decrease the number of 'columns' in the mxArray that *array_ptr* points to. The parameter *n* is the number of 'columns' desired; see `mxSetDimensions`.

Commands 176   (CONTINUED)

`bool mxIsEmpty(const mxArray *array_ptr);`
returns `true` if the mxArray that *arra_ptr* points to is empty.

`bool mxIsFromGlobalWS(const mxArray *array_ptr);`
returns `true` if the mxArray that *array_ptr* points to has been copied from the global MATLAB workspace.

`bool mxIsNumeric(const mxArray *array_ptr);`
returns `true` if the mxArray that *array_ptr* points to is of numeric or string type.

`bool mxIsInt8(const mxArray *array_ptr);`
8 bit integer.

`bool mxIsUint8(const mxArray *array_ptr);`
8 bit unsigned integer.

`bool mxIsInt16(const mxArray *array_ptr);`
16 bit integer.

`bool mxIsUint16(const mxArray *array_ptr);`
16 bit unsigned integer.

`bool mxIsInt32(const mxArray *array_ptr);`
32 bit integer.

`bool mxIsUint32(const mxArray *array_ptr);`
32 bit unsigned integer.

`bool mxIsSingle(const mxArray *array_ptr);`
single precision floating point number.

`bool mxIsDouble(const mxArray *array_ptr);`
double precision floating point number.

`bool mxIsComplex(const mxArray *array_ptr);`
complex numbers. It returns `true` if the mxArray that *array_ptr* points to stores its data in the format indicated after the function.

`int mxCalcSingleSubscript(const mxArray *array_ptr,int nsubs,int *subs)`
converts a coordinate vector in a multidimensional order to a scalar index in a lexicographic order. The parameter *nsubs* is usually the number of dimensions in the mxArray that *array_ptr* points to and *subs* is a pointer to the coordinate vector that is to be converted. Use `helpdesk` to get more information.

The routines below are used to create and handle mxArrays that are full two-dimensional $m \times n$ matrices containing double precision floating point numbers.

Commands 177   HANDLING OF FULL MATRICES IN C

```
mxArray *mxCreateDoubleMatrix(int m,int n,mxComplexity
Complexflag);
```
is analogous to mxCreateCellMatrix (see Commands 181), but here a two-dimensional $m \times n$ matrix with double precision floating point numbers is created. The parameter *Complexflag* is mxCOMPLEX if complex numbers will be stored in the matrix, mxREAL otherwise.

```
double *mxGetPr(const mxArray *array_ptr);
```
returns a pointer to the first real element in the mxArray that *array_ptr* points to. It returns NULL if the mxArray does not contain any real elements.

```
void mxSetPr(mxArray *array_ptr,double *pr);
```
sets the real elements in the full mxArray that *array_ptr* points to. The parameter *pr* is a pointer to a vector that contains the values that should be used. This vector must be dynamically allocated using mxCalloc; see Commands 175.

```
double *mxGetPi(const mxArray *array_ptr);
```
is analogous to mxGetPr, but for the imaginary elements.

```
void mxSetPi(mxArray *array_ptr,double *pi);
```
is analogous to mxSetPr, but for the imaginary elements.

The routines below are used to create and handle mxArrays that are sparse two-dimensional $m \times n$ matrices containing double precision floating point numbers.

Commands 178   HANDLING OF SPARSE MATRICES IN C

```
mxArray *mxCreateSparse(int m,int n,int nzmax,mxComplexity
ComplexFlag);
```
creates a sparse, two-dimensional $m \times n$ matrix. The parameter *nzmax* is the number of non-zero elements that will be stored in the matrix. The parameter *ComplexFlag* is mxCOMPLEX if complex numbers will be stored in the matrix, mxREAL otherwise. It returns a pointer to the matrix if the operation was successful, NULL otherwise. Free the memory used by the mxArray with mxDestroyArray when it is no longer needed; see Commands 175.

```
int mxGetNzmax(const mxArray *array_ptr);
```
returns the value *nzmax* (see above) used by the sparse mxArray that *array_ptr* points to. It returns an undetermined value if any error occured.

```
void mxSetNzmax(mxArray *array_ptr,int nzmax);
```
sets the value *nzmax* (see above) used by the sparse mxArray that *array_ptr* points to. If *nzmaz* is changed then the size of the vectors **ir**, **pr** and **pi**, if they exist, must also be changed; use helpdesk to get more information.

Commands 178 (CONTINUED)

```
int *mxGetIr(const mxArray *array_ptr);
```
returns a pointer to an integer vector containing the numbers of the rows, where the first row has number 0, that have non-zero elements in the sparse mxArray that *array_ptr* points to. It returns NULL if the operation failed.

```
void mxSetIr(mxArray *array_ptr,int *ir);
```
defines the rows in which the sparse mxArray that *array_ptr* points to have non-zero elements. The parameter *ir* is a pointer to an integer vector containing the row numbers which will be used and these must be sorted in column order. The row numbering starts at 0. Use helpdesk to get more information.

```
int *mxGetJc(const mxArray *array_ptr);
```
is analogous to mxGetIr, but returns a pointer to an integer vector that indirectly indicates the columns having non-zero entries. Use helpdesk to get more information.

```
void mxSetJc(mxArray *array_ptr,int *jc);
```
is analogous to mxSetIr, but sets the vector that indirectly indicates the columns with non-zero entries. Use helpdesk to get more information.

```
bool mxIsSparse(const mxArray *array_ptr);
```
returns true if the mxArray that *array_ptr* points to is of sparse type.

The routines below are used to create and handle string mxArrays.

Commands 179 HANDLING OF STRINGS IN C

```
mxChar
```
is a data type used by string mxArrays to store data elements.

```
mxArray *mxCreateCharArray(int ndim,const int *dims);
```
is analogous to mxCreateCellArray, but here an *n* dimensional character matrix is created; see Commands 181.

```
mxArray *mxCreateCharMatrixFromStrings(int m,char **str);
```
is analogous to mxCreateCellMatrix (see Commands 181), but creates a two-dimensional character matrix from the string vector that *str* points to; *m* is the number of strings in the string vector.

```
mxArray *mxCreateString(const char *str);
```
creates a string mxArray from the string **str**. It returns a pointer to the string mxArray if the operation succeeded, otherwise NULL. Free the memory used by the mxArray with mxDestroyArray when it is no longer needed; see Commands 175.

```
int mxGetString(const mxArray *array_ptr,char *buf,int buflen);
```
copies a string from the string mxArray that *array_ptr* points to. The string is stored in **buf** and *buflen* is the maximum number of characters that can be stored in **buf**. It returns 0 if the operation succeeded, otherwise 1.

Commands 179   (CONTINUED)

bool mxIsChar(const mxArray *array_ptr);
returns true if the mxArray that *array_ptr* points to is of string type.

A new data type in MATLAB 5 is multidimensional matrices; see Section 2.2. To handle this type of mxArrays there are the following routines below.

Note: in C it is possible to create and compute using mxArrays that have 8, 16, or 32 bit integer numbers with or without sign and single precision floating point numbers. However, it is currently not possible to use these in the MATLAB environment in any other way than just listing them.

Commands 180   HANDLING OF MULTIDIMENSIONAL MATRICES IN C

mxArray *mxCreateNumericArray(int ndim,const int *dims,mxClassID
class,MxComplexity ComplexFlag);
works as mxCreateCellArray; see Commands 181, but here an *n* dimensional matrix of numbers is created. The numbers are of type *class*, see mxClassID in Commands 176, and if complex numbers are stored *Complexflag* is set to mxCOMPLEX, otherwise mxREAL.

void *mxGetData(const mxArray *array_ptr);
works as mxGetPr, see Commands 177, but returns a void pointer. It is used for numerical matrices containing something other than double precision floating point numbers.

void mxSetData(mxArray *array_ptr,void *data_ptr);
works as mxSetPr, see Commands 177, but returns a void pointer. It is used for numerical matrices containing something other than double precision floating point numbers.

void *mxGetImagData(const mxArray *array_ptr);
works as mxGetPi, see Commands 177, but returns a void pointer. It is used for numerical matrices containing something other than double precision floating point numbers.

void mxSetImagData(mxArray *array_ptr,void *pi);
works as mxSetPi, see Commands 177, but returns a void pointer. It is used for numerical matrices containing something other than double precision floating point numbers.

void mxSetLogical(mxArray *array_ptr);
sets the logical flag in the numerical mxArray that *array_ptr* points to. This instructs MATLAB that the data of the mxArray should be treated as logical variables, that is 0 is false and the other values are true.

Commands 180   (CONTINUED)

```
void mxClearLogical(mxArray *array_ptr);
```
removes the logical flag in the numerical mxArray, see above.

```
bool mxIsLogical(const mxArray *array_ptr);
```
checks if the logical flag in the numerical mxArray is set, see above. It returns `true` if that is the case, otherwise `false`.

A new data type in MATLAB 5 is the cell matrix, also called cell array; see Section 5.5. To handle this type of mxArrays there are the following routines:

Commands 181   HANDLING OF CELL MATRICES IN C

```
mxArray *mxCreateCellArray(int ndim,const int *dims)
```
creates an empty *n* dimensional cell matrix. The parameter *ndim* is the number of dimensions and *dims* is a pointer to a vector containing the size in each dimension. It returns a pointer to the cell matrix if the creation succeeded, otherwise NULL or the execution stops.

```
mxArray *mxCreateCellMatrix(int m,int n);
```
is analogous to the function above, but creates a two-dimensional cell matrix of size $m \times n$.

```
mxArray *mxGetCell(const mxArray *array_ptr,int index);
```
copies a cell from a cell mxArray. The parameter *array_ptr* is a pointer to the cell mxArray, and *index* is the number of cells between the first cell and the cell to be copied; see `mxCalcSingleSubscript` in Commands 176. It returns a pointer to a cell mxArray if the operation succeeded, otherwise NULL.

```
void mxSetCell(mxArray *array_ptr,int index,mxArray *value);
```
sets a cell in a cell mxArray. The parameter *index* is the number of cells between the first cell and the cell to be set; see `mxCalcSingleSubscript` in Commands 176. The parameter *value* is a pointer to the cell whose value will be set in the mxArray pointed to by *array_ptr*.

```
bool mxIsCell(const mxArray *array_ptr);
```
returns `true` if the mxArray that *array_ptr* points to is of cell type.

Another new data type in MATLAB 5 is structs; see Section 12.5. To handle this type of mxArrays there are the following routines:

Commands 182	HANDLING OF STRUCTS IN C

```
mxArray *mxCreateStructArray(int ndim,const int *dims,int
nfields,const char **field_names);
```
is analogous to mxCreateCellArray (see Commands 181), but here an *n* dimensional structure matrix is created. The parameter *nfields* is the number of fields in each element and *field_names* is a pointer to a string vector containing the names of the fields.

```
mxArray *mxCreateStructMatrix(int m,int n,int nfields,const char
**field_names);
```
is analogous to the function above, but creates a two-dimensional structure matrix of size $m \times n$.

```
int mxGetNumberOfFields(const mxArray *array_ptr);
```
returns the number of fields in the structure mxArray that *array_ptr* points to. It returns 0 if the operation failed.

```
mxArray *mxGetField(const mxArray *array_ptr,int index,const char
*field_name);
```
returns the value of a field in one of the elements in the structure mxArray that *array_ptr* points to. The parameter *index* is the number of elements between the first element and the element of interest; see mxCalcSingleSubscript in Commands 176. The parameter **field_name** is a string indicating the name of the field in the element. It returns a pointer to the field if the operation succeeded, otherwise NULL.

```
void mxSetField(mxArray *array_ptr,int index,const char
*field_name,mxArray *value);
```
is analogous to the function above, but sets the field to the value that the pointer *value* points to.

```
int mxGetFieldNumber(const mxArray *array_ptr,const char
*field_name);
```
returns the field number of a field in the structure mxArray that *array_ptr* points to. The string **field_name** indicates the name of the field. It returns the field number in the structure (starts at 0) if the operation succeeded, otherwise -1.

```
const char *mxGetFieldNameByNumber(const mxArray *array_ptr,int
field_number);
```
returns a name of a field in the structure mxArray that *array_ptr* points to. The parameter *field_number* is the sequence number (starts at 0) for the field in the structure.

```
mxArray *mxGetFieldByNumber(const mxArray *array_ptr,int index,int
field_number);
```
is analogous to mxGetField, but instead of the name of the field, the *field_number* (sequence number, starts at 0) for the field in the structure is indicated.

Commands 182 (CONTINUED)

```
void mxSetFieldByNumber(mxArray *array_ptr,int index,int
field_number,mxArray *value);
```
is analogous to `mxSetField`, but instead of the name of the field, the *field_number* (sequence number, starts at 0) for the field in the structure is indicated.

```
bool mxIsStruct(const mxArray *array_ptr);
```
returns `true` if the mxArray that *array_ptr* points to is of struct type.

```
int mxSetClassName(mxArray *array_ptr,const char *classname);
```
converts the MATLAB structure that *array_ptr* points to into a MATLAB object by giving it a **classname**. Returns 0 if the operation succeded, otherwise a non-zero number. When the object is read into MATLAB via `load`, a check is made as to whether the class **classname** exists; if not then the object is converted back to a structure.

The following routines are used to get the values of special constants in C, for example machine epsilon and positive infinity. There are also routines for checking whether the value of a variable is equal to any of these constants.

Commands 183 SPECIAL CONSTANTS IN C

```
double mxGetEps(void);
```
returns the value of machine epsilon in MATLAB.

```
double mxGetInf(void);
```
returns the value of `inf`, that is positive infinity, in MATLAB.

```
bool mxIsInf(double value);
```
returns `true` if *value* is `inf`, otherwise `false`.

```
double mxGetNaN(void);
```
returns the value of NaN, Not a Number, in MATLAB.

```
bool mxIsNaN(double value);
```
returns `true` if *value* is NaN, otherwise `false`.

```
bool mxIsFinite(double value);
```
returns `true` if *value* is not `inf` or NaN, otherwise `false`.

The routines below are used when debugging a C program:

Commands 184 DEBUGGING ROUTINES IN C

```
void mxAssert(int expr,char *error_message);
```
is used when debugging. If *expr* is `false` then the program is stopped and *expr*, filename, line number and **error_message** are printed. If *expr* is `true` nothing happens.

Commands 184 (CONTINUED)

```
void mxAssertS(int expr,char *error_message);
```
is used as above, but *expr* is not printed if *expr* is false.

Some routines in MATLAB 4.2 have been replaced by new ones. But old routines still exist to make MATLAB 5 backwards compatible, though these should **not** be used in new C programs.

Commands 185 OBSOLETE MATRIX ROUTINES IN C

```
mxCreateFull    mxIsFull    mxIsString    mxFreeMatrix
```

15.2.2 Handling of MAT-files in C

Below is an example of how to read and write a MAT-file, that is, a file containing data stored in the internal binary format used by MATLAB.

■ **Example 15.1**

Suppose we need a matrix with normally distributed random elements in a C program. This apparently simple matrix can be quite difficult to generate, so instead we create it in MATLAB with a single command. We first define a normally distributed 10×10 matrix and save it using the save command:

```
OldMatrix = randn(10);   % Creates a random matrix.
save data OldMatrix;     % Saves matrix OldMatrix on file
                         % data.mat.
```

Then we create a C program that reads this random matrix, multiplies all elements by 2, and then adds it as a new matrix to the file **data.mat**. The C program is saved in the file **matex.c**.

```
#include "mat.h"

void main()
{
  MATFile *mfp;
  mxArray *A_ptr, *B_ptr;
  double *A, *B;
  int M, N, i, j;
```

```
/* Read matrix from file. */
mfp = matOpen("data.mat", "u");
A_ptr = matGetArray(mfp, "OldMatrix");
M = mxGetM(A_ptr);
N = mxGetN(A_ptr);
A = mxGetPr(A_ptr);

/* Create a new matrix. */
B_ptr = mxCreateDoubleMatrix(M, N, mxREAL);
mxSetName(B_ptr, "NewMatrix");
B = mxGetPr(B_ptr);

/* Set the new matrix to the old*2. */
for (i = 0; i < M; i++)
{
  for (j = 0; j < N; j++)
  {
    B[i + M * j] = 2 * A[i + M * j];
  }
}

/* Save the new matrix and finish. */
matPutArray(mfp, B_ptr);
matClose(mfp);
mxDestroyArray(A_ptr);
mxDestroyArray(B_ptr);
exit(0);
}
```

This program is compiled in UNIX by (written as one unbroken line at the system prompt):

```
gcc -ansi -I/opt/matlab52/extern/include -o matex matex.c
-L/opt/matlab52/extern/lib/sol2 -R/opt/matlab52/extern/lib/sol2
-lmat -lmx -lmi -lut
```

Note that all paths are system dependent. When this program is run the file **data.mat** is extended with the matrix **NewMatrix**, which is 2***OldMatrix**.

■

Below we list the routines for MAT-files. By using these, we can read and write the binary files of MATLAB, and in that way send data between MATLAB and a program written in C. In order to use these routines the header file **mat.h** must be included in the program, that is the program header must contain the following line:

```
#include "mat.h"
```

Before writing to or reading from a MAT-file, it must be opened, and afterwards it must be closed. These operations are done by the following routines:

Commands 186 OPENING AND CLOSING OF MAT-FILES IN C

```
MATFile
```
is the data type for binary MAT-files.

```
MATFile *matOpen(const char *filename,const char *mode);
```
opens the file **filename** in the mode **mode**. There are four modes: "r" for reading, "w" for writing, "u" for reading/writing and "w4" for writing in the MATLAB 4 MAT-file format. If the opening succeeded a pointer to the MAT-file is returned, otherwise NULL.

```
FILE *matGetFp(MATFile *mfp);
```
returns a C file pointer to the MAT-file that mfp points to. It is used, for example, in the C function ferror().

```
int matClose(MATFile *mfp);
```
closes the MAT-file that mfp points to. It returns 0 if it succeeded, otherwise EOF.

When the MAT-file is opened, writing to or reading from the file is done by the following routines:

Commands 187 READING AND WRITING OF MAT-FILES IN C

```
char **matGetDir(MATFile *mfp,int *num);
```
gives a pointer to a list of the names of the mxArrays that are stored in the MAT-file that mfp points to. The parameter *num* is the address of a variable that will hold the number of mxArrays. If the operation failed, NULL is returned and *num* becomes a negative number. The memory to the list of mxArrays must be freed by mxFree when there is no need for it any more; see Commands 175.

```
mxArray *matGetArray(MATFile *mfp,const char *name);
```
copies the mxArray **name** from the MAT-file that mfp points to. Returns a pointer to the mxArray if it succeeded, otherwise NULL. Free the memory of the mxArray by mxDestroyArray when there is no need for it any more; see Commands 175.

```
mxArray *matGetArrayHeader(MATFile *mfp,const char *name);
```
is analogous to the function above, but copies only the information in the array header.

```
mxArray *matGetNextArray(MATFile *mfp);
```
copies the next mxArray in the MAT-file that mfp points to. Returns a pointer to the mxArray if it succeeded, otherwise NULL. Free the memory of the mxArray by mxDestroyArray when there is no need for it any more; see Commands 175.

```
mxArray *matGetNextArrayHeader(MATFile *mfp);
```
is analogous to the function above, but copies only the information in the array header.

Commands 187 (CONTINUED)

`int matPutArray(MATFile *mfp,const mxArray *mp);`
writes the mxArray that *mp* points to into the MAT-file that *mfp* points to. If the mxArray already exists in the MAT-file it is overwritten. Returns 0 if it succeeded, otherwise a non-zero value.

`int matPutArrayAsGlobal(MATFile *mfp,const mxArray *mp);`
is analogous to the function above, but when the mxArray is read into MATLAB it is stored in the global workspace with a reference to it in the local workspace.

`int matDeleteArray(MATFile *mfp,const char *name);`
deletes the mxArray **name** from the MAT-file that *mfp* points to. Returns 0 if it succeeded, otherwise a non-zero value.

Some routines in MATLAB 4.2 have been replaced by new ones. The old routines still exist to make MATLAB 5 backwards compatible, but should **not** be used in new C programs.

Commands 188 OBSOLETE MAT-FILE ROUTINES IN C

matGetFull	matGetMatrix	matGetNextMatrix	matGetString
matPutFull	matPutMatrix	matPutString	matDeleteMatrix

For compilation and linking of C programs that use MAT-files, use the following commands:

- **UNIX:** Write the following at the system prompt as one unbroken line:

  ```
  gcc -ansi -I/.../matlab/extern/include -o programname sourcecode.c
  -L/.../matlab/extern/lib/... -R/.../matlab/extern/lib/...
  -lmat -lmx -lmi -lut
  ```

  The three dots, . . . , in the paths above indicate that these parts of the paths are system dependent, **programname** is what one wishes to call the program and **sourcecode.c** is a list of the files of source code in C that one wishes to compile. Here the compiler `gcc` is used, but, of course, other compilers can be used as long as they comply with the ANSI C standard. If desired, debug and optimization flags can be set; see the documentation for the compiler.

- **Windows:** Write the following at the MATLAB prompt:

  ```
  mex sourcecode.c -f optfil
  ```

  Where **optfil** is **watengmatopts.bat** (Watcom C), **msvcengmatopts.bat** (Microsoft Visual C) or **bccengmatopts.bat** (Borland C). The parameter **sourcecode.c** is a list of the files of source code in C that one wishes to compile.

- **Macintosh:** See the MATLAB 5 manual *Application Program Interface Guide*.

15.2.3 Calling MATLAB from C

To call MATLAB from C, a MATLAB engine must first be started. This is very simple, and is done by a call to engOpen; see Commands 189.

The next thing to do is to transfer the mxArrays that are to be manipulated in MATLAB. This is performed in two steps:

1. The first step is to convert the mxArrays to a format understood by MATLAB, and this can be done in two different ways. One can choose to work from the beginning with the data in the format that MATLAB uses, and create mxArrays with the routines starting with mxCreate and name them with mxSetName. These routines are described in Section 15.2.1. Alternatively, one can choose to copy a data structure of one's own to an mxArray. It is important, however, to note that MATLAB stores matrices in the column direction, while C stores matrices in the row direction, that is, one has to swap indices.

2. The second step is to put the matrices in the MATLAB workspace. This is done by the routines that start with engPut; see Commands 189.

MATLAB is now ready to receive commands. These are given just as in the ordinary command window, but now in a string passed to the function engEvalString.

Finally, a conversion and transfer from MATLAB to C might be necessary.

This may sound rather complicated, but an example makes it more clear.

■ **Example 15.2**

Suppose we have a matrix in a C program which we want to study using computer graphics in some way. Then it is a good idea to use MATLAB for the visualizations. We write the following C program and store it in the file **plotm.c**:

```
# include "engine.h"

void main()
{
  Engine *ep;
  mxArray *A_ptr;
  double* A;
  int i, j;

  /* Create a new matrix. */
  A_ptr = mxCreateDoubleMatrix(10, 10, mxREAL);
  mxSetName(A_ptr, "A");
```

```
A = mxGetPr(A_ptr);
for (i = 0; i < 10; i++)
{
  for (j = 0; j < 10; j++)
  {
    A[i + 10 * j] = (j + 1) * (j + 1) * (i + 1) * (i + 1);
  }
}

/* Start the MATLAB Engine. */
ep = engOpen("/opt/matlab52/bin/matlab");
/* Transfer the new matrix. */
engPutArray(ep, A_ptr);
/* Preform the command mesh(A) and save. */
engEvalString(ep, "mesh(A);");
engEvalString(ep, "print picture.eps -deps;");

/* Finish. */
engClose(ep);
mxDestroyArray(A_ptr);
exit(0);
}
```

To compile the program in a UNIX environment, write the following at the system prompt as one unbroken line:

```
gcc -ansi -I/opt/matlab52/extern/include -o plotm plotm.c
-L/opt/matlab52/extern/lib/sol2 -R/opt/matlab52/extern/lib/sol2
-leng -lmat -lmx -lmi -lut
```

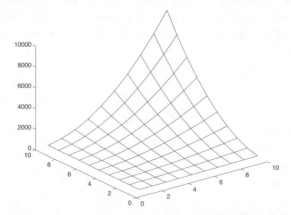

Figure 15.1 *A matrix created in a C program and drawn by MATLAB.*

Note that all paths are system dependent. When the program is executed we get Figure 15.1.

■

Calls to MATLAB are handled by the following **engine routines**. Note that these routines are currently not available for Macintosh. In order to use these routines the header file **engine.h** must be included in the program, that is, the program header must contain the following line:

```
#include "engine.h"
```

Commands 189 MATLAB ENGINE ROUTINES IN C

```
Engine
```
is the data type for MATLAB engines.

```
Engine *engOpen(const char *startcmd);
```
starts a MATLAB engine, where **startcmd** is a string containing the starting command, usually "matlab". It returns a pointer to the MATLAB engine if it succeeded, otherwise NULL.

```
int engOutputBuffer(Engine *ep,char *p,int n);
```
defines a text buffer **p** of size *n* to the MATLAB engine that *ep* points to. The text that is normally written on the screen is stored here.

```
int engEvalString(Engine *ep,const char *string);
```
evaluates the MATLAB commands in the string **string** in the MATLAB engine that *ep* points to. Returns 0 if it succeeded, otherwise a non-zero value.

```
mxArray *engGetArray(Engine *ep,const char *name);
```
copies the mxArray **name** from the workspace in the MATLAB engine that *ep* points to. It returns a pointer to the mxArray if it succeeded, otherwise NULL. Free the memory used by the mxArray with mxDestroyArray when it is no longer needed; see Commands 175.

```
int engPutArray(Engine *ep,const mxArray *mp);
```
copies the mxArray that *mp* points to, to the workspace in the MATLAB engine that *ep* points to. It returns 0 if it succeeded, otherwise 1.

```
int engClose(Engine *ep);
```
closes the MATLAB engine that *ep* points to. It returns 0 if it succeeded, otherwise 1.

Some routines in MATLAB 4.2 have been replaced by new ones. The old routines still exist to make MATLAB 5 backwards compatible, but should **not** be used in new C programs.

Commands 190	OBSOLETE MATLAB ENGINE ROUTINES IN C

engGetFull	enGetMatrix	engPutFull	engPutMatrix
engSetEvalCallback	engSetEvalTimeout	engWinInit	

For compilation and linking of C programs which call MATLAB, use the following commands:

- **UNIX:** Write the following at the system prompt as one unbroken line:

```
gcc -ansi -I/.../matlab/extern/include -o programname
sourcecode.c
-L/.../matlab52/extern/lib/...
-R/.../matlab/extern/lib/...
-leng -lmat -lmx -lmi -lut
```

  The three dots, ..., in the paths above indicate that these parts of the paths are system dependent, **programname** is what one wishes to call the program and **sourcecode.c** is a list of the files of source code in C that one wishes to compile. Here the compiler gcc is used, but, of course, other compilers can be used as long as they comply with the ANSI C standard. If desired, debug and optimization flags can be set; see the documentation for the compiler.

- **Windows**: Write the following at the MATLAB prompt:

```
mex sourcecode.c -f optfil
```

  Where **optfil** is **watengmatopts.bat** (Watcom C), **msvcengmatopts.bat** (Microsoft Visual C) or **bccengmatopts.bat** (Borland C). The parameter **sourcecode.c** is a list of the files of source code in C that one wishes to compile.

15.2.4 Calling C from MATLAB

This section starts with a simple example describing calls to C from MATLAB. A call to C in MATLAB is done in the same way as a call to an ordinary function file, that is an M-file.

A MEX-file uses the same routines and matrix format that one uses in C to call MATLAB. However, now the so called MEX routines are also used.

The file must have a main function called mexFunction, which is the function MATLAB calls. This routine has four parameters: the number of input arguments, the number of output arguments, and two arrays of pointers to these arguments. This function will thereafter call any computing routines.

■ Example 15.3

We create a MEX-file that from a given matrix returns a matrix where the elements have been multiplied with their row indices. The following C routines are stored in the file **rmult.c**.

```c
# include "mex.h"


/* A routine multiplying the elements with their row indices. */
void radMult(double *Out, double *In, int M, int N)
{
  int i, j;

  for (i = 0; i <  M; i++)
  {
    for (j = 0; j < N; j++)
    {
      Out[i + M * j] = (i + 1) * In[i + M * j];
    }
  }
}


/* This routine is called by MATLAB. */
void mexFunction(int nlhs, mxArray *plhs[],
                 int nrhs, const mxArray *prhs[])
{
  mxArray *In_ptr, *Out_ptr;
  double  *In, *Out;
  int M, N;

  /* Check the number of arguments and their type. */
  In_ptr = prhs[0];
  In = mxGetPr(In_ptr);
  if (nrhs != 1)
    mexErrMsgTxt("Only one input argument allowed!");
  else if (nlhs != 1)
    mexErrMsgTxt("Only one output argument allowed!");
  if ( !mxIsNumeric(In_ptr) || mxIsComplex(In_ptr) ||
       mxIsSparse(In_ptr) || !mxIsDouble(In_ptr) )
    mexErrMsgTxt
      ("Input argument must be a full floating point matrix!");

  /* Create a new matrix. */
  M = mxGetM(In_ptr);
  N = mxGetN(In_ptr);
```

```
    Out_ptr = mxCreateDoubleMatrix(M, N, mxREAL);
    Out = mxGetPr(Out_ptr);

    /* Calls a routine that operates on the matrix. */
    radMult(Out, In, M, N);

    /* Returns the new matrix ... */
    plhs[0] = Out_ptr;
}
```

This program is compiled in UNIX by (written at the system prompt):

```
/opt/matlab52/bin/mex rmult.c
```

Note that the path is system dependent.

When the program has been compiled, we can write the following at the MATLAB prompt to execute the program:

```
New =
     1     2     3
     2     4     6
     3     6     9
```

∎

In the command tables below we describe all the MEX routines. These are used in MEX-files and can be seen as compiled M-files written in C. In order to use these routines the header file **mex.h** must be included in the program, that is, the program header must contain the following line:

```
#include "mex.h"
```

To let MATLAB be able to call a routine written in C, one has to write an interface function called mexFunction. From the MEX-file one can also make calls in the 'other direction', that is, to MATLAB from C, by the routines mexCallMATLAB and mexEvalString.

Commands 191   INTERFACE TO MATLAB IN C

```
void mexFunction(int nlhs,mxArray *plhs[],int nrhs,const mxArray
*prhs[]);
```
is the interface function to MATLAB. The parameter *nlhs* is the number of output arguments and *plhs* is a pointer to a vector of pointers to these arguments (set to NULL). Similarly, *nrhs* is the number of input arguments and *prhs* is a pointer to a vector of pointers to these arguments. The input arguments must not be altered in the C program.

```
int mexCallMATLAB(int nlhs,mxArray *plhs[],int nrhs,mxArray
*prhs[],const char *command_name);
```
calls a MATLAB function, an M-file or a MEX-file. The parameter *nlhs* is the number of output arguments (must be less than or equal to 50) and *plhs* is a pointer to a vector of pointers to these arguments (set to NULL). Similarly, *nrhs* is the number of input arguments (must be less than or equal to 50) and *prhs* is a pointer to a vector of pointers to these arguments. The string **command_name** contains the name of the function one wants to call, and if it is an operator it must be placed within single quote characters, for example `'+'`. It returns 0 if the operation succeeded, otherwise a non-zero value. Free the memory used by the mxArrays that *plhs* points to by `mxDestroyArray` when they are no longer in use; see Commands 175.

```
void mexSetTrapFlag(int trap_flag);
```
is used for handling errors when using `mexCallMATLAB`. If MATLAB discovers an error in the call to `mexCallMATLAB` the execution of the MEX-file is stopped and one gets back to the MATLAB prompt. Exactly the same thing happens if $trap\_flag$ is set to 0, but if, on the other hand, it is set to 1, then the MEX-file will regain control.

```
int mexEvalString(const char *command);
```
executes the MATLAB command **command** in the caller's workspace. There is no possibility of transferring the results back to the MEX program. All input arguments to the **command** must be found in the caller's workspace. It returns 0 if the operation succeeded, otherwise a non-zero value.

```
int mexAtExit(void (*ExitFcn)(void));
```
defines a function that is called when the MEX program is about to exit. Is used for example to close files. Always returns 0.

In addition to transferring data as parameters in `mexFunction` it is also possible to read and write data directly in the workspaces of MATLAB.

Commands 192   TRANSFERRING DATA TO AND FROM MATLAB IN C

```
mxArray *mexGetArray(const char *name,const char *workspace);
```
copies an mxArray from a workspace. The string **name** is the name of the mxArray and **workspace** indicates from which workspace the mxArray should be copied. The following alternatives are available:

Commands 192   (CONTINUED)

"base"   searches for the variable **name** in the current MATLAB workspace.
"caller"   searches for the variable **name** in the workspace of the calling function.
"global"   searches for the variable **name** in the list of global variables.

It returns a pointer to the copied mxArray if the operation succeded, otherwise NULL.
Free the memory used by the mxArray by mxDestroyArray when it is no longer in use;
see Commands 175.

```
int mexPutArray(mxArray *array_ptr,const char *workspace);
```
is analogous to the function above, but copies an mxArray to a workspace. It returns 0
if the operation succeeded, otherwise 1.

```
const mxArray *mexGetArrayPtr(const char *name,const char
*workspace);
```
returns a read-only pointer to an mxArray in a different workspace. The string **name** is
the name of the mxArray and **workspace** indicates from which workspace the mxArray
should be copied (see mexGetArray). It returns NULL if the operation failed. Note that
it is only possible to read from the mxArray, not alter its values.

The following routines are used to write error messages, warnings and other text in the
MATLAB command window:

Commands 193   ERROR HANDLING AND PRINTING IN C

```
int mexPrintf(const char *format,arg1,arg2,...);
```
writes, in ANSI C printf style, a string in the MATLAB window. The parameter
format is an ANSI C format string, and $arg1$, $arg2$, ... are optional arguments to
printf.

```
void mexErrMsgTxt(const char *error_msg);
```
writes the error message **error_msg** in the MATLAB window and stops the execution
of the MEX-file.

```
void mexWarnMsgTxt(const char *warning_msg);
```
displays the string **warning_msg** in the MATLAB window, but does not stop the execution of the MEX program.

The following C routines do different things in the MATLAB environment. For example
one can use these to handle graphical objects; see Section 14.2.

Commands 194   OTHER MEX ROUTINES IN C

```
bool mexIsGlobal(const mxArray *array_ptr);
```
returns true if the mxArray that $array\_ptr$ points to is a global variable.

Commands 194   (CONTINUED)

```
const mxArray *mexGet(double handle,const char *property);
```
is used to get the value of a property of one of the graphical objects in MATLAB. The parameter *handle* is an object pointer (handle) to the graphical object, and the string **property** is the property. It returns a pointer to an mxArray containing the value of the property if the operation succeeded, otherwise NULL. See also Section 14.2.

```
int mexSet(double handle,const char *property,mxArray *value);
```
is analogous to the function above, but instead sets a property in one of the graphical objects in MATLAB. The parameter *value* is a pointer to a mxArray that contains the value that is assigned to the property. It returns 0 if the operation succeeded, otherwise 1. See also Section 14.2.

```
void mexAddFlops(int count);
```
adds *count* to the internal counter in MATLAB that counts the number of floating point operations.

The following routines are used to control the way the memory in the MEX routines is handled. These routines make it possible to let variables keep their values in between successive calls to MEX routines.

Commands 195   MEMORY HANDLING IN C

```
void mexMakeArrayPersistent(mxArray *array_ptr);
```
Normally, the memory used for an mxArray is freed when the MEX program exits. If one does not want this to happen, that is, one wants the mxArray to keep its data in between successive calls to the MEX program, then this function can be used. The parameter *array_ptr* is a pointer to the mxArray.

```
void mexMakeMemoryPersistent(void *ptr);
```
is analogous to the functions above, but is used instead for the memory area that has been allocated by mxCalloc. The parameter *ptr* is a pointer to the start of the memory area.

```
void mexLock(void);
```
locks the MEX-file, that is makes it impossible to delete from memory.

```
void mexUnlock(void);
```
unlocks the MEX-file; see above.

```
bool mexIsLocked(void);
```
returns true if the MEX-file is locked; see above.

Some routines in MATLAB 4.2 have been replaced by new ones. The old routines still exist to make MATLAB 5 backwards compatible, but should **not** be used in new C programs.

Commands 196	OBSOLETE MEX ROUTINES IN C		
mexGetMatrix	mexGetGlobal	mexPutMatrix	mxGetMatrixPtr
mexGetFull	mexGetGlobal	mexPutMatrix	mxGetMatrixPtr
mexIsInf	mexGetNaN	mexIsNaN	mexIsFinite

For compilation and linking of C programs that are called from MATLAB, use the following commands:

- **UNIX:** Write the following at the system prompt as one unbroken line:

  ```
  .../matlab52/bin/mex sourcecode.c
  ```

  The three dots, ..., in the path above indicate that the path is system dependent. The parameter **sourcecode.c** is a list of the files of source code in C that one wishes to compile. Possibly one should configure the compilation or linking; see the MATLAB 5 manual *Application Program Interface Guide*.

- **Windows:** Write the following at the MATLAB prompt:

  ```
  mex sourcecode.c
  ```

  Possibly one should configure the compilation or linking; see the MATLAB 5 manual *Application Program Interface Guide*.

- **Macintosh:** See the MATLAB 5 manual *Application Program Interface Guide* for configuration. When this is done one can write the following at the MATLAB prompt:

  ```
  mex sourcecode.c
  ```

The created MEX-file will get a suffix that is system dependent. One can check what suffix is used by the system with the help of the MATLAB command mexext.

It is possible to debug MEX programs, but then the compiler flag −g must be added. In a UNIX environment, after compilation, matlab −Ddbx is entered at the system prompt, followed by run when MATLAB has been loaded. At the MATLAB prompt dbmex on is entered and then the MEX-file one wants to debug is executed. Before the MEX-file is executed one will, however, get back to the debugger and have the chance to list the program, set break points, etc. From the MATLAB prompt one can go to the debugger by writing dbmex stop, and in the debugger one writes continue to get back to MATLAB. For debugging in Windows and on Macintosh see the MATLAB 5 manual *Application Program Interface Guide*.

15.3 MATLAB and FORTRAN

One difference between FORTRAN and C is that the MATLAB FORTRAN library can only handle strings and two-dimensional matrices, full and sparse, which contain double precision floating point numbers.

15.3.1 Handling of mxArrays in FORTRAN

Manipulation of mxArrays is done by the routines in the tables below. Here, an 'mxArray' is either a string or a two-dimensional matrix, full or sparse, containing double precision floating point numbers.

In C it is natural to work with pointers. In FORTRAN, however, pointers are not a data type of their own, and they are very clumsy to work with. In FORTRAN a MATLAB pointer is represented by a 4 byte integer on all platforms except on the Alpha and the SGI64 where they are represented by 8 byte integers (the calls in the command tables must be adjusted accordingly). All operations on matrices etc. must now be done via the converting routines which start with mxCopy.

Yet, some compilers support the %val construction. This is an extension of FOR-TRAN 77 and FORTRAN 90 which means that the value of a variable can be sent in subroutine calls, so called 'call by value'. Normally, only the address of the variable is sent in a subroutine call, so called 'call by reference'. If this construction is available there is no need to convert pointers to data, that is, the pointers that are returned by mxGetPr and mxGetPi; see Commands 200. Instead these pointers can be sent with %val to a subroutine where they are declared as FORTRAN matrices that contain double precision floating point numbers; see Example 15.6 below. Consult the FORTRAN compiler manual to see if it supports the %val construction.

The %val construction is also needed if one wants to allocate memory dynamically; see the MATLAB 5 manual *Application Program Interface Guide* and the Example 15.6 below.

Commands 197 HANDLING OF POINTERS IN FORTRAN

```
subroutine mxCopyPtrToInteger4(px,y,n)
integer*4 y(n)
integer*4 px,n
```
copies *n* integers from the MATLAB integer vector that *px* points to to a standard integer vector **y** in FORTRAN. The parameter *px* points to either an **ir** or a **jc** vector; see mxGetIr and mxGetJc in Commands 201.

```
subroutine mxCopyInteger4ToPtr(y,px,n)
integer*4 y(n)
integer*4 px,n
```
copies *n* integers from an ordinary integer vector **y** in FORTRAN to the MATLAB integer vector that *px* points to. The parameter *px* points to either an **ir** or a **jc** vector; see mxGetIr and mxGetJc in Commands 201.

Commands 197   (CONTINUED)

```
subroutine mxCopyPtrToPtrArray(px,y,n)
integer*4 y(n)
integer*4 px,n
```
copies a pointer *px* to an ordinary integer vector **y** in FORTRAN. The parameter *px* points to either an **ir** or a **jc** vector; see mxGetIr and mxGetJc in Commands 201.

```
subroutine mxCopyPtrToReal8(px,y,n)
real*8 y(n)
integer*4 px,n
```
copies *n* floating point numbers from the MATLAB floating point vector that *px* points to to an ordinary floating point vector **y** in FORTRAN. The parameter *px* points to either a **pr** or a **pi** vector; see mxGetPr and mxGetPr in Commands 200.

```
subroutine mxCopyReal8ToPtr(y,px,n)
real*8 y(n)
integer*4 px,n
```
copies *n* floating point numbers from an ordinary floating point vector **y** in FORTRAN to the MATLAB floating point vector that *px* points to. The parameter *px* points to either a **pr** or a **pi** vector; see mxGetPr and mxGetPr in Commands 200.

```
subroutine mxCopyPtrToComplex16(pr,pi,y,n)
complex*16 y(n)
integer*4 pr,pi,n
```
copies *n* complex numbers from the MATLAB vectors that *pr* (real part) and *pi* (imaginary part) point to to an ordinary complex vector **y** in FORTRAN. See mxGetPr and mxGetPi in Commands 200.

```
subroutine mxCopyComplex16ToPtr(y,pr,pi,n)
complex*16 y(n)
integer*4 pr,pi,n
```
copies *n* complex numbers from an ordinary complex vector **y** in FORTRAN to the MATLAB vectors that *pr* (real part) and *pi* (imaginary part) point to. See mxGetPr and mxGetPi in Commands 200.

```
subroutine mxCopyPtrToCharacter(px,y,n)
character*(*) y
integer*4 px,n
```
copies *n* characters from the MATLAB character vector that *px* points to to an ordinary character vector **y** in FORTRAN. See mxGetString in Commands 202.

```
subroutine mxCopyCharacterToPtr(y,px,n)
character*(*) y
integer*4 px,n
```
copies *n* characters from an ordinary character vector **y** in FORTRAN to the MATLAB character vector that *px* points to. See mxGetString in Commands 202.

The routines in the tables below are used to allocate and free memory. It is good programming practice to free memory which is no longer needed. If one only uses MATLAB routines to create data structures this is not necessary because this is done automatically by MATLAB after the program terminates, but if one is careful this should be done anyway.

Commands 198   MEMORY MANAGEMENT IN FORTRAN

```
integer*4 function mxCalloc(n,size)
integer*4 n,size
```
allocates memory. The parameter *n* is the number of elements being allocated and *size* is the number of bytes per element. It returns a pointer to the beginning of the allocated memory if the allocation was successful, otherwise 0 or the execution is stopped. Use mxFree to free the memory when it is no longer use.

```
subroutine mxFree(ptr)
integer*4 ptr
```
frees the memory that *ptr* points to.

```
subroutine mxFreeMatrix(pm)
integer*4 pm
```
frees the memory that has been allocated by mxCreateFull or mxCreateSparse. The parameter *pm* is a pointer to the mxArray in question.

Commands 199   COMMON ROUTINES USED TO HANDLE MXARRAYS IN FORTRAN

```
character*32 function mxGetName(pm)
integer*4 pm
```
returns a pointer to a character vector (of maximum 32 characters) which contains the name of the mxArray that *pm* points to. If the operation failed, 0 is returned.

```
subroutine mxSetName(pm,name)
integer*4 pm
character*(32) name
```
gives the mxArray that *pm* points to the name **name** (maximum 32 characters).

```
real*8 function mxGetScalar(pm)
integer*4 pm
```
returns the value of the first real element of the mxArray that *pm* points to. If the mxArray is of sparse type the value of the first non-zero real element is returned and if the mxArray is empty an undetermined value is returned.

```
integer*4 function mxGetM(pm)
integer*4 pm
```
returns the number of rows in the mxArray that *pm* points to.

Commands 199   (CONTINUED)

```
subroutine mxSetM(pm,m)
integer*4 pm,m
```
is used to reshape or increase/decrease the number of rows in the mxArray that *pm* points to. The parameter *m* is the number of rows desired. If one wants to increase/decrease the number of rows then memory must be allocated/deallocated; see helpdesk for more information.

```
integer*4 function mxGetN(pm)
integer*4 pm
```
returns the number of columns in the mxArray that *pm* points to.

```
subroutine mxSetN(pm,n)
integer*4 pm,n
```
is used to reshape or increase/decrease the number of columns in the mxArray that *pm* points to. The parameter *n* is the number of columns one wants. If the number of columns should be increased/decreased, then the memory must be allocated/deallocated; see helpdesk for more information.

```
integer*4 function mxIsNumeric(pm)
integer*4 pm
```
returns 1 if the mxArray that *pm* points to contains numerical data, otherwise 0.

```
integer*4 function mxIsDouble(pm)
integer*4 pm
```
returns 1 if the mxArray that *pm* points to contains double precision floating point numbers, otherwise 0. If 0 is returned, the mxArray cannot be used by FORTRAN programs.

```
integer*4 function mxIsComplex(pm)
integer*4 pm
```
returns 1 if the mxArray that *pm* points to contains complex numbers, otherwise 0.

The routines below are used to create and handle mxArrays that are full two-dimensional $m \times n$ matrices containing double precision floating point numbers.

Commands 200   HANDLING OF FULL MATRICES IN FORTRAN

```
integer*4 function mxCreateFull(m,n,ComplexFlag)
integer*4 m,n,ComplexFlag
```
creates a two-dimensional $m \times n$ matrix (mxArray) with double precision floating point numbers. The parameter *Complexflag* is 1 if complex numbers are to be stored in the matrix, otherwise 0. Use mxFreeMatrix to free the memory used by the matrix when it is no longer in use; see Commands 198.

Commands 200 (CONTINUED)

```
integer*4 function mxGetPr(pm)
integer*4 pm
```
returns a pointer to the first real element in the mxArray that *pm* points to. It returns 0 if the mxArray does not contain any real elements.

```
subroutine mxSetPr(pm,pr)
integer*4 pm,pr
```
sets the real elements in the full mxArray that *pm* points to. The parameter *pr* is a pointer to a vector that contains the values that should be used, this vector must be dynamically allocated using mxCalloc; see Commands 198.

```
integer*4 function mxGetPi(pm)
integer*4 pm
```
is analogous to mxGetPr, but for the imaginary elements.

```
subroutine mxSetPi(pm,pi)
integer*4 pm,pi
```
is analogous to mxSetPr, but for the imaginary elements.

```
integer*4 function mxIsFull(pm)
integer*4 pm
```
returns 1 if the mxArray that *pm* points to is a full matrix, 0 if it is a sparse matrix.

The routines below are used to create and handle mxArrays that are sparse two-dimensional $m \times n$ matrices containing double precision floating point numbers.

Commands 201 HANDLING OF SPARSE MATRICES IN FORTRAN

```
integer*4 function mxCreateSparse(m,n,nzmax,ComplexFlag)
integer*4 m,n,nzmax,ComplexFlag
```
creates a sparse, two-dimensional $m \times n$ matrix. The parameter *nzmax* is the number of non-zero elements that will be stored in the matrix. The parameter *ComplexFlag* is 1 if complex numbers will be stored in the matrix, 0 otherwise. It returns a pointer to the matrix if the operation was successful, 0 otherwise.

```
integer*4 function mxGetNzmax(pm)
integer*4 pm
```
returns the value *nzmax* (see above) used by the sparse mxArray that *pm* points to. It returns an undetermined value if any error occurred.

```
subroutine mxSetNzmax(pm,nzmax)
integer*4 pm,nzmax
```
sets the value *nzmax* (see above) used by the sparse mxArray that *pm* points to. If *nzmaz* is changed then the size of the vectors **ir**, **pr** and **pi**, if they exist, must also be changed; use helpdesk to get more information.

Commands 201 (CONTINUED)

```
integer*4 function mxGetIr(pm)
integer*4 pm
```
returns a pointer to an integer vector containing the numbers of the rows, where the first row has number 0, that have non-zero elements in the sparse mxArray that *pm* points to. It returns 0 if the operation failed.

```
subroutine mxSetIr(pm,ir)
integer*4 pm,ir
```
defines the rows in which the sparse mxArray that *pm* points to have non-zero elements. The parameter *ir* is a pointer to an integer vector containing the row numbers which will be used and these must be sorted in column order. The row numbering starts at 0. Use helpdesk to get more information.

```
integer*4 function mxGetJc(pm)
integer*4 pm
```
is analogous to mxGetIr, but returns a pointer to an integer vector that indirectly indicates the columns having non-zero entries. Use helpdesk to get more information.

```
subroutine mxSetJc(pm,jc)
integer*4 pm,jc
```
is analogous to mxSetIr, but sets the vector that indirectly indicates the columns with non-zero entries. Use helpdesk to get more information.

```
integer*4 function mxIsSparse(pm)
integer*4 pm
```
returns 1 if the mxArray that *pm* points to is of sparse type, otherwise 0.

The routines below are used to create and handle string mxArrays.

Commands 202 HANDLING OF STRINGS IN FORTRAN

```
integer*4 function mxCreateString(str)
character*(*) str
```
creates a string mxArray from the string **str**. It returns a pointer to the string mxArray if the operation succeeded, otherwise 0.

```
integer*4 function mxGetString(pm,str,strlen)
integer*4 pm,strlen
character*(*) str
```
copies a string from the string mxArray that *pm* points to. The string is stored in the FORTRAN string vector **str** and *strlen* is the maximum number of characters which can be stored in **str**. It returns a pointer to the string mxArray if the operation succeeded, otherwise 0.

```
integer*4 function mxIsString(pm)
integer*4 pm
```
returns 1 if the mxArray that *pm* points to is of string type, otherwise 0.

15.3.2 Handling of MAT-files in FORTRAN

Below is an example of how to read and write a MAT-file, that is, a file containing data stored in the internal binary format used by MATLAB.

■ **Example 15.4**

Suppose we need a matrix with normally distributed random elements in a FORTRAN program. This apparently simple matrix can be quite difficult to generate, so instead we create it in MATLAB with a single command. We first define a normally distributed 10×10 matrix and save it using the save command:

```
OldMatrix = randn(10);   % Creates a random matrix.
save data OldMatrix;     % Saves matrix OldMatrix on file
                         % data.mat.
```

We now create a FORTRAN program that reads this random matrix, multiplies all elements by 2, and then adds it as a new matrix to the file **data.mat**. The FORTRAN program is saved in the file **matex.for**.

```
      program main
      implicit none

      integer mfp
      integer A_ptr, B_ptr
      double precision Temp(10, 10)
      integer A, B
      integer i, j
      integer matOpen, matGetMatrix, mxCreateFull
      integer mxGetPr, matPutMatrix, stat, matClose, stat

C     Read matrix from file.
      mfp = matOpen("data.mat", "u")
      A_ptr = matGetMatrix(mfp, "OldMatrix")
      A = mxGetPr(A_ptr)
      call mxCopyPtrToReal8(A, Temp, 100)

C     Create a new matrix.
      B_ptr = mxCreateFull(10, 10, 0)
      call mxSetName(B_ptr, "NewMatrix")
      B = mxGetPr(B_ptr)

C     Set the new matrix to the old*2.
      do 100 i = 1, 10
```

```
          do 110 j = 1, 10
             Temp(i, j) = 2.0 * Temp(i, j)
110       continue
100    continue
       call mxCopyReal8ToPtr(Temp, B, 100)

C      Save the new matrix and finish.
       stat = matPutMatrix(mfp, B_ptr)
       stat = matClose(mfp)
       call mxFreeMatrix(A_ptr)
       call mxFreeMatrix(B_ptr)
       stop

       end
```

This program is compiled in UNIX by (written as one unbroken line at the system prompt):

```
f77 -I/opt/matlab52/extern/include -o matex matex.for
-L/opt/matlab52/extern/lib/sol2 -R/opt/matlab52/extern/lib/sol2
-lmat -lmx -lmi -lut
```

Note that all paths are system dependent. When this is run the file **data.mat** is extended with the matrix **NewMatrix**, which is 2***OldMatrix**. ∎

Below we list the routines for MAT-files. By using these, we can read and write the binary files of MATLAB, and in that way send data between MATLAB and a program written in FORTRAN. Note that these routines are currently not available in Windows, but they are nevertheless available in C.

Before writing to or reading from a MAT-file, it must be opened, and afterwards it must be closed. These operations are done by the following routines:

Commands 203   OPENING AND CLOSING OF MAT-FILES IN FORTRAN

```
integer*4 function matOpen(filename,mode)
integer*4 mfp
character*(*) filename,mode
```
opens the file **filename** in the mode **mode**. There are four modes: "r" for reading, "w" for writing, "u" for reading/writing and "w4" for writing in the MATLAB 4 MAT-file format. If the opening succeeded a pointer mfp to the MAT-file is returned, otherwise 0.

```
integer*4 function matClose(mfp)
integer*4 mfp
```
closes the MAT-file that mfp points to. It returns 0 if it succeeded, otherwise -1.

When the MAT-file is opened, writing to or reading from the file is done by the following routines:

Commands 204   READING AND WRITING OF MAT-FILES IN FORTRAN

```
integer*4 function matGetDir(mfp,num)
integer*4 mfp,num
```
gives a pointer to a vector containing pointers to the names of the mxArrays that are stored in the MAT-file that mfp points to. The parameter *num* is a variable that will hold the number of mxArrays. If the operation failed, 0 is returned and *num* becomes a negative number. The memory for the list of mxArrays must be freed by `mxFree` when there is no need for it any more; see Commands 198.

```
integer*4 function matGetMatrix(mfp,name)
integer*4 mfp
character*(*) name
```
copies the mxArray **name** from the MAT-file that mfp points to. It returns a pointer to the mxArray if it succeeded, otherwise 0. Free the memory of the mxArray by `mxFreeMatrix` when there is no need for it any more; see Commands 198.

```
integer*4 function matGetNextMatrix(mfp)
integer*4 mfp
```
copies the next mxArray in the MAT-file that mfp points to. It returns a pointer to the mxArray if it succeeded, otherwise 0. Free the memory of the mxArray by `mxFreeMatrix` when there is no need for it any more; see Commands 198.

```
integer*4 function matPutMatrix(mfp,name)
integer*4 mp,mfp
character*(*) name
```
writes the mxArray **name** to the MAT-file that mfp points to. If the mxArray already exists in the MAT-file it is overwritten. It returns 0 if it succeeded, otherwise a non-zero value.

```
integer*4 function matGetFull(mfp,name,m,n,pr,pi)
integer*4 mfp,m,n,pr,pi
character*(*) name
```
copies the full $m \times n$ matrix **name**, containing double precision floating point numbers, from the MAT-file that mfp points to. The parameter *pr* is a pointer to the real part of the matrix and *pi* is a pointer to the imaginary part. The parameters m, n, *pr* and *pi* are set by the function. It returns 0 if the operation succeeded, otherwise 1. Free the memory used by the real and imaginary parts of the matrix by `mxFree` when there is no need for it any more; see Commands 198.

| Commands 204 | (CONTINUED) |

```
integer*4 function matPutFull(mfp,name,m,n,pr,pi)
integer*4 mfp,m,n,pr,pi
character*(*) name
```
is analogous to the function above, but instead writes the full $m \times n$ matrix **name**, containing double precision floating point numbers, to the MAT-file. If the mxArray already exists in the MAT-file it is overwritten.

```
integer*4 function matGetString(mfp,name,str,strlen)
integer*4 mfp,strlen
character*(*) name,str
```
copies the string **str** of maximal length *strlen* from the MAT-file that mfp points to. It returns 0 if the operation succeeded, 1 if **str** is not a string, 2 if **str** is longer than *strlen* and 3 if a file error occurred.

```
integer*4 function matPutString(mfp,name,str)
integer*4 mfp
character*(*) name,str
```
writes the string **str** as a string mxArray by the name **name** on the MAT-file that mfp points to. It returns 0 if the operation succeeded, otherwise 1.

```
subroutine matDeleteMatrix(mfp,name)
integer*4 mfp
character*(*) name
```
deletes the mxArray **name** from the MAT-file that mfp points to. It returns 0 if it succeeded, otherwise a non-zero value.

For compilation and linking of FORTRAN programs that use MAT-files, use the following commands:

- **UNIX:** Write the following at the system prompt, as one unbroken line:

  ```
  f77 -I/.../matlab/extern/include -o programname sourcecode.for
  -L/.../matlab/extern/lib/... -R/.../matlab/extern/lib/...
  -lmat -lmx -lmi -lut
  ```

  The three dots, . . ., in the paths above indicate that these parts of the paths are system dependent, **programname** is what one wishes to call the program and **sourcecode.for** is a list of the files of source code in FORTRAN that one wishes to compile. If desired, debug and optimization flags can be set; see the documentation for the compiler.

- **Macintosh:** See the MATLAB 5 manual *Application Program Interface Guide*.

15.3.3 Calling MATLAB from FORTRAN

To call MATLAB from FORTRAN, a MATLAB engine must first be started. This is very simple, and is done by a call to engOpen; see Commands 205.

The next thing to do is to transfer the mxArrays that are to be manipulated in MATLAB. This is performed in two steps:

1. The first step is to convert the mxArrays to a format understood by MATLAB. The routines starting with mxCreate are used to create an mxArray of the same size as the data type that is to be transferred, and it is named by mxSetName. All routines are described in Section 15.3.1. Thereafter the data type is copied from the FORTRAN format to the MATLAB format, which is something not needed in C. This is done by the routines starting with mxCopy; see Commands 197.

2. The second step is to put the matrices in the MATLAB workspace. This is done by the routines that start with engPutMatrix or engPutFull; see Commands 205.

MATLAB is now ready to receive commands. These are given as in the ordinary command window, but now in a string passed to the function engEvalString.

Thereafter it remains to perform the process of conversion in the other direction.

This may sound rather complicated, but an example makes it clearer.

■ **Example 15.5**

Suppose we have a matrix in a FORTRAN program which we want to study using computer graphics in some way. Then it is a good idea to use MATLAB for the visualizations. We write the following FORTRAN program and store it in the file **plotm.for**:

```fortran
      program main
      implicit none

      integer ep
      integer A_ptr
      integer A
      integer i, j
      double precision Temp(10, 10)
      integer mxCreateFull, mxGetPr, engOpen
      integer engPutMatrix, engEvalString, engClose, stat

C     Create a new matrix.
```

```
        A_ptr = mxCreateFull(10, 10, 0)
        call mxSetName(A_ptr, "A")
        A = mxGetPr(A_ptr)
        do 100 i = 1, 10
           do 110 j = 1, 10
              Temp(i, j) = j * j * i * i
110        continue
100     continue
        call mxCopyReal8ToPtr(Temp, A, 100)

C       Start the MATLAB Engine.
        ep = engOpen("/opt/matlab52/bin/matlab")
C       Transfer the new matrix.
        stat = engPutMatrix(ep, A_ptr)
C       Preform the command mesh(A) and save.
        stat = engEvalString(ep, "mesh(A);")
        stat = engEvalString(ep, "print picture.eps -deps;")

C       Finish.
        stat = engClose(ep)
        call mxFreeMatrix(A_ptr)
        stop
        end
```

To compile the program in a UNIX environment, write the following at the system prompt, as one unbroken line:

```
f77 -I/opt/matlab52/extern/include -o plotm plotm.for
-L/opt/matlab52/extern/lib/sol2 -R/opt/matlab52/extern/lib/sol2
-leng -lmat -lmx -lmi -lut
```

Note that all paths are system dependent. When the program is executed we get Figure 15.1.

■

Calls to MATLAB are handled by the following **engine routines**. Note that these routines are currently not available for Windows or Macintosh, but for Windows they are nevertheless available in C.

Commands 205   MATLAB ENGINE ROUTINES IN FORTRAN

```
integer*4 function engOpen(startcmd)
integer*4 ep
character*(*) startcmd
```
starts a MATLAB engine, where **startcmd** is a string containing the starting command, usually "matlab". It returns a pointer *ep* to the MATLAB engine if it succeeded, otherwise 0.

```
subroutine engOutputBuffer(ep,p,n)
integer*4 ep,n
character *(*) p
```
defines a text buffer **p** of size *n* to the MATLAB engine that *ep* points to. The text that is normally written on the screen is stored here.

```
integer*4 function engEvalString(ep,command)
integer*4 ep
character*(*) command
```
evaluates the MATLAB commands in the string **command** in the MATLAB engine that *ep* points to. It returns 0 if it succeeded, otherwise a non-zero value.

```
integer*4 function engGetMatrix(ep,name)
integer*4 ep
character*(*) name
```
copies the mxArray **name** from the workspace in the MATLAB engine that *ep* points to. It returns a pointer to the mxArray if it succeeded, otherwise 0. Free the memory used by the mxArray with mxFreeMatrix when it is no longer needed, see Commands 198.

```
integer*4 function engPutMatrix(ep,mp)
integer*4 mp, ep
```
copies the mxArray that *mp* points to to the workspace in the MATLAB engine that *ep* points to. If the mxArray already exists in the workspace it is replaced. It returns 0 if the operation succeeded, otherwise 1.

```
integer*4 function engGetFull(ep,name,m,n,pr,pi)
integer*4 ep,m,n,pr,pi
character*(*) name
```
copies the full $m \times n$ matrix **name**, containing double precision floating point numbers, from the workspace in the MATLAB engine that *ep* points to. The parameter *pr* is a pointer to the real part of the matrix and *pi* is a pointer to the imaginary part. The parameters *m, n, pr* and *pi* are set by the function. It returns 0 if the operation succeeded, otherwise 1. Free the memory used by the real and imaginary parts of the matrix by mxFree when there is no need for it any more; see Commands 198.

Commands 205	(CONTINUED)

```
integer*4 function engPutFull(ep,name,m,n,pr,pi)
integer*4 ep,m,n,pr,pi
character*(*) name
```
is analogous to the function above, but instead copies the full $m \times n$ matrix **name**, which contains double precision floating point numbers, to the workspace. If the mxArray already exists in the workspace it is overwritten.

```
integer*4 function engClose(ep)
integer*4 ep
```
closes the MATLAB engine that *ep* points to. It returns 0 if it succeeded, otherwise 1.

For compilation and linking of FORTRAN programs which call MATLAB, use the following commands:

- **UNIX**: Write the following at the system prompt, as one unbroken line:

  ```
  f77 -I/.../matlab/extern/include -o programname sourcecode.for
  -L/.../matlab/extern/lib/... -R/.../matlab/extern/lib/...
  -leng -lmat -lmx -lmi -lut
  ```

  The three dots, . . ., in the paths above indicate that these parts of the paths are system dependent, **programname** is what one wishes to call the program and **sourcecode.for** is a list of the files of source code in FORTRAN that one wishes to compile. If desired, debug and optimization flags can be set; see the documentation for the compiler.

15.3.4 Calling FORTRAN from MATLAB

This section starts with a simple example describing calls to FORTRAN from MATLAB. A call to FORTRAN in MATLAB is done in the same way as a call to an ordinary function file, that is an M-file.

A MEX-file uses the same routines and matrix format that one uses in FORTRAN to call MATLAB. However, now the so called MEX routines are also used.

The file must have a main function called `mexFunction`, which is the function MATLAB calls. This routine has four parameters: the number of input arguments, the number of output arguments, and two arrays of pointers to these arguments. This function will thereafter call any computing routines.

■ **Example 15.6**

We create a MEX-file that from a given matrix returns a matrix where the elements have been multiplied with their row indices. The following FORTRAN program is stored in the file **rmult.for**.

```fortran
C     A routine multiplying the elements with their row indices.
      subroutine radMult(Out, In, M, N)
      integer M, N
C     Dynamic memory in Fortran 77!
      real*8 Out(M, N), In(M, N)

      integer i, j

      do 100 i = 1, M
         do 110 j = 1, N
            Out(i, j) = real(i * In(i, j))
110      continue
100   continue

      return
      end
C     This routine is called by MATLAB.
      subroutine mexFunction(nlhs, plhs, nrhs, prhs)
      integer nlhs, nrhs
      integer plhs(*), prhs(*)

      integer In_ptr, Out_ptr
      integer In, Out
      integer M, N
      integer mxGetPr, mxGetM, mxGetN
      integer mxCreateFull, mxIsFull, mxIsDouble

C     Check the number of arguments and their type.
      In_ptr = prhs(1)
      In = mxGetPr(In_ptr)
      if (nrhs .ne. 1) then
         call mexErrMsgTxt("Only one input argument allowed!")
      elseif(nlhs .ne. 1) then
         call mexErrMsgTxt("Only one output argument allowed!")
      endif
      if ((mxIsFull(In_ptr) .ne. 1) .or.
     $   (mxIsDouble(In_ptr) .ne. 1)) then
         call mexErrMsgTxt ("Input argument must be a full
     $        floating point matrix!")
      endif

C     Create a new matrix.
      M = mxGetM(In_ptr)
      N = mxGetN(In_ptr)
      Out_ptr = mxCreateFull(M, N, 0)
      Out = mxGetPr(Out_ptr)
```

```
C       Calls a routine that operates on the matrix.
        call radMult(%val(Out), %val(In), M, N)

C       Returns the new matrix ...
        plhs(1) = Out_ptr
        return
        end
```

Before compilation in a UNIX environment, one has to copy the file

/opt/matlab52/bin/mexopts.sh

to the same directory as the program. Then one should edit this file and under the title sol2) set:

```
LDFLAGS=$"$-G -M $MATLAB/extern/lib/sol2/$MAPFILE
                    -R $MATLAB/extern/lib/sol2
                    -L $MATLAB/extern/lib/sol2
                    -leng -lmat -lmx -lmi -lut$"$
```

Now it is possible to compile the program by (written at the system prompt):

```
/opt/matlab52/bin/mex rmult.for
```

Note that the paths are system dependent.

When the program has been compiled, we can write the following at the MATLAB prompt:

```
New = rmult([1 2 3;1 2 3;1 2 3])

New =
        1       2       3
        2       4       6
        3       6       9
```

∎

In the command tables below we describe all the MEX routines. These are used in MEX-files and can be seen as compiled M-files written in FORTRAN.

To let MATLAB be able to call a routine written in FORTRAN, one has to write an interface function called mexFunction. From the MEX-file one can also make calls in the 'other direction', that is to MATLAB from FORTRAN, by the routines mexCallMATLAB and mexEvalString.

Commands 206   INTERFACE TO MATLAB IN FORTRAN

```
subroutine mexFunction(nlhs,plhs,nrhs,prhs)
integer*4 nlhs,nrhs,plhs(*),prhs(*)
```
is the interface function to MATLAB. The parameter *nlhs* is the number of output arguments and **plhs** is a vector of pointers to these arguments. Similarly, *nrhs* is the number of input arguments and **prhs** is a vector of pointers to these arguments. The input arguments must not be altered in the FORTRAN program.

```
integer*4 function mexCallMATLAB(nlhs,plhs,nrhs,prhs,name)
integer*4 nlhs,nrhs,plhs(*),prhs(*)
character*(*) name
```
calls a MATLAB function, an M-file or a MEX-file. The parameter *nlhs* is the number of output arguments (must be less than or equal to 50) and **plhs** is a vector of pointers to these arguments. Similarly, *nrhs* is the number of input arguments (must be less than or equal to 50) and **prhs** is a vector of pointers to these arguments. The string **name** contains the name of the function one wants to call, and if it is an operator it must be placed within single quote characters, for example '+'. It returns 0 if the operation succeeded, otherwise a non-zero value. Free the memory used by the mxArrays that **plhs** points to by mxFree when they are no longer in use; see Commands 198.

```
integer*8 function mexCallMATLAB(nlhs,plhs,nrhs,prhs,name)
integer*4 nlhs,nrhs
integer*8 plhs(*),prhs(*)
character*(*) name
```
is analogous to the function above, but for the Alpha and SGI64 platforms.

```
subroutine mexSetTrapFlag(trap_flag)
integer*4 trap_flag
```
is used for handling errors when using mexCallMATLAB. If MATLAB discovers an error in the call to mexCallMATLAB the execution of the MEX-file is stopped and one gets back to the MATLAB prompt. Exactly the same thing happens if *trap_flag* is set to 0, but if, on the other hand, it is set to 1, then the MEX-file will regain control.

```
integer*4 function mexEvalString(command)
character*(*) command
```
executes the MATLAB command **command** in the caller's workspace. There is no possibility to transfer the results back to the MEX program. All input arguments to the **command** must be found in the caller's workspace. It returns 0 if the operation succeeded, otherwise a non-zero value.

```
integer*4 function mexAtExit(ExitFcn)
subroutine ExitFcn()
```
defines a function that is called when the MEX program is about to exit. It is used, for example, to close files. Always returns 0.

In addition to transferring data as parameters in mexFunction it is also possible to read and write data directly in the workspaces of MATLAB.

Commands 207	TRANSFERRING DATA TO AND FROM MATLAB IN FORTRAN

```
integer*4 function mexGetMatrix(name)
character*(*) name
```
copies the mxArray **name** from the caller's workspace. It returns a pointer to the copied mxArray if the operation succeeded, otherwise 0. Free the memory used by the mxArray by `mxFree` when it is no longer in use; see Commands 198.

```
integer*4 function mexGetGlobal(name)
character*(*) name
```
is analogous to the function above, but copies the mxArray from the global workspace in MATLAB.

```
integer*4 function mexPutMatrix(mp)
integer*4 mp
```
is analogous to the function `mxGetMatrix`, but copies the mxArray to the caller's workspace. It returns 0 if the operation succeeded, otherwise 1.

```
integer*4 function mexGetMatrixPtr(name)
character*(*) name
```
returns a pointer to the mxArray **name** in the caller's workspace. This makes it possible to read and modify the mxArray in the MEX program. Do not free the memory to this mxArray!

```
integer*4 function mexGetFull(name,m,n,pr,pi)
integer*4 m,n,pr,pi
character*(*) name
```
copies the full $m \times n$ matrix **name**, containing double precision floating point numbers, from the caller's workspace. The parameter pr is a pointer to the real part of the matrix and pi is a pointer to the imaginary part (m, n, pr and pi are set by the function). It returns 0 if the operation succeeded, otherwise 1. Free the memory used by the real and imaginary parts of the matrix by `mxFree` when there is no need for it any more; see Commands 198.

```
integer*4 function mexPutFull(name,m,n,pr,pi)
integer*4 m,n,pr,pi
character*(*) name
```
is analogous to the function above, but instead copies a full $m \times n$ matrix, containing double precision floating point numbers, to the caller's workspace.

The following routines are used to get the values of special constants in FORTRAN, for example machine epsilon and positive infinity. There are also routines for checking whether the value of a variable is equal to any of these constants.

Commands 208   SPECIAL CONSTANTS IN FORTRAN

```
real*8 function mexGetEps()
```
returns the value of machine epsilon in MATLAB.

```
real*8 function mexGetInf()
```
returns the value of inf, that is the positive infinity, in MATLAB.

```
integer*4 function mexIsInf(value)
real*8 value
```
returns 1 if *value* is inf, otherwise 0.

```
real*8 function mexGetNan()
```
returns the value of NaN (Not a Number) in MATLAB.

```
integer*4 function mexIsNaN(value)
real*8 value
```
returns 1 if *value* is NaN, otherwise 0.

```
integer*4 function mexIsFinite(value)
real*8 value
```
returns 1 if *value* is not inf or NaN, otherwise 0.

The following routines are used to write error messages and other text in the MATLAB command window:

Commands 209   ERROR HANDLING AND PRINTING IN FORTRAN

```
subroutine mexPrintf(format,arg1,arg2,...)
character*(*) format,arg1,arg2,...
```
writes, in ANSI C printf style, a string in the MATLAB window. The parameter **format** is an ANSI C format string, and *arg*1, *arg*2, ... are optional arguments to printf.

```
subroutine mexErrMsgTxt(error_msg)
character*(*) error_msg
```
writes the error message **error_msg** in the MATLAB window and stops the execution of the MEX-file.

For compilation and linking of FORTRAN programs that are called from MATLAB, use the following commands:

- **UNIX:** Write the following at the system prompt, as one unbroken line:

  ```
  .../matlab52/bin/mex sourcecode.for
  ```

  The three dots, ..., in the path above indicate that this part of the path is system dependent. The parameter **sourcecode.for** is a list of the files of source code in

FORTRAN that one wishes to compile. Possibly one must configure the compilation or linking; see the MATLAB 5 manual *Application Program Interface Guide* and Example 15.6.

- **Windows:** Write the following at the MATLAB prompt:

```
mex sourcecode.for
```

Possibly one must configure the compilation or linking; see the MATLAB 5 manual *Application Program Interface Guide*.

- **Macintosh:** See the MATLAB 5 manual *Application Program Interface Guide* for configuration. When this is done one can write the following at the MATLAB prompt:

```
mex sourcecode.for
```

The created MEX-file will get a suffix that is system dependent. One can check what suffix is used by the system with the help of the MATLAB command `mexext`.

It is possible to debug MEX programs, but then the compiler flag −g must be added. In a UNIX environment, after compilation, `matlab −Ddbx` is entered at the system prompt, followed by `run` when MATLAB has been loaded. At the MATLAB prompt `dbmex on` is entered and then the MEX-file one wants to debug is executed. Before the MEX-file is executed one will, however, get back to the debugger and have the chance to list the program, set break points, etc. From the MATLAB prompt one can go to the debugger by writing `dbmex stop`, and in the debugger one writes `continue` to get back to MATLAB. For debugging in Windows and on Macintosh see the MATLAB 5 manual *Application Program Interface Guide*.

15.4 MATLAB and advanced file management

In MATLAB, the the following commands can be useful in file management:

Commands 210   FILENAME

`fullfile(dir1,dir2, fname)`	concatenates a string. The strings **dir1, dir2,** ... (directory names) indicate the path to the file **fname**. The returned string will indicate the file **fname** with the complete path. MATLAB inserts directory separator characters between the directory names **dir1, dir2,** ... . This separator character is system dependent, for example, / in UNIX and \ on the PC.
`[path,name,ext,ver] fileparts(file)`	returns path, filename and extension in the variables **path**, **name**, and **ext**. In VMS the variable **ver** contains the version of the file.
`filesep`	returns the directory separator character that is used on the system.

Sometimes it might be necessary to use binary files in MATLAB. Therefore it must be possible to read and write files in any format if another program requires or generates files in a specific format. We begin with an example.

■ **Example 15.7**

Suppose we want to store the Hadamard matrix on a file. This can be done with the command save, as discussed in Section 2.8. However, it is not possible to control the format the matrix is stored in when the commands save and load are used. Using the low-level file handling commands in MATLAB, the format and precision, for example, can be controlled in detail.

We write the following code to export a 64×64 Hadamard matrix to the file **hada.mtl**:

```
fp        = fopen('hada.mtl','w');
antok     = fwrite(fp,hadamard(64),'int8');
[msg,err] = ferror(fp);

if err ~= 0
   disp('An error occurred when writing to the file:')
   disp(msg)
end

err = fclose(fp);

if err ~= 0
   disp('Could not close the file.')
end
```

■

As can be seen in the example, the file must first be opened in writing mode. We also have to close the file afterwards. This was not necessary using the commands save and load.

The commands fopen and fclose are used to open and close files in MATLAB.

| Commands 211 | OPENING AND CLOSING BINARY FILES |

`fopen(filename,op)`	opens the file named in the string **filename** and returns a file pointer, or -1 if an error occurred.
	The string **op** indicates which operations are possible to the file, and can take the following values:

`'r'`	read only.
`'r+'`	read and write.
`'w'`	overwrite old file, or create new if the file does not exist. Read only.
`'w+'`	overwrite old file, or create new if the file does not exist. Read and write.
`'a'`	append an old file, or create new if the file does not exist. Write only.
`'a+'`	append an old file or create a new if it does not exist. Read and write.

	The letters `'r'`, `'w'`, and `'a'` stand for read, write, and append, respectively. PC and VMS users must separate between binary files and text files. This is done with an additional `'t'` in the string **op**; see `help fopen`.
`[fp,msg] = fopen(filename,op, ark)`	does the same as above. If an error occurs, fp is assigned the value -1 and an error message is stored in the string **msg** to interpret the error message, see a textbook on C. The string **arch** determines the machine format in which the data is stored; type `help fopen` to get more information.
`[filename,op,ark] = fopen(fp)`	returns information about which file fp is referring to. The string **filename** is the name of the file, the string **op** the mode the file was opened in, and the string **arch** the machine format the file was opened.
`fclose(fp)`	closes the file fp. It returns -1 if it failed, or 0 if everything went well.
`fclose('all')`	closes all open files. It returns -1 if it failed, or 0 if everything went well.

■ **Example 15.8**

(a) We open the file **hada.mtl** for reading and appending:

```
[fp,msg] = fopen('hada.mtl','a+');

if fp == -1
  disp(msg)
end
```

```
[f,op,ark] = fopen(fp)
err            = fclose(fp)

if err ~= 0
  disp('Could not close the file.')
end

f =
      hada.mtl

op =
      a+

ark =
      ieee-be

err =
      0
```

(b) We close the file opened in (a):
```
err = fclose(fp)

err = 0
```

■

There are two commands, `fwrite` and `fread`, to write and read binary data from the files.

Commands 212	WRITING TO AND READING FROM BINARY FILES

`fwrite(fp,A,prec)`	writes the matrix **A** column by column to the file fp. The function returns the number of written elements. The string **prec** determines the precision used. There are more than 20 different precisions available. Type `help fwrite` for more information. A fourth argument can be used to write empty bytes between the elements of **A**.
`fread(fp)`	reads and returns data from the file fp.
`[A,c] = fread(fp,s,prec)`	reads data from the file fp to the matrix **A**. The size of **A** is determined by s according to:

$s = n$	a column vector of length n.
$s = \text{inf}$	all the data from fp are read into a column vector.
$\mathbf{s} = [m, n]$	an $m \times n$ matrix is read column by column from fp.

The scalar c returns the number of elements read, without error, from the file.

`feof(fp)`	returns 1 if the end of the file fp is reached, and 0 if not.

■ **Example 15.9**

We type the following to read the file **hada.mtl** created in Example 15.7:

```
clear;

fp = fopen('hada.mtl','r');
A  = fread(fp,[64,64],'int8');

fclose(fp);
whos
nnz(A-hadamard(64))     % Just checking...
```

which gives

Name	Size	Elements	Bytes	Density	Complex
A	64 by 64	4096	32768	Full	No
ans	1 by 1	1	8	Full	No
fp	1 by 1	1	8	Full	No

```
Grand total is 4098 elements using 32784 bytes

ans =
      0
```

that is, it is the same Hadamard matrix that we wrote to the file.   ■

MATLAB can create and read formatted text files. In these operations MATLAB reads and writes the elements column by column. However, text files are always read row by row; thus a transposition might be necessary.

Commands 213	WRITING AND READING FORMATTED TEXT FILES

fprintf(fp,fstr,A, ...)	writes the elements of the matrix or matrices **A**, ... to the file fp in the format according to the string **fstr**. This string can contain format characters like in the C programming language. See Table 15.1 for a list of the most important codes, see a textbook in C or type help fprintf for more information. The function returns the number of written elements.
fprintf(fstr,A,..)	writes formatted data to the screen.

Commands 213   (CONTINUED)

`[A,c] =` `fscanf(fp,fstr,s)`	reads data from the file fp to the matrix **A**. If **s** is a scalar, then **A** becomes a column vector. If **s** = $[m, n]$, then **A** becomes an $m \times n$ matrix read column by column from fp. The string **fstr** determines the format of the data to be read, and uses the same format characters as `fprintf`.
`fgetl(fp)`	reads the next line from the file fp to a string. This string is returned.
`fgets(fp)`	reads the next line from the file fp to a string including `eol` (end of line) characters. This string is returned.

The characters used in the format string of the commands `fprintf` and `fscanf`, and also in the commands `sprintf` and `sscanf` defined in Section 5.1.2, are listed in Table 15.1.

Table 15.1   FORMAT CODES TO THE COMMANDS
                    FPRINTF AND SPRINTF

Control characters		Format codes	
`\n`	new line	`%e`	scientific format, lower-case e
`\r`	beginning of the line	`%E`	scientific format, upper-case E
`\b`	back space	`%f`	decimal format
`\t`	tab	`%s`	string
`\f`	new page	`%u`	integer
`''`	apostrophe, '	`%i`	follows the type
`\\`	back slash	`%X`	hexadecimal, upper-case
`\a`	bell	`%x`	hexadecimal, lower-case

In addition to these, the width, the number of decimals, and the justification can be specified. MATLAB usually aligns the numbers with right justification, but a minus sign between the percentage sign and the format code changes this to left justification. The field width and the number of decimals are also specified between the percentage sign and the format code, according to `%[-][#.#]F`, where the brackets indicate that the entry is optional, and the F is the format code; see Table 15.1.

■ **Example 15.10**

(a) Let us write the number π in different formats with the command `sprintf`:

```
twodec = sprintf('%4.2f',pi)   % Two decimals.

twodec =
          3.14
```

```
ninedec = ...
    sprintf('The number pi = %11.9f',pi)    % Nine decimals.
```

ninedec =

The number pi = 3.141592654

```
scfform = sprintf('%E',pi)    % Scientific large E.
```

scfform =

3.141593E+00

(b) The following program writes a formatted table of the function $f(x) = 1/x$ in the interval [0,4], to the next file **tab.txt**.

```
% Writes a formatted table of the function f(x) = 1/x.
% Right column is written as  integer in four positions,
% and the right column with three decimals in six positions.

x = 1:4;  Y = zeros(4,2);

Y(:,1) = x';%                        % First  column of Y.
Y(:,2) = 1 ./ x';                    % Second column of Y.

fp = fopen('tab.txt','w+');    % Opens file tab.txt.

fprintf(fp,'%4.0f \t %6.3f \n',Y');
fclose(fp);
```

When executing, these statements generate the file **tab.txt**. We can check the contents of this file with: `type tab.txt`.

```
1       1.000
2       0.500
3       0.333
4       0.250
```

(c) To read the file created in (b) we type:

```
fp      = fopen('tab.txt','r');
[Tab,c] = fscanf(fp,'%f %f',[2,4]);

fclose(fp);
Tab = Tab'
```

Tab =

1.0000   1.0000
2.0000   0.5000
3.0000   0.3330
4.0000   0.2500

Again, note that the read matrix must be transposed, since MATLAB creates matrices column by column, while the file is read row by row.

∎

In every file operation, an error can occur. This should generally be controlled after every file operation, something we have not done except in Example 15.7. The control is done by a call to the function `ferror` that generates an error code, and an error message if an error occurred in the last file operation.

Commands 214	ERROR MESSAGES

`msg = ferror(fp)`	returns an error message if an error occurred during the latest I/O operation on the file *fp*.
`[msg,errn] = ferror (fp,'clear')`	returns an error message as in the previous command, but also returns an error code that can be checked with a C language reference manual. If `'clear'` is specified, the error message buffer is cleared.

∎ **Example 15.11**

Preferably an error check should be done after each file operation:

```
fp          = fopen('tab.txt','r');
[Tab,c]     = fscanf(fp,'%f %f',[3,4]);
[msg,errn]  = ferror(fp);

if errn ~= 0
  disp('An error occurred when reading from tab.txt!')
  disp(msg)
end

fclose(fp);
Tab = Tab'
```

If **tab.txt** is the file we created in Example 15.10(b) the statements above give:

```
An error occurred when reading from tab.txt!
At end-of-file.

Tab =
    1.0000    1.0000    2.0000
    0.5000    3.0000    0.3330
    4.0000    0.2500         0
```

∎

There are three functions to control the position of the file pointer fp: `fseek`, `ftell`, and `frewind`. These can be used to move around in the file, and to check the position of the file pointer.

Commands 215   POSITION OF THE FILE POINTER

`frewind(fp)`	moves the file pointer fp to the beginning of the file.
`fseek(fp,nb,u)`	moves the file pointer to the position determined by u and nb, where nb is the number of bytes from the start specified by u as:

-1	the beginning of the file.
0	the current position.
1	the end of the file.

If

$nb < 0$	move the pointer nb bytes from u towards the beginning of the file.
$nb = 0$	move the pointer to u.
$nb > 0$	move the pointer nb bytes from u towards the end of the file.

`ftell(fp)`	returns the position of the file pointer as the number of bytes read from the beginning of the file. A negative number indicates that an error has occurred.

15.5 Additional cooperation with other programs

The possibilities of using MATLAB together with other programs are machine dependent. To see what is possible, read the manuals or ask the system manager. We mention a few examples in this section.

It is possible to read and write files in the Lotus 1-2-3 spreadsheet format WK1 and in an ASCII spreadsheet format. MATLAB 5.2 also has commands which make it possible to read and write hdf files and to write vrml files.

Commands 216	READ/WRITE SPECIAL FILE FORMATS

dlmread(fname,st,*r*, *c*,*v*)	reads an ASCII spreadsheet from the file **fname**. The cells in the spreadsheet have the delimiter **st**, for example, '\t' indicates tab. If *r* and *c* are given, the cells are read with the beginning in row *r* and column *c* (the numbering starts from 0). If the vector **v** = [*r*1, *c*1, *r*2, *c*2] is given, a part of the spreadsheet is read, where (*r*1, *c*1) is the upper left cell and (*r*2, *c*2) is the bottom right cell in the part to be read.
dlmwrite(fname,A, st,*r*,*c*)	converts a MATLAB matrix **A** to an ASCII spreadsheet which is saved in the file **fname**. The cells in the spreadsheet get the delimiter **st**. If *r* and *c* are given, the matrix **A** is written with the beginning in the spreadsheet cell in row *r* and column *c* (the numbering starts from 0).
wk1read(fname,*r*,*c*, *v*)	reads a Lotus 1-2-3 WK1 spreadsheet from the file **fname**. If *r* and *c* are given, the cells are read with the beginning in row *r* and column *c* (the numbering starts from 0). If **v** is given as a vector **v** = [*r*1, *c*1, *r*2, *c*2], a part of the spreadsheet is read, where (*r*1, *c*1) is the upper left cell and (*r*2, *c*2) is the bottom right cell in the part to be read. It is also possible to give an interval **v** as a string, for example 'a1...c5' or 'sales'.
wk1write(fname,A, st,*r*,*c*)	converts a MATLAB matrix **A** to a Lotus 1-2-3 WK1 spreadsheet which is saved in the file **fname**. If *r* and *c* are given, the matrix **A** is written with the beginning in the spreadsheet cell in row *r* and column *c* (the numbering starts from 0).
hdf	makes it possible to read and write files of the hdf format. For more information use help hdf. To be able to use the functions in MATLAB for hdf files, one must be familiar with the hdf library; information about this can be found at http://hdf.ncsa.uiuc.edu. See also the commands imread and imwrite in Commands 162.
vrml(h, *filename*)	writes a vrml 2.0 file that contains the graphical object with handle *h* and its children (if any). The file gets the name filename and, if no suffix is given, the suffix .wrl is added. If no filename is given, the file gets the name matlab.wrl.

If MATLAB is run under Microsoft Windows, it is possible to exchange data with other programs using DDE (Dynamic Data Exchange). This is specially developed between MS Word and MATLAB. Users who have access to the MATLAB Notebook Suite can write their own MATLAB commands interactively in Word, and mix the code with plain text and graphics generated by MATLAB. Furthermore, matrices can be handled via a matrix editor, etc.

In UNIX networks it is possible to start MATLAB engines on other computers, and thus perform computations on the computer with the most free computer capacity, while having the graphics and command windows on one's own computer.

There are many toolboxes for MATLAB. Here we mention a few important ones:

- The Signal Processing Toolbox   used for signal processing.
- The Optimization Toolbox   used for optimization.
- The Symbolic Math Toolbox   used for symbolic mathematics via a link to Maple V.

More information about these and other toolboxes can be found by typing `expo` and then choosing `TOOLBOXES`; see also Appendix C. Generally, they can be described as collections of M-files, where each collection is dedicated to a separate subject area.

The existing possibilities for using MATLAB together with other programs are large, and are likely to be further developed in future versions of MATLAB.

Appendix A
Step-by-Step
Introduction

This is a short introduction to MATLAB. We recommend that the commands are tried while reading. For detailed information about the commands used see references given for each section, and/or use help *or* helpdesk. *Almost all commands appear in Appendix D and the List of Command Tables, p. 535.*

A.1 Starting and quitting MATLAB

MATLAB is started by clicking on an icon or by typing matlab, depending on the computer in use. For more information read Section 2.1. The following appears in the MATLAB Command Window:

```
            < M A T L A B (R) >
    (c) Copyright 1984-98 The MathWorks, Inc.
            All Rights Reserved
            Version 5.2.0.3084
              Jan 17 1998


  To get started, type one of these: helpwin, helpdesk, or demo.
  For product information, type tour or visit www.mathworks.com.
```

It is a good idea to try some of these commands. The commands tour and demo should prove worthwhile. A command is given after the MATLAB prompt, and is processed when the return key is hit.

```
>> tour ↩
```

For the rest of this book we will **not** print the MATLAB prompt because it makes it more difficult to read. The commands are to be typed at the prompt, >>, but it will not be listed for each row.

Note that the book uses different fonts for what the user types at the prompt and for what MATLAB returns for an answer; see Section 1.2.

To quit MATLAB simply type `quit` and press return. From here on we do not stress the return at the end of the command lines.

```
>> quit
```

If you want to abort current computations in MATLAB press the 'CTRL' button and the 'c' button simultaneously. MATLAB stops whatever it is doing and the screen prompter returns indicating MATLAB is ready to start running:

```
>>
```

A.2 Basic assignments and calculations

MATLAB can be used as an ordinary calculator in a natural way:

```
5011 + 13
```

```
ans =
        5024
```

Several commands on the same line:

```
2^5, 2*(3+2)
```

```
ans =
     32
```

```
ans =
     10
```

Normally variables are used for assigned values or results. If no assignment is made, MATLAB stores the result in the variable named *ans*. Now let us define and assign some variables:

```
x = 14
```

```
x =
     14
```

```
y = 3*x
```

```
y =
    42
```

All the elementary mathematical functions are defined in MATLAB (see Section 2.4):

```
sin(x)
```

```
ans =
    0.9906
```

Parentheses, '( )', can be used as in mathematics.

```
u = 2*x - y;
w = 2*(x-y);
exp((2-u)/(w-2))
```

```
ans =
    0.7589
```

Note that a semicolon, ';', at the end of the command makes MATLAB do the assignment 'quietly': nothing is echoed to the screen by MATLAB, but the computation is performed as usual.

Variables in MATLAB are usually vectors or matrices:

```
vcol = [1;2;3;4], vrow = [5 6 7 8]
```

```
vcol =
    1
    2
    3
    4
```

```
vrow =
    5    6    7    8
```

```
A = [1 2 3 4;5 6 7 8;9 10 11 12]
```

```
A =
    1    2    3    4
    5    6    7    8
    9   10   11   12
```

Note that the rows are separated by semicolons.

Functions can be applied on vectors or matrices in a single command:

```
sqrt(vcol)
```

```
ans =
    1.0000
    1.4142
    1.7321
    2.0000
```

By now we have several variables defined. To get a list of these we can type:

```
who
```

```
Your variables are:
```

A	u	vrow	x
ans	vcol	w	y

The command whos will also show current variables but with some additional information about each variable. Try the command and see how to distinguish whether the variable is a scalar or a vector.

MATLAB remembers all variables defined during a session. To remove variables, type:

```
clear
```

All previous variables are now deleted. If who is typed nothing is returned; see Section 2.3. Vectors can be generated by the colon operator; see Section 4.3.

```
vector = 0:8
```

```
vector =
    0    1    2    3    4    5    6    7    8
```

```
vector2 = 0:0.5:2
```

```
vector2 =
    0    0.5000    1.0000    1.5000    2.0000
```

The commands `linspace` and `logspace` can also be used to create vectors; see Section 4.3. Computations can be carried out on the vectors directly by elementwise operations:

```
values = 2.^vector
```

```
values =
    1    2    4    8   16   32   64  128  256
```

Note the period prior to the operator `^`. It indicates that the operation should be carried out for each element in the vector; see Section 3.5.

It is possible to repeat previously given commands with the help of the arrow keys; see Section 2.1. It is very time-saving to avoid rewriting a long statement if a typing error was made.

Vectors or matrices can be included inside the brackets defining a new expression, but of course the sizes must now match:

```
Table = [vector;vector.^2;vector.^3]
```

```
Table =
    0    1    2    3    4    5    6    7    8
    0    1    4    9   16   25   36   49   64
    0    1    8   27   64  125  216  343  512
```

A.3 Simple graphics

MATLAB is an excellent tool for simple, as well as advanced, figures. To draw graphics in MATLAB the data has to be computed and stored in vectors or matrices. To plot a graph of the first powers of 2, for example, there are three steps. First, generate a vector of values. Second, evaluate the function for these values. Third, plot the vectors versus each other; see Section 13.1. Since we already have created the variables `vector` and `values` in Section A.2, we can directly plot the graph with:

```
plot(vector,values)
```

The result is a simple graph for which the scaling is automatically done; see Figure A.1.

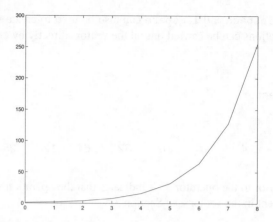

Figure A.1 *The function 2^x as a piecewise linear graph.*

To obtain a smoother graph, use more values, for example 100 values between 0 and 8. The linspace command is very useful when creating long vectors: try typing:

```
vector = linspace(0,8,100);
values = 2.^vector;
clf;
plot(vector,values);
```

The command clf clears the graphical window before plotting the function. Now let us try different line types. Give the command plot as above, now including the extra argument ':' or '+'. These can be combined with colors; for example, for a blue dash-dotted curve:

```
plot(vector,values,'b-.');
```

Other line styles and colors can be found in Section 13.1, especially Table 13.1.

Three-dimensional graphics are drawn in much the same way. Generate the data into matrices and plot them, now using, for example, the surf or the mesh commands. To generate the values needed when plotting a function of two variables is a little bit more tricky. These values, or grid points, are discrete points in a plane. The best way to generate this grid is to use the command meshgrid, as described in Section 13.4.

```
vector2 = 0:0.5:8;
[X,Y] = meshgrid(vector2);
mesh(X,Y,2.^X+2.^Y);
```

The brackets, '[ ]', are used to receive more than one return argument. Recollect that the semicolon, ';', supresses the echoing of the result. This is worth remembering if the matrix is big. The resulting mesh plot can be seen in Figure A.2.

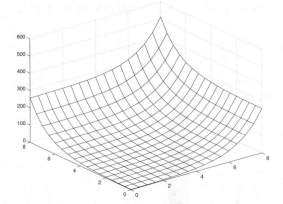

Figure A.2 *The function* $2^x + 2^y$ *plotted with mesh.*

A surf plot is quite similar to a mesh plot, but now the actual surface is drawn instead of the grid lines, see Figure A.3. Surf plots are generated with the command `surf`.

```
surf(X,Y,cos(X./2).*sin(Y./2));
```

This result is shown in Figure A.3.

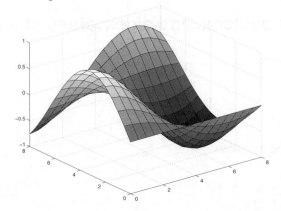

Figure A.3 *The surface graph of the function* $\cos(x/2)\sin(y/2)$ *using the* `surf` *command.*

To draw statistical diagrams, use the command `hist`; see Section 6.5. To illustrate, we generate a random vector of numbers in the interval [0, 1] with the command `rand`, which is described in Section 4.1.

```
random = rand(1,7)
```

```
random =
     0.4553 0.3495 0.4523 0.8089 0.9317 0.6516 0.2152
```

```
hist(random);
```

The `hist` result is shown in Figure A.4. Try other commands on the same vector, for example `stairs` and `bar`; see Section 6.5.

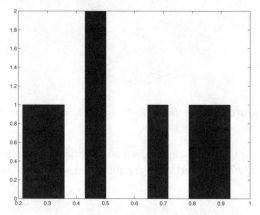

Figure A.4 *A histogram plot.*

A.4 Linear systems and eigenvalues of matrices

We define the matrices:

$$\mathbf{A} = \begin{pmatrix} 3 & 4 & 5 \\ 5 & 2 & 2 \\ 1 & 2 & 3 \end{pmatrix} \qquad \mathbf{B} = \begin{pmatrix} 1 & 2 & 3 \\ 1 & 1 & 1 \end{pmatrix}$$

with the following statements:

```
A = [3 4 5;5 2 2;1 2 3];
B = [1 2 3;1 1 1];
```

The matrices can be multiplied by the command B*A, which results in:

```
ans =
     16    14    18
      9     8    10
```

But A*B results in:

```
??? Error using ==> *
Inner matrix dimensions must agree.
```

since this matrix multiplication is not defined! See Section 3.2.

To compute the determinant of **A**, use the command `det`:

```
det(A)
```

```
ans =
    -6
```

The determinant of **B** is not defined. Also try `trace`, `null`, `orth` and `inv` on the same matrices. These commands are all defined in Section 7.1.

Now we focus on the system of linear equations:

$$3x_1 + 4x_2 + 5x_3 = 25$$
$$5x_1 + 2x_2 + 2x_3 = 18$$
$$x_1 + 2x_2 + 3x_3 = 13$$

or in matrix notation $\mathbf{Ax} = \mathbf{b}$, with **A** as above and **b**:

$$\mathbf{b} = \begin{pmatrix} 25 \\ 18 \\ 13 \end{pmatrix}$$

This system is solved with the backslash operator, '\':

```
b = [25;18;13];
A\b
```

```
ans =
    2.0000
    1.0000
    3.0000
```

Overdetermined systems are solved in the same way. Since these systems usually do not have true solutions, MATLAB uses the method of least squares to solve them. See Sections 7.2 and 7.7.

Eigenvalues and eigenvectors are determined with the command `eig`, for example for the matrix **A** from above:

```
[EigenVectors,EigenValues] = eig(A)
```

```
EigenVectors =
   -0.7111    -0.4501    -0.0210
   -0.6185     0.8459    -0.7756
   -0.3342    -0.2863     0.6309
```

```
EigenValues =
    8.8291          0          0
         0    -1.3373          0
         0          0     0.5082
```

The columns of the matrix **EigenVectors** form the eigenvectors, and the diagonal elements of the matrix **EigenValues** are the eigenvalues; see Section 8.1.

A.5 Curve fitting and polynomials

Polynomials are represented by vectors with the coefficients as components; see Section 10.1. The polynomial:

$$p(x) = 2x^3 + x^2 + 5x + 17$$

is represented by the vector $\mathbf{p} = (2 \quad 1 \quad 5 \quad 17)$, and can be evaluated for any value with the command polyval:

```
p = [2 1 5 17];
polyval(p,0), polyval(p,2)
```

```
ans =
    17
```

```
ans =
    47
```

Polynomials can be differentiated with the command polyder, and multiplied with the command conv:

```
pprim = polyder(p)
```

```
pprim =
     6     2     5
```

which represents $p'(x) = 6x^2 + 2x + 5$.

```
psquare = conv(p,p)

psquare =
     4    4    21    78    59    170    289
```

which represents $p(x)^2 = 4x^6 + 4x^5 + 21x^4 + 78x^3 + 59x^2 + 170x + 289$.

Let us now plot all three polynomials using three subplots in the same figure. The command `subplot` is described in Section 13.3.

```
x = linspace(-2,2,50);

clf;
subplot(2,2,1);
plot(x,polyval(p,x));
xlabel('p(x)');

subplot(2,2,2);
plot(x,polyval(pprim,x));
xlabel('p''(x)');

subplot(2,2,3);
plot(x,polyval(psquare,x));
xlabel('p(x)^2');
```

The command `xlabel` writes a string below the current picture, at the x axis; see Figure A.5.

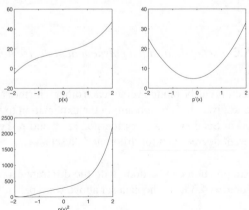

Figure A.5 *The polynomial* $p(x) = 2x^3 + x^2 + 5x + 17$, *its derivative and the polynomial* $p(x)^2$.

Polynomials can be used to fit curves to data. Assume that the following data has been acquired in an experiment, and entered into MATLAB:

```
x = 1:10;
y = [1 5 3 3 2 3 6 11 17 34];
```

Now the command `polyfit` returns the polynomial, that is the coefficients of the polynomial, of a specified degree that best fits the data in the least squares sense; see Section 10.4. As an example, the best polynomial of degree 4 is determined. Also, the original data is plotted in the same graph as the polynomial:

```
clf;
ypol = polyfit(x,y,4);
plot(x,y,'*',x,polyval(ypol,x),'b-');
legend('Experimental data','Least squares polynomial');
```

The result can be seen in Figure A.6.

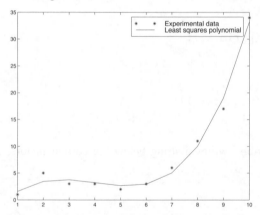

Figure A.6 *A set of data with a polynomial of degree 4 fitted to it.*

Notice that several vectors can be plotted versus each other with the same `plot` command. The command `legend` gives the box containing the explanation to the different vectors plotted. It is defined in Section 13.3. Try the `polyfit` and `polyval` commands for polynomials of different degrees and for different data sets.

Interpolation and extrapolation can be done with the different `interp` commands. To interpolate a value for $x = 4.3$ from the data set above we type:

```
interp1(x,y,4.3)
```

```
ans =
   2.7000
```

This is linear interpolation, also referred to as 'table look up'. Several other possibilities exist: type help interp1 to see them. Interpolation is described in Section 10.4.

A.6 Simple programming

A program is a sequence of MATLAB statements, often controlled by conditional statements and loops. It is convenient to store these commands in an M-file, which is a text file with the extension **.m**.

Consider the MATLAB statements below stored in the file **draw.m**:

```
% Program plotting functions.
% Comments can be made after %-sign.

% Displays explanatory text.

disp('This program plots f(x) in the interval [a,b]');

% Reads from user.

ftext = input('Give a function: ','s');
a     = input('Give lower bound a: ');
b     = input('Give upper bound b: ');

clf; fplot(ftext,[a b]);        % Plots the function.
```

This program is executed by typing draw after the MATLAB prompt. As an example:

```
This program plots f(x) in the interval [a,b].
Give a function: 2.*x.*cos(x.^2)
Give lower bound a:  0
Give upper bound b:  2.*pi
```

The result of the program with this input can be seen in Figure A.7.

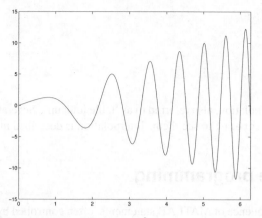

Figure A.7 *The function* $2x \cos x^2$ *drawn with the M-file* ***draw***.

The program **draw.m** is an example of a command file. There are also function files. A function file must also have the extension **.m**, and have the keyword `function` in the first line. As an example, consider the following functions, stored in the M-file **div.m**:

```
function y = div(n,d);

% This function computes the integer division
% thus n = rem(n,d) + y*d

y = (n-rem(n,d))/d;
```

This function can now be called as any other MATLAB function:

```
div(1234,7), check = 1234/7


ans =
    176


check =
    176.2857
```

Information about M-files can be found in Sections 2.9 and 12.3.

A.7 Analysis of functions

Finding a local minimum of a function of one variable is done with the command `fmin`, and for several variables with the command `fmins`; see Section 10.3.

We want to find a minimum of the function:

$$f(x) = \frac{x - 1.96}{x^2 + 1.15}$$

First, we create a function file that computes the value of the function $f(x)$. The file is named **f.m**.

```
function y = f(x)

y = (x-1.96)./(x.^2+1.15);
```

The command:

```
fmin('f',-1,1)
```

gives us the answer:

```
ans =
    -0.2742
```

To see if this is correct we plot the function by giving the command:

```
fplot('f',[-10 10]);
title('f(x) = (x-1.96)./(x.^2+1.15)');
grid;
```

The command `title` gave us a title to the figure. It is described in Section 13.3. The command `grid` added the grid and it is also described in Section 13.3. We can also find the exact location of the zeros, i.e., the x values for which $f(x) = 0$. This is done by the command `fzero` that requires a starting value for the iteration; see Section 10.2. In Figure A.8 we see that 2 is close to $f(x) = 0$ so we type:

```
fzero('f',2)
```

```
ans =
    1.9600
```

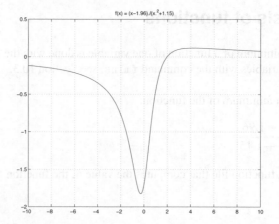

Figure A.8 *An M-file function plotted with* `fplot`.

A.8 Integrals

We can compute a definite integral by using the command quad described in Section 11.1. For computing:

$$\int_0^\pi \frac{\sin(x)}{x} \, dx$$

we must define the function $\sin(x)/x$ in an M-file which we name **sinx_x.m**:

```
function y = sinx_x(x)

y = sin(x)./x;
```

Now we simply type:

```
quad('sinx_x',1E-8,pi)
```

The result will be:

```
ans =
     1.8520
```

Note that this integral cannot be solved analytically. The function is shown in Figure A.9.

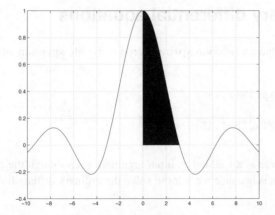

Figure A.9 *The function* $\sin(x)/x$ *in the interval* $-10 \le x \le 10$.

The area marked is the value of the integral. This area has been filled with the graphical object patch described in Section 14.2. First we plot the function **sinx_x** with the fplot command and add a grid.

```
fplot('sinx_x',[-10 10]); grid on;
```

Now we give the command patch and keep a 'handle' so that properties of the patch can be changed later on.

```
h = patch([0.001 0.001:0.01:pi pi], ...
    [0 sinx_x(0.001:0.01:pi) 0], 'r' )

h =
    73.0005
```

The first argument to patch defines the x coordinates of the edges of the plot. The second argument defines the y coordinates. The last argument defines the color in which the patch is drawn, in this case 'r' for red. We can now change the edge color of the patch by typing:

```
set(h,'EdgeColor',[0 0 1]);
```

To see other properties that can be manipulated with the set command type get(h). These commands are described in Section 14.2.

A.9 Ordinary differential equations

Suppose that we have a function **xprim**, stored in the file **xprim.m** and defined as:

```
function y = xprim(x,t)

y = (x-1.96)./(x.^3+1.15);
```

Besides the x, there is a t added as input argument even though the function does not depend on t. This is because we want to solve the ordinary differential equation:

$$\frac{dx}{dt} = \frac{x - 1.96}{x^3 + 1.15} \qquad (*)$$

with the MATLAB command ode45 described in Section 11.2.

First let us solve (∗) in the interval $0 \le t \le 10$ with initial condition $x(0) = 1$. The call to the ode45 command looks like:

```
[x1,t1] = ode45('xprim',[0 10],1);
```

The result is the two vectors **x1** and **t1** which we can plot:

```
clf;
plot(x1,t1);
```

Let us now solve equation (∗) in the same t-interval but with a different initial value $x(0) = -1$:

```
[x2,t2] = ode45('xprim',[0 10],-1);
```

We want this function to be plotted in the same figure so we give the command hold on before plotting the new vectors.

```
hold on;
plot(x2,t2,':');
hold off;
```

This gives us Figure A.10.

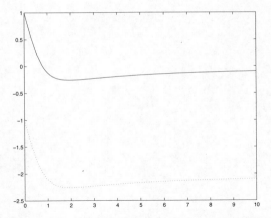

Figure A.10 *The solutions of the ordinary differential equation with two different initial values.*

Appendix B
Definitions and Basic Concepts in Linear Algebra

This is a concise presentation of basics in linear algebra and matrix algebra. All concepts treated are also included in MATLAB.

B.1 Vectors

A **linear space** consists of **vectors** which can be added and multiplied by scalars.

The linear space $\mathbb{R}^n$ consists of column vectors:

$$\mathbf{x} = \begin{pmatrix} x_1 \\ x_2 \\ \vdots \\ x_n \end{pmatrix} \qquad \mathbf{y} = \begin{pmatrix} y_1 \\ y_2 \\ \vdots \\ y_n \end{pmatrix}$$

with real **elements** x_k and y_k and **length** n.

In the linear space $\mathbb{C}^n$, the elements can be complex.

Addition is defined element by element:

$$\mathbf{x} + \mathbf{y} = \begin{pmatrix} x_1 + y_1 \\ x_2 + y_2 \\ \vdots \\ x_n + y_n \end{pmatrix}$$

Multiplication by a scalar α is defined element by element:

$$\alpha \mathbf{x} = \begin{pmatrix} \alpha x_1 \\ \alpha x_2 \\ \vdots \\ \alpha x_n \end{pmatrix}$$

The **null vector** has all its elements equal to zero:

$$\mathbf{0} = \begin{pmatrix} 0 \\ 0 \\ \vdots \\ 0 \end{pmatrix}$$

A set of p vectors $\mathbf{x}_1, \mathbf{x}_2, \dots, \mathbf{x}_p$ in the linear space are said to be **linearly dependent** if at least one of the vectors can be written as a linear combination of the others:

$$\mathbf{x}_p = \alpha_1 \mathbf{x}_1 + \cdots + \alpha_{p-1} \mathbf{x}_{p-1}$$

where α_i are scalars.

If this is not possible, the vectors are said to be **linearly independent**. The most common definition of linear independence is that $\alpha_1 \mathbf{x}_1 + \alpha_2 \mathbf{x}_2 + \cdots + \alpha_p \mathbf{x}_p = \mathbf{0}$ holds only for $\alpha_1 = \alpha_2 = \cdots = \alpha_p = 0$.

■ **Example B.1**

The vectors

$$\mathbf{x}_1 = \begin{pmatrix} 1 \\ 0 \\ 0 \end{pmatrix} \quad \mathbf{x}_2 = \begin{pmatrix} 1 \\ 1 \\ 0 \end{pmatrix} \quad \mathbf{x}_3 = \begin{pmatrix} 1 \\ 1 \\ 1 \end{pmatrix}$$

are linearly independent in $\mathbb{R}^3$.

■

The maximum number of linearly independent vectors in a space is called the **dimension** of the space. The spaces $\mathbb{R}^n$ and $\mathbb{C}^n$ have the dimension n. Note that in some cases it is convenient to say that $\mathbb{C}^n$ has the dimension $2n$, thus separating the real and imaginary parts.

A **basis** in a linear space is a set of vectors such that all vectors in that space can be written as a linear combination of these. The number of vectors in a basis is equal to the dimension of the space. There is an infinite number of bases in a linear space.

■ **Example B.2**

The vectors in Example B.1 form a basis in $\mathbb{R}^3$ and $\mathbb{C}^3$. The vectors:

$$\mathbf{e}_1 = \begin{pmatrix} 1 \\ 0 \\ 0 \end{pmatrix} \quad \mathbf{e}_2 = \begin{pmatrix} 0 \\ 1 \\ 0 \end{pmatrix} \quad \mathbf{e}_3 = \begin{pmatrix} 0 \\ 0 \\ 1 \end{pmatrix}$$

form a more common basis in the same space. We have:

$$\mathbf{x} = \begin{pmatrix} x_1 \\ x_2 \\ x_3 \end{pmatrix} = x_1 \mathbf{e}_1 + x_2 \mathbf{e}_2 + x_3 \mathbf{e}_3$$

that is an arbitrary vector in $\mathbb{R}^3$ can be expressed as a linear combination of the vectors of the basis. This is illustrated in Figure B.1.

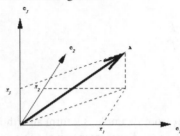

Figure B.1 *A vector and its components.*

■

The **scalar product** or **dot product** of two vectors $\mathbf{x}$ and $\mathbf{y}$ in $\mathbb{C}^n$, usually written $(\mathbf{x}, \mathbf{y})$ or $\langle \mathbf{x}, \mathbf{y} \rangle$ is defined by:

$$(\mathbf{x}, \mathbf{y}) = \sum_{i=1}^{n} \bar{x}_i y_i$$

The complex conjugate of x_i is not necessary if we restrict ourselves to $\mathbb{R}^n$. Using notations introduced in the next section, it holds that $(\mathbf{x}, \mathbf{y}) = \mathbf{x}^H \mathbf{y}$.

The **Euclidean norm** $\|\mathbf{x}\|_2$ of a vector in $\mathbb{C}^n$ is defined by:

$$\|\mathbf{x}\|_2^2 = (\mathbf{x}, \mathbf{x}) = \sum_{i=1}^{n} |x_i|^2 = \mathbf{x}^H \mathbf{x}$$

The norm measures the size or the length of a vector. There are also other norms, and some of them are introduced in Section B.6.

Two vectors $\mathbf{x}$ and $\mathbf{y}$ are said to be **orthogonal** if $(\mathbf{x}, \mathbf{y}) = 0$.

The **angle** θ between two vectors $\mathbf{x}$ and $\mathbf{y}$ is defined by:

$$\cos \theta = \frac{(\mathbf{x}, \mathbf{y})}{\|\mathbf{x}\|_2 \|\mathbf{y}\|_2}$$

We see that the angle between two orthogonal vectors is $\pi/2$ or 90 degrees, that is the vectors are perpendicular. The null vector is orthogonal to all vectors.

A set of non-zero vectors $\mathbf{x}_1, \mathbf{x}_2, \ldots, \mathbf{x}_p$ forms an **orthogonal system** if all vectors are mutually orthogonal. The vectors are also linearly independent, and thus orthogonality is stronger than linear independence. The vectors $\mathbf{x}_1, \mathbf{x}_2, \ldots, \mathbf{x}_p$ form an **orthonormal system** if they form an orthogonal system, and all have the Euclidean norm equal to one. The following holds for the vectors in an orthonormal system:

$$(\mathbf{x}_j, \mathbf{x}_k) = \begin{cases} 0 & j \neq k \\ 1 & j = k \end{cases}$$

■ **Example B.3**

The vectors $\mathbf{e}_1$, $\mathbf{e}_2$ and $\mathbf{e}_3$ from Example B.2 form an orthonormal system in $\mathbb{R}^3$ (and in $\mathbb{C}^3$). They represent the x, y, z axes, respectively, in a normal Cartesian coordinate system.

■

We could also have defined all the above concepts in terms of row vectors

$$\mathbf{v} = (v_1, v_2, \ldots, v_p)$$

instead of in terms of column vectors. However, there are several advantages in working with column vectors.

B.2 Matrices, an introduction

A **matrix** is a rectangular array of numbers arranged in **rows** and **columns**. A matrix with m rows and n columns is referred to as an $m \times n$ matrix. For instance, this is a 2×3 matrix:

$$\begin{pmatrix} 2 & 1 & 3 \\ 3 & -2 & 0 \end{pmatrix} = \begin{pmatrix} a_{11} & a_{12} & a_{13} \\ a_{21} & a_{22} & a_{23} \end{pmatrix}$$

The numbers in the matrix are referred to as the **elements** or the **components** of the matrix. If the matrix is denoted by $\mathbf{A}$, the elements of $\mathbf{A}$ are called a_{ij}, where i indicates the **row index** and j the **column index**, that is a_{ij} denotes the element in row i and column j.

An $n \times n$ matrix is said to be **square**.

The **size** of a matrix is given by the number of rows, m, and the number of columns, n. For square matrices, n is sometimes referred to as the **order** of the matrix.

The **main diagonal** starts in the top left-hand corner of the matrix and continues diagonally downwards to the right. The elements of the main diagonal are referred to as the **diagonal elements** a_{ii}. The **anti-diagonal** starts in the top right-hand corner, and continues diagonally to the left. The diagonals over and under the main diagonal are called the **super-diagonals** and **sub-diagonals**, respectively.

Addition of two matrices of the same size is defined element by element. The matrix $C = A + B$ has the elements $c_{ij} = a_{ij} + b_{ij}$.

Multiplication by a scalar is also defined element by element. The matrix αA has the elements αa_{ij}.

Multiplication of matrices is only defined if the number of columns in the left matrix is equal to the number of rows in the right matrix. The matrix $C = AB$, where A is an $m \times p$ matrix and B is a $p \times n$ matrix, is an $m \times n$ matrix with the elements:

$$c_{ij} = \sum_{k=1}^{p} a_{ik} b_{kj}$$

The element c_{ij} is the scalar product of row i in A and column j in B.

Even if AB is defined, BA may not be. If both A and B are square matrices of order n, then AB and BA are both defined, but usually $AB \neq BA$. Matrix multiplication is **not commutative**.

The **identity matrix** of order n, denoted by I or I_n, is an $n \times n$ matrix in which all the diagonal elements are 1 and all the off-diagonal elements are 0. A matrix multiplied with the identity matrix remains unchanged, thus it holds that $IA = A$ and $AI = A$.

A **column vector** can be seen as an $n \times 1$ matrix, and a **row vector** as a $1 \times n$ matrix. Sometimes it can be useful to regard a scalar as a 1×1 matrix.

If x is a column vector with n components, and A is an $n \times n$ matrix, then Ax is also a column vector with n components. This is called **matrix–vector multiplication**.

A **transposition** is a reflection in the main diagonal. The transposition operator is written ^{T}. If A is an $m \times n$ matrix with the elements a_{ij}, then the **transposed matrix** A^T is an $n \times m$ matrix with elements a_{ji}. A transposition can also be described as an interchange between rows and columns of a matrix in the sense that the first column of A is the first row in the transposed matrix, the second column of A the second row in the transposed matrix, and so on.

The **conjugate** of a matrix is a matrix in which all the elements are replaced by their complex conjugates. The result is written $\bar{\mathbf{A}}$. A common operation is conjugation and transposition, that is forming the matrix $\bar{\mathbf{A}}^T$ or the equivalent $\overline{\mathbf{A}^T}$. This matrix is usually written A^H, A^*, and in MATLAB $\mathbf{A}'$.

The **scalar product** of two column vectors $\mathbf{x}$ and $\mathbf{y}$ can now be written:

$$(\mathbf{x}, \mathbf{y}) = \sum_{i=1}^{n} \bar{x}_i y_i = \mathbf{x}^H \mathbf{y}$$

and the **Euclidean norm** can be written $\|\mathbf{x}\|_2 = \sqrt{\mathbf{x}^H \mathbf{x}}$. Note that $\mathbf{x}^H \mathbf{y}$ is a scalar, since it is the product of a $1 \times n$ matrix and an $n \times 1$ matrix. On the contrary $\mathbf{x}\mathbf{y}^H$ is an $n \times n$ matrix.

B.3 Matrix concepts

Matrices are not only a set of numbers. Several important and useful mathematical concepts are associated with matrices.

The **rank** of a matrix $\mathbf{A}$, *rank($\mathbf{A}$)*, is the number of linearly independent columns in the matrix $\mathbf{A}$, and this number is always equal to the number of linearly independent rows in $\mathbf{A}$. If $\mathbf{A}$ is an $m \times n$ matrix, then the rank is less than or equal to $\min(m, n)$.

The **determinant** of a square matrix $\mathbf{A}$, $\det(\mathbf{A})$, is a scalar that can be defined and computed in different ways. The following holds:

1. $\det(\mathbf{A}) = \det(\mathbf{A}^T)$.

2. $\det(\mathbf{A}^H) = \overline{\det(\mathbf{A})}$.

3. $\det(\mathbf{A}) = 0$ if $\mathbf{A}$ has two rows that are equal, or a row that is a linear combination of the other rows. The same holds for the columns of $\mathbf{A}$.

4. The determinant does not change if a row multiplied with a scalar is subtracted from another row. The same holds for the columns.

5. The sign of the determinant changes if two rows are interchanged. The same holds for the columns.

6. The determinant of an upper triangular matrix, that is a matrix where all the elements below the main diagonal are zero is the product of the diagonal elements. The same holds for a lower triangular matrix.

7. The determinant of a matrix product is the same as the product of the determinants. This is the important multiplication theorem: $\det(\mathbf{AB}) = \det(\mathbf{A})\det(\mathbf{B})$.

8. Computation of the determinant is preferably carried out by Gaussian elimination.

A **system of** n **linear equations** can be written in the explicit form:

$$\begin{cases} a_{11}x_1 + a_{12}x_2 + \cdots + a_{1n}x_n = b_1 \\ a_{21}x_1 + a_{22}x_2 + \cdots + a_{2n}x_n = b_2 \\ \vdots \\ a_{n1}x_1 + a_{2n}x_2 + \cdots + a_{nn}x_n = b_n \end{cases}$$

or with $\mathbf{A} = (a_{ij})$, $\mathbf{x} = (x_1, x_2, \ldots, x_n)^T$ and $\mathbf{b} = (b_1, b_2, \ldots, b_n)^T$ in the compact form:

$$\mathbf{Ax} = \mathbf{b}$$

Introducing the vectors $\mathbf{a}_1, \mathbf{a}_2, \ldots, \mathbf{a}_n$ as the columns of $\mathbf{A}$, the system can be written in the semicompact form:

$$x_1 \mathbf{a}_1 + x_2 \mathbf{a}_2 + \cdots + x_n \mathbf{a}_n = \mathbf{b}$$

The system has a unique solution if and only if $\det(\mathbf{A}) \neq 0$.

The **range**, $\mathcal{R}(\mathbf{A})$, of an $m \times n$ matrix $\mathbf{A}$ is the set of all linear combinations of the columns $\mathbf{a}_1, \mathbf{a}_2, \ldots, \mathbf{a}_n$ of $\mathbf{A}$. This is a linear space, and the dimension of $\mathcal{R}(\mathbf{A})$ is the same as *rank*($\mathbf{A}$).

The **null space**, $\mathcal{N}(\mathbf{A})$ of the matrix $\mathbf{A}$ is the set of vectors $\mathbf{x}$ such that $\mathbf{Ax} = \mathbf{0}$, that is all the solutions of the homogeneous system. This is also a linear space, and its dimension is m-*rank*($\mathbf{A}$).

The range and null space of $\mathbf{A}^T$ are defined in the same way.

The system $\mathbf{AX} = \mathbf{I}$ where $\mathbf{A}$ is an $n \times n$ matrix and $\mathbf{I}$ is the identity matrix of order n is a **matrix equation**. Using the notation $\mathbf{x}_1, \mathbf{x}_2, \ldots, \mathbf{x}_n$ and $\mathbf{e}_1 = (1, 0, \ldots, 0)^T$, $\mathbf{e}_2 = (0, 1, \ldots, 0)^T, \ldots, \mathbf{e}_n = (0, 0, \ldots, 1)^T$ for the columns of $\mathbf{X}$ and $\mathbf{I}$ according to:

$$\mathbf{X} = (\mathbf{x}_1 \quad \mathbf{x}_2 \quad \cdots \quad \mathbf{x}_n) \qquad \mathbf{I} = (\mathbf{e}_1 \quad \mathbf{e}_2 \quad \cdots \quad \mathbf{e}_n)$$

we can write the matrix equation as the set of linear systems:

$$\mathbf{Ax}_k = \mathbf{e}_k \quad k = 1, 2, \ldots, n$$

These have unique solutions if and only if $\det(\mathbf{A}) \neq 0$. The solution $\mathbf{X}$ of $\mathbf{AX} = \mathbf{I}$ is called the **inverse** of $\mathbf{A}$ and is denoted by $\mathbf{A}^{-1}$. It holds that $\mathbf{AA}^{-1} = \mathbf{I}$ and $\mathbf{A}^{-1}\mathbf{A} = \mathbf{I}$.

The computation of the inverse is usually carried out by Gaussian elimination. A matrix that has an inverse is called **non-singular**, and otherwise it is said to be **singular**.

Eigenvalues and **eigenvectors** of a square matrix are defined by the equation:

$$\mathbf{Ax} = \lambda\mathbf{x}$$

This is equivalent to the homogeneous system of equations:

$$(\mathbf{A} - \lambda\mathbf{I})\mathbf{x} = \mathbf{0}$$

For every $\mathbf{A}$ and every λ, the vector $\mathbf{x} = \mathbf{0}$ is a solution, but if $\det(\mathbf{A} - \lambda\mathbf{I}) \neq 0$ there are also non-trivial solutions to the system. These solutions $\mathbf{x}_k \neq \mathbf{0}$ are called **eigenvectors** of $\mathbf{A}$ and the corresponding λ_k are called **eigenvalues** or **characteristic roots**. There are always n eigenvalues $\lambda_1, \lambda_2, \ldots, \lambda_n$ to $\mathbf{A}$ in the complex plane. An eigenvalue and its eigenvector are called an **eigenpair**.

The function $\varphi(\lambda) = \det(\mathbf{A} - \lambda\mathbf{I})$ is a polynomial in λ of exactly degree n, and is called the **characteristic polynomial** of $\mathbf{A}$. The **characteristic equation** is $\varphi(\lambda) = 0$.

It is always true that the matrix polynomial $\varphi(\mathbf{A}) = \mathbf{0}$. This is the **Cayley–Hamilton theorem**.

If $\mathbf{C}$ is a non-singular matrix, and $\mathbf{A}$ and $\mathbf{B}$ are defined as $\mathbf{B} = \mathbf{C}^{-1}\mathbf{A}\mathbf{C}$, then $\mathbf{A}$ and $\mathbf{B}$ are said to be **similar matrices**, and the transformation from $\mathbf{A}$ to $\mathbf{B}$ is called a **similarity transform**. Such a transform does not change the eigenvalues of the matrix.

The **spectral radius** $\rho(\mathbf{A})$ of a matrix $\mathbf{A}$ is defined as $\max_i |\lambda_i|$.

The following rules hold for the inverse, the transpose and the conjugate transpose:

$$(\mathbf{AB})^{-1} = \mathbf{B}^{-1}\mathbf{A}^{-1} \quad \text{if all the inverses exist.}$$
$$(\mathbf{AB})^T = \mathbf{B}^T\mathbf{A}^T$$
$$(\mathbf{AB})^H = \mathbf{B}^H\mathbf{A}^H$$

In the following chain of equivalences most of the above definitions appear. $\mathbf{A}$ is a square matrix of order n.

> The linear system $\mathbf{Ax} = \mathbf{b}$ has a unique solution
> $\Leftrightarrow$
> $\det(\mathbf{A}) \neq 0$
> $\Leftrightarrow$
> $\mathbf{A}^{-1}$ exists
> $\Leftrightarrow$
> the rank of $\mathbf{A}$ is n
> $\Leftrightarrow$
> the columns of $\mathbf{A}$ are linearly independent
> $\Leftrightarrow$
> the rows of $\mathbf{A}$ are linearly independent
> $\Leftrightarrow$
> the range of $\mathbf{A}$ has the dimension n
> $\Leftrightarrow$
> the null space of $\mathbf{A}$ has the dimension 0
> $\Leftrightarrow$
> the homogeneous system $\mathbf{Ax} = \mathbf{0}$ has only the solution $\mathbf{x} = \mathbf{0}$
> $\Leftrightarrow$
> $\lambda = 0$ is not an eigenvalue of $\mathbf{A}$

B.4 Matrix classes

Matrices can be classified in many ways. A matrix is said to be a **diagonal matrix** if all off-diagonal elements are zero. A matrix is said to be **upper triangular** if all elements below the main diagonal are zero. If all the elements on the diagonal are also zero, then the matrix is said to be **strictly upper triangular**. **Lower triangular** and **strictly lower triangular** are defined in the same way.

A matrix is said to be **tridiagonal** if non-zero elements only exist on the main diagonal, on the first super-diagonal and on the first sub-diagonal. More generally, a matrix is said to be a **band matrix** if all its non-zero elements are located in a band around the main diagonal.

A matrix is said to be in **upper Hessenberg form** if all the elements below the first sub-diagonal are zero.

A matrix is said to be **sparse** if most of its elements are zero; otherwise it is said to be **full**. Band matrices are examples of sparse matrices.

It is often useful to work with **block matrices**, that is where the elements of the matrices are also matrices. Arithmetic operations can, in fact, be carried out as usual.

Let $\mathbf{A}$ and $\mathbf{B}$ be defined by:

$$\mathbf{A} = \begin{pmatrix} \mathbf{A}_{11} & \mathbf{A}_{12} \\ \mathbf{A}_{21} & \mathbf{A}_{22} \end{pmatrix} \quad \mathbf{B} = \begin{pmatrix} \mathbf{B}_{11} & \mathbf{B}_{12} \\ \mathbf{B}_{21} & \mathbf{B}_{22} \end{pmatrix}$$

this gives us $\mathbf{C} = \mathbf{AB}$ as:

$$\mathbf{C} = \begin{pmatrix} \mathbf{C}_{11} & \mathbf{C}_{12} \\ \mathbf{C}_{21} & \mathbf{C}_{22} \end{pmatrix}$$

where, for instance. $\mathbf{C}_{11} = \mathbf{A}_{11}\mathbf{B}_{11} + \mathbf{A}_{12}\mathbf{B}_{21}$.

Block matrices are sometimes referred to as **partitioned matrices**. In the previous example, the size of the submatrices must agree. Definitions like **block diagonal** and **block upper triangular** need no further explanation.

Matrices can also be classified according to their mathematical properties. Some concepts have already been introduced but are repeated here.

A matrix $\mathbf{A}$ is said to be **non-singular** if $\det(\mathbf{A}) \neq 0$, and this means that all eigenvalues are non-zero. If $\det(\mathbf{A}) = 0$ then the matrix is **singular** and at least one eigenvalue is zero.

A matrix $\mathbf{A}$ is said to be **Hermitian** if $\mathbf{A}^H = \mathbf{A}$. This is the same as **symmetric** for real matrices. The eigenvalues are real and the eigenvectors form an orthonormal basis.

A matrix $\mathbf{A}$ is said to be **skew-Hermitian** if $\mathbf{A}^H = -\mathbf{A}$. This is the same as **skew-symmetric** for real matrices. The eigenvalues are imaginary and the eigenvectors form an orthonormal basis.

A matrix $\mathbf{A}$ is said to be **normal** if $\mathbf{A}^H\mathbf{A} = \mathbf{A}\mathbf{A}^H$. The eigenvectors form an orthonormal basis.

A matrix $\mathbf{A}$ is said to be **unitary** if $\mathbf{A}^H\mathbf{A} = \mathbf{I}$. This is the same as **orthogonal** for real matrices. Thus it is true that $\mathbf{A}^{-1} = \mathbf{A}^H$. The columns of $\mathbf{A}$ form an orthonormal basis, and so do the rows. The eigenvalues have the absolute value 1 and the eigenvectors form an orthonormal basis.

A Hermitian matrix is said to be **positive definite** if $\mathbf{x}^H\mathbf{A}\mathbf{x} > 0$ for every $\mathbf{x} \neq \mathbf{0}$. All eigenvalues are positive.

Positive semidefinite is defined in the same way with the slightly weaker condition $\mathbf{x}^H\mathbf{A}\mathbf{x} \geq 0$ for every $\mathbf{x}$. The eigenvalues are non-negative.

A matrix is said to be **nilpotent** if $\mathbf{A}^p = \mathbf{0}$ for some integer p. It is said to be **idempotent** if $\mathbf{A}^2 = \mathbf{A}$.

A is **possible to diagonalize** if there exists a similarity transform **C** so that $\mathbf{C}^{-1}\mathbf{A}\mathbf{C}$ is diagonal. This happens if and only if **A** has n linearly independent eigenvectors.

A matrix is **defective** if it has less than n linearly independent eigenvectors.

B.5 Special matrices

A **zero matrix** has all components equal to zero. A **one matrix** has all components equal to one. An **identity matrix** has ones in the main diagonal, and all the other elements are zero. A **random matrix** has random elements.

A **Givens rotation** is a matrix which has the form:

$$
\begin{pmatrix}
1 & & & & & \\
& \ddots & & & & \\
& & \cos\theta & & \sin\theta & \\
& & & \ddots & & \\
& & -\sin\theta & & \cos\theta & \\
& & & & & \ddots \\
& & & & & & 1
\end{pmatrix}
$$

that is it differs from the identity matrix in exactly four entries, (i, i), (i, j), (j, i), and (j, j). Givens rotations are orthogonal.

Householder reflections are matrices defined by $\mathbf{I} - 2\mathbf{w}\mathbf{w}^H$ where $\mathbf{w}^H\mathbf{w} = 1$. These matrices are unitary and Hermitian.

Gauss transforms have the form

$$
\begin{pmatrix}
1 & & & & & & \\
& \ddots & & & & & \\
& & \ddots & & & & \\
& & & \ddots & & & \\
& & & & 1 & & \\
& & & & \times & \ddots & \\
& & & & \times & & \ddots \\
& & & & \vdots & & & \ddots \\
& & & & \times & & & & 1
\end{pmatrix}
$$

where $\times$ denotes non-zero elements. They differ from the identity matrix in one column below the diagonal.

A **permutation matrix** has the same columns as the identity matrix, but in a different order. There is exactly one unit entry in each row and in each column.

B.6 Vector and matrix norms

We previously introduced the **Euclidean norm** or **two-norm** for vectors **x**.

$$\|\mathbf{x}\|_2 = \sqrt{\sum_{i=1}^{n} |x_i|^2} = \sqrt{\mathbf{x}^H \mathbf{x}}.$$

It is also useful to introduce the **maximum norm**:

$$\|\mathbf{x}\|_\infty = \max_{1 \le i \le n} |x_i|.$$

Another norm is the **one-norm**:

$$\|\mathbf{x}\|_1 = \sum_{i=1}^{n} |x_i|.$$

All these are special cases of the more general **p-norms**:

$$\|\mathbf{x}\|_p = \left(\sum_{i=1}^{n} |x_i|^p \right)^{1/p}.$$

Norms are used to measure the size or length of vectors.

Matrix norms are defined by:

$$\|\mathbf{A}\| = \max_{\mathbf{x} \ne \mathbf{0}} \frac{\|\mathbf{A}\mathbf{x}\|}{\|\mathbf{x}\|} = \max_{\|\mathbf{x}\|=1} \|\mathbf{A}\mathbf{x}\|$$

and the following can be derived:

- the **one-norm** of **A** is the maximum of the absolute values of the column sums,

$$\|\mathbf{A}\|_1 = \max_{1 \le j \le n} \sum_{i=1}^{m} |a_{ij}|$$

- the **two-norm** or **spectral norm** of **A**:

$$\|\mathbf{A}\|_2 = \sqrt{\rho(\mathbf{A}^H \mathbf{A})}$$

and the **maximum norm** of **A** is the maximum of the absolute values of the row sums,

$$\|\mathbf{A}\|_\infty = \max_{1 \le i \le m} \sum_{j=1}^{n} |a_{ij}|.$$

There is another often used matrix norm, the **Frobenius norm** $\|A\|_F$, defined by:

$$\|A\|_F^2 = \sum_{i=1}^{m} \sum_{j=1}^{n} |a_{ij}|^2.$$

The Frobenius norm cannot be defined by a vector norm, like the other three matrix norms.

The following inequalities hold:

1. $\rho(A) \le \|A\|$ for every matrix A and for all norms.

2. $\rho(A) = \|A\|_2$ if A is Hermitian.

3. $\|A\|_2 = 1$ if A is unitary.

By matrix norms the sensitivity for perturbations in matrices can be estimated and measured.

The **condition number** for linear systems of equations $Ax = b$ is defined by:

$$\text{cond}(A) = \|A\| \cdot \|A^{-1}\|$$

and we have the relation:

$$\frac{\|\Delta x\|}{\|x\|} \le \text{cond}(A) \frac{\|\Delta b\|}{\|b\|}$$

where Δb is the perturbation in the right-hand side b and Δx the corresponding perturbation in the solution vector x. Notice that both vector and matrix norms occur in the relation. A similar relation exists for perturbations in A.

B.7 Matrix factorizations

1. **LU factorization** or **LU decomposition**
   $PA = LU$ where P is a permutation matrix, L a lower triangular matrix with ones on the diagonal and U an upper triangular matrix.

2. **Cholesky factorization**
   A symmetric and positive definite matrix A can be factorized as $A = GG^T$ where G is lower triangular.

3. **QR factorization**
   $A = QR$, where A is an $m \times n$ matrix, Q an orthogonal $m \times m$ matrix and R is upper triangular of size $m \times n$.

4. Suppose A has n linearly independent eigenvectors. Then a matrix C exists such that $C^{-1}AC = D$ is diagonal, that is $A = CDC^{-1}$. The condition is both sufficient and necessary. A sufficient condition is that all the eigenvalues are different.

5. **Schur decomposition**
   There exists a unitary matrix $\mathbf{U}$ for every matrix $\mathbf{A}$ so that $\mathbf{U}^H \mathbf{A} \mathbf{U} = \mathbf{T}$ is upper triangular, that is $\mathbf{A} = \mathbf{U} \mathbf{T} \mathbf{U}^H$.

6. For a Hermitian matrix $\mathbf{A}$ there exists a unitary matrix $\mathbf{U}$ so that $\mathbf{U}^H \mathbf{A} \mathbf{U} = \mathbf{D}$ diagonal, that is $\mathbf{A} = \mathbf{U} \mathbf{D} \mathbf{U}^H$.

7. **Murnaghan–Winters theorem**
   For all real $\mathbf{A}$, there is a real orthogonal matrix $\mathbf{U}$ so that $\mathbf{U}^T \mathbf{A} \mathbf{U} = \mathbf{B}$ is a real block triangular matrix, where the diagonal blocks are either of size 2×2 or 1×1. Every block of order two represents a complex conjugate pair of eigenvalues.

8. **Jordan normal form**
   For every square matrix $\mathbf{A}$, there exists a non-singular matrix $\mathbf{S}$ such that $\mathbf{S}^{-1} \mathbf{A} \mathbf{S} = \mathbf{J}$, where $\mathbf{J}$ is a block diagonal matrix of the form:

$$
\mathbf{J} = \begin{pmatrix} \mathbf{J}_1 & & & \\ & \mathbf{J}_2 & & \\ & & \ddots & \\ & & & \mathbf{J}_p \end{pmatrix}
\qquad
\mathbf{J}_k = \begin{pmatrix} \lambda_k & 1 & & \\ & \ddots & \ddots & \\ & & \ddots & 1 \\ & & & \lambda_k \end{pmatrix}.
$$

If the block $\mathbf{J}_k$ is of order 1 it holds that $\mathbf{J}_k = (\lambda_k)$. One eigenvector corresponds to every diagonal block, also called a **Jordan box**. The matrix $\mathbf{A}$ has p linearly independent eigenvectors, if the number of Jordan boxes is p.

9. **Singular value decomposition**
   Every $m \times n$ matrix $\mathbf{A}$ can be factorized by the two unitary matrices $\mathbf{U}$ and $\mathbf{V}$ such that $\mathbf{U}^T \mathbf{A} \mathbf{V} = \mathbf{D}$ is a diagonal $m \times n$ matrix. Here, $\mathbf{U}$ is an $m \times m$ matrix, $\mathbf{V}$ an $n \times n$ matrix, and $\mathbf{D}$ has the diagonal elements σ_k. These are ordered so that $\sigma_1 \geq \sigma_2 \geq \cdots \geq \sigma_p \geq 0$ where $p \leq \min(m, n)$. All other σ_k, if any, are zero. The numbers σ_k are called **singular values** of $\mathbf{A}$. Thus $\mathbf{A} = \mathbf{U} \mathbf{D} \mathbf{V}^T$.

   The singular values can be used to define the **pseudo-inverse** $\mathbf{D}^+$ of $\mathbf{D}$. This is illustrated for the case $m \geq n$:

$$
\mathbf{D} = \left[\begin{array}{ccc|c} \sigma_1 & & & \\ & \ddots & & 0 \\ & & \sigma_p & \\ \hline & 0 & & 0 \end{array} \right]
\qquad
\mathbf{D}^+ = \left[\begin{array}{ccc|c} \sigma_1^{-1} & & & \\ & \ddots & & 0 \\ & & \sigma_p^{-1} & \\ \hline & 0 & & 0 \end{array} \right]
$$

but is defined in the same way if $m \leq n$. If $\mathbf{D}$ is of size $m \times n$, then $\mathbf{D}^+$ is of size $n \times m$. The pseudo-inverse $\mathbf{A}^+$ of $\mathbf{A}$ is also of size $n \times m$ and is defined by the singular value decomposition as $\mathbf{A}^+ = \mathbf{V} \mathbf{D}^+ \mathbf{U}^T$.

Appendix C
MATLAB Toolboxes and SIMULINK

This information is given by The MathWorks, Inc., but edited into a form consistent with the rest of The MATLAB 5 Handbook.

MATLAB features a family of application-specific products, for solving problems in different areas, e.g., signal analysis, system identification, simulation etc. These so called **toolboxes** are built on the computational and graphical capabilities of MATLAB. They are usually a collection of M-files and implemented in the high-level MATLAB language in order to make it possible for the user to modify the source code for functions, and also to add new ones. One can easily combine the techniques in different toolboxes to design custom solutions for specific problems.

The toolboxes, which are currently commercially available from The MathWorks, Inc., are listed and briefly described in Table C.1. The lists of toolboxes are not static since, in general, several new toolboxes are created every year.

The Student Edition of MATLAB 5 can only handle matrices with a maximum of 16,384 elements, but contains three complete toolboxes: Signal Processing Toolbox, Control System Toolbox and Symbolic Math Toolbox; see Table C.1. Note that the Student Edition of MATLAB is not designed for use with the professional toolboxes. The Student Edition is published and distributed by Prentice Hall.

Furthermore, there exists a powerful, visual, interactive environment, called **SIMULINK**, for simulating non-linear dynamic systems. SIMULINK provides a graphical user interface for construction of block diagram models of dynamic systems. One may create linear, non-linear, discrete-time, continuous, and hybrid models in a very simple way, since SIMULINK takes full advantage of windowing technology. By the use of click-and-drag operations and mouse interactions, components from a block library may be connected together. It is possible to change parameters during a simulation to do 'what if' analysis. SIMULINK is fully integrated with MATLAB, and together with MATLAB and the MATLAB toolboxes it allows you to move among the various stages of modeling, design, analysis, and simulation.

It is possible to add extensions to SIMULINK. The environment includes a family of optional tools that, for example, enhance simulation speed, as shown in Table C.2. The toolboxes connected with SIMULINK are called blocksets, which extend the block library with specialized design and analysis capabilities; see Table C.3.

FEMLAB is another MATLAB-based software for the solution of partial differential equations (PDEs); for more information, see `http://www.femlab.com`

Stateflow, which is a relatively new product, is a powerful interactive design and developing tool for different kinds of complex control problems. Together with SIMULINK and SIMULINK's block extensions, Stateflow is a unique environment for event controlled and continuous systems.

For more information about SIMULINK, Stateflow, and the toolboxes, use the MATLAB command `demo` or `helpdesk`, or take a look at The MathWorks, Inc. World Wide Web Home Page:

    `http://www.mathworks.com/`

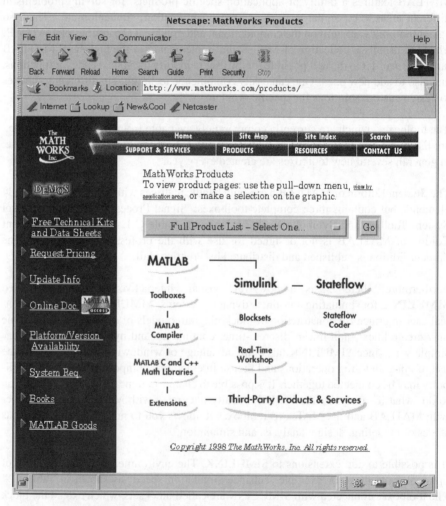

Figure C.1 *http://www.mathworks.com/products/*

Furthermore, The MathWorks, Inc. maintains an archive on the anonymous FTP server

```
ftp.mathworks.com
```

This site contains collections of M-files associated with books, user-contributed and The Mathworks, Inc. contributed software and documentation.

Other software commercially available from The MathWorks, Inc. includes the **MATLAB Compiler** and the **MATLAB C and C++ Math Libraries**. There are also **Applix Link** and **Excel Link** which integrate MATLAB with word processors and spreadsheets, e.g., moving numerical data from MATLAB to Excel. More information is available on:

```
http://www.mathworks.com/products/
```

There are also third party toolboxes, **MATLAB Third Party products**, that complement MATLAB and SIMULINK. These products and services result from collaboration with organizations from all over the world. More information is available on:

```
http://www.mathworks.com/connections
```

Table C.1	MATLAB TOOLBOXES DEVELOPED BY THE MATHWORKS, INC.
'μ'-Analysis and Synthesis	operates with MATLAB and the Signal Processing Toolbox, to be used for analysis and design of robust, linear control systems.
Chemometrics	for quantitative and qualitative analysis of data with chemometrical methods and technics.
Communications	has MATLAB functions and SIMULINK blocks for communication system design, simulation, and analysis.
Control System	for automatic control system design and analysis. Functions from this toolbox are contained in the Signals and Systems Toolbox included with the Student Edition of MATLAB.
Extended Symbolic Math	for extended symbolic mathematics. Adds support for programming in Maple V and gives access to all Maple V libraries. Includes the Symbolic Math Toolbox.
Financial	for financial and quantitative analysis.
Frequency Domain System Identification	for accurate modeling of linear systems with or without delay based on frequency domain data.
Fuzzy Logic	for fuzzy logic modeling for development of intelligently-controlled products and processes. Is especially designed to work with SIMULINK.
Higher-Order Spectral Analysis	for advanced signal processing with higher order spectra.

Table C.1	(CONTINUED)
Image Processing	operates with MATLAB and the Signal Processing Toolbox, to be used for advanced manipulation and analysis of images and two-dimensional signals.
LMI Control	for fast and efficient solution of linear matrix inequalities (LMIs).
Mapping	for analyzing and mapping of geographically-based data.
Model Predictive Control	for control system design and applications involving constraints on the manipulated and/or controlled variables.
NAG Foundation	provides interactive access to the mathematical and statistical routines in the NAG Foundation Library.
Neural Network	for design, implementation, and simulation of many kinds of neural networks and adaptive systems. Includes additional blocks to SIMULINK's extensive block library.
Optimization	for optimization of linear and non-linear functions.
Partial Differential Equation (PDE)	for the study and solution of partial differential equations in time and two space dimensions, using the finite element method.
QFT Control Design	operates with MATLAB and the Control System Toolbox, to be used for practical design of robust feedback systems using QFT methods.
Robust Control	operates with MATLAB and the Control System Toolbox, to be used for advanced, robust, multivariable feedback control system design.
Signal Processing	for algorithm development, digital signal processing and time-series analysis.
Spline	for the construction and use of piecewise polynomial functions, curve fitting, and approximation of functions.
Statistics	for statistical data analysis, modeling, and Monte Carlo simulation. Also provides GUI (graphical user interface) tools for fundamental concepts in statistics and probability, and building blocks for your own creation of statistical tools.
Symbolic Math	for symbolic mathematics, equation solving, variable-precision arithmetic, and special mathematical functions. The software is based on Maple V. An educational version is included in the Student Edition of MATLAB.
System Identification	for advanced signal processing and modeling, such as parametric modeling, system identification, and time-series analysis. Signal Processing Toolbox recommended.
Wavelet	for signals and image analysis, compression, and de-noising.

Table C.2	OPTIONAL TOOLS FOR SIMULINK
SIMULINK Real-Time Workshop	for automatic generation of C code for real-time implementation directly from SIMULINK block diagrams.
Stateflow Coder	for automatic generation of C code in the part of the SIMULINK model generated with Stateflow. Connected to the C code generator of SIMULINK, SIMULINK Real-Time Workshop.

Table C.3	SIMULINK BLOCKSETS
DSP Blockset	operates with MATLAB, SIMULINK, and the Signal Processing Toolbox, to be used for extension of the use of SIMULINK and Real-Time Workshop to digital design.
Fixed-Point Blocksets	for extension of the SIMULINK block library to fixed-point applications, for example, choice of 8-, 16-, or 32-bit fixed-point results.
Non-linear Control Design (NCD)	operates with MATLAB and SIMULINK to be used for time-domain-based control design. Includes additional blocks to SIMULINK's extensive block library.
Power System Blockset	for simulation of systems with electrical power nets using SIMULINK.

In this handbook some pictures have been generated by the PDE Toolbox. See Figures 1.11 and 1.12 in Chapter 1.

Appendix D
Quick Reference

This is a short presentation of the commands mainly following the structure of The MATLAB Handbook.

Editing and Special Keys

Some of the special keys are system dependent. Usually 'or' in the following means keys on different systems. Some keys do not exist at all on some systems.

↑ or Ctrl-P and ↓ or Ctrl-N	Browse among and recall previous commands
← or Ctrl-B	Move left one character
→ or Ctrl-F	Move right one character
Ctrl-L or Ctrl-←	Move left to next word
Ctrl-R or Ctrl-→	Move right to next word
Ctrl-A or Home	Move to beginning of line
Delete or Backspace	Delete character
Ctrl-K	Delete to end of line
Ctrl-C	Stop running calculations
cedit	Switch key modes

Basic System Commands

exit, quit	Leave MATLAB
diary	Diary of session
save	Save workspace on file
load	Load workspace from file
type, dbtype	List file
what, dir, ls	List contents of directory
cd	Change directory
pwd	Show current directory
path	Show and set current path
!	Command to the operating system follows

Help and Demonstration Commands

In the Macintosh and Windows versions, help is most easily obtained from the help menu.

help	Help on topic
lookfor	Search for text
expo, demo	Demonstration programs
whatsnew	List of new features
info	General information

Variables and Workspace

who, whos	List variables
clear	Clear variable
size, length	Size of matrix and vector
exist	Existence
pack	Restructure workspace
format	Output format
casesen	Differentiate on upper- and lower-case letters

Standard Constants and Variables

ans	Last unassigned answer
pi	π, 3.141 592 653 589 79
eps	Relative accuracy
realmax, realmin	Largest and smallest number
inf	Infinity, defined as $1/0$
NaN	Not a number, e.g. $0/0$
i, j	Imaginary unit, $\sqrt{-1}$
nargin, nargout	Number of arguments

User I/O

The easiest way to obtain the value of a variable is to type the variable name and press return.

disp	Display value or text
input	Input from keyboard
ginput	Read coordinates
pause	Pause execution
waitforbuttonpress	Wait for user action
format	Output format
more	Scroll format
casesen	Differentiate on upper- and lower-case letters
menu	Pop-up menu with choices
lasterr	Last error message string

For information on graphics commands and graphical user interface see the sections Graphics and Handle Graphics below.

Time-keeping Functions

flops	Number of flops
tic, toc, etime	Time keeping
clock, date	Time and date
cputime	Time since MATLAB start

Special System Commands

computer, getenv	Type of computer
terminal	Set terminal type
ver	Information on version etc.
version	MATLAB version
hostid	Server host id no.

Mathematical Functions

The standard mathematical functions are carried out elementwise.

Elementary mathematical functions

abs	Absolute value
sign	Sign function
sqrt	Square root
pow2	Power of 2
exp	Exponential function
log, log2, log10	Logarithmic functions
sin, cos, tan, cot, sec, csc	Trigonometric functions
asin, acos, atan2, atan, acot, asec, acsc	Inverse trigonometric functions
sinh, cosh, tanh, coth, asinh, acosh, atanh, acoth, sech, csch, asech, acsch	Hyperbolic functions and inverses

Advanced mathematical functions

legendre	Legendre functions
bessel, bessely	Bessel functions
gamma, gammaln, gammainc	Gamma functions
beta, betaln, betainc	Beta functions
expint	Exponential integral
erf, erfinv, erfc, erfcx	Error functions
ellipke, ellipj	Elliptic integrals

Coordinate transformations

cart2pol, pol2cart	Cartesian and polar
cart2sph, sph2cart	Cartesian and spherical

Integers and Floating Point Numbers

round, fix, floor, ceil	Rounding functions
rat	Rational approximation
rats	Rational number to string
rem	Remainder after division
gcd	Greatest common divisor
lcm	Least common multiplier

Complex Numbers

real, imag	Real and imaginary parts
conj	Conjugate
angle	Phase angle
unwrap	Adjust arguments
cplxpair	Complex pairs

Matrix Operations and Functions

A dot prior to the operator indicates an elementwise operation.

Matrix operators

+, -	Addition and subtraction
, ., cross, dot, kron	Multiplication
/, \, ./, .\	Division
', .'	Conjugation, transposition
^, .^	Power
>, <, >=, <=, ==, ~=	Relational operators
&, |, ~, xor	Logical operators

Matrix functions

det, trace, rank	Determinant, trace and rank
inv, pinv	Inverse and pseudo-inverse
orth, null	Basic subspaces
subspace	Angle between subspaces
expm, logm, sqrtm, funm, polyvalm	Matrix functions
size, length	Size and length of matrices and vectors
any, all, isnan, isinf, isieee, issparse, isstr, isempty, finite	Logical functions
find	Find under condition

Defining Vectors and Matrices

The colon, :, is used to generate and extract vectors and matrices.

:	Index operator
linspace, logspace	Generate vectors
eye	Identity matrix
ones, zeros	Matrices of ones and zeros
rand, randn	Random matrices
diag	Diagonal matrices
triu, tril	Triangular matrices
fliplr, flipud, rot90, reshape	Changing matrices
hilb, invhilb, toeplitz, compan, gallery, hadamard, hankel, magic, pascal, rosser, vander, wilkinson	Special matrices

Strings

Strings are enclosed by apostrophes, 'text'.

strcmp	String compare
strtok, strrep	Extract strings
findstr	Search for a string
isstr, isletter, isspace	Logic on strings
strmat	Matrix of strings
blanks, deblank	Blanks in string
lower, upper, abs,	Case conversion
setstr, num2str, int2str, rats, hex2num, hex2dec, dec2hex	String conversion
sprintf, sscanf	Formatted I/O
eval, feval	Evaluate strings

Data Analysis and Statistics

sum, cumsum	Sums
prod, cumprod	Products
diff, gradient, del2	Differences
max, min	Maxima and minima
mean, median	Mean and median values
std	Standard deviation
cov	Variance and covariance
corrcoef	Correlation matrix
sort	Sorting
hist, bar, stairs	Histogram plots, etc.

Linear Systems

Systems of linear equations are usually solved with the backslash operator, \.

\	Left divison, solution operator
det, rank	Determinant and rank
inv	Inverse of matrix
norm, normest	Norm of matrix
cond, condest	Condition numbers
lu	LU decomposition
rref, rrefmovie	Echelon form of matrix
chol	Cholesky factorization
qr	QR factorization
qrinsert, qrdelete	QR manipulations
planerot	Givens rotations

Eigenvalues and Eigenvectors

eig, polyeig	Eigenvalues and eigenvectors
poly	Characteristic polynomial
trace	Trace of matrix
balance	Balance transform
hess	Upper Hessenberg form
qr, qz	QR and QZ decompositions
schur	Schur decompositions
rsf2csf	Real to complex Schur form conversion
cdf2rdf	Complex to real diagonal form conversion
svd	Singular value decomposition

Sparse Matrices

Most of the standard matrix commands can be applied directly on sparse matrices. Notable exceptions are the command norm and some of the graphics commands.

sparse	Full to sparse conversion
full	Sparse to full conversion
find	Find indices
spconvert	Indices to sparse
nnz	Number of non-zero elements
spy	Structure plot
nonzeros	Find non-zero elements
speye	Sparse identity matrix
spones	Ones in non-zero positions
sprandn, sprandsym	Sparse random matrices
spdiags	Sparse diagonal matrix
issparse	Logic on storage
spalloc, nzmax	Sparse allocation
spfun	Evaluate function
sprank	Rank of sparse matrix
normest	2-norm estimate
condest	Condition number estimate
spaugment	Create square matrix to compute least squares solutions
etree	Elimination tree of matrix
etreeplot	Plot of elimination tree
colmmd, symmmd	Minimum degree orderings
symrcm, colperm	Column permutations
randperm	Permuted vector
dmperm	Dulmage–Mendelsohn decomposition
spparms	Sets sparse parameters
symbfact	Analyze chol and lu
gplot	Graph plots

Polynomials and Curve Fitting

polyval, polyvalm	Evaluate polynomials
conv, deconv	convolution, product of polynomials
residue	Partial fractions
polyder	Derivative of polynomials
poly	Characteristic polynomial
compan	Companion matrix
polyfit	Polynomial approximation
interp1–interp6	Interpolation
interpft	Fourier interpolation
spline	Spline interpolation

legendre, bessel, bessely	Orthogonal functions
fft, ifft	Fast Fourier Transform
fft2, ifft2	D FFT
fftshift	Swap quadrants

Zeros, Maxima, and Minima

roots	Zeros of polynomials
fzero	Zeros of functions
fmin, fmins	Minima of functions

Integrals and Differential Equations

trapz, quad, quad8	Computation of definite integrals
ode23, ode45, ode23p	ODE solvers

Programming in MATLAB

Programs can be written by the prompter, or more conveniently, in an M-file. An M-file is a file of MATLAB commands, with the extension **.m**. The M-file is executed by giving the name of the file as a command. Blocks in MATLAB are closed by an end.

Conditional statements

```
if condition
        statement1
        statement2
    ...
```
The general form of an if-else block

```
else
        statement3
end
```
The else part is optional, but an if always has an end

Loops

```
for i=1:2:10
        statement1
    ...
```
Loop i from 1 to 10 using step 2

```
end
```
A block is closed by end

```
while condition
        statement1
    ...
end
```
Loop while condition is true

Control statements

%	Comment follows
return	Leave M-file
pause	Pause execution
break	Terminate current loop
global	Declare variables global
nargin	Number of arguments in
nargout	Number of arguments out

Debugging M-files

keyboard	Keyboard command mode
echo	Echo commands
error	Terminate with error message
dbtype	Type M-file with line no.
dbstop, dbclear	Set and clear breakpoints
dbstatus	List current breakpoints
dbstep, dbcont	Execute statements
dbup, dbdown	Switch workspace
dbstack	Show stack of workspaces
dbquit	Quit debugging mode

Graphics

2D- and 3D-graphics

plot	Plot in two dimensions
plot3	Plot in three dimensions
fplot	Plot function
subplot	Divide current figure into subplots
errorbar	Plot with error bars
comet, comet3	Animated plot, 2D, 3D
polar	Plot in polar coordinates
semilogx, semilogy loglog	Logarithmic plots
quiver, feather, compass, rose	Complex graphics
stem	Data sequence plot
hist, bar, stairs	Histogram plots, etc.

Graphics control

figure	Create or display a figure
clf	Clear figure
hold	Hold the current plot
subplot	Divide current figure into subplots
clc	Clear command window

home	Put cursor home, i.e. top left
axis	Scale of the axes
zoom	Zoom in and out (2D only)
grid	Show or hide gridlines
title, xlabel, ylabel, zlabel	Write basic text items
text	Write text anywhere
gtext	Place text with mouse
ginput	Read coordinates
rbbox	Move rectangular region
hidden	Show or do not show hidden surfaces
view	Position and angle of view
viewmtx	Matrix defining the view
rot90	Rotate matrix

Surface and contour plots

contour	Contour plots
contour3	Contour plots in 3D
clabel	Mark contour lines
meshgrid	Generate grid
cylinder, sphere	Special geometry grids
surf	Surface plot
mesh	Mesh surface plot
meshc, meshz, waterfall	Mesh surface with reference lines
surfl, surfc, surfnorm	Surface plots with special light, contours, and normals
pcolor	Surf plot seen from above
fill, fill3	Filled polygons
slice	Plot of functions of three variables

Color control

shading	Surface color mode
colormap	Read or set color table
colorbar	Display a color bar
rgb2hsv, hsv2rgb	Conversion of color tables
caxis	Scale of the color axis
spinmap	Rotate colors
brighten	Change color map
contrast	Increase contrast
whitebg	Background color
graymon	Black and white parameters

Printing

print	Generate hardcopy
printopt	Print options
orient	Paper orientations

Sound

sound	Play sound
saxis	Sound axis
auread, auwrite	Sun au sound files
mu2lin, lin2mu	Sun sound conversion
wavwrite, wavread	Windows sound files

Handle Graphics

Graphics in MATLAB are object oriented. First there is a root object that may have children, that is figures. These figures can contain one or more axes, plot regions. A plot is built by lines, surfaces, patches, and text objects drawn in the plot region. Each object has a unique handle, and through this handle its properties may be changed.

get	Get properties
set	Set properties
gcf, gca, gco	Get handle to current figure, axis, or object
clf, cla	Clear current figure or axes
close	Close figure
delete	Delete object
rotate	Rotate object
reset	Reset properties of an object
refresh	Refresh figure
drawnow	Flush graphics update
newplot	Set properties for next plot
figure	Set current or create figure
axes	Plot region
line	Line object
text	Text object
patch	Patch (filled polygon) object
surface	Surface object
image	Image object
capture	Bitmap copy
uimenu	User interface menu
dialog	Dialog box
errordlg, warndlg, helpdlg, questdlg	Inherited dialogs

Movies

movie	Show movie
get frame	Get movie frame
moviein	Initialize movie

Binary and Text Files

`fopen`	Open file
`fclose`	Close file
`fwrite`	Write to file
`fread`	Read from file
`fprintf`	Formatted output to file
`fscanf`	Scan data from file
`fegtl, fgets`	Read line from file
`ferror`	Check for file error
`feof`	Check for end of file
`frewind`	Reset file
`fseek`	Set position in file
`ftell`	Get position in file

Bibliography

This bibliography contains books in linear algebra, matrix algebra and applications. The basic MATLAB manuals are also listed.

Backstrom, G. *Practical Mathematics Using MATLAB*. Studentlitteratur (ISBN 91-44-49231-6) and Chartwell Bratt Ltd (ISBN 0-86238-397-8), 1995.

Biran, A. and Breiner, M. G. *MATLAB for Engineers*, Addison-Wesley, 1995 (ISBN 0-201-56524-2).

Borse, G. J. *Numerical Methods with MATLAB: A resource for Scientists and Engineers*, PWS Publishing Company, 1997 (ISBN 0-534-92822-1).

Golub, G. H. and Van Loan, C. F. *Matrix Computations* (2nd edition). The Johns Hopkins Univeristy Press, 1989 (ISBN 0-8018-3739-1).

Hager, W. W. *Applied Numerical Linear Algebra*. Prentice Hall, 1988 (ISBN 0-13-041369-0).

Heath, M. T. *Scientific Computing, an Introductory Survey*, McGraw-Hill, 1997 (ISBN 0-07-027684-6).

Jennings, A. and McKeown, J. J. *Matrix Computation*. John Wiley, 1992 (ISBN 0-471-93527-1).

Lindfield, G. and Penny, J. *Numerical Methods Using MATLAB*. Ellis Horwood, 1995 (ISBN 0-13-030966-4).

Malek-Madani, R. *Advanced Engineering Mathematics with Mathematica and MATLAB*, Addison-Wesley, 1998 (ISBN 0-201-59881-71).

Marcus, M. *Matrices and MATLAB: A Tutorial*. Prentice Hall, 1993 (ISBN 0-13-562901-2).

Ogata, K. *Solving Control Engineering Problems with MATLAB*. Prentice Hall, 1993 (ISBN 0-13-045907-0).

Strang, G. *Introduction to Linear Algebra*. Wellesley-Cambridge Press, 1993 (ISBN 0-9614088-5-5).

Strum, R. D. and Kirk D. E. *Contemporary Linear Systems Using MATLAB*. PWS Publishing, 1994 (ISBN 0-534-93273-8).

MATLAB manuals:

Getting Started with MATLAB, The MathWorks, Inc., 1998.
Late-Breaking News for the MATLAB 5.2 Product Family, The MathWorks, Inc., 1998.
MATLAB 5.2 Product Family New Features, The MathWorks, Inc., 1998.
MATLAB Application Program Interface Guide, The MathWorks, Inc., 1998.
MATLAB Application Program Interface Reference Manual, The MathWorks, Inc., 1998.
MATLAB Functions Reference – Volume 1, The MathWorks, Inc., 1998.
MATLAB Functions Reference – Volume 2, The MathWorks, Inc., 1998.
MATLAB Application Program Interface Reference Manual, The MathWorks, Inc., 1998.

Using MATLAB, The MathWorks, Inc., 1998.

Using MATLAB Graphics, The MathWorks, Inc., 1997.

Student Edition of MATLAB Version 5 User's Guide, Prentice Hall, 1995 (ISBN 0-13-272550-9).

List of Command Tables

Index

Normal font is used for general concepts. `Fixed space font` is used for MATLAB commands.

The beginning of this index comtains a list of all special keys used in MATLAB.